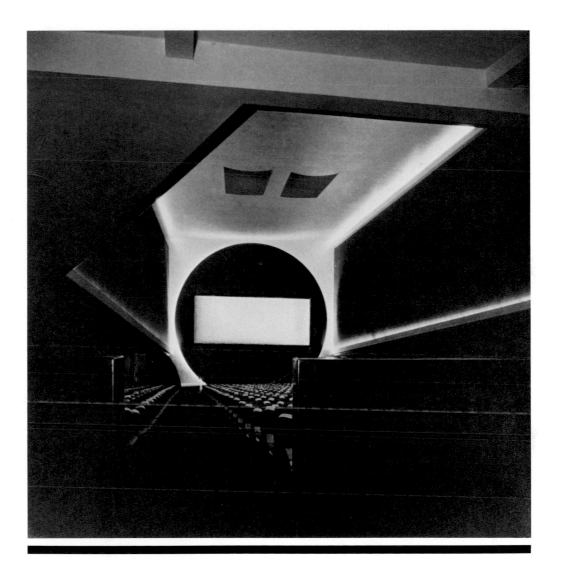

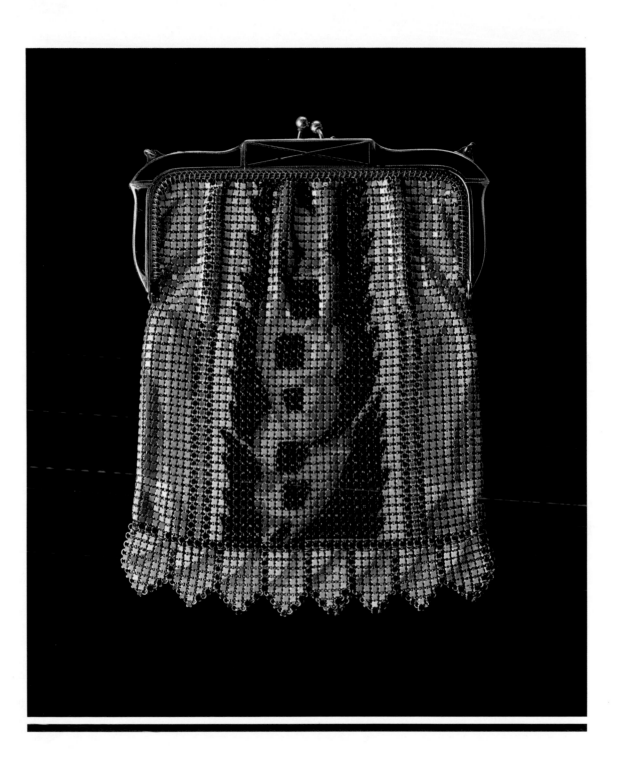

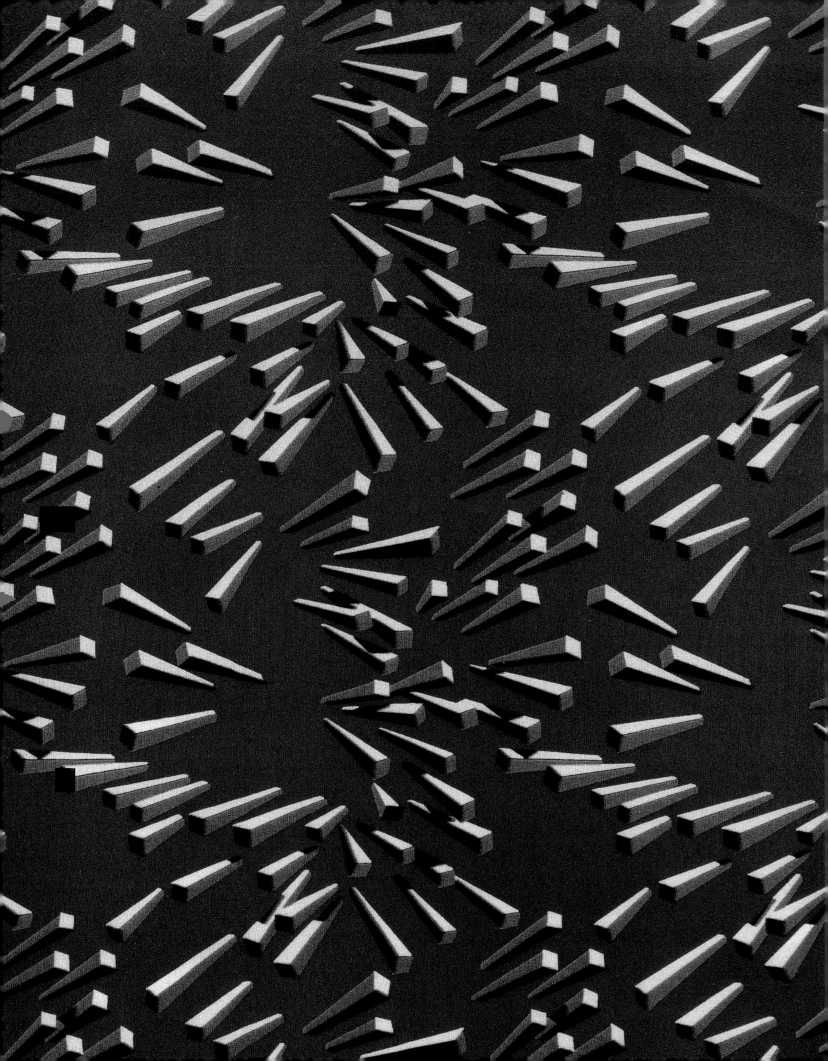

THE MACHINE AGE

Richard Guy Wilson

IN AMERICA

Dianne H. Pilgrim

1918-1941

Dickran Tashjian

THE BROOKLYN MUSEUM

in association with

HARRY N. ABRAMS, INC., PUBLISHERS, NEW YORK

■

Project Director:
   Margaret L. Kaplan

Editor: Beverly Fazio
Designer: Michael Hentges

Published in 1986 by Harry N. Abrams, Incorporated, New York. All rights reserved. No part of the contents of this book may be reproduced without the written permission of the publishers

Times Mirror Books

Printed and bound in Japan

Library of Congress Cataloging-in-Publication Data

Wilson, Richard Guy, 1940–
   The machine age in America, 1918–1941.

   Published in conjunction with a major exhibition that will tour the country after opening at the Brooklyn Museum.
   Bibliography: p. 361
   Includes index.
   1. Design Industrial—United States—History.
I. Pilgrim, Dianne H. II. Tashjian, Dickran, 1940–
III. Brooklyn Museum. IV. Title.
TS23.W55 1986 745.2′0973 86–3590
ISBN 0–8109–1421–2
ISBN 0–8109–2334–3 (pbk.)

Front cover: Adapted from a drawing by Louis Lozowick. *Machine Ornament No. 2* (see fig. 1.20)
Back cover: Gerald Murphy. *Watch* (fig. 7.1)
Endpapers: Thurman Rotan. *Skyscrapers.* 1932. Photomontage. Collection Mark Isaacson, 50-50 Gallery, New York. Courtesy Keith Douglas de Lillis Fine Art Photography. © Thurman Rotan
Page 2: Lewis W. Hine. *Heart of the Turbine* (fig. 7.72)
Page 3: Alfred Stieglitz. *Georgia O'Keeffe* (fig. 7.70)
Page 4: Erik Magnussen. "Cubic" Coffee Set (fig. 8.31)
Page 5: Hugh Ferriss. *Study for the Maximum Mass Permitted by the 1916 New York Zoning Law, Stage 2* (see fig. 6.4)
Page 6: Boiling Flasks (fig. 8.50)
Page 7: Frederick Kiesler. Interior, Film Guild Cinema (fig. 9.7)
Page 8: Berenice Abbott. *Manhattan Bridge: Looking Up* (fig. 7.65)
Page 9: Handbag (fig. 8.21)
Page 10: Ralph Steiner. *Portrait of Louis Lozowick* (fig. 7.47)
Page 11: Theodore Roszak. *Crescent Throat Construction* (fig. 7.52)
Page 12: Charles Buckles Falls. *Pegs* (fig. 8.39)

Exhibition Itinerary

The Brooklyn Museum
   October 17, 1986–February 16, 1987
Museum of Art, Carnegie Institute, Pittsburgh   *April 4–June 28, 1987*
Los Angeles County Museum of Art
   August 16–October 18, 1987
The High Museum of Art, Atlanta
   December 1, 1987–February 14, 1988

The exhibition was organized by The Brooklyn Museum and made possible through grants from the J. M. Kaplan Fund and the National Endowment for the Humanities.
■

Exhibition Curators: Dianne H. Pilgrim
                          Richard Guy Wilson
Exhibition Coordinator: Christopher Wilk
Research Associate: Caroline Mortimer
Special Photography: Schecter Lee

CONTENTS

Foreword

An underlying sensibility can be found in every age, operating at all levels of social organization. Because no period in time is monolithic, this sensibility is visible only with distance. A certain "family" resemblance appears as an essential unity which can be seen to inform many of that society's cultural products and other manifestations. We have no difficulty accepting this unity in the art and culture of such historical periods as Ancient Greece, the Middle Ages, and the Renaissance, but have not yet clearly defined the forces that shaped the first half of this century.

The Machine Age in America 1918–1941, and its accompanying exhibition, demonstrate that the machine in all its many manifestations was the defining force in America during the years between the two great wars. From its founding, the United States has held out the promise to the world of developing a unique civilization. By the early twentieth century many Europeans felt that at last America was on the verge of a new art and ultimately a new culture. What they perceived was the great achievement of American technology and industrialization from which would arise not simply a modern style, but an entirely new way of life.

The period 1918–41 witnessed the struggle of America's artists, designers, and public to acknowledge, understand, accept, and finally control this machine-driven world. These goals, though hardly achieved by the time of our entry into World War II, prepared the way for America's political, economic, and artistic leadership in the 1940s and 1950s, and created a climate in which for the first time in history Europe looked to America for inspiration.

That the machine had a powerful impact on American and European culture in the early twentieth century is hardly a new idea. Monographs are plentiful on cubism, futurism, de Stijl, the Bauhaus, and American precisionism, and there are important recent discussions of industrial design and Art Deco. However, the fact that the machine was the major motivating force behind them has not been generally recognized. The significance of America's contribution to world culture during this period has likewise been insufficiently explored.

This is the first book and exhibition to examine within their social and cultural context the full range of American art and artifacts of this period. Ironically, there was a clearer understanding of the connection between the machine and culture during the 1920s and 1930s than there has been for the past forty years. This book and exhibition follow in the tradition of *The Machine-Age Exposition* of 1927, organized by the magazine *The Little Review*, which also included paintings, sculpture, decorative arts, architecture, photography, and actual machines. Unlike Pontus Hultén's exhibition, *The Machine as Seen at the End of the Mechanical Age*, held at The Museum of Modern Art in 1968, which focused mainly on European painting and sculpture of the twentieth century, this study explores the impact of the American response to the machine.

This project is a natural outgrowth of the 1979 exhibition *The American Renaissance 1876–1917*, organized by Dianne H. Pilgrim, curator of decorative arts, and Richard Guy Wilson, professor of architectural history, University of Virginia, along with Richard N. Murray, then assistant to the director, National Collection of Fine Arts, now director of the Archives of American Art, Smithsonian Institution, under the auspices of The Brooklyn Museum. While working on the *American Renaissance* show, Mrs. Pilgrim and Professor Wilson discovered

that they shared a long-standing interest in the arts of America during the 1920s and 1930s. They decided then to do a modest exhibition on architecture and decorative arts. But like the original conception of the *American Renaissance* exhibition, which was to concentrate on McKim, Mead & White, the present project grew to encompass the totality of the period. Both eras had been ignored or denigrated through misunderstanding. In each case the attempt has been to give an overview, a new way of looking at a part of our cultural heritage. To this end, Dickran Tashjian, professor of comparative culture and social science, University of California, Irvine, has contributed to this endeavor with his knowledge of painting and sculpture. It is the authors' hope that this larger perspective will encourage others to study its myriad facets and individual artists in depth. We are grateful to Professor Wilson and Mrs. Pilgrim for their perception and courage in initiating and organizing this exhibition and publication and to the three authors for their insights into this complex period.

The Brooklyn Museum, since its founding in 1890, has been in the forefront of the advancement of art of all cultures. It has widely promoted American art, even in periods when it was held in low esteem. Since the teens the museum has been involved with contemporary artists, designers, and industry. In 1926 the museum sponsored the influential *International Exhibition of Modern Art* assembled by the Société Anonyme. Through the Department of Industrial Design, which became the Edward C. Blum Design Laboratory in 1948, it has sponsored important exhibitions such as *The American Union of Decorative Artists and Craftsmen* in 1931 and *Contemporary Industrial and Handwrought Silver* in 1937–38. *The Machine Age in America 1918–1941* follows in a long tradition of exploring uncharted territory. With the perspective of some sixty years and the passage of modernism into the past, the time is right to see and understand America's unique contribution to the culture of the 1920s and 1930s.

We wish to express our gratitude to the National Endowment for the Humanities both for planning and implementation grants, and for their continued commitment to a greater understanding of our culture.

We would also like to thank the extraordinary generosity of Joan K. Davidson and the J. M. Kaplan Fund, without whose help this exhibition and book would not have been possible. A fellowship from the John Simon Guggenheim Foundation helped allow Richard Guy Wilson to research and write his contribution to this publication. The generosity of Diane Wolf made possible the purchase of a computer, which has greatly simplified the difficult task of organizing such a mammoth undertaking. We also want to thank Dudley J. Godfrey, Jr., whose contribution made it possible for us to buy additional software for the computer. We are grateful to John R. Lane, director of the Museum of Art, Carnegie Institute; Earl A. Powell III, director of the Los Angeles County Museum of Art; Gudmund Vigtel, director of The High Museum of Art; and their staffs for making the tour of this exhibition possible. Our sincere appreciation goes to all the museums, individuals, collectors, galleries, and corporations who have contributed their time, support, and objects. Their cooperation and generosity throughout have been exceptional.

Robert T. Buck, Director,
The Brooklyn Museum

Acknowledgments

To undertake a book and exhibition of this scope and complexity requires the generosity, cooperation, and dedication of many scholars, gallery owners, collectors, and colleagues. The authors wish to thank all those who have so generously shared their knowledge, time, and encouragement.

We are grateful for the assistance of our colleagues at the following institutions: John Zukowsky, Art Institute of Chicago; Carolyn A. Davis, George Arents Research Library, Syracuse University; Gregg Buttermore, Auburn-Cord-Dusenberg Museum; Janet Parks, Avery Library, Columbia University; Diane W. Camber, Bass Museum of Art; William Jordy, Brown University; Elaine Dee, Margaret Luchars, Katherine Martinez, David Revere McFadden, and Gillian Moss, Cooper-Hewitt Museum; William N. Lacy, Cooper-Union; Helen L. Pickney, Dayton Art Institute; Marcia A. Mullin, Discovery Hall Museum; Samuel Beizer, Harold Coda, and Lynn Felscher, Fashion Institute of Technology; David R. Crippen, Ford Archives, Edison Institute; Allegra Fuller Snyder, Buckminster Fuller Institute; Donald C. Pierce, The High Museum of Art; Paul M. Bailey, W. H. Crain, Hoblitzelle Theatre Arts Library, University of Texas; Barbara Puorro Galasso, International Museum of Photography, George Eastman House; Leslie Bowman, Edward Maeder, Los Angeles County Museum of Art; Karen Meyerhoff, R. Craig Miller, Amelia Peck, Ann Schirrmeister, and Andrew Spahr, The Metropolitan Museum of Art; Robert Rydell, Montana State University; Phillip Johnston, John R. Lane, Museum of Art, Carnegie Institute; Christopher Monkhouse, Museum of Art, Rhode Island School of Design; Robert Coates, Thomas Grischkowsky, J.Stewart Johnson, Cara McCarty, and Clive Phillpot, The Museum of Modern Art, New York; Jennifer Bright, Museum of the City of New York; Ulysses G. Dietz, Gary Reynolds, The Newark Museum; Inez Brooks-Myers, Kenneth R. Trapp, Oakland Museum; Mary Ann Scherr, Parsons School of Design; John Carlisle, Purdue University; Jon Eklund, Bernard S. Finn, Rodris Roth, Carlene Stephens, Robert Vogel, John H. White, and William Withuhn, National Museum of American History, Smithsonian Institution; Robert MacKay, Society for the Preservation of Long Island Antiquities; Arthur Pulos, Syracuse University; Genie Fraula, Troy Historical Society; Maryly Snow, University of California, Berkeley; David Gebhard, Gavin Townsend, University of California, Santa Barbara; Edith Tonelli, University of California, Los Angeles; Walter Creese, University of Illinois; Robert Bruegmann, University of Illinois, Chicago Circle; Jean France, University of Rochester; Jeffrey Meikle, University of Texas; William Middleton, University of Virginia; Eugene Gaddis, William N. Hosley, Jr., Wadsworth Atheneum; Richard Longstreth, George Washington University; Buford Pickens, Washington University; Noel Frackman, Patterson Sims, Whitney Museum of American Art; Carol Alper, Pamela Johnson, and Mitchell Wolfson, Jr., Mitchell Wolfson, Jr., Collection of Decorative and Propaganda Arts; Patricia Kane, Yale University Art Gallery.

The following individuals or firms graciously allowed objects from their collections to be photographed for this book and assisted in our wide-ranging search for objects for the accompanying exhibition: John Axelrod; Alfred Bauman; Nelson Blitz, Jr.; Jalmar Bowden and Larry Whitely, Whitely Gallery; Eric Brill; Charles Carpenter; Ralph Cutler, Mark Isaacson, and Mark McDonald, Fifty-50; Bruce Davis, Academy of Motion Picture Arts and Sciences; Richard DeNatale; Dyan Economakos and Jim Greer; Susan Kelner Freeman; Denis Gallion and Daniel Morris, Historic Design Collection, Inc.; Dr. William S. Greenspon; Nathan G. Horwitt; Dan Inglett and Gene Watson, Inglett-Watson and Ken Forster; The Ziggurat Collection of Michael D. Kinerk and Dennis W. Wilhelm; Catherine Kurland; Alan Moss, Alan Moss Ltd.; Charles Senseman; Jack Solomon, Circle Fine Art; Ilon Specht Case; John C. Waddell; George H. Waterman III; Paul F. Walter; Judy White; Diane Wolf.

We also wish to thank the following individuals, corporations, and galleries for their assistance and expertise: Raymond Goggin and Warren Thomas, As Time Goes By; H. E. B. Anderson, Austin Company; Stafford Archer, Anita McGurn, Texaco; Bonnie Arnold, Rockefeller Center; Lisa W. Baldauf; Joe Bedway and Bob Paulson, Albert Kahn Associates; Edith Lutyens Bel Geddes; Leslie Blacksberg; Scott W. Braznell; Philip M. Bromberg; Dr. Annella Brown; Martha Buskirk; Catheline Cantalupo; Clarence H. Carter; Charles Cecil, Revere Copper & Brass Company; Arnold Chase, WTIC Television; Geoffrey Clements; Jack Cowin, Customer Relations, General Electric; Craven Crowell and William S. Lee, Tennessee Valley Authority; Dale Curth, Arrasmith, Judd, Rapp, Inc.; Karen Davies; Albert Dean, Walter Dean, and John Derrah, Budd Company; Andrea DeNoto; Martin Diamond; Henry DuLaurence; Alastair Duncan; Martin Eidelberg; Scott Elliott, Kelmscott Gallery; Veronica Falkenberry, Barry Novins, and Patty Tinnell, Whiting and Davis Corporation; John A. Fatula, AIA, Philadelphia Savings Fund Society; Robert C. Ferguson, Lockheed Corporation; Karen Fine; Linda Folland, Herman Miller, Inc.; Mr. and Mrs. Richard Foster; Albert Frey; Harry Gann, Douglas Aircraft Company; John Geroski, Department of General Services, City of New York; Barbara Giella; Madeline Gunther; David A. Hanks, Caroline Stern, and Jennifer Toher, David A. Hanks & Associates; Zenon Hansen; John and Norma Hauserman; Bernard Heineman, Jr.; Stuart Feld and M. P. Naud, Hirschl & Adler Galleries, Inc.; David Holls and Floyd Joliet, General Motors Corporation; Courty Andrews Hoyt, Life Picture Service; Gordon and Carol Hyatt; Joyce Jonas; Ivan Karp; Judith Katzman; Grace Keating; Claudia Keenan, formerly of WNYC; Mrs. Lillian

Kiesler; Sandra Kocher; Sue Kohler, Commission of Fine Arts, Washington, D. C.; Michael Lamm; Robert Lepper; Richard Lilly, Strand Bookstore; Suzanne Lipschutz, Secondhand Rose; Mrs. Adele Lozowick; Richard Lukins; John Martin; Jo Mattern, *Fortune* magazine; Melissa Bellinelli and James Maroney, James Maroney, Inc.; Virginia Hagelstein Marquardt; Barbara Mathes Gallery; Pauline Metcalf; Dione Neutra; Bruce Newman; Derek Ostergard; Nicholas Polites, Walter Dorwin Teague Associates; Mary P. Proddow; Julien Reinhart, Bureau of Reclamation; Gilbert L. Rogin; Lee Rohde; Kirsten Rorhs; Sarah Roszak; Jon R. Saffell, Fostoria Glass; George Sakier; Lawrence B. Salander, Salander-O'Reilly Gallerics, Inc.; Anamarie Sandechi; Anne Saunders, Trans World Airlines; Viktor and Don Schreckengost; Michael Smith, Depression Modern; Richard Steiner; Clifford Brooks Stevens; Nina Stritzler; Karen Strom, A. O. Smith Company; Ann Tashjian; Bill Tompkins, Hedrich-Blessing; Suzanne Vanderwoude; Helene Von Rosenstiel; Joan Washburn; Ann Whyte, Pan American World Airways; Susan Fillin Yeh; Catherine Yronwode, Collectible Plastics; Virginia Zabriskie, Zabriskie Gallery; Larry Zim, Zim-Lerner Gallery.

Schecter Lee, with his assistant Leslie Heathcote, brought sensitivity and patience to the photographing of many of the objects in this book. We would especially like to acknowledge the work of the staff of Harry N. Abrams, Inc.: Margaret Kaplan, Senior Vice-President and Executive Editor; Beverly Fazio, Editor; and Michael Hentges, Designer.

The authors would like to express their deep appreciation to the staff of The Brooklyn Museum. We thank Michael Botwinick, John R. Lane, and Brian Rushton for their early support and enthusiasm for this project and Robert T. Buck for his continuing enthusiasm. The following have each given invaluable assistance: Martin Beller, Patrick Cardon, Ann Curtis, Roy Eddey, Linda Ferber, Charlotta Kotik, Barbara LaSalle and her staff, Deirdre Lawrence, Gerald Le Francois, Barbara Millstein, Ken Moser, Ellen Pearlstein, Serena Rattazzi, Elizabeth Reynolds, Deborah Schwartz, Missy Sullivan, Richard Waller, Polly Willman, and Rena Zurofsky.

The true heroes of this endeavor are the staff of the Department of Decorative Arts. Without their dedication, hard work, perseverance, and patience, this book and exhibition would not have been possible. We wish to thank Celestina Ucciferri, Administrative Assistant, James Hayes, Departmental Technician, and Helen Marangos, Volunteer. Special thanks go to Kevin L. Stayton, Associate Curator, for assuming additional responsibilities in the day-to-day operation of the office, and for his wise council and editorial expertise.

The complicated and overwhelming task of gathering photographs and caption information for three authors and working diligently on all the myriad details in connection with the exhibition was performed by Caroline Mortimer, Research Associate, with efficiency, diplomacy, perseverance, and good humor. Overseeing all of the logistical and scholarly complexities of organizing a book and exhibition of this magnitude was Christopher Wilk, Assistant Curator and Exhibition Coordinator. He managed this enormous undertaking with determination, commitment to quality, and great knowledge and perception. To Christopher and Caroline we wish to express our deep respect and heartfelt gratitude.

R.G.W., D.H.P., D.T.

1.1

CHAPTER 1

AMERICA AND THE MACHINE AGE

Entranced with the mechanism of his recently purchased Akeley motion picture camera, Paul Strand began in 1922 to create portraits of its working parts. Strand went on to photograph a number of other machines, including lathes and drills, and to write an essay claiming that man has "consummated a new creative act, a new Trinity: God the Machine, Materialistic Empiricism the Son, and Science the Holy Ghost.... The deeper significance of a machine, the camera, has emerged here in America, the supreme altar of the new God." But he also observed, "not only the new God but the whole Trinity must be humanized unless it in turn dehumanizes us." In this way, Strand serves as a paradigm of the machine age artist; he early recognized the fascination and beauty of the machine, but also its threat.[1]

The machine age in America refers to the dominance of the machine in all areas of American life and culture and the creation of that special sensibility informing modernism. No age is completely homogeneous: several themes and concerns can be recognized in America during the period between the two world wars, 1918 to 1941. Although the two decades have different orientations—business and boom in the 1920s, depression and social concern in the 1930s—many Americans could see a unified period of science and industry, resulting in fast communications and new products. For many people the period marked a new age, brought into being by the machine. From the clock that awakened one in the morning, to the flicked switch, the faucet handle, the vehicle for transportation, and the radio and motion picture, machines and their products increasingly pervaded all aspects of American life. Machines were everywhere; their impact went beyond the fact of their physical existence to challenge perceptions of both the self and the world. This new consciousness implied a whole new culture that could be built as readily as the machine; history seemed irrelevant, traditional styles and pieties outmoded. The machine in all its manifestations—as an object, a process, and ultimately a symbol—became the fundamental fact of modernism. The art and theater critics Sheldon and Martha Cheney applauded what they saw as a "spreading machine-age consciousness"; they claimed that the "age of machine-implemented culture" had begun.[2]

From an artistic and cultural perspective, the machine was central to those years. A great number of different-ap-

1.1 Paul Strand (1890–1976) *Double Akeley, New York, 1922.* 1922. Gelatin-silver print, 10 × 8″. © 1976 The Paul Strand Foundation, as published in *Paul Strand: Sixty Years of Photographs* (Millerton, N.Y.: Aperture, 1976)

1.2 Charles Sheeler (1883–1965) *Industry.* 1932. Gelatin-silver print, triptych, side panels 7¾ × 2¾"; center panel 7¾ × 6⅜". The Art Institute of Chicago. Julien Levy Collection

1.3 Walter Dorwin Teague, Jr. (b. 1910) Prototype for Marmon 12. ca. 1932. Painted wood and metal, 6 × 6 × 20". Cooper-Hewitt Museum, the Smithsonian Institution's National Museum of Design, New York

pearing "modern" styles were created, but at bottom they all contained a family resemblance: all were based upon the machine. Avant-garde painters and sculptors first grasped the possibilities of the machine in the 1910s and early 1920s. In succeeding years the other arts began to recognize the machine as a source of beauty. Some furniture designers and architects in the late 1920s began to cast off the traditional styles and search for a machine expression. Although the Depression of the 1930s raised doubts about the future of an industrial civilization, for many the machine retained its social promise. Business, its back to the wall, retooled and restyled its products, helping to create a new artist-hero of the machine age, the industrial designer. The world of machine

art encompassed not simply the traditional arts, but electric clocks, pencil sharpeners, and new, streamlined cars and trains. For the creative individual the machine age offered the chance to invent a singularly American art, one that ranged from products for the home to the great building enterprises of the day. Artists were quick to recognize the uniqueness of America. Charles Sheeler, the painter-photographer, enamored of Henry Ford's River Rouge plant, raised up coal bunkers, conveyor tubes, and body presses as the American equivalent to European monuments of civilization (see fig. 1.2). Sheeler believed "Our factories are our substitutes for religious expression."[3]

A NEW AGE

The identification of a machine age in the 1920s and 1930s by many Americans and foreigners heralded a break with the past. The French social scientist André Siegfried wrote in his popular (fourteen printings between 1927 and 1929) *America Comes of Age*: "Today, as a result of the revolutionary changes brought about by modern methods of production, [America] has again become a new world. . . . The American people are now creating on a vast scale an entirely original social structure which bears only a superficial resemblance to the European. It may even be a new age. . . ."[4] In Europe the machine, though exalted, remained essentially a plaything of the elite, and for the designer handicraft processes dominated even products with a machine appearance. In America the machine proliferated throughout society; it included the expensive *Streamlined Monel Metal Sink*, inexpensive Sears, Roebuck kitchen implements, and the cast-offs of industrial civilization, the automobile junkyard. The machine age meant actual machines such as giant turbines and new machine materials such as Bakelite, Formica, chrome, aluminum, and stainless steel. The machine age meant new processes—mass production, "Fordism"—factories, great corporations, and new ways of living. Individuals from the factory worker to the housewife became machine operators and had at their fingertips and feet more power than their grandparents ever imagined. Science in all its branches, argued historian Charles Beard, upheld the machine system. The machine age encompassed the vast new skyscraper city, with its transportation systems compacted one on top of the other, and the new horizontal city composed of filling stations, drive-ins, and superhighways. Even human beings were viewed as machines in the scientific management and time-motion studies of Frederick Taylor and his disciples, Frank and Lillian Gilbreth. John B. Watson, the father of behavioralism, claimed he could "build any man, starting at birth."[5]

The physical and social transformation of America begun in the nineteenth century reached a new tempo and range in the 1920s and 1930s. Electricity, while not new, came to be widely applied. Electrification of American homes rose from 24 percent in 1917 to nearly 90 percent by 1940. New, individually controlled machines such as coffee pots, vacuum clean-

1.4 Raymond Loewy (1893–1986)
Pencil Sharpener. 1933. Prototype, metal and wood (handle replaced), 4¾ × 5½ × 2¼". Collection Jack Solomon, Circle Fine Art Corp.

1.5 Alfonso Iannelli (1888–1965)
Faucet. 1931. Prototype, designed for Mueller Mixing Valve Co., Decatur, Ill. Chrome-plated metal, 4½ × 2³⁄₁₆ × 7¹⁄₁₆"

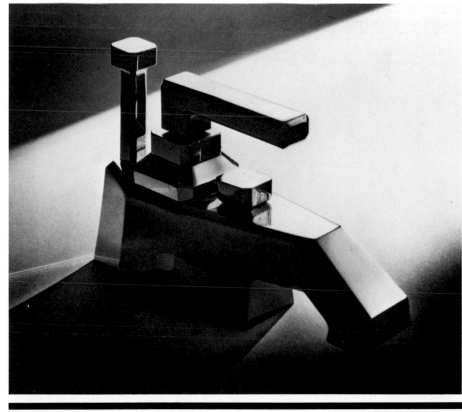

1.6 Walter Dorwin Teague (1883–1960) "Bluebird" Radio. 1937–40. Manufactured by Sparton Corp., Jackson, Mich. Glass, metal, and wood, 45½ × 43½ × 15½″. Collection Michael D. Kinerk and Dennis W. Wilhelm

ers, and washing machines added a new dimension to daily life. There were only 65,000 mechanical refrigerators in 1924, as opposed to 7 million ten years later. Wider availability of electricity made possible microphones at political rallies and the telephone linking people across town, across the country, and across the ocean. In 1900 about 1 million phones existed, by 1920 7.5 million, and by 1930 over 20 million. The first radio station, KDKA of Pittsburgh, appeared in 1920, and by 1925 there were 571 stations and over 2.75 million receivers. Through the formation of the radio networks listeners became intimately linked to a new culture of mass entertainment and advertising. Radio's status can be seen in Rockefeller Center, initially intended to be the home of the Metropolitan Opera (see fig. 6.15). When the opera pulled out, the Radio Corporation of America leased the centerpiece building; the entire complex became known as Radio City. While on one level the radio and telephone tied people together, on another they made possible increased separation. Both the radio and the telephone—carrying the human voice by electro-mechanical means—substituted an illusion of immediacy for real encounters. In entertainment, choice became individualistic and passive. One simply sat and received; reaction involved turning on and off, nothing else was necessary.[6]

Americans were also entertained by another product of the machine, the motion picture. By the 1920s a nationwide ritual had been established of the family attending the movie house at least once a week. The audience had broadened to include the middle class, and by 1927 there were seventeen thousand theaters in the United States. In many towns the movie house was the most impressive piece of new architecture. Television, a sort of motion-picture radio for the home, was forecast in the 1920s; however, partly because of the Depression, but also owing to technical problems, it did not appear until 1939.[7]

The machine that most changed American life—and became in its own right both a symbol and a cult object—was the automobile. From fewer than 500,000 cars and trucks in America in 1910, nearly 10 million were registered in 1920, over 26 million in 1930, and 32 million by 1940. From one hundred fiftieth in product value among American industries in 1900, automobile manufacturing leaped to twenty-first position by 1910 and to first by the mid-1920s. The streets of American cities in 1910 were primarily crowded with streetcars, horse-drawn wagons, and buggies, with only an occasional automobile seen. By 1920, the streets were more crowded and the horse was a rarity: the automobile existed everywhere. Automobile ownership became a status symbol for the working class, as Robert S. and Helen Lynd found in their seminal *Middletown* studies of the 1920s and 1930s. To people of all classes the automobile represented freedom, the ultimate democratic transportation machine, which allowed one—within reason—to roam widely and at will. W. J. Cash discovered that for the southern millworker, the automobile was both "toy and symbol of modernity." Paradoxically, the automobile became also a necessity, and in binding people even more to the machine it made them more dependent on the government to provide the setting in which the symbol could operate.[8]

Contributing to the consciousness of a new age was World War I, the first full-scale, all-mechanized conflict. While the history of war is in one sense the history of the mechanics of killing, this war—with its horrific casualties and the way the machine not simply killed, but chewed up, disfigured, and so tore apart the human body that often it could neither be found nor identified—made apparent a new level of destruction. Not only did the individual disappear into the rank and file necessary for organized warfare, the rank and file was now subsumed by the new machines: long-distance artillery, machine guns, armored transports, tanks, airplanes, and machine products such as aerial bombardments, poison gas, and barbed wire. The victory of the allies was in a sense a machine victory: the American ability to supply in overwhelming numbers the new war machines was the force that tipped the balance.[9]

Historically, America has always been the land of the machine. Even the earliest Americans, faced with abundant natural resources and limited labor, looked to machines to help with their work. No ma-

chine was considered too complicated or too costly if it could save expensive man-hours. Yet in spite of the legend of "Yankee ingenuity," Europeans invented such machines as the spinning jenny, the flying shuttle, the steam engine, the factory, the locomotive, and even the automobile. (A major exception was powered flight, pioneered by Orville and Wilbur Wright in 1903.) American genius took these European machines, altered, perfected, and exploited them, and placed them in a system to produce a flood of goods never before imagined.[10]

1.9 Walker Evans
Brooklyn Bridge. 1929. Gelatin-silver print, 8¾ × 5½″. The Museum of Modern Art, New York. Mr. and Mrs. John Spencer Fund

Americans in the nineteenth century exalted machines, and tended to decorate them. Walt Whitman sang, "By thud of machinery and shrill steam-whistle undismay'd," and Horatio Greenough announced that sailing ship design should be the basis for a new art. Early in the twentieth century Henry Adams speculated that the dynamo might serve as the symbol of modern civilization in the same way that the Virgin of Chartres symbolized the Middle Ages. However, the dominant cultural and artistic values of America—or at least elite America—throughout the nineteenth and early twentieth centuries were genteel, European, and historical in origin. Machines were used, but to imitate the past.[11]

The recognition of industrial civilization marked the break with this orientation to past culture. Photographs by Alfred Stieglitz and Alvin Langdon Coburn taken about 1910 turn to the industrial environment for its inherent beauty, drama, and emotion, seen through a soft focus of steam and smoke. Interpretations of the Brooklyn Bridge indicate the change. While hailed throughout its construction from 1869 until its completion in 1883 as an example of American engineering prowess, the bridge did not enter the realm of high art until the 1910s and the paintings of John Marin. The apotheosis of the Brooklyn Bridge came in the 1920s with the paintings of Joseph Stella, photographs of Walker Evans, and poems of Hart Crane. This wider sensibility was anticipated by Robert J. Coady, the editor of the little art and letters magazine *The Soil*, who wrote in 1917: "Our art is, as yet, outside of our art world." In a Whitmanesque catalogue Coady listed as American art examples as diverse as the Panama Canal, the steam shovel, the Portland Cement Works, and Charlie Chaplin.[12]

1.10 Louis Lozowick (1892–1973) *High Voltage–Cos Cob*. 1930. Oil on canvas, 18 × 24″. Hirschl & Adler Galleries, Inc.

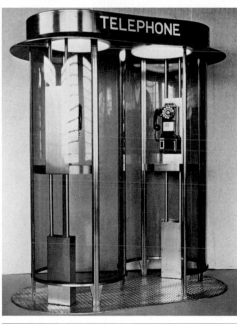

1.11 Sherron Metalic Corporation, Brooklyn, New York "Ying-Yang" Telephone Booth. 1938–39. Designed for 1939 New York World's Fair. Steel, brass, aluminum, and plexiglass, 84 × 50 × 28″ (approx.). Original lost or destroyed

THE AGENDA

The reality of the machine age could not be denied: America dominated the world in the number of automobiles, the amount of electricity consumed, and in steel produced. But that did not make an art or a culture. Some Americans, such as the critic Walter Pach in 1922, probed beneath the raw statistics to predict "the study that will one day be given to the American art that is not yet recognized by its public or its makers. . . . The steel bridges, the steel

1.12 Stuart Davis (1894–1964) *Study for History of Communications Mural.* 1939. Ink on paper, 9⅝ × 29⅞". Minnesota Museum of Art, St. Paul

1.13 Charlie Chaplin (1889–1977) *Modern Times.* 1936. The Museum of Modern Art, New York. Film Stills Archive

1.14 Frank Hultzberg *Fantasy New York.* 1935. Oil on canvas, 54 × 40". Collection Steven De Arakie

buildings, the newly designed machines and utensils of all kinds."[13]

Lewis Mumford, writing in 1921, cited the New York subways and "cheap popular lunchrooms" as the "two main sources of the modern style at present." "How is it that the modern style has been so slow to realize itself—is still so timid, so partial, so inadequate?" he lamented. The next year he saw a sign of hope: "With the beginning of the second decade of this century, there is some evidence of an attempt to make a genuine culture out of industrialization."[14]

The art director of the New York City schools, James P. Haney, arguing in 1919 for more integration of art in industry, claimed it was "a question . . . of practical patriotism . . . a question of national pride." Noting the accomplishments of foreign nations in setting up schools for industrial designers and in establishing national unions of art in industry, Haney felt that by contrast, America, "A great industrial nation without an industrial art," had failed.[15]

What should the new art be like? The photographer Margaret Bourke-White saw an America where "Dynamos were more beautiful . . . than pearls." For her, "any important art coming out of the industrial age will draw inspiration from industry, because industry is alive and vital. The beauty of industry lies within its truth and simplicity: every line is essential and therefore beautiful."[16]

Writing on "The Americanization of Art," part of the important *Machine-Age* exhibition catalogue of 1927, Louis Lozowick noted America's "meager cultural heritage" and argued that "The history of America is a history of stubborn and ceaseless effort to harness the forces of nature . . . of gigantic engineering feats and colossal mechanical construction," and in that history lay a source for art. This environment was "only raw material"; the artist could not make from it "a literal soulless transcription," but must interpret it. Behind and animating this new world was an "industrialization and standardization" that had a "structure," a "function," and "objectivity," which brought forth a new vision of "shapes and colors not paralleled in nature." "Chaos and confusion" existed, Lozowick admitted, but so did "order and organization," observable in the "rigid geometry of the American city: in the verticals of its smoke stacks, in the parallels of its car tracks, the squares of its streets, the cubes of its factories, the arcs of its bridges, the cylinders of its gas tanks." This order offered a mathematical pattern upon which a "plastic structure" of an art would catch the "flowing rhythm of modern America" in a native idiom.[17]

The new vertical monuments of the city afforded one possibility for displaying a native art. While the skyscraper as a building form can be traced back to the 1870s, the period after 1910 and especially in the 1920s is when the skyscraper came to be considered, in the words of the historian Thomas Tallmadge, "the most important architectural achievement of America." In 1911 the philosopher George Santayana had personified the skyscraper as inhabited by the "American Will"; the

1.15

1.15 Margaret Bourke-White (1904–1971)
Niagara Falls Generators. 1928. Gelatin-silver print, 17½ × 13⅛″. International Museum of Photography at George Eastman House, Rochester, N.Y.

1.16 Alvin Langdon Coburn (1882–1966)
Untitled (Steam Shovel and Train). ca. 1910. Gum-platinum print, 13 ⅜ × 16⅜″. International Museum of Photography at George Eastman House, Rochester, N.Y.

1.17 John Gutmann (b. 1905)
Elevator Garage, Chicago. 1936. Gelatin-silver print, 8 × 10″

1.18 Hugh Ferriss (1889–1962) *To Tomorrow with Lehigh Cement.* ca. 1928. Charcoal on paper, 25½ × 19½". Published in *The Metropolis of Tomorrow* (New York: Ives Washburn, 1929). Avery Architectural and Fine Arts Library, Columbia University, New York

1.19 Alfred Stieglitz (1864–1946) *From the Shelton, Looking West.* 1933. Gelatin-silver print, 9⅝ × 3⅝". International Museum of Photography at George Eastman House, Rochester, N.Y.

"American Intellect," on the other hand, resided in a "neat reproduction of the colonial mansion." The skyscrapers of New York particularly moved John Marin, who decided, "they too must have life. Thus the whole city is alive,... influences of one mass on another greater or smaller mass.... I try to express graphically what a great city is doing. Within the frame there must be a balance, a controlling of these warring, pushing pulling forces." Marin saw the skyscrapers of Fifth Avenue as great, man-made mountains of energy, excitement, and agitation. Similarly affected was Hugh Ferriss, whose *Metropolis of Tomorrow* celebrates vast cliffs of man-made setback towers of stone, steel,

glass, and concrete (see fig. 1.18). Ferriss tried to deny the contemporary view of the skyscraper city as "the embodiment of some blind and mechanical force that has imposed itself, as though from without, on a helpless humanity." Yet his drawings showed cities either devoid of humanity or full of rushing, swirling people and cars in multilevel, multilane superhighways that tunneled through buildings, rooftop airports, skyscraper bridges with apartments in the pylons, and towers of unimaginable heights. The modern American skyscraper city became to most people a "giant machine," as Stieglitz called it and portrayed it in his photographs, especially those of the RCA Building.[18]

Music also came under the agenda of the machine age. In Europe a vigorous avant-garde performed a new music incorporating nontraditional sounds that reflected the machine. Both Edgard Varèse's *Ameriques* and Arthur Honegger's *Pacific 231* reflect the machine and the primacy of America. Although this new music was seldom played in the United States, the idea of music from machines was known. George Antheil, an American in Paris in the 1920s, wrote a *Ballet mécanique,* a composition with brutish machine noisemaking. Frederick Shepard Converse's "epic tone poem," *Flivver Ten Million,* inspired by the ten-millionth *Model T,* was premiered by Serge Koussevitzky and the Boston Symphony Orchestra in 1927. In addition to the usual instruments, Converse employed a Ford horn, a factory whistle, and wind and anvil machines; he titled movements "Dawn in Detroit," "The Call to Labor," "May Night by the Roadside," and other equally evocative machine age phrases. In the 1920s jazz, among some advanced composers, also appeared to have a mechanical noise element. The fre-

1.19

1.20 Louis Lozowick
Machine Ornament No. 2. ca. 1927. Brush and ink on paper, 22 × 15¹⁄₁₆″. Hirshhorn Museum and Sculpture Garden, Smithsonian Institution, Washington, D.C.

girl dancers in *Footlight Parade* of 1933, for example, strongly resembled a Curtis radial aircraft engine (fig. 1.21).[19]

The quest for a machine age culture in literature involved both subject matter and technique. The machine appears in novels such as Sinclair Lewis's *Babbitt* (1922), where the characters engage in "worship of machinery" and George Babbitt fondles the shiny new fixtures of his bathroom and revels in the smell of his new car. Carl Sandburg's book of poems *Smoke and Steel* (1920) and many novels of social protest, such as Robert Cantwell's *Land of Plenty* (1934), use machine age landscapes as settings. The machine as subject began to surface in poems such as MacKnight Black's *Machinery* (1929):

> Look, these are all
> We have for symbols

and

> Dynamos are bosoms,
> Round with the sweet first-filling of a
>   new
> Mother's milk.[20]

For some writers the new machine culture would suggest a new technique. John Dos Passos experimented with new methods of transcription in his trilogy *U.S.A.* (1930–37). The interwoven stories of various real and fictional characters trying to adjust to the new world of the machine are interspersed with two machine-like, documentary-appearing devices—"Newsreel" and "The Camera Eye." The choice of photography as the controlling and recording element is a particularly apt one: for the true artist of the machine age it was not enough to try to portray the impact of the machine or make it a symbol; he must himself become a machinist and utilize the machine as technique.

netic sounds of the city became the basic material for *Skyscrapers*, a jazz ballet by John Alden Carpenter. From music based on machines to dance based on machines was but a short step. Earl Carroll's *Vanities* of 1928 contained a ballet drawn from "a visit to the Ford motor plant." The dance director was Busby Berkeley, who in a few years would move to Hollywood and use in his films motorized stages and platforms for dances that recalled machines. Sometimes specific machine images were evoked: the radiating spread of

1.21 Busby Berkeley (1895–1976)
Footlight Parade. 1933

1.22 Charles Lindbergh with *Spirit of St. Louis*. 1927

1.23 Niles Spencer (1893–1952)
Western Pennsylvania. 1937. Mural in Aliquippa, Pa., Post Office. Oil on canvas, 15'4" × 5'7"

1.24 Grant Wood (1892–1942)
Death on the Ridge Road. 1935. Oil on masonite, 32 × 39″. Williams College Museum of Art, Williamstown, Mass. Gift of Cole Porter

1.25 Charles E. Burchfield (1893–1967)
Black Iron. 1935. Watercolor on paper, 29 × 41″. Private collection

The machine age required new heroes capable of understanding and controlling the new forces. In the 1920s the businessman was the popular hero, but he was replaced in the 1930s by the more creative engineer, scientist, and industrial designer. For the left wing in the 1930s, the anonymous, muscular, proletarian worker came to the fore, especially in painting and sculpture. Still, a need existed for a single personality to symbolize the hero incarnate. To many people Charles Lindbergh, already strongly identified with the machine age, filled the role. Harry Crosby, the expatriate novelist, recorded the feeling at Le Bourget, France, on May 21, 1927: "A small white hawk of a plane swoops hawk-like down across the field . . . it seems as if all the hands in the world are touching or trying to touch the new

Christ and that the new Cross is the Plane. . . . *Ce n'est pas un homme, c'est un Oiseau!*"[21]

Certainly not every American felt the creation of a machine age art and culture to be a high priority. A traditional academic viewpoint dominated many art and architecture schools. Allegorical maidens in gowns were still painted, and neoclassical and colonial revival buildings were still built: in 1932 the first buildings of Colonial Williamsburg opened to the public. The regionalist movement in literature and painting, which held agrarian values supreme, claimed a wide following, yet much of the imagery of American Scene painters such as Charles Burchfield dealt with the machine landscape of upper New York State. Even Grant Wood, the most vociferous of the regionalists, who retreated to Stone City to create a pastoral vision of rural Iowa life, could not ignore the machine as it rushed in, a sleek, impatient city car creating certain tragedy in *Death on the Ridge Road* (fig. 1.24). And the modern machine also appeared in public murals for the Works Progress Administration (WPA) and other organizations.[22]

An inspection of almost any house from the late 1920s and 1930s shows a dichotomy between the historical facade and period furnishings and the new, machine-made service areas. Writing about the traditionalist, Palladian-inspired A. Everett Austin, Jr., House in Hartford, Connecticut (figs. 1.26, 1.27), Philip Goodwin (later an associate architect on the new Museum of Modern Art in New York) noted, "Modernism is creeping right into the fabric of the whole house—kitchen, pantry, laundry, bedrooms and bath, have all capitulated to the machine; only the exterior, the dining-room and living rooms are holding out, and the dining-room is quite ready to be converted."[23]

1.26 A. Everett Austin, Jr. (1900–1957) and Leigh H. French, Jr. (1894–1946) A. Everett Austin, Jr., House. 1930. Hartford, Conn. Wadsworth Atheneum Archives, Hartford, Conn.

1.27 Dressing Room, A. Everett Austin, Jr., House

1.28 New York World's Fair, viewed from midtown Manhattan, with *Perisphere* and *Trylon* seen in the background. 1939

1.29 Henry Dreyfuss (1904–1972) *Democracity.* 1939. Model inside the *Perisphere*, New York World's Fair, 1939–40

1.30 Arthur J. Hammond *Semi Lunar.* 1939–40. Gelatin-silver print, 10¼ × 13½″. The Brooklyn Museum. Gift of the artist

The agenda for the machine age not only included the traditional arts of painting, sculpture, and architecture, but also envisioned a total transformation. Everything needed to be redesigned, claimed Norman Bel Geddes; as Walter Dorwin Teague remarked, "we are not building big and little gadgets—we are building an environment." Attempts were made to create the new world in microcosm in the pavilions of two World's Fairs, the *Centu-*

ry of Progress, Chicago, 1933–34, and the *World of Tomorrow*, New York, 1939–40. Their names offered a utopian promise, and through their displays, from the model General Motors assembly line by Albert Kahn at Chicago to *Democracity* by Henry Dreyfuss at New York, the visitor entered the machine-made future (see figs. 1.29, 3.12). Exiting from Dreyfuss's model city inside the two-hundred-foot-diameter *Perisphere*, the visitor passed through the seven-hundred-foot-tall *Trylon*—and then down a ramp, the *Helicene*, to the ground. Envisioned was a future where the entire man-made world was art, for as Teague claimed, "every man who plans the shape and line and color of an object—whether it is a painting, statue, chair, sewing machine, house, bridge, or locomotive—is an artist."[24]

A machine age culture had been created, ahistorical and nontraditional, constantly changing and always new. Production and consumption were the keys to the new world, and art, from painting to advertising, heralded its triumphs. So successful was this new culture that Henry Ford claimed, "Machinery is accomplishing in the world what man has failed to do by preaching, propaganda, or the written word."[25]

Americans adopted the machine as reality and as symbol. It appeared to promise blessings and benefits and a way of life free from want. Yet it needed to be controlled as well. Alfred H. Barr pointed out in The Museum of Modern Art's 1934 *Machine Art* catalogue, "Not only must we bind Frankenstein—but we must make him beautiful." Perhaps Stuart Chase, the popular economist and machine advocate-critic, summed up the situation best: "The machine has ruthlessly destroyed a whole age of art, but is busy creating a new age."[26]

40

2.1

CHAPTER 2

MACHINE AESTHETICS

To the industrial designer Raymond Loewy the evolution of design, whether in telephones or locomotives, followed a pattern. In a series of mid-1930s charts Loewy showed machines of all types evolving from primitive assemblages of parts into smooth, cohesive shapes (fig. 2.2). He predicted the trend would continue well into the future, even extending to the female form and women's fashions. A will to similar form encompassed all objects.[1]

Loewy's evolutionary charts exemplify the attempt by many designers, artists, and critics to project an aesthetic system that would offer a common visual continuum in which the automobile, the house, the dining-room chairs, the electric toaster, and a painting could exist in harmony. A fundamentally new approach to aesthetics—or, as Walter Dorwin Teague wrote, "A new style as right and satisfying and as true to our time as Gothic was to the Middle Ages in which it flourished"—appeared necessary. While a single, all-encompassing aesthetic was sought, stylistic terms proliferated: "modern," "modernistic," "moderne," "Manhattan Style," "cubistic," "jazz," "streamlined," "International Style,"

"functionalist," "organic," and others. No single machine style or aesthetic approach won the day. Some approaches to the machine claimed the allegiance of many, others were entirely personal. Some reflected a priori aesthetics, others reflected different machines. The issue of "sales" or "appeal to the purchaser" was frequently the underlying motive, sometimes openly acknowledged, other times hidden.[2]

The different attitudes to the machine expressed in the 1920s and 1930s show one of two reactions: exaltation or rejection. Rejection implied a dislike of the machine and the tendency to disguise it, for example by covering electrical appliances with Louis XVI patterns, or treating automobiles as coaches and homes as eighteenth-century colonial mansions. Exaltation meant recognition of the primacy of the machine for the new age and the attempt to make it into art. Exaltation could also imply disguise of the object, since artists and designers tended to emphasize certain aspects, such as the angular geometry of gears, simple chrome shells covering complex electric appliances, or chairs contoured out of molded plywood. These different positive re-

2.1 Charles Demuth (1883–1935) *My Egypt*. 1927. Oil on composition board, 35¾ × 30″. Whitney Museum of American Art, New York

2.2 Raymond Loewy
Evolution Chart of the Desk Telephone
and *Evolution Chart of Female Dress.*
1934

sponses may be called machine aesthetics—the belief that a machine beauty exists that can be enhanced by an artist or a designer.

Four stylistic interpretations emerge out of machine aesthetics of the 1920s and 1930s: moderne, machine purity, streamline, and biomorphic. Each style involves a fundamentally different response to the machine and chooses different prime objects or images as its primary design inspiration. The power of an image both realistically and abstractly conceived has many ramifications: a powerful, dominant image can generate a family of like forms for very different purposes and products. For example, the setback skyscraper gave form to interior furnishings and decor, kitchen appliances, and two-dimensional advertising design.[3]

Obviously prime images can change because of new cultural and artistic perceptions. In the 1920s the prime objects were complex arrays of machine parts, machines with a variety of parts, gear boxes, setback skyscrapers, and the automobile, with its separate elements: wheels, spare tire, headlights, hood cover, radiator, doors, and top. The moderne, a decorative style, was one response to this machine-as-parts syndrome. In *Egg Beater #1* by Stuart Davis (fig. 2.4), the machine's parts and motions become a decorative pattern with similarities to many of the interiors designed by Kem Weber in the late 1920s. Opposed to such decorative elaboration was machine purity, which also saw the machine as angular geometry. Charles Sheeler's *Upper Deck*, (fig. 2.6), seems to be a true-to-life depiction of motors, stacks, and parts, and is in fact based on a photograph. But Sheeler had carefully composed the scene, cropping and lighting it, and adjusting the

2.3 Abel Faidy (1895–1965) Armchair. 1927. Maple with leather upholstery, 55½ × 21⅝ × 22″. Collection Chicago Historical Society

solids, voids, and planes. Not even a smudge of oil mars the pristine forms.

With the streamlining of the 1930s, more cohesive units, such as aerodynamic monocoque shapes of airplanes, serve as the inspiration. Kem Weber's "airline chair," 1935, uses simple curved shapes in place of angular geometry (fig. 2.5). In the late 1930s with the biomorphic aesthetic, multicontoured forms and natural shapes, such as amoebas, become the prime object, as in Charles Eames and Eero Saarinen's molded plywood chair of 1941 (fig. 2.20).

2.4 Stuart Davis
Eggbeater #1. 1927. Oil on canvas, 27 × 38½″. The Phillips Collection, Washington, D.C.

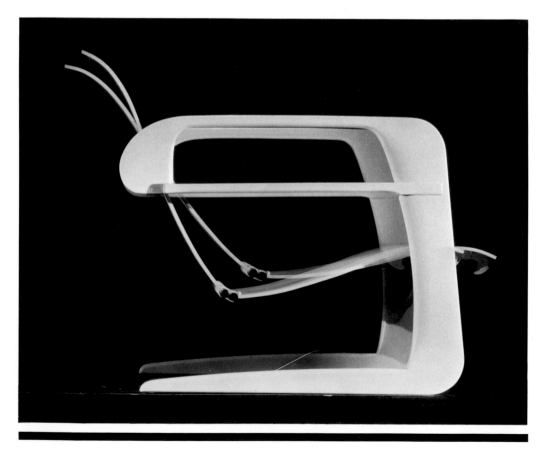

2.5 Kem Weber (1889–1963)
Airline Chair. 1934–35. Manufactured by Airline Chair Co., Los Angeles. Wood and naugahyde, 30½ × 25 × 34″. University Art Museum, University of California, Santa Barbara. Gift of Mrs. Erika Weber

Not every designer can be pigeonholed into one stylistic aesthetic. Some, such as Paul T. Frankl, a German immigrant with offices first in New York and then in Los Angeles, actually mastered several of them—in Frankl's case three of the four. In the late 1920s he designed "skyscraper" furniture with a multiplicity of parts, exemplifying the moderne. In the early 1930s his emphasis changed from the vertical to the horizontal. He described the form of his armchair from 1932–33 (fig. 2.23) as "borrowed from the streamlines of the boat cutting through the water at fast speed." And in the late 1930s Frankl moved to biomorphic shapes, as seen in the cocktail tables he designed for the Johnson Furniture Company.[4]

MODERNE OR DECORATIVE GEOMETRY

Machine-styled art and design of the 1920s appear to have been influenced by the perception of the machine as a combination of parts—gears, cams, axles—or of factory complexes involving many buildings and multiple smokestacks. Machines, as in Ralph Steiner's *Typewriter as Design* (fig. 2.7), were simple geometrical elements arranged in complex patterns. The moderne (or "modernistic," or more recently "Art Deco") style took as its primary clue the multiple geometrical elements of machines arranged in a decorative pattern.

The moderne style in America grew out of a number of European art movements. Geometrical simplification had first arisen in the English Arts and Crafts movement of the 1880s, and by the turn of the century, the Secessionists in Vienna were creating total environments—paintings, furniture, and architecture—based upon geometrical simplification. English designers, through the Craftsman move-

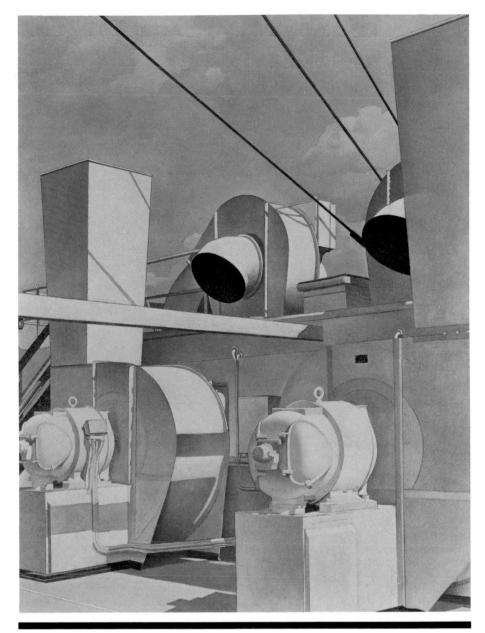

2.6 Charles Sheeler
Upper Deck. 1929. Oil on canvas, 29 × 22⅛". Fogg Art Museum, Harvard University, Cambridge, Mass. Purchase, Louise E. Bettens Fund

ment of Gustav Stickley, and the Viennese, through displays at world's fairs, became known in America. Artists allied with the Secessionists, Joseph Urban, Paul Frankl, and Kem Weber all arrived before World War I broke out, and Viennese and German Secessionist–style designs were shown periodically in department stores, museums, and specialty shops. Between 1922 and 1924 Joseph Urban ran a New York branch of the Wiener Werkstätte and held exhibitions in a number of American cities.[5]

Futurism, committed to glorifying the machine, and cubism, with its emphasis upon simple geometrical shapes—abstractions of real objects—arrayed in

2.7

complex patterns of varying spatial depth, were important sources for the moderne. To many Americans futurism and cubism were largely indistinguishable, both seen as machine oriented. Which style was first responsible for inserting mechanical elements in paintings is problematical. By 1912 two futurists, Giacomo Balla and Umberto Boccioni, portrayed street lamps and the modern city. Marcel Duchamp's 1912 cubist-futurist painting, *Nude Descending a Staircase, No. 2* (fig. 2.8), used a mechanical, mannequin-like figure in motion derived from, as he later noted, "the cinema, still in its infancy, and the separation of static positions in the photochronographs of Marey in France, Eakins and Muybridge in America." Francis Picabia's object portraits—such as *Portrait d'une jeune fille américaine dans l'état de nudité* (fig. 2.9), in which a sparkplug is the central feature, or *Ici, c'est ici Stieglitz*, which offers a camera as the central feature—began to appear in 1915. There is no apparent influence of machines on the early analytical cubism of Pablo Picasso and Georges Braque, yet the rhythmical geometrical shapes certainly could have been associated with machines.[6]

The *Exposition International des Arts Décoratifs et Industriels Modernes* held in Paris in 1925 helped to popularize European modern art, making it acceptable for American architecture, decorative arts, and industrial products. From the Paris exposition came the terms "Art Moderne," "modernistic," and the recent sobriquet "Art Deco." The exposition contained many different examples of art—from the highly sophisticated, hand-crafted furniture of Emile-Jacques Ruhlmann, to low-relief, neoclassical sculpture and the geometrical purism of Le Corbusier and Amédée Ozenfant's

2.7 Ralph Steiner (1899–1986) *Typewriter as Design*. 1921–22. Gelatin-silver print, 8 × 6″. Worcester Art Museum, Worcester, Mass.

2.8 Marcel Duchamp (1887–1968) *Nude Descending a Staircase, No. 2*. 1912. Oil on canvas, 58 × 35″. Philadelphia Museum of Art. Louise and Walter Arensberg Collection

Pavillon de l'Esprit Nouveau—but the American observers tended to overlook the differences, choosing instead to view the entire ensemble as an example of the moderne movement or Art Moderne. The overall impression was of an ornamental effect: lush, rich, and exotic materials, colors, and forms competing on the interiors and exteriors. Helen Appleton Read, a prominent art critic, compared the exposition's "cubistic shapes and futurist colors" to "a Picasso abstraction."[7]

Few if any of the exhibits were really machine produced or machine styled, but in certain ways the exposition did serve as a source for machine age aesthetics. First, of course, was the name, which linked the notions of industry and modernity. In addition, some of the materials used, such as the reinforced concrete in Auguste Perret's *Exhibition Theatre*, were interpreted as very modern and industrial. Many of the exhibition buildings, both on their exteriors and interiors, also used stylized and abstract patterns with a geometrical—hence machine-like—character. Finally, there were explicit machine motifs, from highly realistic murals of automobiles in *La Cour des Métiers*, to

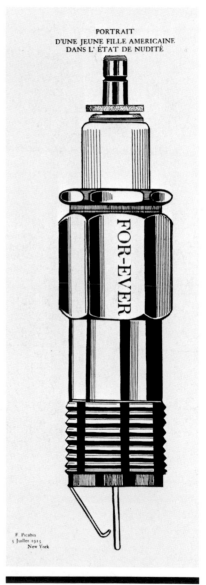

PORTRAIT
D'UNE JEUNE FILLE AMÉRICAINE
DANS L' ÉTAT DE NUDITÉ

FOR-EVER

F. Picabia
5 Juillet 1915
New York

2.9 Francis Picabia (1879–1953) *Portrait d'une jeune fille américaine dans l'état de nudité, 1915*. 1915. (From *291*, Nos. 5–6, July–August 1915). San Francisco Museum of Modern Art

2.10 Charles Loupot (1892–1971)
*Exposition Internationale Arts Décoratifs
et Industriels Modernes.* 1925. Lithograph
poster, 36 × 22¼". Collection Bob Hels-
ley and David Bergman

2.11 Henri Favier and André Ventre,
architects
*Gates of Honor. Exposition Internationale
des Arts Décoratifs et Industriels Modernes*, Paris. 1925. Edgar Brandt, metal-
work; Navarre, sculptor; René Lalique,
glasswork

cubistic renditions of trains and other
transportation machines in a frieze inside
Le Pavillon de Tourisme.[8]

The decorative geometry of the Paris
Arts Décoratifs et Industriels Modernes
exhibition fit comfortably into the already
developing view of the machine as
parts—interconnected gears—arranged
in a complex way. Read compared Cé-
zanne's aesthetic of angular geometry to
the development of "the age of scientific
reason and the glorification of the machine." A few months later she interpreted the exposition as part of the new
aesthetic: "The whole trend of modern
design toward the geometric and the unadorned, had its inception through the
omnipresence of the machine. Because
we had absorbed the shapes of the machine into our consciousness, we ended
up by creating designs which reflected it,
and which in turn are most suitable for
machine-made processes."[9]

The moderne style being touted in Paris was not altogether new in the United
States. Since 1920 several magazines had
been publishing French designs, and in
1923 Paul Poiret, a French moderne interior and dress designer, had made a successful lecture tour of several American
cities. American architects such as Frank
Lloyd Wright and Bertram Goodhue had
created a native American moderne or
Art Deco, which emphasized interrelated
flat and angular geometrical patterns.[10]

Nonmachine in source and yet also in-
strumental in forming the geometrical
cast of moderne machine aesthetics were
primitive or vernacular art sources such as
American Indian pottery and rugs and
Middle Eastern textiles. The connection
was a recognized sympathy of forms, repetitive patterns, simple geometrical
shapes, and strong colors. Some artists,
such as Allen True, a painter from Denver, exploited these similarities. True,

2.12 Allen Tupper True (1881–1955) Floor Tile Design. 1936. Boulder Dam, Boulder City, Nev.

who directed the color scheme and interior decoration at Hoover Dam in 1935–36, chose for the floor terrazzo decoration patterns based upon Pueblo, Acoma, and Pima pottery, basketry, and sand paintings (fig. 2.12). As an explanation of his choice True wrote: "A little study of its central portion will reveal its striking similarity to what might be termed an engineer's basic diagram of a generator or turbine, with valves, gates, and a suggestion of centrifugal motion."[11]

MACHINE PURITY

A purified style of machine aesthetics began to replace the decorative modernistic in the late 1920s, and by the early 1930s assumed an almost canonical position. Its preeminence in America was due in part to increasing knowledge of the avantgarde European design—the German Bauhaus, Dutch de Stijl, and French purism—and an American equivalent, the objectivist photographers and painters Paul Strand, Charles Sheeler, and Charles Demuth. A two-way street of interest and influence existed, however, as many Europeans sought inspiration in American factories, grain elevators, and machines.

The French purist group—Fernand Léger, Le Corbusier, and Ozenfant—owing to their Paris location, which for many Americans was the center of art, became

the most influential. All extolled, along with Léger, unconscious "Machine Beauty, without artistic intention," and "the true creator . . . who daily, modestly, unconsciously, creates and invents these handsome objects, these beautiful machines which make us live." Enamored with American subjects, Léger traded a group of his prints for a set of American mechanical drawings. Louis Lozowick reported after a European trip in the mid-1920s that the work of Léger "pleads with American artists for an American orientation, a closer contact with their industrial civilization so rich in plastic possibilities, and a consequent fluorescence of an original indigenous art."[12]

The publication in English of Le Corbusier's *Towards a New Architecture* (1927) gave added impact to the aesthetic of machine purity. Even though Le Corbusier tried to distance himself from the *Arts Décoratifs*, preferring simpler patterns, he saw the machine as a series of simple geometric shapes arrayed in a complex pattern, as he showed with his cut-away illustration of a Delage front-wheel brake (fig. 2.13). The governing assumption was the existence of a universal order of geometry that could be found in ancient and classical art as well. The caption under the Delage brake illustration summed up the connection: "This precision, this cleanness in execution go further back

2.13 Le Corbusier [Charles Edouard Jeanneret-Gris] (1887–1965) Delage Front-Wheel Brake. Drawing from *Vers une Architecture*, 1927. © SPA-DEM, Paris/VAGA, New York, 1986

than our re-born mechanical sense. Phidias felt this way: the entablature of the Parthenon is a witness. So did the Egyptians when they polished the Pyramids. This at a time when Euclid and Pythagoras dictated to their contemporaries."[13]

Le Corbusier's aesthetic was a rationale for the utilization of similar geometric forms in both his painting and his architecture. His writings had a direct impact on artists and designers in the United States: his aphorism "A house is a machine for living in" became a rallying cry both for those who admired the new machine age and for those who despised it. An American review from 1927 claimed: "He sees the greatness of our future in a scientific expression of the possibilities of steel beams, mass production units, bare concrete walls and a complete avoidance of all unnecessary detail." Others responded negatively. Ralph Walker, whose New York Telephone Building had appeared as a frontispiece in Le Corbusier's book, implying a sympathy of interests, described such geometric reductivism as fit only for a "robot."[14]

A number of Americans responded to Le Corbusier's emphasis on classic geometry. Paul Frankl saw classic geometry as the key to all good design. Walter Dorwin Teague returned from Europe in 1926 convinced that "Machine Age" beauty was actually "familiar in Athens, the beauty of precision, of exact relationships of rhythmical proportions; the beauty whose first law is perfect fitness and performance, whose second is candor and direct simplicity, whose third is a harmony of elements mathematically exact." Later, in his 1940 book, *Design This Day: The Technique of Order in the Machine Age*, he became more explicit, publishing diagrams and descriptions of proportional schemes—"The Parthenon, based on the square, the golden section rectangle, the root-five rectangle and their diagonals"—and "Dynamic Symmetry." Geometry, Teague claimed, ruled all design.[15]

The aesthetic of machine purity received major American academic imprimatur with The Museum of Modern Art's major exhibitions of the 1930s, the *International Exhibition of Modern Architecture* of 1932 and the *Machine Art* show of 1934. The *Machine Art* show extended the notion presented by the 1932 architecture exhibition—that of a true universal modern style composed of simple geometric forms (emphasized by black-and-white photographs) with complex details. Curated by Philip Johnson, it drew tremendous crowds. Based on classical ideals of beauty, the aesthetic developed by Alfred H. Barr, Jr., the museum's director, and Johnson involved geometrical shapes in pure forms, proportions, and surface treatment, properties that could come from the handicraft tradition as well as the machine. The exhibition contained 402 items that confirmed Barr and Johnson's view of beauty: boat propellers, ball

bearings, and springs mounted on pedestals like valuable art objects. Ironically, some of the items they included, such as the Dunhill pipe—a popular shape included in French cubist and purist paintings—was in fact not machine made, but handmade. Dunhill refused to participate until the Rockefellers, who both supported the museum and rented space to the Dunhill shop in Rockefeller Center, intervened.[16]

By 1934 machine purity displaced the more ornamental moderne and modernistic, terms that became the whipping boys of the purists. Philip Johnson claimed that "the problem in America has not been the conflict against a strong handicraft tradition but rather against a 'modernistic' French machine-age aesthetic."[17]

To this canonical view of machine puri-ty, several caveats must be noted. A striking discrepancy can occur between concepts on paper and real objects. Many of the designs of Teague, Dreyfuss, Frankl, and others have little to do with their printed words. Also many of the terms used—for example, "simplicity," "function," and "cleanliness"—were also used with the more ornamental modernistic, streamlined, and biomorphic, but with obviously different interpretations. While the machine purists proclaimed the principles of simplicity, function, and cleanliness, some of them could see that machines were complex, imperfect, and messy. Ultimately such conflicts were resolved by aesthetic feelings, or as Frankl described, deciding what one was going to express and doing it in a clear, simple, and pure manner.[18]

STREAMLINE

Streamlining began to appear around 1930, and was in time applied to a great range of designs, from transportation machines to architecture, home appliances to advertising. Heavily promoted by Norman Bel Geddes in *Horizons* (1932), streamlining gave the appearance of efficiency and speed. Unlike the ideals of machine purity and modernism, the streamlined object had few parts and was not a geometrical form; rather, it was aerodynamically contoured, with the ultimate shape resembling a teardrop. The concept of machine motion changed from an almost primitive rhythm of watch gears turning to a new, smooth, constantly accelerating motion.

The airplane was the most important stimulus for this changed aesthetic. Airplanes had been admired earlier by Le Corbusier and others; however, they showed primitive, multiangular planes with several wings, guy wires, struts, and a clear separation of parts. While Lindbergh's 1927 flight across the Atlantic, other record-setting voyages, and the possibility of air travel for everyone increased public interest in the airplane, the main source of the aesthetic was the appearance of several new streamlined planes in the late 1920s and early 1930s. The Lockheed *Sirius*, 1929, and the Douglas *DC-1*, *2*, and *3*, developed between 1931 and 1935, were the most successful; they provided a totally new image with their bright, shiny, sheer surfaces, their rounded noses, contoured bodies, tapered wings, smooth engine cowls, and parabolic tails. Designers recognized a new prime object had been born. The frontispiece of the Cheneys' 1936 *Art and the Machine* (fig. 2.15) was a photograph of the tail of a *DC-3*, accompanied by the caption: "Sources of idioms of machine-age art: streamline, long hard edge, sheer surface, and repetition of simple motives as seen in an airplane."[19]

Several other transportation machines also acted as form-givers. The torpedo-shaped dirigible seemed in the 1920s and early 1930s a viable alternative for long-distance travel, and its projectile imagery contributed to some designs. Ships and ocean liners were also tremendously popular, and nautical elements appeared in many designs, but instead of concentrating upon the multiple geometric parts of their superstructures—which Le Corbusier had praised and Sheeler and Gerald Murphy had painted—streamlining found a source for imagery in their sheer hulls fit for cleaving water with the least resistance. Trains and automobiles also began to change their appearance in the early 1930s, moving away from the boxy assemblage of parts to more cohesive monocoque forms.

Technological change also made possible the appearance of the rounded, contoured, streamlined shape. New body die-pressing machines capable of creating more complex and modeled automobiles and appliances, and new materials such as shiny stainless steel and polished flat-sheet aluminum came on the market in

2.16 Goodyear Tire & Rubber Company *Pilgrim* (NC-9A) Airship. ca. 1925

2.15 Dmitri Kessel (b. 1902) *Airplane Tail*. 1936. Gelatin-silver print. As published in Sheldon and Martha Cheney, *Art and the Machine* (New York: Whittlesey, 1936)

2.17 Norman Bel Geddes (1893–1958) Model of Aerial Restaurant. 1929–30. For *Century of Progress Exposition*, 1933. Norman Bel Geddes Collection, Theatre Arts Library, Harry Ransom Humanities Research Center, University of Texas at Austin. By permission of Edith Lutyens Bel Geddes, Executrix (hereafter: Bel Geddes Collection)

2.18 Otto Kuhler (1894–1977) Rear Observation "Beaver Tail" Car, *Hiawatha* Train. 1938. Manufactured for the Chicago, Milwaukee, St. Paul and Pacific Railroad

the mid-1920s and into wide usage by the early 1930s. Bakelite and other plastics offered the possibility of molded, self-supporting shells that could be contoured to the streamlined image.[20]

For many designers the work of the German architect Erich Mendelsohn offered a source for streamlined objects expressing speed. Through publications, exhibitions, and visits, Mendelsohn was far better known in America than either Walter Gropius or Mies van der Rohe, and until the rise of the Nazis he was the most successful modern architect in Germany. He had been shown at the *Contempora Exposition* in New York in 1929, and his work was widely praised by Wright, Ferriss, Cheney, and Bel Geddes. In both sketches, which stretched as far back as 1915, and completed works Mendelsohn showed building designs with long, low, horizontal lines, closely spaced; horizontal, finlike projections; rounded corners; curving windows; and machine-like projections—all of which suggested speed. Mendelsohn's influence permeated all mediums; even advertising artists took cognizance of him. Bel Geddes discovered Mendelsohn as early as 1924, and many of the streamlined designs in *Horizons*, as well as his exhortation "speed is the cry of our era," betray Mendelsohn's impact on him.[21]

Mendelsohn introduced a new ornament to machine age America: closely spaced horizontal lines called "speed lines." Appearing as raised fluting in stainless-steel railway cars by the Budd Company, as fins on the observation cars of Otto Kuhler for the Milwaukee Road (fig. 2.18), as a large vertical fin on Henry Dreyfuss's *20th Century Limited* locomotive (fig. 5.23) and thin, incised lines on his thermos of 1935 (fig. 8.2), and in advertising design by Egmont Arens, speed

lines became ubiquitous. In 1940 the editors of *Architectural Forum* noted the "curious cult of the 'three little lines' . . . few objects have escaped the plague of this unholy trinity."[22]

Streamlining by the mid-1930s had conquered much of American product design, and its impact was felt in areas such as architecture, painting, and sculpture. It not only implied speed and efficiency, but also offered a subliminal, yet obvious, sexual reference. Streamlining was touted for women's underwear and silhouettes, and along with the projectile phallic imagery of some products it gave spice to the cold machine. Such popularity added fuel to the raging debate between the geometric machine purists of The Museum of Modern Art and the streamliners of industrial design. In spite of the superficial application of much streamlining, some machine purists, such as Lewis Mumford, felt called upon to acknowledge "the superior economy of nature: on actual tests, the blunt heads of many species of fish and the long tapering tail proved against naive intuition to be the most economic shape of moving through air or water." In streamlined transportation design a shift takes place from the blunt and rear-inclined noses such as in the Chrysler *Airflow*, 1934, to more projectile and penetrating shapes as in Loewy's *K-4S* of 1936. To interpret all visual design of the period as containing phallic or anatomical symbols would be outrageous, yet Teague positioned within a few pages of each other female breasts and rounded machine forms, and Loewy's pose in front of his locomotive certainly implied a phallic message (see fig. 5.22).[24]

2.19 Erich Mendelsohn (1887–1953) Drawing for Optical Factory. 1917. Ink on paper

2.20 Eero Saarinen (1910–1961) and Charles Eames (1907–1978)
Armchair. 1941. Manufactured by Haskelite Corp. and Heywood Wakefield Co. Plywood, sponge rubber, covered with fabric designed by Marli Ehrman, 42 × 32 × 23″. The Museum of Modern Art, New York. Purchase Fund

2.21 E. McKnight Kauffer (1890–1954) Cover for *Organic Design in Home Furnishings* exhibition catalogue. 1941. Courtesy The Museum of Modern Art, New York

BIOMORPHIC

The biomorphic machine aesthetic—in which chairs, instead of resembling setback skyscrapers or rectilinear chrome tubes or sweepback-winged planes, accepted the undulations of the body—was an attempt to humanize the machine. The biomorphic aesthetic interpreted the machine as capable of creating forms more in sympathy with nature, the human body, and psychology. The machine was no longer the prime object; instead the new source was nature or organic forms such as the amoeba.

"Organic," a word frequently applied to the art and products of biomorphism, can be a synonym for "biomorphic," but to many of the mechanicophile theorists, organicism implied only a relationship between form and function. Eliot Noyes, the curator for The Museum of Modern Art's 1941 *Organic Design* exhibition and competition, claimed, "A design may be called organic when there is an harmonious organization of the parts within the whole, according to structure, material, and purpose." This, he explained, meant no ornamentation or excess in form. The other meanings of organic, relating to a bodily organ, or derived from living organisms, did not figure in Noyes's definition. However, the cover of the catalogue showed in outline a human hand (fig. 2.21), and the shape of the winning design, the Charles Eames and Eero Saarinen chair (fig. 2.20), appeared to be derived from the human body. Noyes never referred to the Eames and Saarinen chair as being molded by the human body; rather it was interpreted as offering better support for the human body than either conventional or modern chairs, and exemplifying new machine techniques and materials in its use of a molded plywood shell. Only the museum's publicity releases mentioned the chair as molded "to fit the contours of the human anatomy."[25]

2.22 Louis Lozowick
Above the City. 1932. Lithograph, 17 ×
7⅝″. National Museum of American Art,
Smithsonian Institution, Washington,
D.C. Gift of Adele Lozowick

2.23 Paul T. Frankl (1887–1958) Streamlined Armchair. ca. 1932–33. Leather arms, lapin cloth cushions

New perceptions of the human body play an important role in the biomorphic machine aesthetic. Loewy's evolutionary charts of female form had implied that women would reduce away to a sleek stick by about 1936 (fig 2.2). Beginning with a woman in angular dress shown for 1925, similar to the angular geometry of the *Arts Décoratifs*, Loewy proceeds to make her progressively thinner, more flat-chested, and slimmer-hipped. However, Loewy's idea was already passé by 1935. A Mae Westian, amply contoured voluptuousness came onto the fashion scene by 1933. Women's underwear advertisements were "illustrating a new creation with pictures of young women whose breasts were separately and sharply conspicuous." The shift to more ample and well-endowed shapes had been prefigured in Picasso's monumental and classic nudes of the 1920s and in American muscular, proletarian art of the early 1930s. In Lozowick's machine and urban views of the 1920s, man is almost entirely absent, but in the 1930s, muscular workers abound, making and controlling the environment. Even Teague, trying to encompass all the possibilities of design for the machine age, included in his book *Design This Day*, along with pictures of planes and camshafts, photographs of the

human body. Nude male and female torsos, both well-endowed, were captioned: "Adaption to the specific functions of the male and female animal is the source of beauty in the human body."[26]

Like streamlining, biomorphic designs also contain some obvious sexual references. Automotive grilles such as the 1937 Buick *Y-Job* designed by Harley Earl, or Loewy's 1938 Studebaker *President*, have mouthlike appearances, and in the "cheesecake" advertisements from Studebaker that same year, the car was clearly a sexual symbol.[27]

Support for the sexuality of some biomorphic design comes from the quite apparent relationship of Eames and Saarinen's chair and Earl's *Y-Job* grille to the liquid forms of Salvador Dali and the biomorphism of Joan Miró and Jean Arp. When the surrealist art of Dali, Miró, and Arp was shown in New York galleries in the late 1920s and in an exhibition at The Museum of Modern Art in 1936, the overt sexuality, dreamlike forms, psychological references, and primitivism of the canvases drew both protests and immediate emulation. *Harper's Bazaar* reported that dress design, advertising, and window display fell immediately into surrealism.[28]

Surrealism, though European by origin, fed into a native American strain of biomorphism, the abstract nature painting of Arthur Dove, Charles Burchfield, and Georgia O'Keeffe. O'Keeffe was a precisionist and painted both natural forms and machines, sometimes combining them. Also, straight or objective photographers such as Paul Strand, Edward Weston, and Ralph Steiner photographed machines and natural forms with the same intense technique: Weston could make a wrecked car look like an organic contoured pepper.

Feeding into the biomorphic aesthetic was the interest in primitive and vernacu-

2.24 Harley J. Earl (1893–1954) Buick *Y-Job*. 1937. Manufactured by General Motors

2.25 Raymond Loewy Pennsylvania Railroad Locomotive *K4S* (Engine 3768). 1936

2.26 Raymond Loewy Studebaker *Champion* Cruising Sedan. 1938

2.27 Russel Wright (1904–1976) "American Modern" Dinnerware. Designed 1937, introduced 1939. Manufactured by Stubenville Pottery, East Liverpool, Ohio. Glazed earthenware, pitcher ht.: 10⅝″; plate dia.: 10″. The Brooklyn Museum. Gifts of Russel Wright, Paul F. Walter, and Andrew and Ina Feuerstein

lar design. The industrial designers Roy Sheldon and Egmont Arens claimed: "Those who have to do with designing for mass production by the machine will do well to go to the museums and study the handiwork of those early men who loved the feel of things in their hands." Instead of the angular geometry admired by modernistic designers, this new primitivism chose more anthropomorphic and natural shapes. The interest in vernacular design, especially early American, emerged in Russel Wright's mass-produced "American Modern" ceramics of the later 1930s (fig. 2.27), described by the artist as "humanizing functional design." The water pitcher contained similarities to an eighteenth-century American coal shuttle as well as to the organic sensuality of an Arp sculpture.[29]

The architecture of Frank Lloyd Wright displays some affinity with biomorphic machine design. Visually his work encompassed a wide variety of approaches, from a multiplication of parts to streamlined forms. Wright was acknowledged by nearly every machine age designer as a seminal influence, but by the early 1930s he removed himself from their company, criticizing art and architecture that resembled machines. His approach he now called "organic," claiming that it fit in with the landscape and was more natural to man. *Fallingwater*, 1935–36, the most popular image of his organic approach, is in one sense a machine in the wilderness with its broad, machine-produced, reinforced-concrete decks (fig. 2.28). Yet *Fallingwater* is tied to the site, part of the waterfall. Rocks push up through the living-room floor, and substantial stone piers carry the machine-like decks. Wright's arguments for, and use of, materials in their nearly natural state—wood with the grain, stone in the rough, and the application of "natural" colors or finishes to the concrete, copper, and brick—became a hallmark of organic design, and allied him tangentially with biomorphism.[30]

Lewis Mumford came closest to articulating a theoretical position incorporating biomorphism. In the 1920s he had argued for machine purism, but by 1934, in his *Technics and Civilization*, Mumford foresaw a "biotechnic phase" of human history. Basing his ideas on the concept of the evolution of machines in different periods—for example, the Paleotechnic encompassed the blood and iron of the industrial revolution—Mumford claimed new machines were shrinking in size yet increasing in productivity, power, and concern for the natural world. Instead of

allowing machines to destroy life, Mumford argued, "We can now act directly upon the nature of the machine itself, and create another race of these creatures, more effectively adapted to the environment and to the uses of life."[31]

By 1938 and his *Culture of Cities*, Mumford prophesied a biotechnic community where machinery would build houses and make life easier, but would not be in control. Instead, extensive greenery, open space, and community feeling would prevail. His prime example, however, was Ernst May's Frankfort-Romerstadt housing, celebrated in The Museum of Modern Art's 1932 *International Style* exhibition. Mumford's visual aesthetics were still those of the machine purist; however, in his suggestions for a larger regional order that would encompass the geology and ecology of an area, and his

promotion of greenbelt towns, the biomorphic aesthetic is evident.[32]

Machine aesthetics was a controversial subject in the 1920s and 1930s. Americans, while responding to European ideas and examples, came up with a wide variety of stylistic expressions that were uniquely American. On one level, machine aesthetics and the various styles involved were a sectarian argument among a small group of artists, designers, and critics; yet, from the larger perspective of the capitalistic culture, the various ideas of machine aesthetics succeeded in changing the face of America. America became modern, and simultaneously the way was paved for post–World War II developments, when American art and design, from the work of the abstract expressionists to thin-legged aluminum and plastic furniture, dominated the world.

2.28 Frank Lloyd Wright (1867–1959) *Fallingwater*—the Edgar J. Kaufmann House. Bear Run, Pa. 1935–36. Colored pencil on paper, 17 × 33″. © 1959 The Frank Lloyd Wright Foundation

CHAPTER 3

SELLING THE MACHINE AGE

Advertisements proclaiming "Contrived in the modern spirit" and filled with "modern products" served to lure approximately forty thousand visitors to the department store R. H. Macy and Company's *Art in Trade* exhibition between May 2 and 6, 1927. Countless thousands more experienced it vicariously through the press and over radio station WJZ. Daily talks by twenty-two notables, including Paul Frankl on "The Skyscraper in Decoration" and Bruce Barton, the advertising executive and author, lauded a new day for American art. Another speaker was the president of The Metropolitan Museum of Art, Robert W. de Forest, who claimed, "Much as I am interested in bringing art to the museum, I am more interested in bringing good art to the home." Although the exhibition contained European products, it was the American designs, such as René Clarke's *Stadium* pattern for Cheney Brothers Silk, and Edward Steichen's *Cigarettes and Matches* for Stehli Silk, that captured public attention. The installation by Lee Simonson was constructed of modern materials, including Celotex, Onyx Rubber, and Craftex, and was characterized as an "affair of angle and straight line, not a curve anywhere." Elizabeth Cary, a critic for *The New York Times*, summed up: "American artists, in league with the mighty gods of the machine, provide the most significant, and naturally the most sympathetic expression of life."[1]

Though indeed significant, the *Art in Trade* exhibition was not the first time a department store had brought machine art to public attention. The previous year Louis Lozowick had used his machine-ornament schemes as a backdrop for a Lord & Taylor fashion show (fig. 3.2). He also designed a dress containing cubistic machine patterns for Gilda Gray, the Ziegfeld Follies shimmy girl, which was included in the display. In 1927 Norman Bel Geddes, as one of his first commissions, did Franklin Simon store windows that contained expressionistic cubistic pyramids, dramatically lighted; metallic mannequins; and cut-up A. M. Cassandre railroad posters (fig. 3.3). The publicity engendered by these displays and exhibits spawned exhibitions in other department stores. In 1928 in New York alone, Macy's, B. Altman's, Abraham & Straus, and Lord & Taylor held exhibitions of industrial art, both American and foreign. The success of these and similar exhibi-

3.1 Edward Steichen (1879–1973) *Buttons and Thread*. 1927. Manufactured by Stehli Silk Corp., New York. Printed silk crepe-de-chine, 40 × 72″. The Newark Museum

3.2 Louis Lozowick
Backdrop for Fashion Show, Lord & Taylor. New York. 1926. Collection University of Wisconsin, Madison

tions across the country led John Cotton Dana, the director of The Newark Museum and a long-time advocate of art in everyday objects, to proclaim that in kitchens and bathrooms could be seen the best of American art. Dana argued that "the industrialist is an artist" and that the products of business were worthy of exhibition in any museum.[2]

This intermingling of business and the arts demonstrates that machine age America was not simply an aesthetic debate among artists and theorists, but an expression of American consumer capitalism. Paul Frankl explained the issue in 1928: "America is a nation of consumers. We are not interested in abstract excellence, in impersonal aesthetic values. We are pragmatists." The machine age mentality called for mass production and its corollary, mass consumption, which needed to be stimulated by appealing designs, advertising, packaging, and marketing. Thus the machine age was sold to the American public. Any understanding of the machine age must be based on an understanding of the interrelatedness of consumption, the image of business, advertising, and the emergence of the industrial designer.[3]

CONSUMPTION

Economists saw heavy consumption as the major issue confronting both the continuously booming America of the 1920s and the recovering America of the 1930s. Consumption became a verifiable phenomenon in the 1920s, and came to be used as a synonym for new ideas of advertising and marketing as well as to point out the problems of American capitalism. Most Americans liked to believe they lived in a free, capitalist, market economy, guided by the unseen hand of production and want, supply and demand. In such an Adam Smith fairyland, the balancing of consumer demand is met by production. Theoretically, low demand, or absence of want, meant a producer had to either slack off or change products to meet new demands. In some areas this did happen: for instance, bridle and wagon manufacture slowed as automobiles became the new dominant mode of transportation. But the development of mass production of goods and the growth of large corporations with large investments and staffs necessitated a change in business practices as manufacturers attempted to hang on to, and even increase, their share of the market, even when demand was low. By the mid-1920s, for example, the automobile market in the United States had reached a saturation point: the *Model T* had been fully successful. But instead of scaling back to meet the replacement demand, automobile manufacturers forged ahead to increase sales. They developed the annual model change, which created product obsolescence—to be up-to-date, one needed the latest model, which frequently had little to do with mechanical efficiency—and turned to advertising to stress the associative powers of status, sex, the good life, and modern art that would accrue to the purchaser of a new car.[4]

A new ethic developed by which products were sold—and purchased—not simply on their mechanical benefits but on their appearance or style. The "progress" took place in product design. Raymond Loewy and his industrial design staff spent considerable time between 1935 and 1938 producing annual models for Sears, Roebuck and Company's Coldspot refrigerator. Although its inner workings remained basically the same, the moldings on the Coldspot cabinet were changed from vertical skyscraper setbacks in 1935 to rounded-off corners in 1937, and to a "v" press similar to the hood of an automobile in the door for 1938 (see figs. 3.4, 3.5). Loewy also instituted changes in the feet, chrome moldings, and door latches. Creating demand became as important as making a quality product.[5]

In one sense the consumption ethic broadened the American materialist strain noted earlier. The consumption ethic of the 1920s, however, entailed a fundamental break with traditional American virtues, or what Malcolm Cowley, the literary critic, defined as the "*Saturday Evening Post* business-Christian ethic" of "industry, foresight, thrift and personal initiative." The selling of automobiles on the installment plan, tentatively introduced shortly before World War I, caught on with General Motors in the 1920s. Henry Ford, trying to uphold traditional American virtues, refused to allow credit buying until 1928, when his share of the market dropped from over 50 percent to less than 30 percent. Installment plans and credit purchasing became a way of life, and gratification of wants became almost immediate.[6]

The consumption ethic meant a personal self-realization through purchase. Sinclair Lewis caricatured the consumption ethic in *Babbitt*. George Babbitt, the ulti-

mate consumer, increases his stature with his family by discussing the purchase of a new car. An argument ensues over the body type—"Aw, gee whiz, if the Doppelbraus can afford a closed car, I guess we can!" The omniscient narrator comments, "It was an aspiration for knightly rank...where Babbitt as a boy had aspired to the presidency, his son, Ed, aspired to a Packard twin-six and an established position in the motored gentry." Throughout the novel Babbitt lusts for products, from electric cigar lighters to cameras, and hot-water heaters: "The large national advertisers fix the surface of his life, fix what he believed to be his individuality."[7]

THE IMAGE OF BUSINESS

The machine age romanticized American industry. Between the booming 1920s and the Depression of the 1930s the image of business changed drastically: glorification gave way to questioning and sometimes condemnation. Business adapted itself to this new environment by adopting the garb of science and research.

Certainly in the 1920s, under three Republican presidents, Harding, Coolidge, and Hoover, business never ranked higher. Frederick Lewis Allen, looking back from 1931, noted the development in the

3.3 Norman Bel Geddes
Window Display, Franklin Simon Department Store. New York. 1927. Bel Geddes Collection

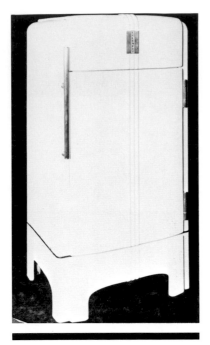

3.4 Raymond Loewy
Coldspot Refrigerator. 1935. Manufactured by Sears, Roebuck and Co., Chicago

3.5 Raymond Loewy
Coldspot Refrigerator. 1938. Manufactured by Sears, Roebuck and Co., Chicago

1920s of a "new veneration" for American business. Businessmen, previously considered crass and undignified, now ranked with clergymen or even above. Bruce Barton's *The Man Nobody Knows* portrayed Jesus Christ as a very successful businessman. According to Barton, if Christ were alive in the 1920s, he would be in advertising. New heroes appeared —Walter P. Chrysler, David Sarnoff, Henry Ford. Ford's popularity knew no bounds. Widely viewed as the inventor of mass production, which some economists claimed was a new economic system, Ford probably could have been president had he wanted. Ford enthusiastically supported the idea of a machine age. In his Greenfield Village, which pays tribute to the history of America, behind the re-creation of Independence Hall, he set up a museum of machines, the first of the age.[8]

The fatuous glamorization of business in the 1920s did not go unopposed. Intellectuals such as H. L. Mencken, Lewis Mumford, and Stuart Chase wrote incisive criticism. Literary culture in the United States never had much use for business, and in the 1920s the younger generation either condemned it, as did John Dos Passos, or ignored it and fled to Europe.[9]

With the fall of the stock market in October 1929 and the ensuing Depression, the businessman ceased to be much of a hero. Most literary and intellectual life in the 1930s was left-wing, and while hymns were still sung to the machine, business was frequently seized upon as the source of the economic catastrophe. Yet for some, business still offered romance, as Henry Luce conveyed in the first issue (February 1930) of *Fortune* magazine:

Business takes *Fortune* to the tip of the wing of the airplane and through the depths of the ocean along be-barnacled

cables. It forces *Fortune* to peer into dazzling furnaces and into the faces of bankers. *Fortune* must follow the chemist to the brink of worlds newer than Columbus found and it must jog with freight cars across Nevada's desert.[10]

Fortune cost one dollar per issue: Luce aimed to influence the opinion of industrial leaders, not the worker. He hired some of the best writers and photographers in America, and examined specific industries and companies as well as changing phenomena such as modern architecture and industrial design. Graphically *Fortune* was superb: Thomas M. Cleland laid out the magazine with exciting covers and photographs, and well-designed advertisements were demanded.

3.6 Fred Chance
Cover of *Fortune*. November 1939. 14 × 11¼". The Mitchell Wolfson Jr. Collection of Decorative and Propaganda Arts, Miami-Dade Community College (hereafter: Wolfson Collection)

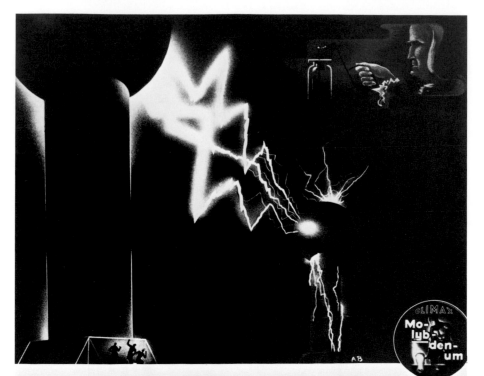

DISCOVERY GOES ON

From the time of the first crude Leyden Jar to the 5-million-volt "atom smasher," science has been restless with exploration. Endlessly new discoveries have made "the survival of the fittest" as axiomatic of industry as it is of man.

Metallurgy presents no exception. Thousands of ferrous products which a few years ago "couldn't be bettered," today offer greatly increased service values and

production economies because of the use of Molybdenum irons and steels. Example:

Rapid wear of certain parts in heavy-duty crushers and grinders has always been a problem. Climax developed a wear-resistant Chrome-Molybdenum steel that adds enormously to the life of these vital parts.

What does your concern make that would gain through lighter weight, higher strength, greater resistance to impact and

abrasion; or by cost-cutting through easier forging, welding, machining, heat-treating, and fewer rejects? Investigate Moly irons and steels. A wealth of practical data is at your service.

"Molybdenum in Industry," our non-technical outline of Molybdenum characteristics and economies, is free to executive, sales and production heads. Climax Molybdenum Co., 500 Fifth Ave., New York.

Climax Mo-lyb-den-um Company

3.7 Alexey Brodovitch (1898–1971) Advertisement for Climax Molybdenum Company. 1937. As published in *Fortune* (June 1937)

By 1930 a new, publicity-conscious image for business, applied science, and research emerged. While manufacturers had always shown some interest in applied research, the devotion of considerable dollars and personnel to "science," as it was called, was practically nonexistent before 1900, and only came about in a large way in the 1920s. Of course the definition of research varied widely depending on the company: some sponsored impressive basic research resulting in Nobel prizes, but most other research was on product development—producing new products or restyling and improving old—or on consumer research and opinion polling. Countless demonstration houses, model kitchens and bathrooms, and products of the future—all from re-

search laboratories of large corporations—littered the decade.[11]

Research provided a positive business image: hence when the A. O. Smith Company of Milwaukee, a manufacturer of automobile frames and metal products, built a new headquarters, they named it the "Research and Engineering Building" (fig. 3.8). The building did contain research and engineering facilities for Smith's large staff, but also held the company offices and a large showroom. John Wellborn Root II, of the Chicago firm of Holabird and Root, worked closely with the Smith engineers to develop a steel frame and curtain wall that would provide an image of modernity while it displayed the company's products. Extensive aluminum trim gave the appearance of a business "fundamentally based on the metal industry." The interior was a sealed environment. The entrance lobby was a modernistic extravaganza of shiny aluminum paneling, Formica panels, and a black terrazzo floor inset with glass brick in cubistic swirls. The furniture was also suitably machine-like, made of aluminum sheathing and including tables each with a large gear for a base (see fig. 8.35). Brilliantly lighted at night, the A. O. Smith Building attempted to give a picture of a better world through research.[12]

A positive image of science was apparent with the *Century of Progress* in Chicago and the *World of Tomorrow* in New York. Their themes of science and business sprung from the involvement of the National Research Council (NRC). The NRC stood at the center of American scientific research. Funded by big business and supported by the academic community, the NRC promoted and sought publicity for science. For the Chicago exposition an NRC committee of scientists and

3.8 Holabird and Root (John A. Holabird, 1886–1945, and John Wellborn Root II, 1887–1963)
A. O. Smith Company Research and Engineering Building. Milwaukee, Wis. 1929–31.

3.9 Interior, A. O. Smith Research and Engineering Building

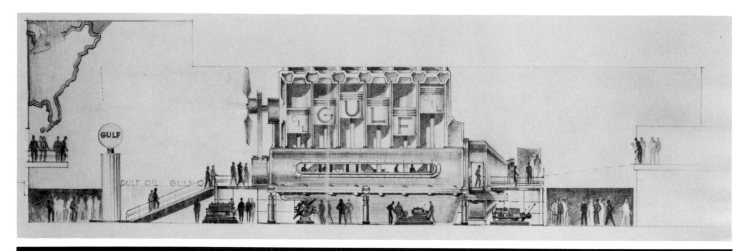

3.10 Holabird and Root
Design for Gulf Oil Station Exhibit, *Century of Progress Exposition*, Chicago. 1933. Pencil on tracing paper, 25 × 27″. Collection Chicago Historical Society

businessmen developed "a philosophy of showmanship for the contributions of science and their application," which led the exposition's organizers to develop plans significantly different from the *beaux arts* festival schemes originally put forward by the architectural advisory board. The official themes of the Chicago fair became "Science Finds—Industry Applies—Man Conforms," or, "The transformation of life through the ministrations of science." The fair's buildings were consciously designed to show "the new methods of construction...provided by science" with metallic skins, electric cascades, suspended roofs, and a general science-fiction, "Buck Rogers" air. Exhibits attempted to be pedagogically entertaining: a giant cutaway engine one could walk through for the Gulf Oil exhibit, Ford and General Motors mass-production lines contrasted with machine shops of a hundred years before (fig. 1.8), and houses of tomorrow (see figs. 6.35, 6.60).[13]

A similar "scientific idealism" continued with the New York fair, which, in the words of its president, Grover Whalen, offered the visitor "a glimpse of the community of the future—a future conditioned by science." An Advisory Committee on Science was organized; its membership comprised the NRC secretary and prominent scientists and businessmen. Albert Einstein—the personification of science to the American public—served as nominal chairman of the committee, though he never attended a meeting and contributed nothing. Originally the fair's organizers had

not intended to have a science building, but ultimately, at the prodding of scientists, one was erected. Containing exhibits on scientific methods of thought and the history of science, the Science and Education Pavilion's most popular attraction was the movie *The City*, photographed and directed by Ralph Steiner and Willard Van Dyke, written by Pare Lorentz and Lewis Mumford, and with musical score by Aaron Copland. *The City* was largely a panegyric to greenbelt towns, which it claimed were clean, healthy, and fun to live in. Set against the decaying industrial cities of old were the new cities, where "science serves the worker and you can't tell where the playing ends and work begins."[14]

The image of science prevailed in many of the fair's other exhibits. The business pavilions attempted to look like futuristic laboratories. The most popular, the General Motors Pavilion, known overall as *Highways and Horizons*, had several exhibits including *Previews of Progress in Science*, product displays, and *Futurama*, designed by Norman Bel Geddes. Bel Geddes tried to remove "the curse of the advertising angle" from *Futurama* by claiming it resulted from "independent research," even though the project had originally started with the Shell Oil Company and had been used in advertisements in 1937.[15] The entrance to *Futurama* was a gigantic curving wall painted in a silver Duco metallic-like automobile finish (fig. 3.11). The visitor entered a large, black auditorium dominated by a map of the United States that

3.11 Norman Bel Geddes and Albert
Kahn Associates
Entrance to *Futurama*, General Motors
Pavilion, New York World's Fair. 1939

3.12 Norman Bel Geddes
Interior, *Futurama*. Bel Geddes Collection

3.13 Norman Bel Geddes
Interior of *Futurama*, full-sized street intersection seen through car windshield. Bel Geddes Collection

electronically compared traffic in 1939 with predictions for 1960. Climbing aboard a rubber-tired train, the visitor took a simulated airplane trip across the United States of 1960, passing over a modern superhighway system, sweeping through towns and out into the country. From the sound of a synchronized voice the visitor learned about farming of the future—with orchards and crops under glass, hydroelectric dams, and regional planning. Fifty thousand miniature automobiles were used, ten thousand of them in motion. At the end, after approaching a modern metropolis filled with high-rise modern buildings, and viewing up-close a model street intersection (figs. 3.12, 3.13), the visitor exited into a full-scale re-creation of the model intersection, populated with the latest General Motors products. Industrial design had turned into scientific research, with business holding the key to a better future.

Thus a new image of business was created. Its appeal to Depression America was obvious: technology and the machine were not the problem, but the salvation. Long-range planning by corporate scientists was a necessity. That a conflict existed between the tradition of American free enterprise and the implications of extensive planning and conformity did not seem to be considered, especially since big business would do the planning.

ADVERTISING

Advertising was fundamental to machine age America. Through it Americans learned that even if Norman Bel Geddes did not design the Chrysler *Airflow*, he approved of it. The line between industrial design and advertising was frequently very thin, and many industrial designers got their start in advertising. Advertising helped to create and popularize the iconography of the machine age. José Arentz's advertisements for B. F. Goodrich brought Hugh Ferriss's *Metropolis of Tomorrow* to millions (see fig. 3.15). If a person could see, it was hard to escape the impact of Otis Shepard's or A. M. Cassandre's billboard designs. Through the ephemera of a commercial culture—insurance brochures, sales catalogues, magazine advertisements, and packages: a virtual public museum of modern art—Americans learned about modern design.

In the 1920s advertising emerged as a significant formulator of public opinion and as an essential component of mass production. Calvin Coolidge, addressing the American Association of Advertising Agencies in 1926, linked the "preeminence of America in industry" to advertising, "the most potent influence in adopting and changing the habits and modes of life, affecting what we eat, what we wear, and the work and play of the whole nation." Coolidge's view was not

3.14 A.M. Cassandre [Adolphe Edouard Mourron] (1901–1968)
Watch the Fords Go By. 1937. Offset lithograph poster, 12′8″ × 19′5⅞″. The Museum of Modern Art, New York. Gift of the designer

3.15 José Arentz
Painting for advertisement, *Goodrich Silvertown Tires*. ca. 1935. Pen and ink, 18¾ × 19½″. Collection Charles Martignette

shared by all; negative opinions about inflated product claims, misstatements of fact, and manipulative appeal were frequently aired. In spite of the naysayers, however, advertising as an institution grew tremendously and began to take on a distinctive character, claiming at times the status of an independent art form.[16]

The question of whether advertising could be really considered an art was approached gingerly by the American art establishment. Portraying commercial products could debase art. But advertising did provide employment, and some proponents claimed that through advertising public taste might be improved. The defensiveness of the artist engaged in commercial work can be easily seen in

Carl Sandburg's book on Edward Steichen, his brother-in-law, published in 1929. Steichen had been an "art" photographer, a founding member of the Photo-Secession, and a frequent exhibitor at Alfred Stieglitz's gallery, "291". After World War I he became the chief photographer of the Condé Nast publications *Vogue* and *Vanity Fair*; soon he began doing advertising work for J. Walter Thompson and, in time, other agencies. Steichen's work now was commercial: celebrity portraits, abstract patterns for silk, new clothing fashion, and hands peeling potatoes for Jergens lotion. Sandburg pointed out that artists such as Michelangelo, Leonardo, and Rembrandt also worked commercially. Steichen agreed, claiming that all great art was the product of either commerce or the revolutionaries opposed to that commerce, and saying that he "welcome[d] the chance to work in commercial art . . . we live in a commercial age." "Art for art's sake," according to Steichen, was "still-born."[17]

Of course, not every photographer or critic agreed with Steichen's aggrandizement of commercial art. Incensed, Paul Strand denied any value in "the passionate penetration of life gleaming on the billboard of the young Adonis who would walk a mile for a Camel!" Nonetheless, the list of artists who worked in advertising or lent their names is impressive, and includes practically all the machine age photographers, painters such as O'Keeffe and Ernest Fiene, architects such as Richard Neutra and Ferriss, and of course all the industrial designers.[18]

The concept of advertising as art was promoted by Earnest Elmo Calkins of the New York agency Calkins and Holden.

Until 1900 most advertising agencies simply acted as space brokers, and copy was randomly produced by manufacturers, printers, or writers. A prolific writer and public speaker, Calkins argued that just as in the fifteenth century, the church offered great artistic opportunity, now in the twentieth century, business offered a new field for art. In 1920 Calkins helped found the Art Directors Club of New York, which through its annual exhibitions attempted to improve the status of advertising art. He also supported *Advertising Arts*, an important periodical of the 1930s devoted to promoting modern design in advertising. Modernism, Calkins felt, "afforded the opportunity of expressing the inexpressible, of suggesting not so much a motor car as speed, not so much a gown as style." Yet, he noted, advertising should never get too far ahead of the buying public. The Calkins and Holden stable of artists included Joseph Leyendecker of Arrow collar fame, Earl Horter, who used *Arts Décoratifs* motifs, and Walter Dorwin Teague, who popularized decorative borders. René Clarke—born James A. Clark in Springfield, Massachusetts—became Calkins's art director, well-known for a flat, abstract style. His design for the Snowdrift shortening can—related by one critic to Matisse's reductionism—contained pure white abstractions of boiling fat on a blue background (fig. 3.17). The package design was praised as attention-grabbing and responsible for converting many housewives from cooking fat to purchasing canned shortening. In the late 1920s Calkins established a division of "Industrial Styling" headed by Egmont Arens to provide design services for clients.[19]

3.16 Edward Steichen
Douglas Lighters. 1928. Gelatin-silver print, 9⅜ × 7½". International Museum of Photography at George Eastman House, Rochester, N.Y. Bequest of Edward Steichen by direction of Joanna T. Steichen

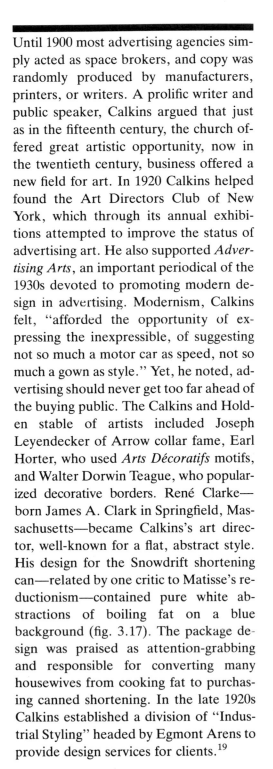

3.17 René [James A.] Clarke (1886–1969)
Snowdrift Shortening Can and Label. ca. 1930. Designed for Calkins and Holden Agency. From *Advertising Arts* (July 9, 1930)

3.18 Norman Bel Geddes
Conference Room for J. Walter Thompson Advertising Agency. New York. 1928. Bel Geddes Collection

Vaughn Flannery, the art director at the Philadelphia agency of N. W. Ayer & Son, also helped to promote innovative modern ads in the 1920s. Flannery hired his friend Charles Sheeler to take photographs of the Ford River Rouge complex as part of a campaign for the introduction of the *Model A* in 1927. (Sheeler also worked on advertisements for Ford, Canada Dry, and Koehler plumbing.) The Flannery Ford campaign was the first to portray a beauty and heroism in the manufacturing process in order to spur sales. The Rouge ads started a fad, as many advertisers found that industrial views could be used in popular, mass-circulation magazines as well as in trade journals. Other Flannery advertising campaigns at Ayer included the modernist George Gershwin

ads with illustrations by the Mexican artist Miguel Covarrubias, and Earl Horter for Steinway pianos (see fig. 8.26). Vibrant in their Art Deco motifs, the Ayer advertisements caused considerable comment. Flannery left Ayer in 1930, but the agency continued to produce modern ads for Climax Molybdenum (see fig. 3.7) and for Ford.[20]

The J. Walter Thompson Agency of New York, headed by Stanley and Helen Resor, was the largest agency of the period and one of the most innovative. The Resors hired the psychologist John B. Watson in the early 1920s, although Watson later claimed his ideas on behavior modification had no value to advertising. The Resors also hired Edward Steichen, whose photographs caused a small revolution in advertising. Reflecting a cubist sensibility, Steichen's advertising photographs were composed of simple forms and backgrounds of either deep black pools, or layers of shadows (see fig. 3.16). To advise clients on design and also to design some new interiors for the Thompson offices in the Graybar Building, the Resors engaged Norman Bel Geddes in 1928. All but one of Bel Geddes's pre-Depression clients came through the Thompson Agency contact. His interior design for Thompson included an auditorium and conference room complex done in the severely geometrical modernistic idiom (fig. 3.18). Round, tublike chairs in the conference room contrasted with angular, zig-zag paneling with strips of black Vitrolite glass. Wall lighting was concealed behind frosty glass and controlled by twenty-second dimmers. Radiators and air-conditioning ducts were concealed behind brass grills. Colors were subdued grays, greens, and blues, and

The New 112 H.P. Chrysler Imperial "80"

A car of today for the sophisticated tastes of today! Chrysler's New 112 h.p. Imperial "80" has enriched even the experience of those most accustomed to and appreciative of the finest in motor cars . . . ¶ Not merely by building one of the world's most powerful motor cars, but by translating that power into terms of flawless performance—power that flashes or purrs as the driver demands . . . ¶ Not by excess of ornament but by creating in the hand-built bodies by Chrysler, Locke, LeBaron and Dietrich, that well-defined note of restraint that speaks true smartness . . . ¶ Longer, wider bodies, finest upholstery and grooming, longer springs, chassis and engine rubber insulated—"Red-Head" high-compression power—the New 112 h. p. Imperial "80" leaves nothing to be desired for performance, with superlative comfort . . ¶ The fourteen custom body types present a wide range, suitable for all town and country uses.

Open and closed custom-built body types by Chrysler, Dietrich, Locke and LeBaron, ranging in price from $2795 to $6795. All prices f. o. b. Detroit, subject to current Federal excise tax. Chrysler dealers are in position to extend the convenience of time payments.

3.19 McCann-Erickson Agency
The New 112 H.P. Chrysler Imperial 80. 1928. Advertisement from *House and Garden* (April 1928)

black and white. Bel Geddes claimed the interior space was "machine-like in its efficiency, in its ability to help its occupant get through his day's work with the minimum of interference and distractions." (While Helen Resor personally was committed to modern art, her agency had to appear ecumenical: the decoration of the executive dining room imitated that of a seventeenth-century New England keeping room, with pine paneling and an iron kettle for the fireplace.)[21]

The visual shift in American advertising closely follows the development of the various machine aesthetics. Modernistic raylines and flat cubistic forms began to appear in the mid-1920s as foreign-trained artists, both European and American, swarmed through the breach. Features of the new trend were sans-serif type, little black dots, the air brush, and dynamic symmetry. From the obvious modernistic quality of a 1928 Chrysler advertisement by the McCann-Erickson agency (fig.

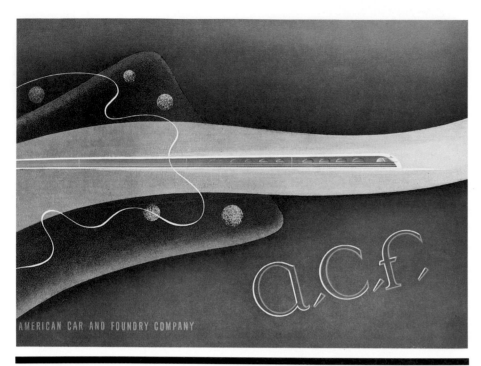

AMERICAN CAR AND FOUNDRY COMPANY

3.20 Leo Rackow (b. 1901)
Book Cover: *A.C.F.* ca. 1938. 10 × 14″.
For American Car and Foundry Company. Wolfson Collection

3.21 Fuller, Smith and Russ Agency
Speed—The World Salutes Each Victor.
1930. Advertisement for The Austin Company from *Fortune* (May 1930)

3.19) emerged a new, flat geometry of shape, where text was treated as block. This same design structure was picked up by the Austin Company advertisements of the early 1930s by Fuller, Smith and Russ (see fig. 3.21). These energy-charged ads, portraying the company as fully up-to-date with the machine age, helped to change the company's architectural image. A large design-build firm, the Austin Company had been stylistically conservative. The success of the modern ads, however, induced the president, George A. Bryant, to have a company architect, Robert Smith, Jr., produce models of contemporary styled structures for advertisements. From these ads, the Austin Company obtained commissions for buildings such as the NBC headquarters in Los Angeles, 1938.[22]

In quick succession and overlapping with the flat geometry of machine purity, streamlining and biomorphism also made an appearance in advertising in the early and mid-1930s. Streamlined ads generally illustrated streamlined designs, while biomorphism was applied to many different products. Leo Rackow's design for the American Car and Foundry Company booklet used a multicontoured protoplasmic shape (fig. 3.20). Sans-serif type became mandatory, and while type designs by Bauhaus artists like László Moholy-

Nagy and Herbert Bayer were well-known, several American types became popular as well. Lucian Bernhard, an immigrant from Germany in 1923, designed for the American Type Founders Company a variety of sans-serif types ranging from very thin, delicate, and angular, to a heavier, rounded style known as "Bernhard Gothic" (fig. 3.22).[23]

Advertising art—which includes subject, illustration, layout, and type—cannot be considered the only, or even the consummate maker of public taste and opinion. Obviously, a dialectic exists between what the public wants—and will accept—and what advertising provides. Even the best advertisement will not cause one product to totally dominate a market; many other factors are involved, including the excellence of the product and customer preference. Yet advertising does present a fantasy world wherein the consumer becomes part of a vast, nationwide, social group. Individual differences are subsumed to the group, and ideas become slogans and snappy phrases. It can be inferred that the American public was willing to accept the machine as an image as well as modern design from the great number of advertisements which either explicitly or implicitly carried these messages. Comparison of an early 1920s advertisement with one from around 1940 suggests the visual revolution America had accepted. That the country looked different in 1940 has to some degree to be credited to advertising.[24]

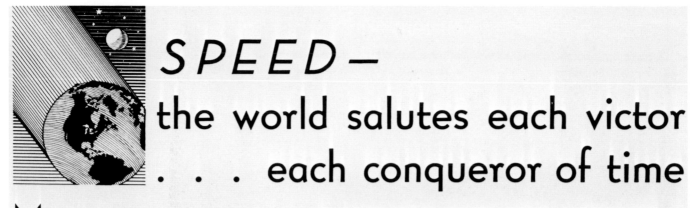

SPEED –
the world salutes each victor
. . . each conqueror of time

MOUTHS stood agape when headlines told of an ocean liner clipping nearly nine hours from the trans-Atlantic voyage . . . eyes popped when a racing car attained a speed of nearly four miles a minute . . . when a roaring plane hurtled through the air to establish a new mark of 355 miles an hour.

. . . and business executives, too, have commented as Austin, international engineers and builders, created amazing speed records . . . erecting a mammoth six-story manufacturing building in Northern Jersey 23 working days ahead of the guaranteed 90-day completion date . . . in the Midwest, designing and constructing a complete plant of 125,000 square feet for efficient straight line production, in the short span of 60 working days.

Years of research and toil precede the perfected machine that sets a record. In like manner, the Austin organization has progressed by ever seeking out and applying better methods . . . by developing and sponsoring the improvements which provide low cost design and rapid construction of industrial plants and commercial buildings.

Speed, not to the exclusion of all else . . . but speed that permits occupancy of your buildings weeks before you had expected . . . speed that puts you into production on that new article before competition is aware of its existence . . . speed covered by a rigid bonus and penalty clause in the contract if you desire . . . *that is Austin speed!*

Helpful building data and approximate costs on any project you may be planning will be gladly furnished. Wire, phone or write today.

THE AUSTIN COMPANY

The AUSTIN METHOD *of Undivided Responsibility*

Design, construction and building equipment . . . separate responsibilities ordinarily . . . become one unified responsibility under The Austin Method. One nation-wide organization handles the complete project under one contract which specifically guarantees in advance, total cost, time of completion with bonus and penalty clause if desired; and quality of materials and workmanship.

THE
AUSTIN
METHOD
Ⓐ

ENGINEERS AND BUILDERS . . . CLEVELAND

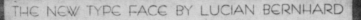

THE NEW TYPE FACE BY LUCIAN BERNHARD

FASHION

IS DESIGNED TO FULFILL THE DEMAND FOR
A MOST DELICATE TYPE STYLE WHICH
IS EXPRESSIVE OF EVERYTHING
WIT...
C...

BERNHA...
from T...
«includi...
point»...
HARDES...

TYP...

BERNHARD GOTHIC MEDIUM

is the first of several

sans-serif type faces

recently designed by

Lucian Bernhard for

the American Type

Founders Company

INDUSTRIAL DESIGN

Industrial design was, along with advertising, one of the major art forms of American capitalist consumption. A 1934 *Fortune* article on industrial design quoted the economist Oliver Sprague as claiming that the problem of the Depression stemmed from the "failure of industries to adopt policies designed to open up additional demands for industrial products." The industrial designer gave a new look and appeal to the products of commercial America, cleaning up the oil and grime of the machine and helping to save capitalist America from the crisis of the 1930s.[25]

For many manufacturers prior to the 1930s, product appearance was never a high priority. As late as 1931 a survey by *Product Engineering Magazine* found that only 7 percent of its readers—engineers and manufacturers—felt appearance to be a crucial factor in sales. In many companies the title of designer never existed; a product's appearance simply evolved as part of the manufacturing process or as a gut reaction to the market on the owner's part. In the industries in which appearance was of concern, the product was generally designed by foreign-trained artists and artisans. World War I and the immigration laws of the 1920s choked off the supply of foreign designers. The industrial designer emerged in this vacuum, just at the time when some companies began to realize the importance of product appearance. Also, in several cases, advertising agencies prodded their clients into developing new designs and utilizing an industrial designer.[26]

Helping to further the idea of product appearance as a key to increased sales were the successes of some new designs. *Fortune* magazine in 1934 claimed that John Vassos's Perey turnstile redesign

(fig. 3.23) had actually lowered the cost while it increased sales by 25 percent; Raymond Loewy's redesign of a radio for Colonial had increased sales by 700 percent; and Harold Van Doren's redesign of the Toledo scale—after Bel Geddes's design had been rejected—both lowered the factory costs and increased sales by 900 percent.[27]

Changed appearance did not always mean total redesign; frequently color change alone was enough. Debates raged on what was the best or most appealing color—and could it be predicted? What was the psychological reaction to a red bed? (According to *Fortune*, the older generation would find it "immoral.") Many manufacturers discovered—often reluctantly, as in Henry Ford's case—that

3.23 John Vassos (1898–1985) Turnstile. ca. 1932. Manufactured by Perey Company, New York. Collection George Arents Research Library, Syracuse University

3.22 Lucian Bernhard (1883–1972) Type Design. ca. 1931

3.24 Raymond Loewy and Lee Simonson (1888–1967)
Industrial Designer's Office, *Contemporary American Industrial Art* exhibition, The Metropolitan Museum of Art, New York. 1934

color allowed variety, mitigating to some degree the standardization of mass production. Howard Ketcham, a color engineer responsible for the Duco colors of E. I. duPont Company, which allowed automobile manufacturers in the mid-1920s to offer different color schemes at low expense, claimed: "Color affords the most logical attribute for product excellence."[28]

Industrial design encompassed both the independents such as Loewy, Teague, and Bel Geddes, and the lesser-known company men. In 1927 General Motors set up an Art and Colour Section with Harley Earl in charge. Chrysler followed within a few years, as did others, but Ford refused. Westinghouse hired Donald Dohner as director of art for its heavy-industry division in 1929. With Westinghouse Dohner designed diesel electric locomotives, electric ranges, and a water cooler that reportedly captured 40 percent of the national market, and worked on patterns for Micarta, the Westinghouse brand of Formica. He left Westinghouse in 1935 to found with Peter Müller-Munk and Robert Lepper the first academic program in industrial design at the Carnegie Institute of Technology in Pittsburgh. Ray Patten held a similar position at General Electric from 1928, where he supervised the design of domestic appliances. By 1936 the number of individuals involved in some aspect of product development reached 9,500. By the mid-1930s the large merchandising concerns Sears, Roebuck and Montgomery Ward had discovered the value of having staff designers along with independent consultants to advise on product lines.[29]

The independent industrial designer—more flamboyant than the company man—appeared in the late 1920s and rose to great popularity in the 1930s. While some observers saw humor in industrial design, industrial designers as a group took themselves very seriously, creating public personas with a self-consciousness that verged on narcissism. Norman Bel Geddes became a seer confidently predicting a streamlined, machine-made future. Raymond Loewy, debonair and looking like a stand-in for Clark Gable, exuded confidence and control as he posed in the prototype of an industrial designer's office he designed with Lee Simonson for The Metropolitan Museum of Art's *Contemporary American Industrial Art* exhibit of 1934 (fig. 3.24). The office appeared sleek, efficient, and streamlined, with white Formica walls, chrome bands, tubular metal furniture, blue linoleum floor, recessed lighting, an abstract clock, and sketches of boat designs. A model of Loewy's design for the 1934 *Hupmobile* was strategically placed. Loewy claimed that the office of an industrial designer should be like "a clinic—a place where products are examined, studied and diagnosed." This was the image presented; only rarely did anyone see a messy studio.[30]

The term "industrial design" can be traced as far back as 1913, when it was used as a synonym for "art in industry."

Norman Bel Geddes began using "industrial designer" in 1927, and by the 1930s it was accepted but used interchangeably with "design engineer," "product designer," "creative and inventive engineer," "consumption engineer," "product designer," "packager," and "advertising consultant."[31]

In most cases the leading industrial designers came from advertising offices or the theater, and these backgrounds give a clue to the success of some designers and the relative anonymity of others. Bel Geddes had attended art school and worked in advertising design, and when he opened his industrial design office in 1927 he was known primarily as a theater set designer, an interest he continued to pursue in the 1930s. Teague also attended art school—at night—and was an advertising illustrator with Calkins and Holden before making the shift to industrial design in 1927. Loewy, born in France, first studied to be an engineer. Upon his arrival in New York in 1919 he worked as an advertising artist, primarily in women's fashions. He set up his industrial design office in 1929. Henry Dreyfuss came out of a theater set design background before he set up his own office devoted to consumer products in 1928. Joseph Sinel had worked in advertising before turning to industrial design, as had John Vassos, Egmont Arens, Donald Deskey, Gustav Jensen, Nathan George Horwitt, Lurelle Guild, and many other successful designers. Of course, some industrial designers lacked a theater or advertising background. Kem Weber trained at the Berlin

"Gentlemen—I Am Convinced That Our Next New Biscuit Must Be Styled by Norman Bel Geddes"

Academy of Applied Arts before emigrating to the United States in 1914. Raymond Patten had been educated as an engineer. Architecture also provided a few well-known designers, including David Chapman, Charles Eames, Brooks Stevens, George Nelson, and Eliot Noyes.[32]

For the majority of the leaders of the industrial design profession, however, a background in advertising or, secondarily, the theater was important. As a group they had a keen sense of the value of publicity and drama. Their self-promotion convinced the public that the products of mass production were not anonymously styled, but were the creations of artistic individuals with the best welfare of the American consumer in mind.

The industrial designer as artist had its source in the art in industry or industrial arts movement of the 1910s and 1920s. The models for the American art in industry movement were the Arts and Crafts movement and various European organizations, including the Wiener Werkstätte or Deutsche Werkbund. In America this meant artistic and/or handmade-looking objects. Across the country industrial art exhibitions were held. The Metropolitan Museum inaugurated a series of such exhibitions in 1917. The criteria for selection, according to the curator, Richard F. Bach, were that products, either of the machine or of the hand, "owed their design, color, motive or some other feature to museum inspiration."[33]

The art in industry syndrome had two ramifications for the industrial designers of the 1920s and 1930s. For one, it meant that their product should look "arty," that is, the presence of the designer should be evident. This led almost inevitably to the decorated approach and the use of setbacks, rounded streamlined forms, and "speed whiskers." It also meant that all the industrial designers, in spite of the polemics of designing for mass production, would do custom designs.

The custom-designed industrial arts approach carried over into the department store exhibitions of the later 1920s. While machine-produced fabrics were offered for sale, most of the rest of the displays, such as Paul Frankl's skyscraper bookcases, were custom designs. In 1924 Bach curated an industrial art "quantity production" exhibition, with the usual stipulation that objects entered had to be based on museum collections. The comments of one reviewer—"it is difficult to believe that the objects selected are not authentic antiques"—indicate the participating manufacturers' success in achieving the appearance of handicraft custom design.[34]

Bach and the Metropolitan continued to stress the individuality of industrial arts for many years. The 1929 *Exhibition of American Industrial Art*, known as the "Modernism" exhibit, included custom-

3.26 Kemp Starrett
Cartoon. 1932 (Reproduced in *Fortune*, 1934, with the original caption—"Gentlemen, I am convinced that our next new biscuit should be styled by Norman Bel Geddes"—altered). ©1932, 1960 *The New Yorker*

3.25 Raymond Loewy
Metropolis. 1927. Advertisement for Saks Fifth Avenue from *Vogue* (March 15, 1927)

designed rooms by architects. Few if any of the objects went into quantity production. The 1931 exhibition, reflecting the austerity of the Depression, emphasized manufactured multiple objects. One reviewer commented, "Frankly an exhibit of machine or serial production, items were selected which allowed the machines, without forcing, to turn out things for which they are best fitted." The 1934 exhibition, which featured Loewy and Simonson's industrial designer's office, intermixed custom, one-of-a-kind designs such as Eliel Saarinen's tea urn for International Silver Company (fig. 3.27) and mass-production objects such as Walter von Nessen's inkwell for Chase Brass and Copper.[35]

Industrial design as it emerged in the early 1930s did not have clear boundaries; it encompassed furniture and architecture as well as duplicating machines and cars. The first attempt at a professional industrial arts group was the American Union of Decorative Artists and Craftsmen (AUDAC) founded in 1928. In reaction to being squeezed out by the architect-dominated exhibition at the Metropolitan in 1929, AUDAC, under the direction of Frederick J. Kiesler, held an exhibition in New York in 1930. Kiesler, an Austrian immigrant, had displayed a constructivist *City in Space* sculpture at the *Arts Décoratifs* exposition and had done window displays for New York department stores. The AUDAC exhibit was almost entirely furniture in rooms designed by Kiesler, Deskey, Wolfgang and Pola Hoffmann, and others. In 1931 The Brooklyn Museum held a larger exhibition of AUDAC materials. The catalogue lists as members Frank Lloyd Wright and Hugh Ferriss, as well as Teague, Bel Geddes, and Russel Wright.[36]

Throughout the 1930s there were many more museum exhibits that stressed the beauty to be found in objects of industry and the role of the industrial design. Many of the important exhibitions of The Museum of Modern Art, such as the *International Style*, the *Machine Art*, and the *Organic Design*, were sponsored by and shown at department stores in other cities. With these and other, more commercially inspired exhibits, the American public had spread before it a cornucopia of consumer goods. Ordinary, everyday products intended for the home, the office, the factory, or the road were made into objects of art. Industrial design meant both design for industry and design for consumption. In this way modern design and the machine entered the popular consciousness and became acceptable.

3.27   Eliel Saarinen (1873–1950)
Urn and Tray. 1934. Manufactured by International Silver Co., Meriden, Conn. Silver, urn ht.: 14″; tray dia.: 18″. Cranbrook Academy of Art/Museum, Bloomfield Hills, Mich.

LIFE

NOVEMBER 23, 1936 **10** CENTS

4.1

CHAPTER 4

THE MACHINE IN THE LANDSCAPE

The dramatic immensity of the machine as an icon and in its fundamental physical reality became fully confirmed for millions of Americans with the first issue of Henry Luce's *Life* magazine on November 23, 1936. The cover photograph by Margaret Bourke-White depicted the construction of the flood gates at the Fort Peck Dam in Montana (fig. 4.1). Perhaps never before or since has one photograph so summed up an attitude or given it such an intense presence. On the level of mass culture, for the initial *Life* edition was 600,000 copies, as well as a great work of art, Bourke-White's photograph captured the heroic optimism of the machine age, the belief that a new and better life was possible through the machine. The sequential geometric forms, abstract in their removal from traditional architectural styles, become a series of overlapping cubistic planes. The smooth, rounded surfaces portray a sense of efficiency in the easy flow of water. The emphasis on size is evident in its contrast with the diminutive workers crouching in the foreground. Projected is a gigantic machine, a sublime construction of man that transcends topography to become a geological feature.

The Fort Peck Dam project is but one of a number of great construction feats of the 1920s and 1930s that helped to mold both the physical form and the consciousness of machine age America. America was in a sense rebuilt in these years as superhighways, freeways, and parkways flowed across the landscape carrying automobiles, buses, and trucks with ease to their final destination; from coast to coast great voids were spanned by concrete and steel bridges; and new hydroelectric power and water for irrigation, navigation, and distant populations came as a result of tremendous dams in the West and Southeast. Underwater traffic tunnels were constructed. Giant radio towers and electric transmission lines marched across the distances. To some Americans, such as the editors of *Collier's* magazine, it appeared as if American construction ingenuity were "remaking the world."[1] In a sense they were right. American engineering technology built roads, dams, bridges, and factories from Russia to South America. The American engineer, contractor, and construction "stiff" appeared everywhere, and they were thought heroes. To one writer watching the beginning of construction at

4.1 Margaret Bourke-White *Fort Peck Dam, Montana.* 1936 (First cover of *Life*, November 23, 1936). Silver print. © 1936 Time Inc.; *Life* Picture Service

4.2 Hugh Ferriss
Viaduct in Washington Heights. ca. 1939.
Pencil on paper, 10½ × 16″. Collection
Avery Architectural and Fine Arts Library, Columbia University, New York

Hoover Dam the undertaking was the "Pioneering of the Machine Age."[2]

The scale, comprehensiveness, and design of many of these large projects indicate a fundamental belief in the power of the machine—in the intelligent hands of man—to remake and control the environment. In the earlier landscape the machine was an intruder, and while its power could be admired, seldom was self-conscious beauty or design evident. In this new landscape a special environment was created in which the machine could operate efficiently in concert with nature. Nature brimmed up along the new superhighway, great dams became primal forces creating a new geography, and bridges joined earth and sky in a new pattern. An archaeological analogy caught the fancy of P. H. Elwood, Jr., a parkway designer. He felt future diggers would interpret the early twentieth century as "the

Road-building Age and the people as the machine worshippers." However, Elwood predicted that future archaeologists would find beginning about 1930 a new sensitivity, an "intelligent regard for outdoor life and beauty . . . universally awakening in America." The result, he hoped, would be "Not more roads, but more beauty and enjoyment along the way."[3]

The machine in the landscape has several dimensions. First there is the actual design of dams, bridges, and freeways by engineers, architects, and landscape architects. Second there is the physical construction, a drama in itself. Then there is the interpretation of the project by critics, artists, and others. And finally there is the actual experience of the work by the visitor and user. When these aspects overlap in a positive fashion engineering works leave the realm of pure function to become great art of the machine age.

HIGHWAYS, PARKWAYS, AND FREEWAYS

The concept of the broad freeway or parkway that rolls across the landscape, jumping rivers and valleys, butting through small hills and remodeling larger ones, swinging around towns and small cities, and piercing through the heart of the metropolis in elevated or sunken sections was one of the major accomplishments of machine age America. Drawings by Hugh Ferriss, articles by such polemicists as Lewis Mumford, and models by industrial designers such as Norman Bel Geddes all proclaimed a new synthesis of the road, the city, and the landscape. The new superhighways were major monuments, for as the editors of *Architectural Forum* announced in their "Design Decade" issue of 1940, roads such as the Pennsylvania Turnpike (1937–41) were "bringing a new pattern to the countryside and permitting the car to realize its potentialities."[4] The Swiss architectural historian Sigfried Giedion was enthralled by the parkways he found in America. He wrote: "Full realization is given to the driver and freedom to the machine. Riding up and down the long sweeping grades produces an exhilarating dual feeling, one of being connected with the soil and yet of hovering just above it, a feeling which is nothing else so much as sliding swiftly on skis through untouched snow down the sides of high mountains."[5]

With the increase in automotive traffic, new, specialized professions such as the highway engineer, the highway landscape architect or designer, and the traffic engineer emerged. Motor-car traffic, according to Dr. Miller McClintock of the Harvard University Bureau for Traffic Research, was "a river of steel and rubber and the highway is a river bed, it pursues, now gentle, now sluggish, now a torrent that smashes and churns and breaks out of control." "Friction," whether it was "medial," "intersectional," "marginal," or "internal-stream," was the problem. Limited-access, divided highways were the solution.[6] Americans, enamored of the (reputed) freedom of the motor car, besought their politicians to appropriate funds to construct superhighways so that they could travel in ease and comfort in their new machines. New industries, the long-haul truck, and the long-distance motor coach or bus (such as Greyhound, founded in 1926) appeared and demanded appropriate highways on which to operate. The new ideas for smooth, effortless, high-speed highway travel reached fruition in parkways and freeways in the 1920s and 1930s.

America in 1900 had a fairly sophisticated railroad transportation network and a primitive intercity road system. The railroad, along with streetcars, interurbans, and, to a lesser degree, river traffic, moved most of the passengers and freight in the country. From the 1840s onward the national government had really abdicated in favor of private enterprise the construction of a national transportation network. In the 1890s the development of the "bicycle craze" raised road consciousness, and a few roads were built. The City Beautiful movement at the turn of the century was concerned strictly with inner-city boulevards and roads, though both the McMillan Plan for Washington, D.C. (1901–2), and the Chicago Plan (1906–9), projected parkways and recognized the inter-city road problem. The exponential growth of the motor vehicle between 1900 and 1920 led to an enormous outcry for more and better roads. In 1916 federal legislation allocated funds to the individual states for highway building, provided the states established road-building departments. In 1918 the Bureau of Public Roads, under the U.S. Department of Agriculture, was created to develop standards for road design and construction. The Federal Highway Act of 1921 mandated a national highway system, costs of which were to be split between the states and the federal government. By 1936 the Bureau of Public Roads had spent approximately $2 billion on the improvement and construction of 324,000 miles of federal highways. To this total another $1 billion of WPA funds were added as of 1936.[7]

The litany of troubles, indignities, and hazards Americans underwent on poorly designed roads in the 1920s and 1930s filled newspapers, magazines, books, and movies. There were the problems of the bottleneck; of squeezing twenty-seven lanes down to two lanes to enter the Holland Tunnel; of traffic backed up for miles on two-lane major highways; of wildly driven cars veering on from side roads. Pedestrians became matadors to bullish motor vehicles. Bridges over navigable rivers were a constant source of impediment to the automobile; they were frequently open for river traffic and almost as frequently stuck. A lack of grade separation meant at best endless waits for trains, or at worst a collision of several hundred tons of fast-moving steel and iron with a few tons of tin and wood. Automobile slums of roadside gas stations, garages, and billboards created a visual, auditory, and physical assault. Roadside picnickers had to eat in the midst of traffic jams or directly alongside cars whizzing by at fifty miles per hour. And to make matters worse, motor vehicles were increasing in size and speed faster than the road-builders could keep up with them. In 1936 R. E. Toms, the chief of design at the Bureau of Public Roads, proclaimed that at least one-quarter and possibly one-half of all the roads built in the past twenty years were "unfit."[8]

The solution devised was the creation of a special environment for the motor vehicle: high-speed superhighways in which the car, truck, and bus could operate with a minimum of interruption, so that, as the narrator of *The City* said, "nothing stops you until you are there." Or as Lewis Mumford and Benton MacKay wrote in their seminal article of 1931, "Townless Highways," the highway should be a separate entity, apart from residences, businesses, cross traffic, pedestrians, and other interferences: "The Townless Highway would be, like the railway, an institution in itself, a system."[9]

Throughout the 1920s and 1930s a number of terms were used to identify the new motor-vehicle road system, among them highway, parkway, freeway, superhighway, turnpike, expressway, motorway, and limited way. While semantic differences did exist between the different terms and in their usage by different proponents, three basic terms—highway, parkway, and freeway—sum up the variances in form and meaning.

The highway was composed of two or more lanes of traffic in both directions, generally without a central median strip.

A development in the 1920s was the three-lane highway, in which the central lane was used for turning and passing in both directions. Side-road and cross-traffic access was not limited, and especially near cities the highway could become a forest of stop signs, billboards, and strip business. In general the highway was simply a widening of the old post road or national turnpike system; the motor vehicle, as Mumford and MacKay pointed out, could be seen "still largely crawling along in the ruts laid down by earlier habits."[10]

The parkway's distinctive features were in its landscaped surroundings and limited access. Strictly defined, it was "an attenuated park with a road through it . . . primarily for traffic, but mostly or exclusively for pleasure traffic."[11] Gilmore D. Clarke, the leading parkway designer of the 1920s and 1930s, defined the parkway as a "strip of public land dedicated to recreation, over which abutting owners have no right of light, air, or access."[12] While pleasure or recreation was part of the parkway definition, in actuality it declined as a real governing feature. What remained was the idea of a carefully

landscaped and designed environment, where the motor vehicle would speed through nature. Frequently parkways were limited to automobiles. There could be two or more traffic lanes, perhaps—though not necessarily—divided by a central median strip.

The freeway, according to Clarke, was a "strip of public land dedicated to movement, over which the abutting owners have no right of light, air, or access."[13] The distinctive features of the freeway were multiple traffic lanes and, generally, a central median strip. All types of motorized traffic were permitted on the freeway. The freeway could operate in a parklike or specially landscaped environment, but it could also soar above or through cities as did the Pulaski Skyway over Jersey City, or Chicago's Outer Drive, both constructed in the 1930s.

The origins of the automotive parkway go back to the pleasure drives designed by Frederick Law Olmsted and Calvert Vaux for Central Park, Prospect Park, and the Boston Fens. While Olmsted envisioned his parkways as limited-access and cross traffic separated by different

4.3 Gilmore D. Clarke (1892–1982), landscape architect, and staff, Westchester County Park Commission
Bronx River Parkway, section near Woodlawn, N.Y. 1922. Newton Collection, Frances Loeb Library, Graduate School of Design, Harvard University, Cambridge, Mass.

4.4 Gilmore D. Clarke, landscape architect, and staff, Taconic State Park Commission
Taconic State Parkway. Putnam County, N.Y. 1933

grades and tunnels, the parkway as built in Brooklyn and elsewhere in the United States in the late nineteenth and early twentieth century was really a glorified tree-lined boulevard with cross traffic.

The first automotive parkway was the Bronx River Parkway (fig. 4.3), running from the North Bronx to White Plains in Westchester County and authorized by the New York State legislature in 1907. Agitation for the parkway, which was designed to be a renewal project for a polluted stream as well as a controlled approach to New York City from the north, began in 1905, when it was learned that animals in the Bronx Zoo were dying from drinking water from the river. Construction did not begin until 1913 and then lagged for years until 1919, when new designs and work began in earnest. It

was substantially completed in 1923, though almost immediately extensions were made to the north.[14]

The design of the Bronx River Parkway, while primitive by later standards, laid down the major criteria for parkway design for years to come. Initially the roadway of four lanes, two northbound and two southbound, was without a central median strip, though in several places the lanes did part to slip around hillocks and substantial strands of trees. With the exception of some twists near the beginning—just north of New York City—the concrete roadway had graceful and substantial curves that followed the new course of the Bronx River as laid down by engineers. Long straightaway stretches were avoided; the road swung back and forth in gentle arcs. A constantly changing visual spectacle greeted the driver and passengers. Generous allotments of parkland along the two sides kept billboards and off-the-road businesses at a distance, and in those areas where land could not be purchased, dense plantations of trees blocked the view of noxious commerce. Cross streets were elevated in bridges and faced with local roughcut stone. Traffic access was limited to a few entrances.

Immediately after the popular success of the Bronx River Parkway, the Westchester County Park Commission began a system of other parkways to link together all the recreational areas in Westchester County and also to provide better access for motor vehicles to and from New York City. Between 1923 and 1933 the commission constructed eighty-eight miles of parkways and ten miles of freeways, including the Saw Mill River, the Hutchinson River, Briarcliff-Peekskill, and Cross County parkways. To this network were added recreational parks such as Playland at Rye Beach.[15]

From the Westchester County Parkway Commission came Clarke, the landscape architect for the Bronx River Parkway and Westchester County, who went on to a noteworthy career as the designer of the Taconic State Parkway, an adviser to Robert Moses on the Long Island and New York City parkways, and chief designer on the Bureau of Public Roads' George Washington Memorial Parkway just outside of Washington, D.C. Somewhat of an anomaly as a machine age proponent, Clarke intensely disapproved of most modern architecture, and for the parkways he created a series of vernacular gasoline stations and recreational structures.[16] Still, Clarke designed several of the most distinguished modern parkways.[17] For the Taconic State Parkway in the early 1930s (fig. 4.4) Clarke devised the turnout or overlook as a separate entity from the roadway. The road became more of a visual continuum with sightlines developed so the traveler could see the next section in the distance. The center strip increased in width both for traffic separation and to allow reversal of direction without accidents.

Throughout the 1930s a number of other parkways were designed that advanced and modified the Bronx River model. Robert Moses's Long Island parkways were more extensive and bigger, and the tremendous intersection of the Grand Central Parkway, the Grand Central Parkway Extension, the Union Turnpike, the Interboro Parkway, and Queens Boulevard known as "The Pretzel" became a landmark, a sort of monument to the machine age (fig. 4.5). The cloverleaf intersection was also used in several places on the Long Island parkways.[18] Actually the cloverleaf, invented by the French urbanist architect Eugène Hénard in 1906, was first put into use at Woodbridge, New Jersey, in 1928, at the intersection of State Highways 4 and 25; it then appeared again in the initial section of Chicago's North Shore Drive in 1930–33.[19]

The parkway soon spread beyond the New York area. Stanley W. Abbott, one of several important designers who trained under Clarke, designed the Blue Ridge and Skyline Drive parkways in Virginia and North Carolina, respectively, in the 1930s. These last were entirely recreational or pleasure drives.

Parkways were ideal in principle but not always practicable in their full form as a linear park. The Arroyo Seco Parkway, 1940, between Pasadena and downtown Los Angeles, was, despite its name, really the first section of the Los Angeles freeway system (fig. 4.6). Constructed in a valley, the roadway did not have the usual visual controls.[20] In fact, many of the New York City parkways constructed under Robert Moses's direction, such as the Henry Hudson and the East River Drive, had shrunk the "park" aspect to five-foot right-of-ways on each side. Some designers, such as Charles Downing Lay, a landscape architect and adviser to the New Jersey Highway Department, advocated "straight runs wherever possible," claiming the gracefully curving parkway was a "relic of the horse and buggy days." Lay preferred high-speed freeways like the German *autobahn*. He claimed: "The ideal for which we should strive is a means whereby we can drive from a garage not more than 1/4 mile to a superhighway on which we can continue uninterruptedly until within 5 miles or so of our destination in another city or in a county camp or farm."[21] Lay's suggestion recalls that of Frank Lloyd Wright, whose Broadacre City of the 1930s projected a United States covered by an immense grid of freeways or superhighways complete with cloverleafs.[22]

Still the problem of high-speed access to the inner city remained. Parkways led away from or toward the metropolis, or surrounded it, but did not go inside. Several Europeans and one American did conceive of the high-speed freeway through the heart of the city. Eugène Hénard foresaw limited-access highways through Paris just after the turn of the century.[23] Antonio Sant'Elia, the Italian futurist architect, also projected in his drawings multilevel roadways that can be interpreted—certainly in light of the futurist romance of the machine and speed—as freeways.[24] Le Corbusier picked up on Hénard's and Sant'Elia's ideas for his 1921–22 *Une Ville Contemporaine*, or *City for 3 Million Inhabitants*, and the 1925 Voisin Plan for Paris. In both of Le Corbusier's schemes, two immense superhighways bisect the city into four quadrants and meet at the center in a multilevel interchange.[25]

Undoubtedly Hugh Ferriss was influenced by the European ideas of the superhighway penetrating the city.[26] As early

4.5 Division of Engineering, Long Island State Parkway Commission
Grand Central Parkway, "The Pretzel."
Queens, N.Y. 1941

4.6 Bureau of Engineering, Los Angeles Department of Public Works
Arroyo Seco Parkway (Pasadena Freeway). Los Angeles. 1937–40

as 1922 he projected the separation of pedestrians from road traffic and the elevation of roads on several levels to skirt, and in time penetrate, the immense building masses the new setback laws seemed to suggest.[27] Ferriss's most dramatic renderings of the late 1920s and 1930s show multilevel, high-speed expressways running through the city and its buildings. In his *Imaginary Metropolis* published in *The Metropolis of Tomorrow*, great building blocks are linked by "master highways ... developed for the maximum traffic." In many of his towers "the ground level, practically in entirety, is given over to wheel traffic; parking is beneath the building." While Ferriss claimed his city was "in the image of man," and that true humane values of emotion and sensitivity were present, the overwhelming image is not of people but of gigantic building blocks and large superhighways with cars and trucks rushing to and fro.[28]

By the mid-1930s the idea of superhighways within the city had caught the imagination of many machine age protagonists. Charles Downing Lay showed a scheme based upon the ideas of Le Corbusier for "a high-speed truck highway through a suburban or city district" in which narrow

bands of trees shielded an eight-lane freeway, completely independent of city streets. The freeway backed right up to backyards of houses.[29] Egmont Arens projected a "Roadway Housing Plan" in which "super-highways *from center to center* of cities" would be used to rebuild decayed sections. Apartment blocks would be surrounded by high-speed freeways. The problem of the older big cities as Arens saw it was they were strangling from lack of entrance and egress by automobiles.[30] Miller McClintock, who coined the friction elimination theory mentioned earlier, proposed a specially designed environment in which the motor vehicle reigned as king.[31]

At the June 1937 meetings of the American Society of Planning Officials and the Automobile Manufacturers Association, both in Detroit, McClintock's presentation "Of Things to Come" was accompanied by slides of Norman Bel Geddes's future city recently completed for the Shell Oil Company. McClintock praised Bel Geddes's separation of pedestrians and vehicular traffic, so "that man, as an urban animal, for the first time in centuries is able to use his oldest form of transportation—walking—with some degree of security and dignity." He also admired actual accomplishments such as the Woodbridge, New Jersey, cloverleaf, the new Saint Louis Freeway, the "traffic sorter" approach to New York's Triborough Bridge, and the Arroyo Seco, especially its "tunnels and open cuts which with its efficiency, has a beauty."[32]

Bel Geddes's *Futurama* was in many ways the culmination of the ideas of the 1920s and 1930s on parkways and free-

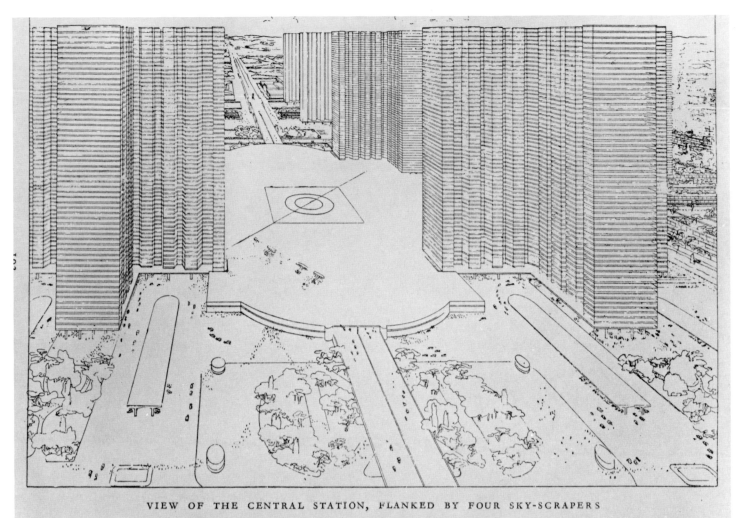

VIEW OF THE CENTRAL STATION, FLANKED BY FOUR SKY-SCRAPERS

The tracks for fast motor traffic pass under the aerodrome. The unobstructed and open ground-floor levels of the sky-scrapers can be seen, as can the piles or "stilts" on which they are built. Covered car-parking places can be perceived on either side. To the right are restaurants, shops, etc., set amidst trees and open spaces.

ways. While derided by some people—Robert Moses called it a "work of the imagination"—both the model and Bel Geddes's book *Magic Motorways* (1940) effectively laid down the pattern for the future.[33] The book, a product of three years of extensive research, and written for a popular audience, projected a vast, national system of freeways. Respecting the landscape when in the countryside, Bel Geddes's freeways would swing around large cities, and through feeder roads and express boulevards would carry high-speed traffic to the heart. Nothing would impede these magic motorways: mountains would be cut away or tunneled through, vast bodies of water and canyons would be jumped over on slender suspension bridges, and traffic control would monitor and even make driving automatic. Carefully designed by architects,

landscape architects, engineers, traffic experts, and the all-knowing industrial designer, the superhighway, motorway, or freeway would become a new American art form.

The ideas of Bel Geddes and other parkway prophets were the background for the great American post–World War II achievement, the Interstate Highway System, which girdled the country in a belt of concrete and asphalt. The negative consequences of this American love affair with the automobile and the open highway are well recognized, yet the parkway and freeway represent a substantial accomplishment not only of technology, engineering, and construction, but in the creation of an aesthetic of speed and motion; broad, long, and continuous surfaces; a cinematic view of nature; and the machine as the dominant fact.

4.7 Le Corbusier
View of the Central Station, Flanked by Four Sky-Scrapers. 1927. From *City of Tomorrow*, 1929. © SPADEM, Paris/VAGA, New York, 1986

101

4.8

BRIDGES

For the viewers of The Museum of Modern Art's American mural exhibition of May 1932, the overwhelming visual presence was provided not by the paintings of social commentary by Ben Shahn, the abstractions of skyscrapers by Georgia O'Keeffe, or the laboratory research by Henry Billings. Instead photographs dominated, especially the one large photomural that Edward Steichen showed (fig. 4.8).[34] The viewer was literally engulfed in the George Washington Bridge. Drawn by the emphatic repetition of its web trusses and parallel catenary arcs, the viewer entered into a world of pure structure, and was led by a receding ground plane toward the further suspension tower and infinity beyond.

Shrugging off the historical references that had dominated early bridge designs, American bridge engineers and architects of the 1920s and 1930s sought expression and meaning in the structure and its purpose. Thus the resulting bridges, like the George Washington, were also works of art, great pieces of sculpture that tugged at the base of emotions in their daring spanning of large voids. David B. Steinman, one of the leading bridge designers of the period, saw bridges as akin to religious ecstasy. He liked to quote from Franklin Delano Roosevelt's 1931 dedication speech at the George Washington Bridge: "There can be little doubt that in many ways the story of bridge-building is the story of civilization." The "ugly civilization" of the nineteenth and early twentieth centuries had been left behind, according to Steinman; an era of "beauty of bridges" had occurred: "instead of re-sorting to concealment or extraneous decoration, bridge designers are now directing their efforts toward producing the most beautiful designs in the steel itself, by developing and perfecting forms and proportions that will most beautifully express the dominant spirit of this material—its strength, its power, and its grace."[35]

Bridge-building was avidly followed by the American public throughout the 1930s. Of course, construction meant considerable work to Depression America, but its fascination went beyond that—it also represented heroism and accomplishment. The daring workers, suspended hundreds of feet in the air, driving pins to trusses, slinging the cables, and fitting it all together, were seen as courageous men performing noble endeavors. Construction photographs helped convey the special drama of high steel balancing acts (see fig. 4.17).

Several thousand bridges of all sizes and types—reinforced concrete, metal arch, cantilever truss, suspension—were executed in the United States in the 1920s and 1930s. In a sense this was the great age of American bridge building. As architects became interested in bridge design, the Beaux-Arts Institute of Design in New York helped to sponsor annual competitions among architecture and engineering students. Accompanying and contributing to this interest was the apotheosis of the Brooklyn Bridge by artists and critics such as Hart Crane, Joseph Stella, Walker Evans, and Lewis Mumford.[36] New figures were added to the pantheon of engineering heros: Othmar H. Ammann of the New York Port Au-

4.8 Edward Steichen *George Washington Bridge.* 1931. Gelatin-silver print, 9⅝ × 7⅞". International Museum of Photography at George Eastman House, Rochester, N.Y. Bequest of Edward Steichen by direction of Joanna T. Steichen

thority and chief engineer on the George Washington, Goethals, Kill van Kull, Triborough, and Bronx–Whitestone bridges, and adviser on the Golden Gate Bridge and later the Verrazano-Narrows Bridge; Joseph B. Strauss of the Golden Gate Bridge; Charles H. Purcell of the San Francisco–Oakland Bay Bridge; and David B. Steinman of the Henry Hudson, Mount Hope, Waldo Hancock, and the Mackinac Strait bridges, and adviser on the George Washington Bridge. These individuals helped to create an American art of bridge design.

Suspension bridges clearly dominated the bridge-building art in America in the 1920s and 1930s, but a few other types of bridges should be noted. Of steel arch bridges, the Kill van Kull, between Bayonne, New Jersey, and Staten Island, New York, is the most dramatic and beautiful (fig. 4.9). A single span of 1,675

feet—an enormous length—the bridge is composed of a continuous parabolic arch carrying the roadway, or deck, for most of its length by cable suspenders. The open truss is vibrant in its reiterated pattern, and while the arch appears symmetrical, the crown is actually located somewhat to the south, since the Staten Island end is the shorter. The top chords of the arch do not really function as an arch—it is a stiffening element—and consequently in the open lattice abutments only the bottom chords are provided with a substantial terminus, indicating the purely functional approach to the design. No visual connections were used for the top chord since that would have been functionally false.[37]

American concrete arch bridges were of two major types, open and closed. The closed-arch bridge usually signified the involvement of a traditional or conservatively oriented architect. The Calvert Street Bridge, Washington, D.C., by Ralph Modjeski as engineer and Paul P. Cret as architect, took as its basis the Roman masonry arch aqueduct (fig. 4.10). A concrete-arched structure faced with sheets of Indiana limestone, its detailing is extremely simple; setbacks for the abutments and narrow grooves provide shadow-line details. Cret's Calvert Street Bridge has four sculptural panels by Leon Hermant which contain heavy neoclassical, seminude figures and transportation machines. To functionalist critics, such closed-arch bridges were regressive.[38] Considered far more modern and truthful were open concrete spans such as the Russian Gulch Bridge on the California coast, designed by F. W. Panhorst of the California State Division of Highways (fig. 4.11). Each of the elements—the roadway, the elliptical arch, and the piers—was clearly separated. Also, the piers and graceful arch state their carrying capacities with their profiles growing slimmer as the load decreases.[39]

The George Washington Bridge over the Hudson River (fig. 4.12) had been dreamed about for years before the state legislatures of New York and New Jersey passed the necessary bills allowing its design and construction between 1927 and 1931. Its span of 3,500 feet nearly doubled the preexisting record of suspension spans. O. H. Ammann was the chief engineer, Allston Dana and Leon Moisseiff were the designing engineers, and Cass Gilbert and Aymar Embury II were the consulting architects. The great span and double-decked roadway determined the massive trussed towers—or really vertical space frames—and the deep anchorages for the cables. Gilbert, a traditional architect of the American Renaissance generation, designed a smooth granite cladding

4.10 Ralph Modjeski (1861–1940) and Paul Cret (1876–1945)
Calvert Street Bridge (now Duke Ellington Memorial Bridge). Washington, D.C. 1931

4.11 F. W. Panhorst, chief engineer Russian Gulch Bridge. On the Mendocino Coast Road, South of Fort Bragg, Calif. 1940

4.12 Othmar H. Ammann, chief engineer
George Washington Bridge. New York side. 1927–31

for the towers, decked out with classical moldings, and anchorages decorated with small, classical openings. For economical, functional, and aesthetic reasons most of Gilbert's design was dispensed with by Embury, who became the consulting architect after Gilbert's death in 1934, though the semicircular arches of the towers remain as a reminder of his classical intentions.[40] As completed the George Washington Bridge exemplifies the 1920s impulse to create a visual complication of parts, to glorify the mechanical elements as the main image.

The Bronx–Whitestone Bridge for the New York Triborough Bridge Authority, 1937–39, with Ammann as chief engineer, Dana as chief designing engineer, and Embury as architect, shows a completely different approach (fig. 4.13). The bridge is simple and refined, a product of the aesthetic of the machine as a cohesive unit. Extremely elegant, the Bronx–Whitestone Bridge is composed of few parts. The rigid-frame towers with semicircular stiffener arches were reduced to ephemeral posts. The roadbed, elegantly suspended by long, thin cables, was a plate girder, unusual in its ribbon thinness from the customary deep truss. The ratio of girder depth to span was a mere 1 to 210. Because of the failure of the Tacoma Bridge in Washington in 1940, also built with a thin girder roadway, the Bronx–Whitestone roadway was reinforced with a truss. Although the original thin proportions are marred, the Bronx–Whitestone still shows the elegant visual refinement of American bridge design in the late 1930s.[41]

The barebones aesthetic of open-web trusses made an appearance at the *Century of Progress Exposition* in *Skyride* (fig. 4.14), designed by David B. Steinman. Funded by Goodyear-Zeppelin, Mississippi Valley Steel, and Otis Elevator, each of whose products appeared to good advantage, *Skyride* was simply a suspension bridge adapted to a carnival thrill ride. Two 628-foot-tall towers—the tallest man-made structures west of New York—were situated at each side of the grounds and linked by steel cables. Spectators either zoomed across the 200-foot-high, one-third-of-a-mile span in rocket cars designed by John Root, or took a high-speed elevator to the top to view the spectacle below.

Out in the San Francisco Bay Area two other great landmarks were constructed. From an aesthetic point of view, the San Francisco–Oakland Bay Bridge (fig. 4.15) lacks the cohesiveness and drama of its neighbor, the Golden Gate Bridge, both 1933–37 (fig. 4.18). However, the Bay Bridge triumphed technically in engineering ingenuity. Composed of a combination of cantilever truss span, an island—Yerba Buena—with a tunnel in the middle, and a pair of suspension bridges, back-to-back, with a span of 9,260 feet, the total length of

4.13 Othmar H. Ammann, chief engineer
The Bronx–Whitestone Bridge, from the northeast, 1937–39

4.14 Nathaniel A. Owings (1903–1985), architect, and David B. Steinman (1886–1960), chief engineer
Skyway. Century of Progress Exposition, Chicago. 1933

4.15 Charles Purcell (1883–1951), chief engineer
San Francisco–Oakland Bay Bridge. San Francisco. 1933–37

4.16 Timothy Pflueger (1892–1946), architect
Yerba Buena Island Tunnel, San Francisco–Oakland Bay Bridge. Photograph during construction

4.17 San Francisco–Oakland Bay Bridge
during construction. Gabriel Moulin photograph ca. 1936

4.18 Joseph B. Strauss (1870–1938), chief engineer
Golden Gate Bridge. San Francisco. 1933–37. Photograph ca. 1937

the mega-structure, including approaches, was 8½ miles. Originally fitted out with classical detailing supplied by Arthur Brown, Jr., the leading Bay Area classicist, the architectural elements of the design were reworked by Timothy Pflueger, an "exponent of the modern" and the designer of several moderne high rises.[42] Pflueger stripped away most of the ornament, allowing chief engineer C. H. Purcell's great X-braced towers, painted in silver, to stand out. Pflueger's tunnel entrances to Yerba Buena (fig. 4.16) were masterpieces of design, with repeated recessed archings that emerge as setback blocks to each side.

The Golden Gate Bridge was the largest span ever attempted at the time, 4,200 feet. Constructed in treacherous waters over a sizable geological fault, with the possibility of earthquakes necessarily considered in the design, the Golden Gate was also hindered by the weather, mostly violent winds and dense fog. Ships rammed the construction piers. It was designed by Joseph B. Strauss, chief engineer, and with a consulting board that included O. H. Ammann, but some of the impact of the Golden Gate Bridge must be attributed to the consulting architect, Irving F. Morrow, who also had modernist sympathies. The towers, which stand 746 feet above water level, are extraordinary. Built of carbon and silicon steel plate welded and riveted into cells for the structural members, the towers were drastically reduced in thickness. As the towers progressed upward their profile diminished. Morrow convinced the engineers to cover the towers with small, riveted panels to emphasize their natural setbacks. The spandrel stiffeners were faced with faceted projections, and corbel blocks helped tie them to the posts. After much consultation Morrow also convinced the bridge authorities to paint the structure international orange and not gold as originally intended. Instead of fitting into the golden California landscape, the bridge stands apart, a graceful effortless leap.[43]

The Golden Gate Bridge is one of the great designs of the period, a monument of the machine moderne style. As an experience it is overwhelming and moving. The approach from either side is through natural landscape, the brown hills of Marin County or the green park of the Presidio; then the setback towers of the bridge soar upward into view. On the bridge the landmasses recede, the buildings of San Francisco and the suburbs across the bay diminish in size. The sky is high overhead and the water, with its ships like toys, miniature models, far below. The tires of passing automobiles sing, the cables glisten as they swing down to the roadway, and for a brief instant nature and the machine merge.

DAMS

Standing on the rim of Black Canyon in the middle of the desert in 1936, J. B. Priestley, the British writer and critic, observed "an inspiring image...a kind of giant symbol. It is the symbol of the new man, a new world, a new way of life." Recognizing that some people might not see the Hoover Dam as art, Priestley was still "enchanted by its clean functional lines...it is a thing of beauty...the impression it makes on any sensitive observer is not unlike that made by a massive work of art."[44]

In the 1930s the massive, multipurpose dam emerged as one of the most distinctive examples of American machine age modernism. Great dams such as Hoover in the Southwest, Shasta in northern California, Grand Coulee and Bonneville in the Northwest, Fort Peck in Montana, and the Tennessee Valley Authority dams in the East were hailed at home and abroad. Constructed by various branches of the government, these great dams and the many smaller ones transformed vast areas of the continent, taming rivers and preventing floods, providing new water-transportation routes, storing water for irrigation and distant populations, creating new agricultural land and recreation areas, generating electricity for industry and the home, and substantially changing the living standards of millions of people. Additionally, these great dams represented the coming of age of a new source of power, hydroelectricity.

The massive multipurpose dam caught the imagination of everyone: it represented work for a Depression-affected economy and indicated the benevolent aspects of governmental planning and the ability of man to significantly alter and control his environment. Of course, dams were not invented in the 1930s; they have a long and ancient history. More recently,

there were constructed in the 1910s and 1920s several large dams—the Arrowrock, 1912–16, and the Deadwood, 1929–30, both in Idaho—that contributed technological knowledge to the great dams of the 1930s.[45] But in the 1930s the size and impact of large dams increased substantially. Hoover Dam (figs. 4.19, 4.21), when completed in 1936, ranked, at over 726 feet, as the highest dam in the world. It had the largest reservoir, Lake Mead, with some 28,537,000 acre-feet of water, and was also the largest in volume of concrete with 3,400,000 cubic yards, and had the largest power capacity. If all its generators had been put on the line, the total horsepower would have equaled one-eighth of all the horsepower available for generating electricity in the United States.[46] In the next few years Hoover was outclassed in all areas except height. The Fort Peck Dam on the Missouri River in Montana, 1933–40, became the largest in the volume of both its reservoir and its earth-fill. The Grand Coulee Dam (fig. 4.20) on the Columbia River in Washington became the largest generator of power and also the largest in total volume of masonry or concrete with 11,976,000 cubic yards—the first structure in forty-seven centuries to exceed the volume of the Great Pyramid at Khufu.[47]

4.19 Bureau of Reclamation Engineers, Gordon B. Kaufmann (1888–1949), consulting architect
Hoover Dam, aerial view. Boulder City, Nev. 1930–36

Hoover Dam, the first and most famous of the 1930s dams, best exemplifies the development of an aesthetic and an iconography. (Begun as Hoover Dam, its name was changed to Boulder Dam in 1933 when Roosevelt entered the White House, then changed back to Hoover Dam in 1947 by a Republican congress.) Located in a desolate and inhospitable area—as were most dams—it was built in the desert, thirty miles from Las Vegas, at the time no more than a ramshackle group of buildings acting as a division point on the Union Pacific Railroad. Boulder City, a model town with housing and facilities for the work force and their families, was constructed in the desert about eight miles from the dam site. Ideas for harnessing the Colorado River had been advanced from the turn of the century; in the 1920s, after a series of devastating floods, the engineers of the Bureau of Reclamation began to investigate the possibilities of building a large dam.[48]

By 1930 the site and general plans were ready. Herbert Hoover, himself a professional engineer, had an interest in the dam as both an engineering marvel and an economic stay. Perceiving the signs of a large depression and enormous unemployment, President Hoover pushed an appropriation bill through congress. The bureau's engineers hurriedly drew up specifications and began preliminary site work, and in March 1931 the bids for construction were opened. The winning bid, for $48,890,995.50—the largest labor contract the government had let up to that time—was by a consortium of contractors known as Six Companies Inc. At the peak of construction some five thousand men were employed; the total employment for the six years was about twenty thousand. Insurance companies estimated that two hundred men would lose their lives in the first year alone. That

the official loss of life was only ninety-six was due to a strike in the summer of 1931 that resulted in a renewed governmental commitment to work and living conditions in the model city. Certainly the weather circumstances were daunting: the temperature could hit 126 degrees at the canyon rim, and over 140 in the bottom of the canyon and in the diversion tunnels; during winter temperatures dropped below 20 degrees, often accompanied by strong winds. The dangerous Colorado was another problem, as it threatened to break through the tempo-

4.21 Hugh Ferriss, renderer
Boulder Dam Overlook. 1941. Charcoal and pen on board with varnish, 25½ × 17½". Collection Avery Architectural and Fine Arts Library, Columbia University, New York

4.20 Bureau of Reclamation, architects, Hugh Ferriss, renderer
Grand Coulee Dam, Snake River, Washington. 1942. Charcoal and pen on board, 28 × 22". Cooper-Hewitt Museum, the Smithsonian Institution's National Museum of Design, New York

4.22 Hoover Dam, Arizona side, during construction. 1934. Photograph by Ben Glaha (1899–1971)

draglines; Caterpillar tractors; "jumbo" drilling rigs; and cableways carrying men and equipment back and forth and up and down the canyon. It seemed as if a new race of giants had inhabited the earth. A balletic poise, a choreography of dance steps appeared to control the actions of the workers, as they swung down the canyon walls with jackhammers and crowbars to scale away loose rock. Eight-yard "Crowe" concrete buckets came sailing down from up high, hand signals directed them, their bottoms opened, and out rushed concrete ready to be tamped and vibrated into place. Photographs captured the concrete cliffs, endlessly repeated concrete forms entirely abstract in their removal from both a human scale and a functional dimension. They were pieces of a larger whole, and yet at the same time they had an eternal beauty and finality all their own. Especially important in conveying to the outside world the drama of Hoover Dam was the photography of Ben Glaha, the official photographer for the Bureau of Reclamation (see fig. 4.22).[49]

Essentially the construction plan involved diverting the Colorado River through tunnels drilled in the solid rock walls of the canyon, building temporary cofferdams to block the river, and then excavating the site before constructing the dam and power plant. The concrete of the dam presented special difficulties: if it were simply poured and left to harden it would have taken about a century to cool, and the shrinkage would have cracked the dam and left it unusable. The problem was solved by a controlled pouring of slabs and the circulation of artificially refrigerated water through tubing placed in the wet concrete. This cooled each pour in seventy-two hours.

rary cofferdams and flood away the entire project.

The building of Hoover Dam intrigued Americans of all classes. Artists, reporters, writers, and tourists, coming by auto or by the Union Pacific Railroad's special excursion train, descended on the site. Construction went on twenty-four hours a day. At night the construction site, with its brilliant lights, resembled a movie set. There were large machines, some of them new to construction sites: 250-horsepower Mack trucks with sixteen-yard dump bodies; dinosaur-like Bucyrus Erie, Marmon, and P & H cranes, shovels, and

The design of Hoover Dam can be attributed to both engineers and an architect. Bureau of Reclamation engineers did the technical designing and then added some debased classical ornamentation. Sensing this was inappropriate, the bureau turned to Gordon B. Kaufmann, a Los Angeles architect known for his work in the moderne style. Kaufmann recognized the primacy of engineering as the basic form giver, but stripped away all the classical elements. The setback outlines of the towers on the dam's crest and the water intake towers emerged from Lake Mead. He also redesigned the powerhouse at the base of the dam and used horizontal aluminum fins for windows. Shiny metal-covered transformers were placed in front of the powerhouse in full view. Together with the bureau's engineers, Kaufmann designed the spillways in the streamlined mode. For the interior, Kaufmann had Allen True engaged to design floor patterns and color schemes for the powerhouse. Kaufmann also supervised the competition for the monument to the dam, which was won by Oskar J. W. Hansen, who also designed the ornamental elevator tower panels. The monument consists of two thirty-foot-tall winged figures, made of bronze; each figure's wings and arms are molded into a single unit (fig. 4.23). The terrazzo floor of the monument contains a celestial map that locates the precise astronomical time—September 30, 1935, 8:56:2.25 in the evening—when President Roosevelt dedicated the dam. The pattern of the map recalls the straight lines, circles, and triangles of the Russian constructivists of the 1920s.[51]

Hoover Dam, though conceived by conservative administrations, became for Roosevelt's New Dealers the prototype

4.23 Oskar J. W. Hansen (1892–1971) *Winged Figures of the Republic,* Hoover Dam. 1935–38. Bronze, ht.: 30′

for the rebuilding of America through extensive public works projects. The work of the Tennessee Valley Authority demonstrates the logical extension of this concept and its application to a wider area.

Argument had existed for years about the control of the Tennessee River, a 650-mile watercourse running from Knoxville, Tennessee, through part of Alabama, draining areas of seven states, and terminating at Paducah, Kentucky, on the Ohio River. The Tennessee Valley Authority Act of May 18, 1933, created a public-governmental corporation charged with not simply controlling the river, but developing an extremely depressed and rural portion of the nation. Viewed by conservatives as creeping state socialism, TVA's board of directors included Dr.

4.24

Arthur E. Morgan, a civil engineer, as chairman, David E. Lilienthal, a lawyer with public power experience, and Harcourt A. Morgan, president of the University of Tennessee and an agriculturalist. All three had substantial social goals in mind.[52]

In addition to the eight dams either completed or under construction by 1941, the TVA became involved in a host of other projects, including fertilizer manufacture, crop seed production, reforestation, recreation, nurseries, ceramics, nutrition, and education. The attempt was made to "socially engineer" or improve the life of workers; mobile vans brought health care to the area, and teachers and social workers worked with the entire community. Several workers' towns or villages were built, the most noted being Norris, named for the Nebraska senator who sponsored the federal legislation. Taking its cue from Boulder City, Nevada, Norris was seen by Arthur Morgan as an answer to the usually squalid and depressed living conditions of most construction camps. The Norris Freeway, a two-lane, limited-access road that curved gracefully through the landscape, connected the dam to Knoxville (about thirty-five miles away), and improved connections to the town. At other dam sites prefabricated mobile housing was attempted. Morgan and his fellow directors foresaw a cooperative-agrarian-industrial community with high social ideals.[53]

TVA architecture—the dams, powerhouses, locks, visitors centers, and associated buildings—exhibits a common aesthetic, the attempt to monumentalize and emphasize machine iconography. Simple forms, great sheer surfaces where possible, the particularization of details, and the machines themselves—whether gan-

try cranes at Kentucky Dam, 1938–41, or the turbines at the Pickwick Landing Dam, 1934–38—make the dams more than functional engineering; they became works of great art. The approaches to the dams were carefully studied, and while engineering and hydrological considerations dictated a dam's location, the visitor was brought to the dam in a dramatic manner, always seeing the structures within the landscape, as symbols of man's control of nature. An engineering force of over one thousand under the direction of chief engineer Theodore B. Parker and chief designing engineer Carl A. Bock provided the basic outlines for the designs. The architectural design and much of the high quality of the TVA's work came from Roland A. Wank.

Wank, a native Hungarian, came to the United States in 1924. In company with other Eastern Europeans—notably Urban, Frankl, Schindler, Neutra—Wank had the Viennese Secessionist attitude toward form and decoration: he liked texture, pattern, and where appropriate, shiny surfaces.[54] He worked with Fellheimer and Wagner, a large New York industrial architecture firm, and was chief designer on their Cincinnati Union Terminal, 1929–33, a large concrete struc-

4.25 Fellheimer and Wagner, architects, Roland A. Wank, chief designer Cincinnati Union Terminal. Cincinnati. 1929–33.

4.24 Roland A. Wank (1898–1970), principal architect, and staff, Tennessee Valley Authority; Seth Harrison Gurnee, renderer
Norris Dam and Powerhouse. ca. 1933. Charcoal on tracing paper, 16½ × 20″

4.26 Roland A. Wank, principal architect, and staff, Tennessee Valley Authority; Seth Harrison Gurnee, renderer
Guntersville Dam Powerhouse. 1937. Pencil on tracing paper, 30 × 11½″

4.27 Roland A. Wank, architect, and staff, Tennessee Valley Authority
Control Room, Pickwick Landing Dam. 1934–38

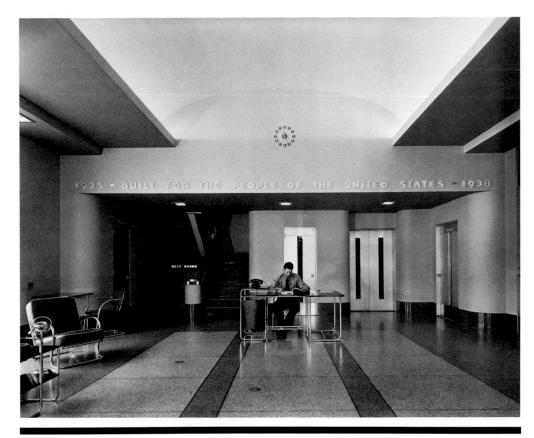

4.28 Visitor's Lobby, Pickwick Landing Dam

ture (fig. 4.25). Lurking inside the vast sculptural shape of the terminal can be felt the cryptic drawings of Erich Mendelsohn.[55] Mendelsohn's machine like forms, huge molded or bended concrete or metal structures, influenced Wank's TVA work. In 1941 The Museum of Modern Art gave Wank's TVA architecture a special exhibition, implying—at least to some people—that his work was in the International Style.[56] While there were some similarities—flat roofs, ribbon windows, tubular furniture—Wank's designs came more out of the Eastern European Secessionist and Mendelsohnian romantic tradition, modified by the American moderne style of the late 1920s, as well as the already-developed dam aesthetic as seen at Hoover Dam. Gordon Kaufmann was brought in as an adviser to Wank on Norris and Wheeler dams, and his experience with working with patterned concrete and treating large masses is apparent. Wank wanted "to make the dams look as functional as the engineers have designed them," a sentiment similar to Kaufmann's.[57] Finally, while Wank is listed as the principal architect for TVA, 1933–43, he was a strong proponent of team design

and would claim the work was a team project of architects and engineers.[58]

Wank joined TVA in 1933 with intention of working on housing, but quickly he became involved with the first dam. Construction of Norris Dam (fig. 4.24) began on October 1, 1933, scarcely four months after the TVA became operational, because the Bureau of Reclamation and the Army Corps of Engineers had designed a dam for the site in the 1920s. After modifications, such as redesigning the powerhouse, removing the engineers' pilasters and the arches atop the dam, and greatly simplifying the outline of the huge concrete masses, Norris Dam was built. The major feature of Norris Dam—a straight gravity dam—is the spillway, a huge wall of textured concrete, 265 feet tall. The spillway gates and roadway across the top are integrated as a continuous horizontal line, interrupted only by the extrusion of the access tower. The powerhouse, a clean-cut, rectangular block, has a fenestration grid of narrow rectangular openings, which increase the apparent size and give a nonresidential, machine-like character. Constructed of preformed concrete panels, the rough-cut

4.29 Hoover Dam Powerhouse, Nevada wing

4.30 Powerhouse, Pickwick Landing Dam

formwork created an alternating checkerboard pattern, reminiscent of the Viennese Secession.[59]

Very different in character (reflecting its function as a main-river control dam, not a flood-storage dam like Norris) is Wank's Guntersville Dam, 1935–37 (fig. 4.26). Gray concrete with a checkerboard pattern from the formwork created a subtle texture against buff brick for the powerhouse.

The scale and emphasis Wank sought were superhuman. His dams were designed on the machine scale. Dropped were all references to traditional architecture and residential scale. Because he worked on a number of dams and buildings, Wank developed an aesthetic capable of being repeated. Window frames were of aluminum, as was all the large lettering. Everything looked "clean," and "efficient."[60] Each detail—the flagpoles, the doors, the drinking fountains—was carefully studied and standardized. Visitor lobbies, with the carefully uniformed guard, the metal tubular furniture, the subdued light reflected from the curved ceiling, the rectilinear patterned terrazzo floor, the aluminum doors, the particulated clock, and the lettering of TVA's motto—"Built for the People of the United States"—helped to carry the message that here was the modern technocratic state. Control rooms, with their shiny glazed surfaces and myriads of dials, levers, and buttons, were carefully crafted displays that visitors could inspect through large glass windows. The magic and the success of the TVA message was caught by a writer in 1939: "In a dozen control buildings a handful of men will sit, and as they push buttons and turn switches the river will do as they wish."[61]

All the dams—TVA, Hoover, and others—were designed not only as functional structures but also as great visitor experiences. The culmination of every visit was the powerhouse. At TVA's Pickwick Landing Dam the generators sat as icons in their dark green and white metal casings; the wainscoting was a dark green tile, the walls were lemon yellow and light green, and overhead was an open truss ceiling (fig. 4.30). Perhaps the greatest experience is at Hoover Dam, where the visitor parks on the roadway on top of the dam, enters the elevator lobby of black, green, bronze, and aluminum, and then drops 528 feet inside the dam. Exiting into a gleaming white glazed-tile tunnel with Indian patterns in the floor, the visitor finally arrives at the viewing platform for the turbines. Set against the repetitive concrete piers with overhead cranes painted a jade green, valves and pipings picked out in vermilion, blue, and yellow, are the turbines, nine on each side of the dam, gleaming in their deep-red casings and aluminum and stainless steel trim. The experience recalls Henry Adams's earlier confrontation with a dynamo: "he began to feel the forty-foot dynamo as a moral force, much as the early Christians felt the Cross. The planet itself seemed less impressive, in its old-fashioned deliberate, annual or daily revolution, than this huge wheel, revolving within arm's-length at some vertiginous speed. . . . Before the end, one began to pray to it."[62] The machine has taken over.

4.31 Charles Sheeler *Suspended Power*. 1939. Oil on canvas, 15 × 30″. Dallas Museum of Art. Gift of Edmund J. Kahn

5.1

CHAPTER 5

TRANSPORTATION MACHINE DESIGN

"Speed," wrote Norman Bel Geddes in 1932, "is the cry of our era, and greater speed one of the goals of tomorrow." For transportation designers in the 1930s speed transcended the notion of mere movement to become a symbol, and ultimately—as in Gordon Buehrig's design for the Cord *810* of 1935 (fig. 5.1)—a form to be developed. A long, narrow hood articulated by a lower band of horizontal ventilator bars shielded the 115-horsepower, V-8 engine. The wheels were prominent but covered in the smooth, high-pontoon front fenders and teardrop rear fenders. Implied power and flowing body lines gave the impression of speed even when the *810* was at rest. A reviewer of the annual auto shows noted its "scientifically stream lined" features and reached for a metaphor: "This new Cord is as clean-cut as a low winged airplane poised for a take-off."[1]

The aircraft simile was a common one in American transportation design in the late 1920s and 1930s. Aeronautical imagery and names became the norm as shared concerns—efficiency in high-speed travel and fuel consumption, appearance, and enlarged carrying capacity—animated most designers. European experiments in streamlining and aeronautics provided a backdrop for American designers. The wind-tunnel look of cars, boats, trucks, trains, and planes seemingly capable of cleaving the air or water with the least resistance came from aeronautical theory. Certainly not every streamlined car or train was tested in a wind tunnel, but the image and principles of teardrop and streamlined design influenced all industrial designers.

Many designers worked on a variety of different transportation modes. Some designs, such as many of those by Norman Bel Geddes, were total fantasy and existed only on paper or as models. Still, Bel Geddes popularized streamlining for the general public and did have actual commissions (for Graham-Paige, Nash, Chrysler, and Autocar), though they came to nothing. Other independent designers were more successful; Raymond Loewy saw his designs for Studebaker automobiles, Pennsylvania Railroad locomotives, Greyhound buses, International Harvester trucks, and several ships produced. Loewy and Bel Geddes were the exceptions, the high-profile superstars; most transportation design evolved within a company by a group of relatively anonymous designers and engineers involved with only one mode of transportation.

5.1 Gordon M. Buehrig (b. 1904), designer
Cord *810 Westchester* Sedan. 1936. Manufactured by the Auburn Automobile Co., Connersville, Ind. Auburn-Cord-Duesenberg Museum, Auburn, Ind.

5.2 John K. Northrop
Sirius. 1929. Manufactured by Lockheed
Aircraft Company

MACHINES FOR THE AIR

The primary achievement of American aviation design in the 1930s was the creation of a dynamic and streamlined form, in both image and performance. Although America had invented the airplane, or at least achieved the first powered airflight, aeronautical theory until the late 1920s was basically the province of Germany and England. Modern American aircraft design was spurred by the luring in 1921 of Max Munk and in 1929 of Theodore von Karman, leading German theorists; the establishment in 1926 of the Daniel Guggenheim Fund for the Promotion of Aeronautics; and the increasing research throughout the 1920s of the National Advisory Committee for Aeronautics (NACA). The essential challenges facing aircraft designers were weight and air drag reduction, increased payload, and greater reliability.[2]

Throughout the late 1920s and early 1930s a number of technological breakthroughs were achieved. Radial engines by Pratt & Whitney and Curtis-Wright replaced cumbersome in-line engines and also provided increased reliability and horsepower. Cantilever wing design, by which wings were internally braced and attached to the fuselage, meant the elimination of external struts and guy wires. Stressed skin and multicellular wing construction allowed for the creation of streamlined shapes. Similarly, wind-shaped cowls over the radial engine improved cooling efficiency and lessened drag. Some of these ideas appeared in William B. Stout's popular Ford *Tri-motor*, built by Ford's aircraft division. Stout's design was heavily based upon the three-engined German *Fokker*. The Ford *Tri-motor* reflected the 1920s machine-as-parts approach to design: it was a combination of unintegrated parts—a fuselage, wings, a tail, landing gear, and three motors, two of which hung from the wings. Late 1920s designs by John K. Northrop for Lockheed, the *Vega* of 1927 and 1929 and the *Sirius* (fig. 5.2), 1929, showed the possibilities inherent in the new approach. Long streamlined fuselages, streamlined cowls hiding radial engines, wings flared to the body to create a continuous skin, and teardrop-shaped covers on the landing gear provided a more unified form. The *Sirius* and *Vega*, flown by Charles Lindbergh, Amelia Earhart, and Wiley Post, helped set speed and distance records while they mapped air-transport routes.[3]

craft, offered another example of American aviation achievement. Germany led the field with the *DO-X* of 1929 by Claude Dornier, until 1931, when in the United States Igor Sikorsky, a Russian immigrant, designed and built for Pan American Airlines the first *Clippers*. These were followed by Glen Martin's flying boats, the best-known of which was the *M-130* or *China Clipper* of 1934 (fig. 5.3). Martin's *M-130* illustrates the new integration and unity of aircraft design: the wing was integrated with the body, and flared cowling was used on the motors.

The impact of industrial designers on aircraft design was evident more in interiors and in the realm of publicity than in actual flying examples. In 1932 Norman Bel Geddes presented a flying boat, *Air Liner Number 4* (fig. 5.4), designed with the assistance of a leading German aeronautical engineer, Dr. Otto Koller. Begun in 1929, Bel Geddes's design took the shape of a large wing, and had a spread of 528 feet, nine decks, two elevators, and a capacity of 451 passengers and 155 crew members. The enormous pontoons held kitchens, crew quarters, lifeboats, and two airplanes, which could be launched to the rear during flight. Essentially an ocean liner lifted aloft, the plane was also to have luxurious staterooms, a gymnasium, a dining room complete with dance floor, promenade decks, verandas, and a bar. On a secondary upper wing, twenty engines provided power; inside the wing were six reserve engines which the crew could use for replacements, effecting mid-air repairs. Bel Geddes claimed a cruising speed of one hundred miles per hour; with refueling in the air over Newfoundland, a commuting time of forty-two hours would be possible between Chicago and Plymouth, England.[5]

Bel Geddes's wing never went into production, for despite his attempts and those of other industrial designers, most American aircraft styling came from aeronautical engineers. Interiors were a different matter though; in 1934 Bel Geddes received a commission from Pan American to restyle a number of interiors, and several of Martin's *China Clippers* were altered by Worthen Paxton and Frances Waite Geddes of his office. Intended for the long Pacific trips, the *China Clipper* interiors had a permanent lounge and sofa-type seating that converted at night into sleeping berths. To meet weight requirements they introduced

5.3 Glen Martin Aircraft Co. Martin *M-130 China Clipper*. 1934. Manufactured for Pan American Airways

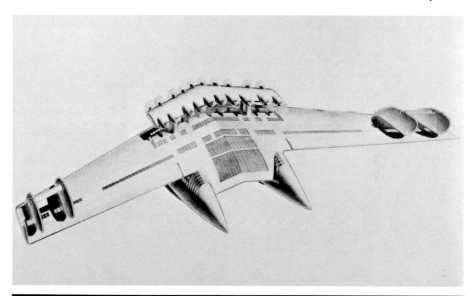

5.4 Norman Bel Geddes and Otto Koller
Airliner Number 4. 1929–32. Charcoal and pencil on paper, 31 × 19″. Bel Geddes Collection

lightweight materials that could easily be removed for cleaning. Other designers, such as Henry Dreyfuss, did custom interiors for private planes; Howard Ketcham, a New York industrial designer, advised on the color for the new *Atlantic Clippers*.[6]

Travel by the *Clippers* gained a romantic resonance as Pan American pushed the American flag into the Caribbean, Latin America, Hawaii, the Far East, and the north and south Atlantic. However,

5.5 Elsie Driggs (b. 1898)
Aeroplane. 1928. Oil on canvas, 44 × 38″.
Private collection. Courtesy James Maroney, Inc.

although waterborne landing strips were less expensive, they were subject to foul-weather conditions, and winter and ice virtually closed down all but warm weather routes. Improved navigation aids for land-based aircraft made the *Clipper*s increasingly vulnerable. While they provided vital service during World War II, by 1945 flying boats were dinosaurs of the machine age.

Dirigibles and blimps offered another alternative to land-based aircraft. During World War I, dirigibles gained notoriety as giant, silent, almost impregnable machines of destruction. After the war Germany led in the technology of dirigibles. The German Zeppelin Company signed an agreement with the American Goodyear Company to build large blimps for commercial service. The *Graf Zeppelin* of 1928 measured 755 feet long, carried about sixty passengers in ocean liner luxu-

ry, and traversed the globe on a demonstration voyage with stops only in Tokyo, Los Angeles, and New York. The *Hindenburg* disaster of 1937 brought to an end thought of passenger travel by dirigibles, but the blimp's smooth, torpedo-like, streamlined shape became an important form-giver, its impact seen in many other machines.[7]

The major breakthrough in American land-based commercial aviation was the almost simultaneous development of the *247* and the *DC-1*, by the Boeing and Douglas companies, respectively. The Boeing *247*, which first flew on February 8, 1933, was an all-metal stressed-skin, streamlined monoplane with a pair of short-cowled radial engines and retractable landing gear. The *247* could carry ten passengers coast-to-coast in twenty hours with seven intermediate stops. The interior was so cramped that passengers had to climb over and sit atop the huge wing, which protruded through the compartment.[8]

The Douglas *DC-1*, which first flew on July 1, 1933, was designed in direct competition to the Boeing *247*. A crash by a Transcontinental and Western Air *Fokker Tri-Motor* in 1931, which killed all the crew and passengers (including the popular Notre Dame football coach Knute Rockne), caused the Federal Aviation Authority to first ground all *Fokker*s and then restrict them to mail service. Casting about for a replacement, the Transcontinental engineering staff drew up specifications for a new tri-motor. Of the several manufacturers approached, only Donald Douglas of Douglas Aircraft expressed interest, and

5.6 Douglas Aircraft Company Douglas *DC-3 Flagship Sleeper*. 1936. Manufactured for American Airlines

in 1932 he flew his engineering staff to New York to secure the contract. Douglas, looking to the future (on the wall of his Santa Monica plant hung a large picture of the *247* with the admonition "Don't copy it! Do it better!"), convinced Transcontinental that the three-engine plane was outmoded. The result—the *DC-1*, which with modifications became the *DC-2* of 1934 and the *DC-3* of 1935–36—far surpassed the *247*. Incorporating design advances initiated by Jack Northrop (Douglas acquired Northrop's company in 1932), the wing was all metal, multicellular, and mounted beneath the fuselage, giving a stronger support and allowing for more passenger comfort and room. The expanded *DC-3* (fig. 5.6) could carry as many as twenty-eight passengers (up from twelve for the *DC-1*). The body, a stressed-skin, semimonocoque construction of lightweight "AL-CLAD NO. 24ST" aluminum riveted to the frame, gave an overall abstract impression of squares arranged in a streamlined pattern. The streamlining profited from tests at the California Institute of Technology's wind tunnels. Controlled-pitch propellers were mounted on Wright and Pratt & Whitney radial engines, placed far in front of the leading edge of the wing to minimize aerodynamic interference. Three-piece NACA "anti-drag rings" or cowls and wing flaps were used for the first time on the *DC-1*.[9]

In both image and performance the new Douglas planes captured the public imagination. Polished to a mirror-like finish from the projectile snout to the long, cigar-shaped body, tapered wings, and parabolic tail, the surfaces flowed into each other, creating a new standard of machine beauty. A Douglas sales brochure lauded the "smooth air flow" of the body and claimed, "the entire external appearance of the Transport is remarkable for its complete freedom from struts and control system parts." The brochure went on to observe that the "Airplane is completely streamlined," and praised the "method of 'flowing' one surface into another, contributing to the high speed performance." The new plane cut coast-to-coast travel to fifteen hours and freed airline companies from the dependence on mail contracts; profits could be earned from passengers alone. Airlines around the world adopted the *DC-2* and *DC-3*; they became the standard commercial airliners for the next twenty years.[10]

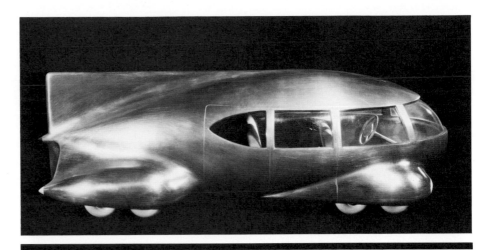

5.8 Norman Bel Geddes
Model of *Motor Car Number 9*. Patented
1933. Brass and plastic, 18 × 6 × 7″. Bel
Geddes Collection

5.9 R. Buckminster Fuller (1895–1983)
Dymaxion Automobile (1933) as exhibited at George Fred Keck's Crystal House,
Century of Progress Exposition, Chicago.
1934

MACHINES FOR THE ROAD

The decade of the 1920s marked a new era in automotive design. Since 1893 and the first American car, the *Duryea*, "automotive design" had really meant simple modifications to the horsedrawn carriage or buggy. Even in the 1920s certain buggy-like features, such as the generally tall and angular bodies and the separation of parts, remained. The two major changes were the development of the closed car (sales rose from 10 percent in 1919 to 85 percent in 1927) and the increased importance attached to body styling.[11]

Until the 1920s most manufacturers stressed the mechanical superiority of their products; appearance and style, though important, were downplayed, seen mainly as a feature of expensive, custom-built cars or bodies. The development at General Motors of the annual model change and the creation of the Art and Colour Section—later called Styling—with Harley Earl in charge changed all that. Earl, coming from a custom-body building background in Los Angeles, and specializing in cars for Hollywood stars, brought a sense of design to the mass-production automobile. Disregarding Henry Ford's dictum of constant improvement on a single design—the *Model T*—Earl and General Motors provided a variety of models for different pocketbooks, and variations within those models in color, body styles, and attachments. Instead of Ford's standard black, the lower-priced, competitive Chevrolet had bright Duco colors as well as a lower profile. Earl's designs were not revolutionary, except for one car, the Buick *Y-Job* of 1937 (fig. 2.24), a custom design that never went into production. Instead of revolution, Earl offered subtle modifications, decided upon two or three years previously, which exactly met public taste when they came out. Even in the mid-1930s, when streamlining was at full tilt, Earl was reticent to accept all the implications; teardrop fenders and chrome speed whiskers would appear on General Motors cars, but the radiator and grille remained flat and perpendicular.[12]

Initially the revolutionaries of automotive design were those who came from

5.7 Chevrolet *Master DeLuxe Sport Coupe*. 1936. As shown at GM exhibition, Waldorf-Astoria Hotel, New York, 1936

5.10 *Airflow.* 1937. Manufactured by the Chrysler Corporation

outside the automotive field. Bel Geddes's Graham-Paige design of 1928 for a car to be in style five years hence was essentially a rounding off of the angular features of the current design. Truly revolutionary were his rear-engined teardrop and finned designs of 1931 and 1933. Aeronautically and wind-tunnel inspired, though never tested or manufactured, Bel Geddes's designs sacrificed detail in favor of an overall harmonious form.[13]

Similar in shape though lacking the fin was Buckminster Fuller's *Dymaxion* design of 1933, of which three prototypes were made. Derived from his own 1927 *4-D Zoomobile*, a design for a vehicle half plane, half car, the *Dymaxion Transport Unit* (fig. 5.9) had a three-point landing gear—two wheels in front, the steering wheel in the rear—and a monocoque shell with a chrome-molybdenum frame. A fatal accident involving the *Dymaxion* and another car in 1934 caused unfavorable publicity, and the *Dymaxion* never went into production.[14]

The concept of reducing the automobile's air resistance goes back to 1910, when "torpedo-shaped" bodies appeared on open sports cars, and as early as 1913

the term "streamline effect" was applied to cars designed with unbroken body lines. But it was not until the early 1930s that such incontrovertibly streamlined features as bullet-shaped headlamps, curved window corners, rolled and tear-dropped fenders, and slanted windshields began to creep into production automobile design. In the wake of such glacial movement, Walter P. Chrysler directed his engineers to come up with a fully streamlined automobile for the 1934 production year. The Chrysler and De Soto *Airflow*s of 1934 were a revolutionary design (see fig. 5.11). Professor Alexander Klemin, the director of the Guggenheim School of Aeronautics at New York University, proclaimed the *Airflow* the most beautiful of American motor cars, "perhaps the most beautiful product of the machine age."[15]

The *Airflow* was a team product and involved four Chrysler engineers (Fred Zeder, vice-president of engineering; Owen Skelton, a chassis engineer; George McCain, a research engineer with wind-tunnel experience; and Carl Breer, the head of Chrysler research), an outside aeronautical adviser, William Earnshaw, and H. V. Henderson, an architectural engineer trained in Paris and the head of Chrysler's art department. Under Breer's direction, a simple wind tunnel was constructed, and experiments began on different configurations. The engineers concluded that any new front-end profile should be matched with changes in the suspension and overall height of the car. A significantly redesigned chassis, with the engine moved forward and down between the front wheels (instead of the normal position behind the front axle), a dropped frame with the passengers placed between the two axles, and an all-steel body welded to an all-steel frame resulted. The interiors of the 1934 models had a machine feel: chrome tubing was used for the seats and marbled rubber for the floor mats. The outer form appeared in good aerodynamic fashion as a parabolic curve with an inclined leading edge rising from the front. Actual styling was by Henderson, who absorbed the front fenders into the front end as a nearly continuous slanted and rounded shape, with a curving grille and flush headlights. The trail edges of both front and rear fenders suggested a teardrop form. Rear fender skirts increased the long, low look and covered up an air-resistant cavity. Speed lines appeared in the three-tiered front bumper, the three horizontal hood vents on each side, chrome belt moldings on the body, and the streamlined bird shape on the fender skirts.[16]

Chrysler's advertising had a romp describing the *Airflow*: "The automobile world learns from aviation." Unfortunately the public response to the *Airflow* fell far short of expectations. The major problem was appearance; one writer claimed you needed two or three days simply to "become accustomed to them." Bel Geddes added his name to *Airflow* supporters in a preliminary advertising campaign; he also signed a contract with "Client Q," as he identified Walter Chrysler, to develop a low-cost, streamlined Plymouth line and to advise on modifications to the *Airflow* styling. Although low *Airflow* sales caused Chrysler to subsequently cancel the contract, Bel Geddes's design for the profile of the Plymouth, based on the *Airflow*, shows a projecting nose (fig. 5.12). For the Chrysler and DeSoto *Airflow*s, Bel Geddes suggested the slanted grille become more upright, and for the next three years Chrysler designers fiddled with it, giving it more of a prowlike shape. Raymond

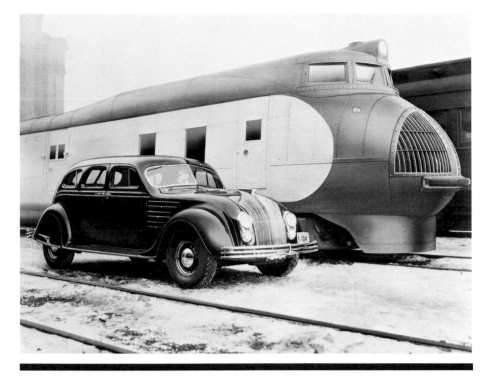

5.11 Chrysler Corporation *Airflow*. 1934; and Pullman Car Corporation *M10,000* (for Union Pacific). 1934

5.12 Norman Bel Geddes & Co. (Artist: Al Liedenfrost) *Drawing for Plymouth*. 1934. Bel Geddes Collection

5.13 Lincoln *Zephyr*. 1936; and *Twin Cities Zephyr*. 1934. Manufactured by Ford Motor Company and Edward G. Budd Company, respectively

Dietrich, a custom-body designer who became head of Chrysler exterior design about 1934, gave the grille its final, vertical shape. Dietrich later observed that the *Airflow*'s profile did not suggest forward motion; in spite of its scientific engineering the *Airflow* gave the appearance of a lumbering, stupid, almost featureless animal, a blank face with nose and eyes reduced to flat surfaces.[17]

The failure of the *Airflow* and the issue of projectile features and implied motion was not lost on Edsel Ford and his design collaborators. Edsel, the artistically inclined, talented son of Henry Ford, had long argued for an increased prominence of style inside the Ford Motor Company. Henry Ford, in spite of the lessons of the *Model T* and *Model A* Fords, still viewed design as a frill and left it to the body or body-dye suppliers. In 1933–34 Edsel, a close acquaintance of Walter Dorwin Teague, who designed the Ford Pavilion for the 1934 *Century of Progress Exposition* (Henry Ford had refused to participate in 1933) and other Ford buildings as well as the Ford *V-8* logo, began to look critically at streamlining. Among the exhibits at the Ford Pavilion was the *Briggs Dream Car*, designed in 1933 by John Tjaarda, a designer for the Briggs Company, Ford's largest body supplier. Designed with a rear engine and a rear-inclined sloping front end, the dream car was aerodynamically styled with teardrop fenders and a low roof line. Under the guidance of Edsel, the dream car was modified—the engine moved to the front, a sharp pointed grille with a taper (a "sailboat prow," one critic commented) added, and protruding headlights and vertical bumper horns included—to become the "small" V-12 Lincoln *Zephyr* of 1936 (see fig. 5.13). The *Zephyr* clearly won over its ill-fated competitors. Along with Gordon Buehrig's Cord *810*, the *Zephyr* captured

5.14 Lincoln *Zephyr Continental Cabriolet*. 1940. Manufactured by Ford Motor Company

public and critical acclaim at the annual New York Automobile Show. Its sharp profile and alligator-type hood influenced lower-priced Ford design for the next four years.[18]

Returning from Europe in 1938, Edsel Ford determined to create for himself a custom-built luxury car. With Eugene T. (Bob) Gregorie and later Ross Cousins of the small Ford design staff, he worked up plaster models of a longer, lower, and more graceful body on a *Zephyr* frame. Edsel's special *Zephyr* convertible hit the road by February 1939, and that summer he drove it to Florida. Beseiged with requests for similar cars from friends and from strangers encountered on the road, Edsel persuaded his father to allow limited production of the special *Zephyr*, renamed in 1940 the Lincoln *Continental* (fig. 5.14). The sharp-nosed *Zephyr* grille was used until 1942, when horizontal bars appeared. The *Continental* drew upon Buehrig's earlier Cord as a source for the distinction between the long hood—shielding the V-12 engine—and the fenders, but where the Cord had a coffin-like

appearance, the *Continental*'s hood came to a firm point. The *Continental*'s front fenders were higher and flared gracefully with a short, vertical drop at the trailing edge merging into the body. Its lines were longer and lower; the trunk bustle dropped against the teardrop rear fenders to provide a more substantial termination. The *Continental* flowed effortlessly, as streamlining should.[19]

By the mid-1930s the idea that production automobiles could have artistic value became commonly accepted. Studebaker hired Raymond Loewy to breathe life into a moribund company, and featured him prominently in Studebaker advertisements. *Arts and Decoration* magazine rhapsodized about the new American mass-production car. No longer a "mere machine of transportation," it was becoming "emancipated through the influence of creative art from the shackles of engineering. . . . The modern automobile is painting and sculpture in motion." In this one object, *Arts and Decoration* concluded, was expressed "the whole principle of a new industrial era."[20]

5.15 Burlington *Zephyr, #9900.* 1934. Manufactured by the Edward G. Budd Company for the Chicago, Burlington and Quincy Railroad

MACHINES FOR THE RAIL

The American entry to the streamlined rail age came on May 26, 1934, when at 5:04 A.M. the Burlington *Zephyr* (fig. 5.15), a streamlined, diesel-electric passenger train, departed the Mile High City's Union Station bound for the Windy City. Scarcely a month old and virtually untested, the little train sped eastward, hitting a top speed of 112 miles per hour. At 7:10 P.M. the train snapped the Western Union timing wire in Chicago, then continued directly to the lakefront site of the *Century of Progress Exposition* and rolled as the grand finale onto the stage of a railroad pageant, "Wings of a Century." The crowd poured from the stands to mob the train. The Denver-to-Chicago run normally took a steam-driven passenger train twenty-six hours (including the changing, rewatering, and refueling of the locomotive), but the *Zephyr* made the 1,015.4-mile trip nonstop—with the help of crossing guards—in thirteen hours and five minutes, at an average speed of 77.61 miles per hour. The total fuel cost, at five cents per gallon, was $14.64. A new day had dawned for American railroading.[21]

The *Zephyr* and her streamlined kin of the 1930s show the impact of aviation upon railroading. Within a few years the entire face of railroading changed: steam, either hidden under streamlined shrouds or replaced by diesel, disappeared from the rails, and more comfortable, modern, passenger cars appeared. The railroad industry in the 1920s and the early 1930s had the reputation of being hide-bound, conservative, resistant to change, and arrogant to passengers. By the early 1930s, however, with passenger revenue off by one-third (owing to the Depression, the lure of the automobile, and the airplane), executives such as Ralph Budd, president of the Burlington Railroad from 1932 on, saw the need for new tactics, an appeal to romance and glamour, to bring back passengers. The original *Zephyr* introduced on the Lincoln–Omaha–Kansas City run increased passenger traffic by 150 to 200 percent; systemwide the later-generation *Zephyrs* added over 26 percent. By the early 1940s railroads that had either converted to diesel-electric or improved their service with streamlined steam and new cars reported significant increases in passenger revenue; surveys proved overwhelmingly that passengers had returned because of new and faster locomotives, streamlined trains, and new comfortable, air-conditioned coaches.[22]

The *Zephyr*, though a watershed in railroad history, was not the first American streamlined train: the Union Pacific *M10,000* (see fig. 5.11) preceded it by two months, while ideas for lowering the wind

5.16 Norman Bel Geddes *Streamlined Locomotive No. 1*. 1931. Bel Geddes Collection

drag on trains had cropped up throughout the nineteenth and early twentieth century. In the late 1920s, as the science of aerodynamics became known in the United States, several individuals contributed suggestions.

Norman Bel Geddes published in *Horizons* his design for a streamlined train consisting of a steam locomotive, encased in a smooth shell of steel and glass with the cab in front, and a number of aluminum cars, including a rear lounge car with a tapered end "to allow the air to pass without forming an eddy" (fig. 5.16). The interior would be air conditioned and fitted out with Monel metal, Bakelite, cork, and modern, easy-to-clean fabrics. Light fixtures were either flush or indirect. The tube-shaped train presented a smooth, almost seamless, appearance; only a small hump at the front indicated the steam boiler.[23]

Contemporary with Bel Geddes in the early 1930s, Dr. O. J. Teitjens of the Westinghouse Research Laboratories in Pittsburgh tested in wind tunnels airfoil shrouding on interurban rail cars. His results indicated that the shroud effected a savings of over 40 percent in fuel consumption and increased top speeds. Teitjens's experiments made an impact on the J. G. Brill Company, a Philadelphia interurban car builder, which in 1931 produced the Brill *Bullet*, a curved, smooth-front design. Otto Kuhler, a German-born designer interested in railroads, who already proposed streamlined shrouding for steam locomotives, was in and out of the Brill Company in these years, and about 1932 he became a design consultant to the American Locomotive Company.[24]

In this climate, with airplanes gaining new speed and distance records almost daily and passenger service revenues declining, the Union Pacific and the Burlington embarked on separate campaigns to put a high-speed, streamlined train on the rails. Officially the Union Pacific won: the *M10,000*, later called the *City of Salina*, rolled out of the Pullman Car Company shops on February 12, 1934, after a year and a half of design and construction. In the fall of 1932, Union Pacific solicited proposals for a new train. Four companies made bids in 1933: the Brill Company, with Kuhler as an adviser; the Edward G. Budd Company; the Ingersoll-Rand Company in joint venture with the St. Louis Car Company; and the Pullman Car Company, with William B. Stout, the aviation designer, as a consultant. On May 24, 1933, the Union Pacific signed a contract with Pullman, the most experienced rail car company. Stout already was designing for Pullman the *Railplane*, a lightweight, streamlined, powered rail car. Round-nosed and with a supergraphics paint job, the prototype *Railplane* made a number of demonstrations in 1934–35, but never went into production. Stout, along with Pullman's chief engineer, E. E. Adams, and others on the Pullman staff, and Ralph H. Upson, an aeronautical dirigible designer, made a number of different models for the Union Pacific and tested them in the University of Michigan's wind tunnels. One early proposal followed Bel Geddes's hump design. The locomotive finally built contained a round, bulbous nose, similar in appearance to a dirigible, that pushed out over the rails and came back to a fender skirt underneath. Large vent automobile grills were mounted in the nose, and a small cab sat high on top. The engine was a Winton (a subsidiary of the Electro-Motive Division of General Motors) V-12

that burned distillate fuel. This supplied power to the electric motors, which drove the axles and wheels. Designed as a unit, the train was three cars in length, each one made of an aluminum, aircraft-type frame with aluminum skin panels. With its prominent rivets and supergraphic yellow and brown paint job, the *M10,000* resembled some type of scaly bug, but it could carry 116 passengers in modernized, air-conditioned comfort.[25]

Widely hailed upon completion, the *M10,000* barnstormed the country; it was toured by 1,195,609 people during its visits to sixty-eight cities, including Chicago for the *Century of Progress Exposition.* Not placed into service until January 1935 on a short Kansas run, the *M10,000* experienced technical problems, including frequent cracks in its aluminum frame and poor engine performance. But it had its value as a source of both publicity and revenue; therefore the Union Pacific ordered from Pullman the *City of Portland* and the *City of Los Angeles*, similar but longer trains with sleepers and diesel engines, which really did serve as high-speed, long-distance passenger movers. In October 1934 the *M10,000* cut twenty hours off the usual fifty-eight-hour trip between Los Angeles and Chicago.[26]

An intense rivalry existed between the Pullman personnel working on the *M10,000* and the Edward G. Budd Company designers working on the *Zephyr.* After all, the Budd Company had lost out on the Union Pacific bid earlier in 1933. Ralph Budd had talked to Edward G. Budd (no relation) in the fall of 1932

about a fast train, but the contract was not signed until June 17, 1933, three weeks after the Pullman contract. At the *Century of Progress Exposition* Ralph Budd had seen displayed a prototype Winton two-stroke diesel engine developed by General Motor's vice-president of research, Charles F. "Boss" Kettering. Assured such engines would be available, Ralph Budd gave the go-ahead to Edward Budd, a quality manufacturer of all-steel car bodies—a concept he developed—with plants in Philadelphia and Detroit concurrently working on the Chrysler *Airflow* body dyes. In the late 1920s Edward G. Budd had become infatuated with stainless steel, a noncorrosive, very high-strength material suitable for both framing and skin covering. The one problem with stainless steel was joining—regular welding made it lose its strength and noncorrosive qualities, and riveting damaged its edges—that is, until a Budd engineer, Colonel E. J. W. Ragsdale, invented and patented a scientific electric welding process for stainless steel. While body production for Ford trucks and all lines of Chrysler, Studebaker, and Chevrolet was Budd's bread and butter, in the early 1930s his engineers began experimenting with stainless steel railroad bodies. A number of demonstration motor-powered rail cars were built, including one in 1932 with fluted stainless steel sides and a faceted angular front.[27]

The design of the *Zephyr* drew upon the earlier Budd experiments but went far beyond them in its merging of contemporary aeronautical theory and function.

The result was a supremely functional and elegant high-speed train that did not rely on supergraphics to make it look fast. Itself a new high-speed symbol, the *Zephyr* represented aircraft technology adapted to the rails. The man most responsible for the exterior design of the *Zephyr* was the chief designer of Budd's high-tensile division, Albert Dean, a twenty-four-year-old graduate of M.I.T.'s aeronautical engineering program. He was assisted by his brother, Walter Dean, a mechanical engineer with aviation design experience, who handled the running gear and power plant. Also assisting was the Philadelphia architect Paul Cret and his partner, John Harbeson, who designed the interiors and made a few suggestions on the exterior—such as narrowing the fluting and the lettering. Holabird and Root were listed as design consultants to the Burlington (John Holabird and Ralph Budd were old friends); they actually contributed little to the *Zephyr*, though they did some later Burlington railroad car interiors and stations. Albert Dean designed the *Zephyr* first for function, then for strength, and finally for appearance. A model was tested in the M.I.T. wind tunnel, but the contours had been developed earlier following aerodynamic theory. As completed, the rounded, shovel-nosed front end, with the engineer sitting in front, and two air-conditioned passenger coaches carrying seventy-two passengers far out-performed comparable trains. As it weighed less than one-third of a conventional steel-and-wood, steam passenger train, the *Zephyr*'s center of gravity was so much lower that curves normally limited to forty mph could be taken at sixty mph. The Cret-Harbeson interiors were modern luxury with silk drapes, spun aluminum and stainless steel seat and table bases, Formica tops, Agosote

paneled ceilings, and indirect and flush-mounted lighting.[28]

The *Zephyr* rolled out of the Budd Philadelphia plant on April 7, 1934, a month and a half behind the *M10,000*, and after East Coast trials and exhibits and the Denver-to-Chicago run barnstormed the country, traveling over thirty thousand miles, visiting 222 cities, and being inspected by 2,016,606 people who paid ten cents each. Millions more saw it only from the exterior in a station or as it flashed by. It also starred in the 1934 movie *Silver Streak*. So successful was the *Zephyr* that the Burlington ordered ten more Budd-built trains slightly larger in size; these linked together the Midwest, the Far West, and the Southwest as they brought streamlining to many small cities and towns.

The *Zephyr* also lent an architectural image to the Burlington. Ticket counters in stations were restyled in sans-serif lettering, and in several stations done by Holabird and Root the *Zephyr* idiom appeared. In the Denver ticket office of 1936 (fig. 5.18), the visitor metaphorically entered streamlining as the polished fluted metal (probably aluminum), echoing the inset ceiling, provided the sensation of the journey ahead.

5.18 Holabird and Root
Denver Ticket Office of the Chicago, Burlington and Quincy Railroad. 1936

5.19 Raymond Loewy
GG1 Locomotive, Pennsylvania Railroad. 1934

5.20 Norman F. Zapf and New York Central Shops
Commodore Vanderbilt. 1934

The extremely simple and aerodynamically sound front end of the *Zephyr* influenced railroad streamlining for the next several years. Nearly duplicate copies of the *Zephyr* were made for the Boston and Maine *Flying Yankee*, and other manufacturers adopted the plain, shovel-faced appearance.[29]

Electric locomotive design also fell under the spell of the *Zephyr*. Electrification had become very important on metropolitan and suburban East Coast lines by the 1930s. The Pennsylvania Railroad's *GG1* of 1934 was the final outcome of a series of prototype studies (fig. 5.19). A large, double-ended electric locomotive with a double cab in the middle and pantographs at the ends for carrying the electric current from the overhead catenary wires to the transformer, the *GG1* was designed by engineers from the Pennsylvania Railroad, General Electric, Wes-

tinghouse Electrical, and the Baldwin Locomotive works. A brute machine, the *GG1* developed 4,620 continuous horsepower and 8,000 horsepower over the short term. The basic streamlined form for the shroud, with its center cab and graceful contoured and tapered hoods allowing visibility for the crew, had been decided upon when Raymond Loewy entered the scene. Loewy recommended welding the shroud instead of riveting it in order to cut manufacturing costs, decrease wind drag, and improve its looks. Loewy changed slightly the contours of the shoulders, restyled the lights to a more horizontal position, and altered the grill. He also provided the lettering and paint job. On dark Pennsylvania green, five narrow gold stripes stretched the length of the locomotive and swept down to a point at the nose. Loewy claimed his cosmetics on the *GG1* were an understatement: "Brute force can have a very sophisticated appearance, almost of great finesse, and at the same time be a monster of power."[30]

Still an allegiance to steam ruled most American railroads; diesels were unproven, and the *Zephyr* and *M10,000* were but small, three-car trains. There was a vast investment in over eighty thousand steam locomotives in the United States, and

even without the Depression, a complete transformation would have been impossible—and to many, undesirable. After all, the steam locomotive, with its large drivers, siderods, cylinders, pistons, cranks, and levers, personified power. The kinetics and sound of steam imparted a totally different and more satisfying sensation of harnessed energy and speed than the *Zephyr* with its silver shrouds could ever do.[31]

To astute railroad personnel the solution was obvious: streamlined steam, either new or rebuilt, coupled with new or remodeled coaches. Still the basic *Zephyr* shovel-nosed profile ruled. Using the designs of a Case Western Reserve student—Norman F. Zapf's studies of shrouding a 4-6-4 Hudson-type locomotive, which tested in a wind tunnel suggested a 91 percent drag reduction at seventy-five mph—the New York Central added a streamlined cover to a locomotive in December 1934 (fig. 5.20). Named the *Commodore Vanderbilt*, it served on the prestigious *20th Century Limited* train between Chicago and New York. Giving the appearance of an inverted bathtub (or seemingly wearing a mask), the *Vanderbilt* and similar locomotives were publicity pieces. Otto Kuhler, as adviser to the American Locomotive Company (ALCO), helped design for the Milwaukee Railroad completely new, streamlined steam locomotives, the *Hiawatha*s, in 1934 (fig. 5.21). The smooth rounded jacket contained a distinctive indentation for air cooling, a recessed smokestack, and a liberal use of color bands: a black stripe across the top; parallel maroon stripes along the sides (one stripe rose to the cab and continued across the tender); and large patches of light gray and orange. The engine number, in red, was positioned on large stain-

5.21 Otto Kuhler
Milwaukee Road *Hiawatha*. 1934. Manufactured by American Locomotive Company

less steel wings that wrapped around the front; the wheels, cylinders, and truck frames protruding beneath the shroud were in brown; all lettering was in gold. Equipped with new ribbed coaches—some of which were known as Beaver Tails—the "*Hi*" turned in faster speeds than the competing *Zephyr*s on the Milwaukee–Chicago run.[32]

satisfy some steam enthusiasts. Raymond Loewy argued for retaining the " 'steam locomotive' feel," and criticized the *Hiawatha* for following too closely the airplane styling of the *Zephyr*. Even Otto Kuhler acknowledged that not every steam locomotive should look the same; rather, "characteristic features of the steam engine" should be retained. Loewy's solutions, such as in his two streamline jobs for the Pennsylvania Railroad in 1936 and 1937, embodied a more organic feel for the steam locomotive parts. His *S–1* design of 1937 for a gigantic locomotive duplex—two complete sets of 84-inch drivers and cranks on one frame stretching over 140 feet including the tender—had a long torpedo-like nose covering the boiler and an extended pilot cowl covering the six-wheel truck (fig. 5.22). Chromium strips acting as speed lines wrapped around the front; several

5.22 Raymond Loewy with his Pennsylvania Railroad *S-1* Locomotive. 1937–39. Collection Larry Zim, World's Fair Collection, Zim-Lerner Gallery

extended all the way down the sides. Capable of sustained 100-mph speeds with a thousand-ton passenger train in tow, the *S–1* helped haul the Pennsy's New York–Chicago *Broadway Limited* with cars designed by Loewy. At the 1939 New York World's Fair, the *S–1* pounded away furiously on a treadmill, thrilling millions.[33]

In direct competition to the Pennsylvania's *Broadway Limited* steamed the train of the era, Henry Dreyfuss's New York Central *20th Century Limited* (fig. 5–23). Earlier, in 1936, Dreyfuss had styled the Central's *Mercury*, a Cleveland–Detroit, later to Chicago, luxury train: following the *Zephyr*'s inclined front, he created a bulky, unappealing bowl, with cutouts for the "white-walled" drivers, which were illuminated at night by concealed spotlights. By 1938 Dreyfuss recognized the essentials of steam power. The *20th Century Limited* had ten new *J3*, 4-6-4 Hudson locomotives with organically contoured shrouds hiding the assemblage of boiler valves, rivets, pipes, and parts, and in an outward swell, covering the cowcatcher and pilot. A minimum of piping and handrails were exposed, and below the boiler magnificently designed solid drivers with counterweight holes, aluminum finished siderods, and steel pistons were displayed. Originally the *J3*'s shroud dropped over the top edge of the drivers, but yard personnel removed

them for ease of inspection and service—the fate of much shrouding. To artists such as Charles Sheeler the harmony of the *20th Century*'s drivers, cranks, and pistons was the very essence of kinetic energy, as can be seen in a painting he did for a *Fortune* magazine portfolio (fig. 5.24). Dreyfuss also designed the cars, using a restrained palette of blues, grays, and silvers. The seating and lounge cars were broken up by partitions and columns to avoid the tunnel look of so many other cars. Smooth, purified round forms, flat surfaces, flush and diffused lighting, Formica, polished aluminum, stainless steel, and metallic paints provided an elegant, cool, "cleanlined" luxury. Pounding up the Hudson River Valley, or across Ohio and Indiana, with its great finned nose—a combination of streamlining and smoke deflection, and reminiscent of ancient warriors' helmets—and great drivers, the train, a symphony of gray and silver, brought the passenger into the heart of the machine age.[34]

Steam, however, would not be the future; rather, the internal-combustion engine conquered. By any measure, diesel power as it developed in the 1930s was more efficient and cost less. General Motors's Electro-Motive Division watched the developments carefully, and in 1935–36 erected a large, $5 million plant at La Grange, Illinois, where it began to design

5.23 Photographer unknown
Untitled (New York Central *20th Century Limited* Locomotives). 1938 (Designed by Henry Dreyfuss, 1938). Gelatin-bromide print, 19 × 23″. Private collection

5.24 Charles Sheeler
Rolling Power, 1939. Oil on canvas, 15 × 30″. Smith College Museum of Art, Northampton, Mass.

5.25 Santa Fe *Super Chief* (westbound in Cajun Pass, Calif.). 1937–38. Manufactured by Electro-Motive Division, General Motors Corporation

and produce entire locomotives. Richard M. Dilworth, the chief engineer, and Charles Kettering of General Motors Research, led in the development of multiple diesel engines harnessed into separate but coupled units. Twin diesel engines were mounted on a frame, each powering an electric motor that drove the axles; these were assembled into combinations of a locomotive and booster unit. The horsepower produced easily equaled that of a large steam locomotive. The initial body configurations were ugly boxes on wheels. Then General Motors styling came to the aid, creating for the Santa Fe *Super Chief* a new profiled body with the smooth, rounded, shovel nose of the *Zephyr*, but with the operating personnel moved up high and slightly back (to avoid injury in collisions) and the stainless steel carried straight back with rounded corners (fig. 5–25). Styled by the Electro-Motive engineers with the help of Leland Knickerbocker from Art and Colour (who evolved the Santa Fe "warbonnet" color scheme of a red nose and cab emblazoned with a bright yellow elliptical herald), the *Chief* marked a departure from standard railroad appearance. The Budd Company, commissioned by General Motors to supply the *Chief*'s stainless steel cars, once again turned to Paul Cret and John Harbeson to design the interiors. Acting on the suggestion of Sterling McDonald, an industrial designer from Chicago, Cret and Harbeson chose an Indian theme, combining the colors of the Pueblo and design patterns based on Hopi Kachina dolls and Navajo rugs with exotic wood paneling and shiny modern metals and metallic paints. The result was distinctly modern interiors.[35]

With slight modifications—a front end a bit more vertical, nautical portholes along the sides of the engine in both the locomotive and booster units, more powerful engines, and slightly different running gear—Electro-Motive transformed the Santa Fe type *E* Unit, into the very popular *F* and *FT* units. Electro-Motive, as a division of the world's largest auto manufacturer, knew mass production was the key. Instead of custom features common to the railroad industry, only custom paint jobs were allowed. The *F* unit, with its double locomotives and twin booster units, replaced steam not only on crack passenger trains but on locals and freights. From November 1939, when the first *F* unit was produced, until production ceased in 1960, Electro-Motive built over 7,600 units, and soon other locomotive manufacturers, including ALCO, Baldwin, and Fairbanks-Morse, copied its essential design. With such standardization, the personality of American railroading was obliterated. An era had come to an end; a new machine ruled.[36]

144

MACHINES FOR THE WATER

Throughout the 1920s and 1930s ocean liner passage was the most common means of trans-oceanic travel. During this time American liner design took a back seat to that of the Europeans. The machine age ocean liners were dominated by such leviathans as the English *Queen Mary*, the German *Bremen*, the Italian *Rex*, and the French *Normandie*. The outflung streamlined bridge decks of the *Queen Mary*, the Art Deco fittings by Lalique and Dupas of the *Normandie*, and "functionalist" boat decks appeared in countless photographs throughout the period. The continuing presence of the ocean liner and the clear division between the streamlined hull and the machine-like superstructure helped keep alive the sharp-angled geometrical approach to machine design in the 1930s.[37]

The indefatigable Norman Bel Geddes tried his hand at ocean liner design as early as 1927, and by *Horizons* in 1932 drawings and models for a streamlined ocean liner were ready (fig. 5.27). Claiming his form came not from external stimuli but from the shipbuilding tradition, Bel Geddes attacked the decoration of ocean liners as "an imitation of . . . floating hotels." His solution, a self-proclaimed "radical departure," was to streamline both hull and superstructure. "Every air

pocket of any kind whatsoever has been eliminated," he claimed. (In a later article on streamlining he wrote, "Were it possible to photograph the path of air passing over a ship it would surely resemble a tangled skein of yarn.") Only the stacks, appropriately streamlined, and the bridge, in the form of an airplane wing, broke the sleek torpedo shape of his ocean liner. Behind the extensive streamlined foil of the front stack lay a dance floor, orchestra box, and bar, and the rear stack foil contained a shop and a hangar for two trimotored sea planes. The stack could be opened to serve as a launching deck. The remainder of his proposed liner was completely covered with a skin composed of moveable glass and light alloy panels. During inclement weather the skin could be closed, making the entire ship airtight; on pleasant days it

5.26 W.F. Gibbs, designer; William Cramp and Sons, Shipbuilders, Philadelphia
Matson Navigation Company *Malolo*. 1927

5.27 Norman Bel Geddes
Ocean Liner Model. 1932. Painted wood, plastic, and wire, 16½ × 12 × 68". Museum of the City of New York

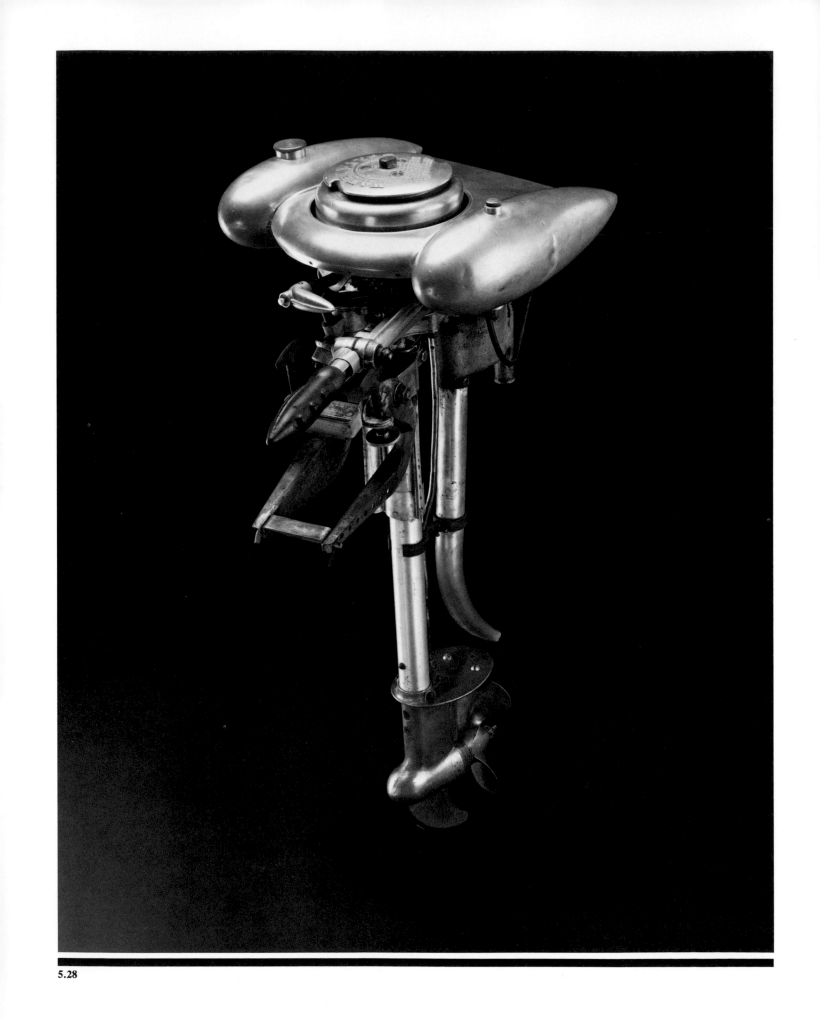

5.28

could roll or slide up. Bel Geddes's liner would be significantly longer and narrower than most other liners, and would displace less weight. For example, the more conventional *Normandie* was 1,028 feet long compared to his 1,808; had a beam of 117 feet instead of 110; and displaced 82,799 tons to Bel Geddes's 70,000.[38]

Actual American contributions were on a smaller scale, such as the Matson Navigation Company's luxury liner for the California–Hawaiian trade, the S.S. *Malolo* of 1927, later renamed the *Matsonia* (fig. 5.26). Designed by William Gibbs and built by the Philadelphia firm of William Cramp, the *Malolo* was 582 feet long, 82 feet at the beam, and displaced 17,232 tons. With its trim curved bridge, slanted stacks, and high enclosed sides that included the main boat deck for over half its length, the *Malolo* also introduced new safety features that became American standards. On a trial run in 1927, the *Malolo* sustained a collision equal to that of the *Titanic* of fifteen years earlier, yet instead of going to the bottom, she sailed back into New York harbor flooded with over 70,000 tons of sea water.[39]

As part of his contract with the Pennsylvania Railroad, Raymond Loewy redesigned in 1933–36 a Chesapeake Bay ferry (fig. 5.29). The *Princess Anne* had a sleek superstructure including a new molded bow placed upon an older hull. A supergraphic paint job helped to emphasize its lines. Whether it was the fastest ship of its kind, as claimed, is doubtful, but the *Princess Anne* was an anomaly with no imitators. Also in 1936 Loewy worked with naval architect George C. Sharp on three ships for the Panama Railway Steamship Company. Sharp did the ship design and Loewy's firm worked on

the interior. Designed in response to the high-styled Art Deco of French liners, the ships had a "simplicity," a "contemporary American" approach expressed by the extensive use of metals, rounded corners, and light colors. With the exception of portholes, the interior lacked any nautical flavor and looked more like an up-to-date hotel lobby.[40]

Ocean liners and ferries really were not consumer objects, perhaps indicating one reason for the lack of American involvement. The small individually controlled motorboat, however, met the consumption requirement, and in this area American design reached some distinction. Several industrial designers, including Loewy and Stevens, advised on the design of outboard motors and boats. The rakish lines of the wooden Chris-Craft "runabouts" with their stainless steel and chromium fittings, the inclined windshield, the gurgling—rising to a deep roar—of the engines provided a totally new sensation of controlled power and speed for the middle-class American.[41] As objects, the fittings of boats—as shown in The Museum of Modern Art's 1934 *Machine Art* exhibit—were some of the finest pieces of art produced by the machine. The highly polished aluminum housing of the Sears Waterwitch outboard motor (fig. 5.28), for example, exudes an iconic presence: it is a piece of machine age sculpture.

5.29 Raymond Loewy
Princess Anne Ferryboat. 1933–36. Manufactured for the Pennsylvania Railroad Company

5.28 John R. Morgan
Waterwitch Outboard Motor. 1936. Manufactured by Sears, Roebuck and Co., Chicago. Steel, aluminum, and rubber, 36 × 16 × 24″. Collection John C. Waddell

6.1

CHAPTER 6

ARCHITECTURE IN THE MACHINE AGE

Opening the symposium on contemporary architecture at the American Institute of Architects' 1930 convention, the moderator asserted:"We are facing a crisis"— a battle raging between the modernists, who argued that a new world had been ushered in by the machine, and the traditionalists, who claimed eternal varieties and styles. On the side of the modernists was George Howe, who, with his partner, William Lescaze, was in the middle of designing the seminal Philadelphia Savings Fund Society (PSFS) Building. Howe presented a functionalist position, defining modernism as essentially technique, the use of "modern construction and modern materials to the full, for architectural expression as well as for practical ends." The traditionalist position was argued by C. Walker Howard of Boston, who in an urbane and witty manner criticized the modernists for displaying neither "manners, courtesies, or finesse." Middle-ground positions were presented by Earl Reed, Jr., and Ralph Walker. Reed, from Chicago, attacked "alien" classicism, holding up Louis Sullivan and Frank Lloyd Wright as ideal mentors. Walker, generally considered a modernist, agreed that grain elevators were more

important than Roman thermae, but worried about raising the machine to the level of a form-giver. He criticized the American tendency to look toward Europe, calling it "a colonial viewpoint," and in the end argued against a formula for modernism, pleading instead for individuality.[1]

The 1930 AIA debate indicated the confusion of American architects as they faced the challenge of the machine age. New materials and technologies such as steel and glass brought into question the traditional notion of the wall as enclosure. Electricity allowed buildings to be floodlit plastic masses or glowing emblems of energy. The automobile created the need for specialized new building types and also affected traditional buildings such as the house, where lodging the car became a major issue. A debate revolved around mass production: if Henry Ford succeeded with cars, why could not housing be similarly produced? Architecture emerged as a social act, a product of European housing experiments in the 1920s and the raised social conscience of the United States in the 1930s. Functionalism became a rallying cry as some architects designed with only practical solutions as criteria, disregarding tradi-

6.1 George Howe (1886–1955) and William Lescaze (1896–1969)
Philadelphia Savings Fund Society Building. Philadelphia. 1928–32

6.2

tional notions of beauty. Finally there was the question of style, or image: what should the new architecture look like?

The architecture of the machine age displays great variety. Some of it falls into the usual stylistic categories, but other designs and buildings go beyond pure style to ideology. To understand the architecture of the 1920s and 1930s it is necessary both to employ the terminology of the period and to view the buildings as representative of the different concerns and approaches to the machine.

THE MODERNE

Most of the American architecture in the 1920s that aspired to be modern tended toward a machine-as-parts aesthetic. Grounded in several different European influences—the Viennese and German Secessionists, with their geometrical patterning; the French *Arts Décoratifs* exhibition; and European modernists such as Eliel Saarinen, whose entry in the Chicago Tribune competition (fig. 6.2) became very popular—the machine-as-parts approach also had an American base. Bertram Goodhue, who died in 1924, was considered by many the most important modernist, more important even than Frank Lloyd Wright. Goodhue's Nebraska State Capitol, 1920–31 (fig. 6.3), retained vestiges of traditional architecture with its strong processional and axial plan, tower, dome, and ornament. Yet the overall form was unique—a setback tower, almost a skyscraper—and the ornament was flattened and geometrical. Goodhue's work here and elsewhere, along with the ornamental contributions of collaborators Lee Lawrie, a sculptor, and Hildreth Meiere, an artist, acted as a prime source for American modernism in the 1920s.[2]

For many architects the major stimulus

150

6.4 Hugh Ferriss for Helmle and Corbett, architects
Study for the Maximum Mass Permitted by the 1916 New York Zoning Law, Stages 1–4. 1922. Crayon, brush, and ink on illustration board, 26⅜ × 20″ each. Cooper-Hewitt Museum, the Smithsonian Institution's National Museum of Design, New York

6.5 Ralph Walker (1889–1973) for McKenzie, Voorhees & Gmelin, architects
The Barclay-Vesey Building (also called the New York Telephone Building). New York. 1922–26

6.6 Lobby, The Barclay-Vesey Building

for the machine-as-parts—or the building-as-parts—setback approach to design was the 1916 New York zoning ordinance, which mandated that a building's height at the street line was limited; as the mass rose, setbacks at different heights were necessary. The architectural renderer Hugh Ferriss made in 1922 a set of drawings of the evolution of a building's zoning envelope (fig. 6.4). Variations of the New York setback law soon were instituted in other cities, and even when not

so legislated, architects attracted by the plastic possibilities of molding form adopted the approach.[3]

While skyscrapers and low-rise buildings in the setback modernistic idiom rose across the country in the late 1920s and the 1930s, most of the important activity centered in New York. Ralph Walker was one of the leading New York modernists. Known as a "little Napoleon" because of his size and peppery personality, Walker had a traditional American *beaux arts*–

oriented education. Before World War I he had worked for Bertram Goodhue. In 1918 he joined a large commercial architectural firm, McKenzie, Voorhees and Gmelin, and around 1922 he began design on a new building for the New York Telephone Company, the Barclay-Vesey (figs. 6.5, 6.6). The site, a parallelogram in shape, prompted Walker to introduce a twist between the base of the building and the tower. Walker's early study shows the building a tall central mass surrounded by small setbacks (fig. 6.7). The skin has a Gothic Revival flavor with its strong verticals and crenellations for cornices, and possibly owes a debt to Saarinen's contemporary Tribune proposal. In successive studies, Walker changed the relation of the central mass to the setbacks and altered the skin. On the completed building, the surrounding setbacks have been raised against the tower, making the mass more integral and also more plastic and more dramatic. The skin is treated as a series of continuous verticals—piers or buttresses—with recessed lighter-colored spandrels. What had been crenellations are now short continuations of the piers, helping to tie the various setbacks into one continuous system. Stylistically, Walker's solution had traces of the earlier Gothic, though greatly simplified. Ornamentally, the motifs were ahistorical, with the exception of a faint Art Nouveau air—a lush covering of floral and seed motifs. The interior was a riot of geometrical plants and vines; Lewis Mumford compared it to a "village street in a strawberry festival." Walker's semi-Gothic, lushly decorated, pier-setback scheme became the standard method of progressive skyscraper design.[4]

6.7 Ralph Walker
Study for The Barclay-Vesey Building. 1922. Pencil on paper, 11⅞ × 8¼″. Collection George Arents Research Library, Syracuse University

6.8 Raymond M. Hood (1881–1934) with Hood, Godley & Fouilhoux American Radiator Building. New York. 1924

6.9 Raymond M. Hood with John Mead Howells and J. André Fouilhoux (1879–1945)
New York Daily News Building. New York. 1929–31. Photograph by Berenice Abbott, 1935

Raymond Hood, another of the "little Napoleons" of New York skyscraper designers, emerged as the most inventive and also the most inscrutable. Hood had attended the Ecole des Beaux Arts in Paris before World War I, and like Walker had worked for Goodhue. Between 1922 and his death in 1934 Hood completed an amazing series of skyscrapers in which he experimented with a variety of expressions. His surface treatment ranged from the American Radiator, 1924, a steel-framed setback structure with a skin of black brick enlivened with gold Gothic ornament (fig. 6.8), to the Daily News, 1929–31, with vertical strips applied in an abstract manner (fig. 6.9), and the McGraw-Hill, 1930–31, with its horizontal orientation of prominent dark green slabs intercut with the short verticals of light green panels and windows (figs. 6.10, 6.11). This horizontalism appeared to be European inspired, and consequently it was included in The Museum of Modern Art's *International Style* exhibition.[5]

Although the McGraw-Hill seemed to indicate Hood was moving away from the masonry massiveness of most modernistic skyscrapers, his work on Rockefeller Center from late 1929 until his death shows the ambiguity of his approach. The genesis of Rockefeller Center can be seen in a series of skyscraper city proposals of the mid- and late 1920s, of which Hugh Ferriss's *Metropolis of Tomorrow* was the best known. Hood had projected a number of his own, including a "City of Towers," with gigantic skyscrapers that completely restructured the traditional street grid pattern of American cities, and a New York City of 1950, with tremendous skyscraper bridges containing set-

6.10 Raymond M. Hood and J. André Fouilhoux
Front entrance, McGraw-Hill Building. New York. 1930–31

6.11 McGraw-Hill Building. Wurts Brothers photograph

6.12 Raymond M. Hood Proposal for *Manhattan 1950*, Skyscraper Bridge. 1929. Charcoal, ink, and watercolor, 17 × 19⅛″. Collection Trientje Hood Reed

back housing blocks (fig. 6.12). As the leading designer in a consortium known as Associated Architects, Hood experimented with a variety of skin and fenestration patterns for Rockefeller Center, but his stated philosophy that architecture was pure utility and the client was always right left him with no aesthetic standards. Hood admired machinery—the steam locomotive, for instance—but he could not accept the machine, modern art, or precedent as a guide; he had only a high-sounding call "to be honest."[6] Consequently, when John D. Rockefeller II demanded Gothic Revival trim on the centerpiece of the RCA Building, Hood and his fellow architects complied.[7] The lack of content in this utilitarian approach led to the hiring of an outside "spiritual counselor," professor of philosophy Hartly Burr Alexander, to devise a theme for the center. The solution, after much revision and the input of many individuals, was "New Frontiers and the March of Civilization." Officially the Rockefeller Center complex was treated as a great milestone in world civilization, while popularly it became known as "Radio City." Banal subthemes and art works—such as Lee Lawrie's entrance sculptures for the RCA Building, *Wisdom: A Voice from the Clouds*—were commissioned. Also attempted were more substantial decorations, such as the ill-fated José Diego Rivera mural *Man at the Crossroads Looking with Uncertainty but with Hope and High Vision to the Choosing of a Course Leading to a New and Better Future*. Rivera's mural showed a complex of machine parts—turbines, drums, propellers—biological and cosmic embryos, marching masses of workers and youth, and a portrait of Lenin. This last was too much for the capitalist Rockefellers (who surprisingly had previously approved the work), and the mural was destroyed amid great outcry.[8]

Still, Rockefeller Center did reveal the possibilities of a new urban order based upon the machine and the skyscraper. The finest piece of American urbanism of the period, Rockefeller Center indicated

6.13 Lee Lawrie (1877–1963)
Genius, Which Interprets to the Human Race the Laws and Cycles of the Cosmic Forces of the Universe Making Cycles of Light and Sound. RCA Building, Rockefeller Center. 1933

6.14 Reinhard & Hofmeister; Corbett, Harrison & MacMurray; Hood, Godley & Fouilhoux, architects; John Weinrich, renderer
Rendering of Rockefeller Center. New York. 1931. Pastel on paper, 18 × 22″. Collection Rockefeller Center

6.15 (Overleaf) John Weinrich, renderer
Overall view of Rockefeller Center. 1931. Pastel on paper, 18 × 22″

GENERAL VIEW LOOKING SOUTH ON 5TH AVENUE

6.15

the new scale possible. Decorations by Paul Manship, Stuart Davis, and others added an intimate nostalgic note, but the greatest impact was due to the overwhelming scale, the soaring shafts of buildings, the overall pattern of mass and void, space and planes overlapping to create a new visual aesthetic.

Implicit in Rockefeller Center and more apparent in other modernistic buildings of the 1920s and 1930s was the idea of the building as advertisement. Of course, a building has always been a source of identity for its owners and occupants, but in general this was provided by the company's association with classical or other historic garb and traditional symbols. The shedding of traditional garb created a void for the image-maker. The glorification of business in the 1920s and the realization that industry and advertising were sources for visual art gave architects with modernist tendencies a new source. Some of Hood's work, such as the gold flame crest of the American Radiator Building, and the large billboard-sized plaque over the entrance of the Daily News, with "THE NEWS" in giant letters across the top and a Joseph Stella composition of the building at the center, had an advertising dimension. For the New York General Electric distributor, Rex Cole, Hood designed showrooms that were virtual advertisements. The Queens showroom was a three-story white icebox with a penthouse that resembled the compressor of a GE refrigerator (fig. 6.16). For Brooklyn's Bay Ridge section, Hood designed a setback cubed composition with the name "Rex Cole" in modernistic lettering as a frieze, and an enlarged refrigerator with the GE logo placed on top as a trophy (fig. 6.17).

6.16 Raymond M. Hood with Hood, Godley & Fouilhoux
Rex Cole Building. Queens, N.Y. 1929–33

6.17 Raymond M. Hood with Hood, Godley & Fouilhoux
Rex Cole Building, rear view. Brooklyn, N.Y. 1929–33

Different aspects of architecture as advertisement can be seen in the two tallest buildings constructed in New York during the period, the Empire State and the Chrysler. The Empire State, 1930–31 (fig. 6.22), by Shreve, Lamb and Harmon, with William Lamb as chief designer, received its distinction through sheer size: at 1,472 feet and 102 stories, it was the tallest inhabitable structure in the world. Designed as a series of progressively smaller rectangular forms linked by the continuous-pier, recessed-spandrel formula, the building had a spectacular top. Originally William Lamb had envisioned the crest as a continuation of orderly setbacks, but with the completion of the Chrysler a stainless steel stem carrying a rounded observation platform similar to a water tank and topped by a dirigible mooring mask was added. By size, and a memorable top, an otherwise undistinguished design became known.[9]

The Chrysler Building (fig. 6.18) is pure advertisement, and perhaps the most obvious tall building-as-machine symbol. William Van Alen, the designer, came from a conventional *beaux arts* background. In the early 1920s, a German-born draftsman with Secessionist sympathies on his staff and the rising clamor of the machine age inspired him to cast about for a new direction.[10] For developer William Reynolds, who had leased the site adjacent to Grand Central Station on Forty-second Street, Van Alen began in the mid-1920s with a scheme for a tall setback building complete with a peaked glass dome. In 1928 Reynolds sold the lease to Walter P. Chrysler, who had recently set up the Chrysler automotive conglomerate and was seeking a New York pied-à-terre and publicity. Van Alen transformed his design, keeping some aspects, but changing the crest

and increasing the height to 1,050 feet and seventy-seven stories. The spire of six floors was retained for Chrysler's own use. It contained an observation platform with Chrysler's own hand tools on display in the lounge. Throughout the building automotive motifs abound: at the thirty-first floor, for example, a frieze of gray and white bricks suggests motion, and Chrysler metal hubcaps were placed within round tirelike and mudguard forms. At the corners perch large abstract eagles that resemble Chrysler radiator ornaments (fig. 6.19). Similar though more realistic eagles made of gleaming, chromium nickel-steel sit at the corners of the sixty-third floor, their beaks pointing outward. Reputedly they served as optical corrections for an illusory widening of the tall building when viewed from the ground. Van Alen ran the conventional continuous vertical-pier, recessed-spandrel arrangement up the center of the main tower and then banded it on the sides with horizontal dark brickwork to create a contrapuntal pattern. The crowning feature was the Krupp "KA 2" stainless steel crest. Triangular windows in the radiating semicircles, brilliantly lighted at night, added a new form to the conven-

6.19 Detail of 31st floor, Chrysler Building

6.18 William Van Alen (1883–1954) Chrysler Building. New York. 1928–31. Wurts Brothers photograph

6.20 Holabird and Root, architects, Gilbert Hall, renderer
Palmolive Building. Chicago. 1928–29

tional rectangularity of New York City. The Chrysler's dimly lit lobby was especially dramatic; repeated geometrical and floral abstractions merged with murals of flight and renditions of the building. All together the Chrysler Building acted as an advertisement for "automotive progress," claimed one critic in 1931; since it was commercial, "why should the architect have hesitated a moment in being the Ziegfeld of his profession?"[11]

The mania for setback buildings swept the country in the late 1920s, and many cities, large and small, received small doses of "metropolitanism," as the style was sometimes called.[13] In the Midwest the leading firm was that of John Holabird and John W. Root II, sons of leading Chicago School architects of the 1880s and 1890s. Conventionally trained at the Beaux Arts, Holabird and Root began to discover modernism in the mid-1920s. A talented draftsman working in the Hugh Ferriss manner of charcoal, Gilbert Hall, helped them to visualize buildings as great stone cliffs, dramatic masses of almost solid masonry skins. In their Palmolive Building (fig. 6.20), the blocky masses are integrated by channels in the skin.

The machine-as-parts aesthetic approach was appropriate to low-rise buildings as well. Holabird and Root's A.O. Smith Research and Engineering Building in Milwaukee, 1929–31 (fig. 3.8), had a facade of crystalline triangular forms in the attempt to project a modern, research-oriented business image. J.R. Davidson, a German émigré architect in Southern California, proposed a "Driv-in Curb-Market" (fig. 6.21) in which an essentially horizontal structure is ornamented with lettering and signs at the corners to add vertical energy. The Niagara Hudson Building, Syracuse, New York,

6.21 J. R. Davidson (1889–1977) Presentation drawing, *Driv-in-Curb-Market*, 1931. India ink and ink wash on vellum, 13¼ × 16⅞". University Art Museum, Santa Barbara. Architectural Drawings Collection

6.22 Shreve, Lamb and Harmon, architects Empire State Building. New York. 1930–31. Collection The New-York Historical Society

6.23 Bley and Lyman, architects
Niagara Hudson Building. Syracuse, N.Y.
1931–32

6.24 Interior lobby, Niagara Hudson
Building

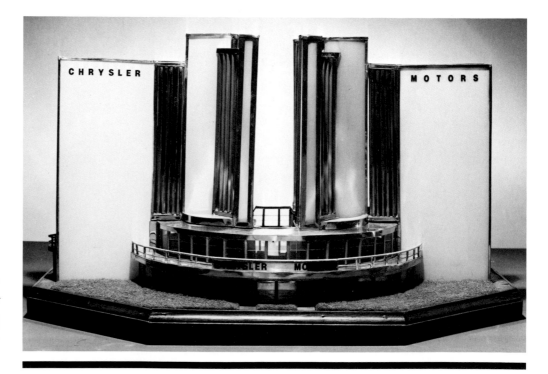

6.25 Holabird and Root
Model for Chrysler Pavilion. *Century of
Progress Exposition*, Chicago. 1932–33.
Aluminum, frosted glass, and wood, 18
× 24 × 33″. Collection Chicago Histori-
cal Society

1931–32 (figs. 6.23, 6.24), by Bley and Lyman is an advertisement for electric power. A setback-shaped, seven-story structure, its exterior of buff brick is covered by shiny stainless steel, black marble, tile, glass and helium lighting strips, incandescent bulbs, tubes, and flood lights. The interior is also a homage to the power of electricity with vibrant Vitrolite murals of generators, transmission lines, gas power, and illumination (see fig. 6.27). The extensive use of stainless steel and other highly polished materials for the railings, trim, and elevator doors, and the novel tubular light fixtures gave the appearance of a futuristic laboratory, one that could be inhabited by Dr. Zarkov. Actually the building predates by several years the *Flash Gordon* serials.[14]

The science-industry theme of the *Century of Progress Exposition* carried modernistic building as advertisement to its apogee. No skyscrapers appeared at Chicago, though David B. Steinman, the bridge engineer, designed the Skyway and Observation Towers, twin 628-feet-tall, open-girder constructions (fig. 4.14). The exhibition buildings ranged from virtual billboards, such as Alfonso Iannelli's inflated thermometer for the Havoline Building (fig. 6.28), to more abstract structures, such as Holabird and Root's Chrysler Pavilion (6.25). The Chrysler Pavilion had gigantic pylons complete with chrome moldings emerging from a two-story glass cylinder that purported to be the central unit of an automotive proving ground.

Movie theaters epitomized the issue of modern architecture as advertising. Thousands of marquees across the country became miniature imitations of the "great white way" of Broadway as they attempted to lure patrons inside. By the late 1920s the historically styled picture

6.26 Thomas Lamb (1871–1942) Trans-Lux Theater. Washington, D.C. 1936. Collection Herbert Striner

palace type of design gave way to the moderne style, which remained the favorite approach to movie theater design well into the 1940s. Only a relatively few theaters, such as Frederick Kiesler's Film Guild Cinema in New York (fig. 9.7) reflected the simpler machine purity of the International Style. Instead the more flamboyant moderne, such as the Trans-Lux in Washington, D.C., by Thomas Lamb (fig. 6.26), emphasized the fantasy of an escape from reality with its illuminated crystalline tower on top of a wave-like marquee. The moderne, or the decorated machine-as-parts approach, advertised modernism, and from skyscrapers to movie theaters it brought Americans the promise of a machine-made future.

6.28 Alfonso Iannelli (1888–1965), designer, Kenneth Olson, renderer Havoline Thermometer Building. *Century of Progress Exposition*, Chicago. 1932. Watercolor, 9½ × 16¾″. Collection Chicago Historical Society

6.27 Artist unknown. *Illumination*. Vitrolite panel, approx. 4′6″ × 3′6″. Niagara Hudson Building

6.29 Installation view, *International Modern Architecture* exhibition, The Museum of Modern Art. 1932. Courtesy The Museum of Modern Art, New York

THE INTERNATIONAL STYLE

By the mid-1930s the setback modernist approach began to give way to a new image, perceptibly lighter and more volumetric in form and purified of excessive decoration. The *International Exhibition of Modern Architecture* shown at The Museum of Modern Art between February 7 and March 23, 1932, and then on the road in various forms to more than thirty American cities in the next six years, assisted in this reorientation. Accompanied by a substantial catalogue, *Modern Architecture*, and a book, *The International Style: Architecture Since 1922*, the exhibit was curated by Henry-Russell Hitchcock and Philip Johnson, assisted by the museum's director, Alfred H. Barr, Jr.[15]

Dominated by European modern architects, the exhibition and catalogue had three parts: a section showing the extent of the International Style (six American examples out of forty buildings from around the world); a section on housing, with a special essay written by Lewis Mumford; and a section on the work of the style's nine leaders, including five Americans, Richard Neutra, the Bowman brothers, Raymond Hood, Howe and Lescaze, and Frank Lloyd Wright.

Wright was included because he was an acknowledged leader of modern architecture—especially by the Europeans—even though, as Barr explained, he didn't fit stylistically; as Hitchcock wrote, at bottom the Europeans were classicists and Wright was a romantic. Raymond Hood's inclusion was due to a combination of the Modern's sensitivity to criticism of being too European-oriented, and the knowledge that the complete omission of New York architects would be criticized. Hood, who with the horizontal orientation of the McGraw-Hill appeared to be moving in the direction mandated by Hitchcock and Johnson, was the one New York architect chosen. The Bowman brothers (Irving and Monroe) of Chicago had built nothing, but they had on the boards several projects of prefabricated machine-like buildings. George Howe and William Lescaze, with their PSFS Building (figs. 6.1, 6.30, 6.31), a thirty-two-story skyscraper nearing completion, approached most closely the strict stylistic requirements of Hitchcock and Johnson. Asymmetrical in the off-centered "T" shape of the tower, lacking in unfunctional setbacks and applied ornament, dynamic with its slightly cantile-

6.30 William Lescaze
Preliminary sketch for base of Philadelphia Savings Fund Society Building. 1929. Charcoal sketch on paper. Collection George Arents Research Library, Syracuse University

vered tower face, and dramatic with its vast, glazed banking floor, the PSFS's different functional elements were clearly stated. The enormous red neon sign on the roof was approvingly noted by Hitchcock and Johnson; criticized was the rounded corner of the elevated banking room; and described as beyond the boundaries of the International Style was the exposed structural frame on the side of the tower.[16]

Though born and trained in Vienna, Richard Neutra was the most sophisticated American working in the International Style. His Lovell "Health" House (figs. 6.32, 6.33)—Dr. Philip Lovell was a prominent body-care propagandizer—easily ranks with the best European works, and went far beyond them in the utilization of machine age technology. The prefabricated steel onto was erected in fewer than forty hours. The planar white walls were of gunite, a concrete mixture shot from hoses onto steel panels. Yet the Lovell House had a rambling quality of composition, a kicked-up parapet, volumetric setbacks, and projections that betray the influence of Frank Lloyd Wright, for whom Neutra had worked in 1924. On the interior certain machine age motifs dominated: a long, polished-aluminum lighting trough stretched through the living room and library; inset into the main stair well were Ford *Model A* headlights and rims. Harwell Hamilton Harris, a student of Neutra's who worked on the designs of the Lovell House, recalls that "for Neutra, Sweet's Catalogue [the supply catalogue of standardized parts] was the Holy Bible and Henry Ford the holy virgin."[17]

6.31 Main floor interior, Philadelphia Savings Fund Society Building. 1932

6.32 Richard Neutra (1892–1970)
Lovell House. Los Angeles. 1927–29

6.33 Interior, Lovell House

While Neutra's Lovell House certainly equaled the quality of the European work, still the feeling at The Museum of Modern Art in those years was that European architecture, design, and art were the most modern and sophisticated and should be the model for Americans. Hence the emphasis of the *International*

Style exhibition was upon the four Europeans, Le Corbusier, Gropius, Mies van der Rohe, and J. J. P. Oud, and the idea that a new "controlling style" had emerged in Europe. The principles of the new architecture, Hitchcock and Johnson explained, were three: "architecture as volume rather than as mass"; "regularity rather than axial symmetry . . . as the chief means of ordering design"; and the absence of "arbitrary applied ornament."[18]

These three principles had little to do with the machine age and mentioned nothing about structure, technology, function, or social responsibility. Hitchcock and Johnson's argument for their primarily aesthetic approach was complex. Although they recognized the importance of function and the incorporation of the expressive possibilities of twentieth-century materials and structure, the style—or aesthetic—that had developed provided a method of arranging facades, fenestration, plans, and details. The International Style, in Hitchcock and Johnson's hands, did not depend upon the ideas of function and materials; this was proven by buildings that looked like thin-walled volumetric containers, but were stucco-covered brick. Although the concept of a new interpenetrating space was recognized by Hitchcock and Johnson, it was not elevated to the height of a principle, but rather subjugated under architecture as volume. Essentially *The International Style* was a recipe book on how to design up-to-date buildings filled with *do*s and *don't*s. A new architectural order, a new classicism, was sought.[19]

The book made a significant impression, and the International Style was interpreted as "an expression of the fast-growing band of scientific-minded who believe in the universal efficacy of machine efficiency."[20] In spite of Hitchcock and Johnson's attempt to disown function and technology as determinants, the International Style became the functionalist expression, its seemingly ahistorical image seen as the expression of necessity and art. Severity, flat Spartan surfaces, revealed structure, and mechanics as objects became its identifying features, the man-made object in the landscape and white interior its trademarks. It was the machine style, even though the forms were rarely made or even dictated by the machine.

As noted, Le Corbusier, Gropius, and other architects of the International Style had been known to some Americans since the mid-1920s. That the style was interpreted as a machine age expression is evident in Lawrence Kocher and Albert Frey's Aluminaire House of 1931 (fig. 6.34). Kocher had received a conventional American *beaux arts*–oriented education and had become known as a critic in the 1920s. In late 1927 he took over *Architectural Record* magazine and helped transform it into a mouthpiece of advanced architectural thought in America. His partner, Albert Frey, a Swiss émigré, had worked for Le Corbusier in the late 1920s until, attracted by the technological marvels of America, he came here in 1930. The Aluminaire House, built in ten days, was a demonstration building for the *New York Architectural League Exhibit* of 1931. Kocher and Frey's Aluminaire was loosely based upon Le Corbusier's Domino and Citrohan house projects, and built of a light steel-and-aluminum frame over which were placed insulation board, tarpaper, and thin, corrugated, polished-aluminum sheets.

Kocher and Frey claimed that in mass production the Aluminaire would cost $3,200, or twenty-five cents per cubic foot, but only the one was built.[21]

Due to The Museum of Modern Art's propagandizing of the International Style, aesthetics were merged with a technological interpretation, so that the style became in many people's opinions the consummate machine age expression; in addition it contributed to a purification of the ornamental excesses of the modernistic approach. Ironically American architecture of the machine age which sought to escape from the embrace of the old world found itself caught in a stylistic term and attitude primarily old world in origin.

6.34 A. Lawrence Kocher (1888–1969) and Albert Frey (b. 1903) Aluminaire House. Syosset, N.Y. 1931

173

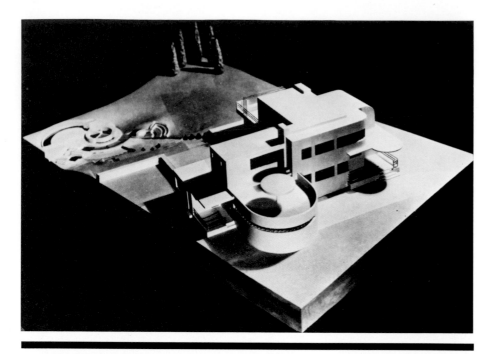

6.35 Norman Bel Geddes
Model, *Ladies Home Journal House #3*.
1931. Bel Geddes Collection

6.36 Edward Durell Stone (1902–1978)
Richard Mandel House. Mt. Kisco, N.Y.
1934

THE STREAMLINED

The other major factor in the changed visual appearance of American architecture in the 1930s was the emergence of the sleek, streamlined body, the machine in motion. Rounded forms had appeared in buildings that became identified as the International Style.[22] However, the major impetus for architectural streamlining came in the early 1930s when Norman Bel Geddes published his House of Tomorrow or *House #3* first in the *Ladies Home Journal* and then in *Horizons* (fig. 6.35). Bel Geddes stressed the machine-like and modern aspects in the accompanying prose. Features such as strip windows, roof terraces, the color white, and pipe railings reflected his knowledge of the European International Style; the rounded forms used for the garage, the entrance canopy, and the front of the main block were examples of streamlining. The crank plan and the elevated area over the living room were more American. The abstract garden grotto, fountain, and terraces had a Mendelsohnian ornamental complexity. Technologically, Bel Geddes claimed, his house was advanced, with built-in lighting, dimmer switches, air conditioning, and a turntable in the garage. Overall it imparted an air of nautical efficiency, of a large liner with sheer hulls, and a superstructure, a self-contained unit for the American family.[23]

Bel Geddes's self-generated publicity helped introduce streamlined forms in a series of American houses in the mid-1930s. The Richard Mandel House by Edward Durell Stone, 1933–34 (fig. 6.36), was compared by one architecture critic to "a giant airplane." Stone had been trained in the American *beaux arts* system but then traveled in Europe during 1927–29 and saw the new architecture. In the early 1930s he worked on the Rockefeller Center project, specifically Radio City Music Hall, where he became acquainted with Donald Deskey. Richard Mandel, a thoroughly committed "modernist," was a partner of Deskey, and together he and Deskey fitted out the interior of his house with the most up-to-date American designs. The house itself had an International Style flavor, but the rounded dining room extrusion, the extended second-floor deck, gave it a machine in motion look.[24]

Even more nautical was the extraordinary E. E. Butler House in Des Moines, Iowa, 1935–36, designed by the owner and George Kraetsch (fig. 6.37). A poured-in-place concrete structure with

6.37 Kraetsch and Kraetsch
Butler House. Des Moines, Iowa. 1936

seven levels bisected by an interior ramp, the Butler House is integrated vertically. Round, triangular, and rectangular forms compete for attention. Designed to be technologically up to date, it was filled with integrated lighting in each room and advanced appliances such as a garbage disposal, dishwasher, and towel dryer in the kitchen.[25]

Streamlining in American architecture was generally restrained, a curving wall or two, a little pipe-railing; however, in Southern California, it became a more aggressive overall expression. Kem Weber, the industrial designer, produced some furniture and several architectural projects including the Art Center School in Los Angeles, 1934–35, designed in conjunction with Art Center students (fig. 6.38). The particularized composition, where each separate activity is given its own space, is mitigated by the use of rounded forms. The spread and overall configuration make it resemble a giant airplane, while the towers add a nautical conning-tower note. Even more aggressive is the Pan Pacific Auditorium, Hollywood, 1935, by Wurdman and Becket (fig. 6.39). A vast, cavernous structure, the major architectural interest is the en-

trance and offices. Tall, finned pylons that appear to have been shaped in a wind tunnel contrast with the more horizontal offices to the sides, with curved corners, strip windows, and pipe railings.

The degree of abstraction obtained in the Pan Pacific Auditorium, where the forms are streamlined but the specific machine reference is hidden, completely disappears for literal replication in Robert Derrah's Coca-Cola Bottling Plant and Office, Los Angeles, 1936, actually a remodeling of four separate buildings on the site (fig. 6.40). Derrah wrapped a wall around the four, added a bridge, and used portholes, watertight bulkhead doors, and ships' ladders on the exterior. Encouragement for the fantasy came from the owner, Stanley Bardee, an avid yachtsman. On the interior Derrah recreated the promenade deck of an ocean liner with simulated steel columns, wooden ceiling beams, rivets (of wood), louvered doors, a pair of davits for life boats, and large ventilators. One interpretation for such a fantasy is that the cleanliness and purity implied by the nautical motifs would be transferred to Coca-Cola, which was frequently attacked as impure and unhealthy.[26]

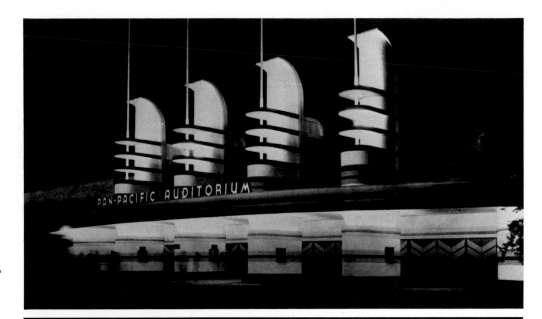

6.39 Wurdman and Becket
Pan Pacific Auditorium. Hollywood.
1935

6.40 Robert Derrah (1895–1946)
Coca-Cola Bottling Plant and Office. Los
Angeles. 1936

6.41 Wischmeyer, Arrasmith & Elswick
Greyhound Terminal. Washington, D.C.
1938

6.42 Henry Hohauser
New Yorker Hotel. Miami Beach, Fla.
1940. © David J. Kaminsky

Naturally streamlining was applied to buildings concerned with transportation, such as bus terminals, a new building type of the machine age. W. S. Arrasmith of Louisville, Kentucky, designed a number of terminals for Greyhound, including one in Washington, D.C., 1939–40 (fig. 6.41). The facade is symmetrical, its focal point the raised tower crowned with a chrome racing greyhound. The entrance is exuberant, with a cantilevered marquee in polished aluminum and curved walls and corners. The building was a conscious effort to reflect an image of speed, efficiency, and modernity; it implied adventure in traveling.[27]

Streamlining became the image for new resort architecture that sprang up in the late 1930s in places such as Miami Beach. These "new" resorts attempted to lure "new" patrons, a middle class affected in only a minor way by the Depression. Miami Beach had the most extensive building campaign of any American city. The totality of the overall ensemble of gaily painted facades with long fins, ribbon windows, towers, portholes, and rounded corners adds up to far more than the frequently banal individual unit. Henry Hohauser, the leading Miami Beach architect, produced some three hundred designs for small hotels and apartment houses (see figs. 6.42, 6.43). His formula (which others copied) was a frontal, axial building with a tower or an explosion of ornament at the entrance. Round-ended strip windows were wrapped around the corners, emphasizing a horizontal orientation. His imagery was generally abstract, though a few references to nautical themes or tropical flora and fauna appear.[28]

Streamlining in American architecture varied between the wholesale usage of the image of speed as in the Pan Pacific Auditorium to the more superficial application of rounded corners, trim, and pipe railings at Miami Beach. Since buildings do not move, streamlining was in many ways an arbitrary application of form and details, yet it provided an image embodying efficiency and the—supposedly—clean lines of machinery.

178

6.43 Henry Hohauser (1896–1963)
Century Hotel. Miami Beach, Fla. 1939.
© David J. Kaminsky

6.44 Paul Cret
Folger Shakespeare Library. Washington, D.C. 1929–32

6.45 Paul Cret
Central Heating and Refrigeration Plant. Washington, D.C. 1933–34. Charcoal on paper, 19 × 14½". Collection National Archives

6.46 Detail of ornamentation, Central Heating and Refrigeration Plant

STRIPPED CLASSICAL MODERNISM OF THE 1930s

By the early 1930s there emerged a distinct American modern style that synthesized the diverse threads of the International Style, the streamlined, the lingering 1920s machine-as-parts setback approach, and the modernistic into a classical bias toward balanced, symmetrical, and hierarchical forms. Essentially a hybrid, this American classic modernism of the 1930s could engage in visual excess, but usually ignored verbal polemics. The designers were, in general, traditionally trained architects who attempted to come to terms with the new language by using it as an appliqué to basically traditional forms. In 1938 Talbot Hamlin, a leading architectural critic, wrote an article identifying "A Contemporary American Style." Hamlin claimed it represented a generic approach that "sometimes, recognizing its classical basis, adopts frankly classical mouldings, cornices or conventional proportions, but . . . avoids the use of orders, and is usually free from historical precedent." Its forms are generally stripped, clean, clear.[29]

The background of this modernized classicism can be seen in the work of Goodhue, Eliel Saarinen, and Paul Cret. Cret's Folger Shakespeare Library in Washington, D.C., 1929–32 (fig. 6.44), uses classical forms without the ornamental language of classicism. A white, marble-clad structure with a tripartite, trabeated division of mass, the traditional orders become fluted piers between the high narrow windows. Simplified neoclassical bas-reliefs appear in the window spandrels. The overall effect is crisp with clean lines and forms. Cret's Central Heating Plant for Washington, D.C., 1933 (fig. 6.45), adapts the stripped classical image to industrial structures. Substantial brick piers enclose vertical window slits. On one of Cret's design studies three turbine-like extrusions appear at the top. On the completed structure relief sculptural panels show mechanical details of the buildings, boilers, and their operations (see fig. 6.46).[30]

As an image for public buildings, stripped classicism dominated a great part of the Public Works Administration (PWA) building programs in the 1930s and early 1940s. As the outcry of some critics grew to avoid all decoration as wasteful, stripped classicism became even more reticent in its ornament. The National Airport in Washington, D.C., 1940 (fig. 6.47), a semicircular structure with a concave entrance and a convex glass wall onto the landing field, constructed under the aegis of the PWA with Howard L.

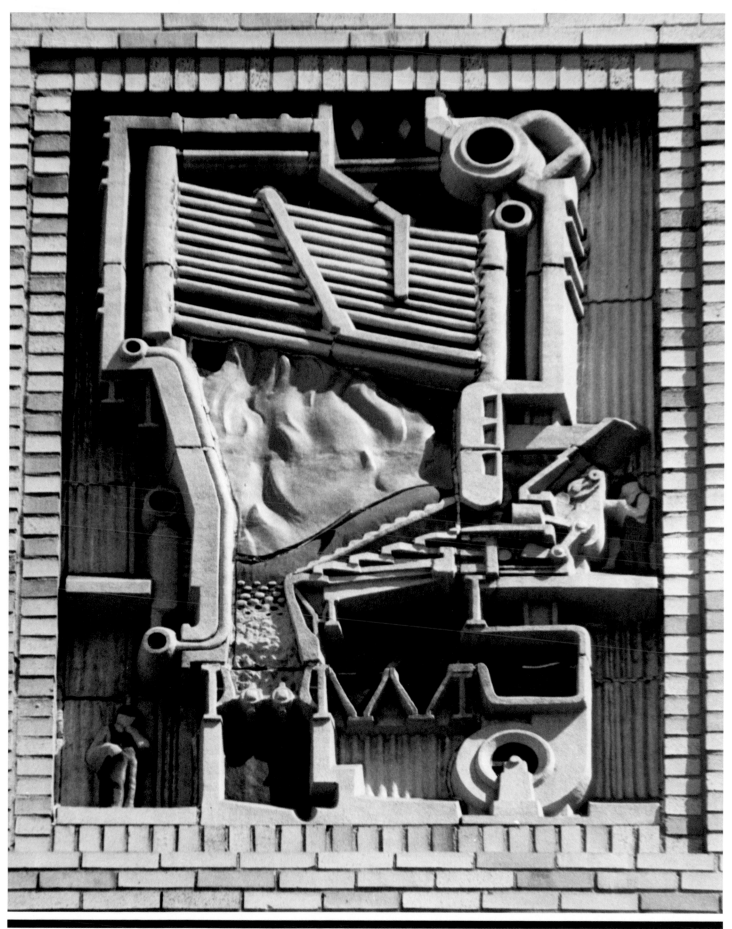

6.46

Graveley Point - Washington, DC

6.47 Howard L. Cheney, architect, Hugh Ferriss, renderer
National Airport. Alexandria, Va. 1939–40. Charcoal on tracing paper mounted on board, 11¼ × 17½". Collection Avery Architectural and Fine Arts Library, Columbia University, New York

Cheney as the consulting architect, shows the apogee of development. Large cylindrical columns placed in antas provide a reference to its classical ancestors.

A stripped classical modernism was applied to numerous commercial structures of the 1930s, such as the Austin Company's large "Radio City of the West" for NBC in Los Angeles, 1937–38 (figs. 6.48, 6.49). Huge, abstract, neoclassical porticos act as corner pivots for two different wings, which are articulated by ribbon windows for offices and round-cornered blank boxes for the studios. Against the monumental classicism of the entrance, the studio wing has a machine air: bent concrete forms in almost baroque swirls led the visitor to glass-block walls trimmed with aluminum and stainless steel strips and sans-serif lettering.

The main designer for the Austin Company, Robert Smith, Jr., also designed a number of prototype buildings such as drive-in laundries (see fig. 6.50). His smaller structures are somewhat abstract, seeking an asymmetrical interweaving of forms and materials, but the larger ones have more classical towers and organization, though decked out in modernistic ornament.[31]

American stripped classicism contains some features similar to public buildings erected in Russia, Italy, France, Germany, and other countries in the 1930s. Certainly an international exchange of ideas and influences occurred, but it would be impossible to label the style as containing specific political ideologies since the governmental systems it housed and represented were fundamentally different. Stripped classicism, while used for commercial buildings, was essentially a public or civic building style intended to represent the power of the state. The boring facelessness or impersonality of the many stripped classical governmental buildings has a certain machine-like repetition and represents—in retrospect— the growing bureaucracy necessary to administer the modern industrial state.

6.48 Austin Company
NBC Studio Building. Los Angeles. 1938

6.49 Detail of facade, NBC Studio Building

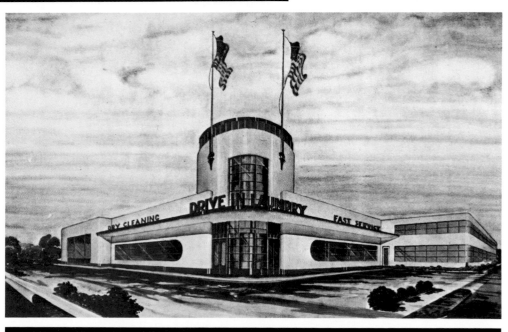

6.50 Austin Company
Model Drive-In Laundry. ca. 1938

6.51 Albert Kahn and Associates
Ohio Steel Foundry Roll and Heavy Machine Shop. Lima, Ohio. 1938

6.52 Interior, Ohio Steel Foundry Roll and Heavy Machine Shop

TOWARD AN AMERICAN MACHINE ARCHITECTURE

At the other extreme from the attempt to graft modern details onto a classical *parti* were those architects who attempted to go beyond style and create a totally machine architecture. This architecture was not stylistically homogeneous: it had elements of the International Style, setback modernism, classicism, and various European idioms such as de Stijl and constructivism. The designers reflected the different machine aesthetics, but stylistic expression was not the uppermost concern. Concern about the look of a building did not disappear, but as a determinant, style was replaced by an attempt to utilize the machine and its processes in creating architectural form.

The touchstone of much machine-oriented architecture of the 1920s and 1930s was the industrial building, especially the factory. Until 1910 the factory had existed in the netherworld of architecture, considered more as engineering than as architectural design. A few architects such as Albert Kahn of Detroit did engage in factory design and had created by 1910 a distinctive American factory idiom. In addition to factories, Kahn, it should be noted, designed public, commercial, and institutional buildings, as well as houses, all of which were very traditional. In 1917 he went to work on the first stage of Ford's River Rouge plant. Ford, convinced of the inefficiency of multistory factories, pushed Kahn to develop steel-frame structures with entire walls of glass, lightweight metal, and/or brick infill.

Kahn became an advocate of "a straightforward attack of the problem," for as he explained, the "avoidance of unnecessary ornamentation, simplicity and proper respect for cost of maintenance make for a type which, though strictly utilitarian and functional, has distinct architectural merit."[32] The River Rouge factory buildings, which so excited artists such as Charles Sheeler, had a direct presence, vast enclosures of steel and glass with cylindrical smokestacks appearing as totems of the machine age.

In the 1930s Kahn further refined factory design, monumentalizing some heretofore neglected features such as the sawtooth clerestory and butterfly roofs. The facades of buildings such as the Dodge Half-ton Plant and the Ohio Steel Foundry Roll and Heavy Machine Shop (figs. 6.51, 6.52) were subdivided into tripartite compositions of a low podium, tall glass walls, and a plain fascia or pediment of stucco or light-colored brick. All the elements were treated as parts of a continuous surface emphasizing the thinness and tautness of the structure. The interiors were great luminous spaces composed of revealed trusses, dropped beams, electrical conduits, and I-beams, scaled not for man but for machines.

6.53 Holabird and Root
Design for Texaco Service Station. 1932.
Colored pencil on tracing paper, 23¾ ×
22¾″. Collection Chicago Historical
Society

The gas or service station provided for much of the American public the most direct contact with architecture of the machine. Standardized stations imparting a company image sprung up in the early 1920s. The Pure Oil and the Sun Oil companies used pitched-roof, domestic-looking structures for their stations. By 1930 many of the large oil companies and their local distributors understood the value of nationally recognized logos and signs—from Mobil's flying horse to the Texaco star—and realized that neat, clean, and efficient buildings were part of an advertising package. Sensing a new market, many steel-building-component manufacturers, along with architects and industrial designers, began to design prototype standardized service stations.[33]

Holabird and Root designed a number of prototype stations for the Chicago distributor of Texaco and Kelly Springfield. Transparent glass boxes for easy display of the products, the stations had flat, overhanging roofs that terminated in billboard-like signs, masterful compositions of American advertising symbols (see figs. 6.53, 6.54). One Boston store sign resembled a Stuart Davis painting.

Porcelain panels or some type of prefabricated metal panel skin, easily erected and maintained, became the norm for service station design in the 1930s. While individual designs in a wide variety of images, from practical to fantastic, continued to appear, most companies tried to standardize. Gulf Oil, using company architects, developed a station with streamlined corners, a large display-waiting room with a curved sheet of glass, horizontal strips and fins, and a setback entrance tower, complete with glass-block infill (fig. 6.55). It was a catalogue of modernism.

Clauss and Daub (Alfred Clauss and George Daub), a young Philadelphia architectural firm and committed followers of George Howe, designed in 1931 for Standard Oil of Ohio a prototype service station with a steel frame and glass and porcelain panel covering (fig. 6.57). Its light and volumetric quality made it acceptable to Hitchcock and Johnson, and the prototype was included in the Modern's *International Style* exhibit. The porcelain panels were colored in red, white, and blue and gave the building both a festive and a functional quality. Constructed by the Austin Company, the prototype was marketed to other oil companies, and with different trim and colors the station appeared across the country.[34]

The most successful and famous standardized service stations of the period were undoubtedly Walter Dorwin Teague's 1936 designs for Texaco. Since the 1920s the Texas Company had experimented with standardized stations for different regions and locations. In the mid-1930s, under aggressive new leadership, Texaco embarked on an extensive marketing campaign. Coupled with Teague's stations was a new program encompassing three new products or services: "Tex-

6.54 Holabird and Root
Design for Texaco Service Station. 1932. Colored pencil on tracing paper, 24¾ × 27". Collection Chicago Historical Society

6.55 Gulf Express Stop Service Station. Pittsburgh. 1937

aco Sky Chief," a premium gasoline "for those who want the best"; uniformed personnel; and what had been an unmentionable—clean rest rooms. Prominent signs advertised "Registered Rest Rooms," and magazine and newspaper advertisements touted Texaco's "White Patrol," an inspection team that crossed the country in white cars checking rest-room cleanliness. Robert Harper of Teague's design staff investigated existing service stations, questioned customers and station operators, and came up with five prototypes based on desired size and location (such as mid-block or corner). Teague's stations could be constructed with a variety of materials—wood and stucco, brick, or the most popular, steel frame and porcelain panel (fig. 6.56). The basic design included large display windows for products, rest rooms entered from outside, one or more bays, precisely labeled—"Lubrication," "Washing," "Service"—and an optional streamlined canopy. Gleaming white in basic color, the fascia contained small Texaco stars and three narrow green bands, which united the building and gave it a "speedy" character. Over the canopy, backed by fins, stood in large sans-serif letters the word "TEXACO." Brilliantly lighted at night and exuding efficiency, hygienic cleanliness, and machine preciseness, the Texaco station would—it was hoped—make the motorist feel in good hands. Teague's designs for Texaco were so successful that by 1940 over five hundred stations had been either erected or remodeled. The image became synonymous with Texaco.[35]

Housing was another area in which architects concentrated their efforts to produce an economical alternative to the hand-built and individually designed house or apartment building. Houses of the future littered the late 1920s and the 1930s, as architects and critics tried to adapt the principles of mass production and standardized machine-produced parts to the American house. Many of the designs never went beyond the paper stage, a few were erected as demonstration buildings, and some were actually inhabited. While the ideal of a machine architecture for the home was not widely realized, a few architects working with some of the less glamorous materials of the machine age did produce an architecture of a new experience.

6.56 Walter Dorwin Teague
Texaco Type "A" Station with canopy.
Oakland, Calif. ca. 1936

6.57 Alfred Clauss (b. 1906) and
George Daub (b. 1901)
Filling Station for the Standard Oil Company of Ohio. Cleveland. 1931. Courtesy
The Museum of Modern Art, New York

Buckminster Fuller illustrated in 1927 the possibilities of a fully machine-generated house. A largely self-taught engineer who had spent some time in the navy during World War I, Fuller determined to create a new approach to housing—and other human problems—by using advanced technology to solve wide-ranging social and ecological problems. His "4-D Utility Unit" of 1927–29 (fig. 6.58) played upon the popular fascination with Einstein by claiming the project embodied the fourth dimension, time. He envisioned a large dirigible circling the world, selecting a site, and dropping a bomb for the foundation, and then setting down "like planting a tree," a stack of 4-D Utility housing units mounted on a central pole. The units, which could be constructed as individual houses as shown in the model, were built of transparent plastic walls, with inflated rubber flooring and an aluminum roof, hung by guide wires from the central utility pole, and carried in tension by struts. The entire composition was designed on a triangular construction module, which created a rigid frame. The central mast was an aluminum pole containing a triangular elevator and utility lines for the air-conditioning and heating systems—making blankets and even clothes unnecessary—and other mechanical gadgets. The bathroom had, in addition to the usual conveniences, a vacuum toothbrush and electric hairclippers. The kitchen was equipped with every imaginable device including a sewage disposal system and dishwasher. A diesel engine supplied power.[36]

Fuller was engaged by the Marshall Field Department Store and Company of Chicago in 1929 to lecture on his design in conjunction with an exhibition of modern furniture. Waldo Warren, an advertising specialist connected with Marshall Field, coined the term "Dymaxion" by fusing the syllables derived from "dynamic," "maximum," and "ions."

The Dymaxion House never did go into production; it existed only on paper and as a model. Fuller was approached to erect one at the 1933 Century of Progress Exposition, but he declined, demanding full-scale production. As a demonstration, Fuller's house summed up many of the marvels of modern technology, and while it contained obvious references to ships and suspension bridges, images of the traditional house also appeared, in the duraluminum pitched roof.

6.58 R. Buckminster Fuller Presentation drawing of Dymaxion House. ca. 1929. Ink drawing

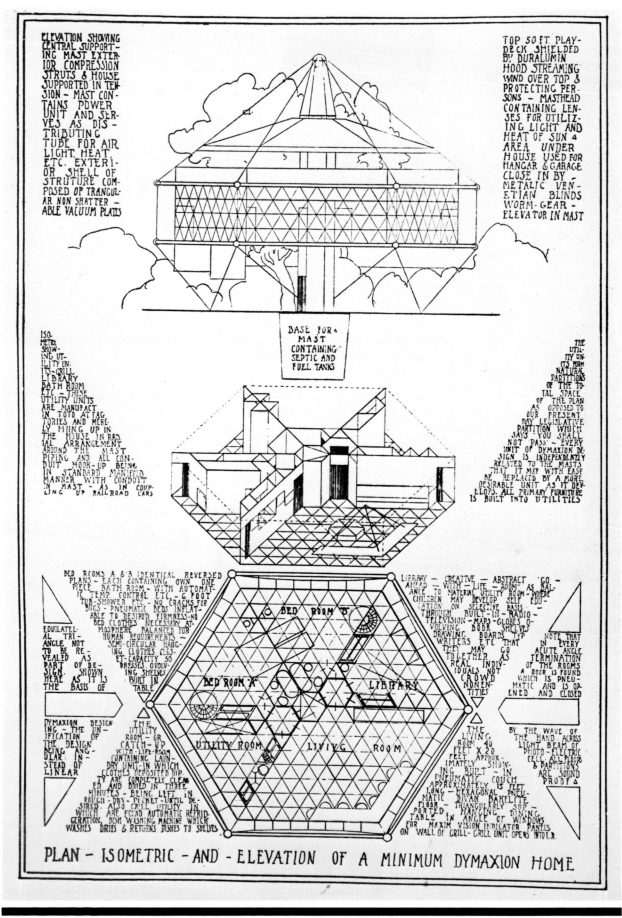

PLAN - ISOMETRIC - AND - ELEVATION OF A MINIMUM DYMAXION HOME

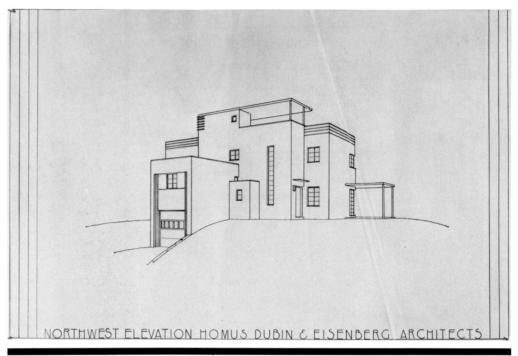

NORTHWEST ELEVATION HOMUS DUBIN & EISENBERG ARCHITECTS

6.59 Henry Dubin (1892–1963) Battledeck House, northwest elevation. Highland Park, Ill. 1929–30. Ink on tracing paper, 9¼ × 14¼". The Art Institute of Chicago. Gift of Arthur Dubin of Dubin, Dubin and Moutoussamy, 1980

6.60 George Fred Keck (1895–1980) House of Tomorrow. *Century of Progress Exposition*, Chicago. 1933

Chicago, reflecting perhaps its heritage of the pragmatic Chicago School and also Frank Lloyd Wright's call for a new American architecture, emerged as one of the centers for machine housing. Henry Dubin described his Battledeck House, 1929–30 (fig. 6.59), as "unhampered by the confining limitations of traditions and 'style.' " In 1928 Dubin had traveled in Europe, where he met Le Corbusier and saw some of his work, including the Villa Stein outside Paris. The house he designed upon his return had as its basis family safety—especially from fire—and economy. The name "Battledeck" came from the floor and roof system of welded steel plate and beams similar to naval vessel construction. Wood was completely eliminated; the walls were made of concrete block, brick, and stucco. With its roof terrace and ribbon windows, the design had a nautical element typical of European modernism. The volumetric asymmetry of the different parts—claimed to spring from functional requirements—could be seen to reflect the influence of de Stijl, but was more probably the result of the impact of Wright. Originally intending to paint the house white, which would have emphasized the European influence, Dubin found that the brick fit in with the natural surroundings and left it buff-colored.[37]

192

6.61 George Fred Keck
Crystal House, night view. *Century of Progress Exposition*, Chicago. 1934

The *Century of Progress Exposition* brought to the public's attention a number of demonstration houses reputedly fit for mass production. George Fred Keck's two houses were the most interesting and far-reaching. Trained in the architectural engineering program at the University of Illinois, Keck was inspired to create machine architecture after reading Le Corbusier's *Towards a New Architecture*. His House of Tomorrow (fig. 6.60) was designed in early 1933 as a demonstration structure to show off a number of new materials and appliances—U.S. Gypsum provided the floors, Libbey-Owens-Ford the glass, Holland Furnace the air-conditioning system, General Electric the appliances, H. W. Howell the metal tubular furniture, and so on. The form, a duodecagon, was inspired, Keck claimed, by mid-nineteenth-century octagon houses designed for maximum efficiency. Keck's House of Tomorrow had a central utility core, reminiscent of Fuller's Dymaxion House, with the floors carried by the core and delicate steel lally columns recessed inside the transparent glass walls. With the exception of the poured concrete foundation and the fiber-concrete floors, the house was prefabricated and took

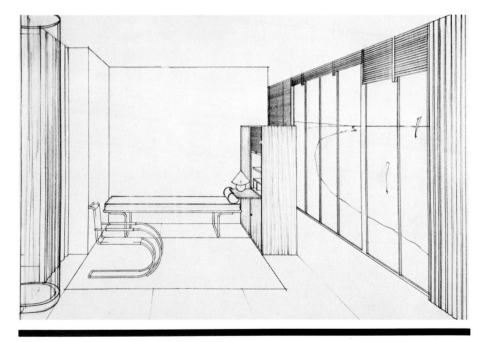

about two months to construct. Conceived as a demonstration of an architectural technique comparable to the technical development in American industries, Keck's design was based on the idea that modern life was so well served by the machine that little permanence was required. The interior spaces were easily rearranged through non–load-bearing insulation board walls. The family would

6.62 Bedroom, Crystal House. Ink on paper, 17 × 21″. Collection State Historical Society of Wisconsin, Madison

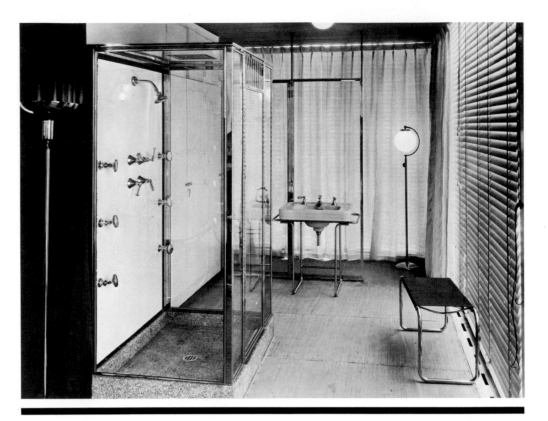

6.63 Lavatory, Crystal House

For us the living...better homes

"Americans want 'living', not 'housing'. We want homes with telephones, radios, automatic heat, mechanical refrigeration, air conditioning. In short, Americans want more copper in their homes, for more copper means better living. That is why industrial research and the new developments in copper now taking place in Revere's laboratories can bring us far greater comfort and pleasure in days to come.

"So, no matter what else results from the all-out effort our country is making, one thing seems certain. When it is over, real enjoyment of life in our homes can be greater, can be available to millions more. For in this great emergency, new standards are being created. Industry is experimenting with new processes. Revere is working out new things in copper. Architects are inventing new methods of building.

"Here is one conception by the famous designer, Norman Bel Geddes. It shows the deep comfort, the complete convenience, the dignity of living which American production methods could easily provide."

G Donald Dallas
President

6.64 Advertisement for prefabricated housing units designed by Norman Bel Geddes. From *Time* (September 15, 1941)

For the second year of the *Century of Progress Exposition* Keck built out of personal funds the Crystal House (figs. 6.61–6.63). Especially dramatic when viewed at night with lighted glazing and the streamlined shape of Fuller's *Dymaxion* automobile visible in the basement, the Crystal House refined some of the technological promise of the House of Tomorrow. Except for a poured-concrete slab, the entire house was prefabricated. A narrow central core contained the utility conduits and steel supporting columns; otherwise, all vertical supports were pushed to the outside, beyond the glazed perimeter, and expressed as narrow and elegant lattice trusses that carried the steel floor and roof plates. The interior was seen as a liquid expanse of space: furniture units provided the major divisions on the main living floor; only the kitchen was enclosed. All exterior walls were of glass, either of clear plate or one of two types of translucent glass, depending on the degree of privacy required. Keck told a reporter that the glass was "employed because it symbolizes the type of material which goes into place readily and once in place is always finished, needing no upkeep." The furnishings were designed by

spend a great deal of time on the various pipe-railed decks, or in the brilliantly lighted interior; darkness would be nonexistent. The family would travel fast and light: both a garage with a Pierce *Silver Arrow* automobile and a hangar with a Curtis-Wright sport biplane were included as part of the package.[38]

6.65 Frank Lloyd Wright
Jacobs House. Madison, Wis. 1937

Leland Atwood, who had contributed to the interior of the House of Tomorrow; for the Crystal House he chose to copy almost directly European styles.[39]

In the succeeding years a few actual examples of machine-produced houses were erected in the Midwest and the East. Howard Fisher, a Chicago architect, formed General Houses, Inc., and constructed his panel-steel dwellings described by *Fortune* in 1933 as "cleanly designed as a pursuit plane." In a Cleveland suburb, the American Rolling Mill Company (ARMCO) constructed a steel-wall house unusual in its extreme lack of beauty and grace.[40] In 1939 Norman Bel Geddes obtained a commission for a mass-produced prefabricated house. Bel Geddes conceived of a package of twenty-seven basic units (see fig. 6.64) that could be combined into a number of different configurations. Stylistically they were far different from his earlier streamlined forms, vaguely resembling Frank Lloyd Wright's earlier Usonian House schemes with their flat overhanging roofs and large

corner windows. The wall and roof units were a combination of an exterior copper sheet, an expanded metal core, and plywood or synthetic interior walls. In spite of extensive promotion and a projected cost of only $1,950, none of the houses was ever built.[41]

Frank Lloyd Wright's relationship to the machine age is ambiguous. Although he appeared at times a prophet of the machine as servant and form-giver, he was unwilling to accept any interpretation of the machine but his own. In 1936–37 he designed his answer to the low-cost, single-family house: the first Usonian House for Herbert Jacobs in Madison, Wisconsin (fig. 6.65). The house, which cost $5,500 including the architect's fee, incorporated several advanced technologies. Wright composed a pavilion form of preassembled wood walls on a slab containing radiant heat and electrical conduits; a flat roof; and only a minimal amount of hand-built brick walls for the fireplace, kitchen core, and one end of the living room. Everything was stan-

6.66 Richard Neutra
Interior, Beard House (with Neutra). Altadena, Calif. 1934

6.67 Beard House, southwest view

dardized: extraneous interior trim was eliminated to the point of bare bulbs dangling from electrical conduits. The house was closed to the street; the main entrance was through a carport—one of the first—and the combined living and dining areas and the bedrooms opened onto the garden. Wright repeated the basic form of the Jacobs House with some modifications for a number of houses in the next few years. To Wright the Usonian House utilized the machine in an organic manner and was far more American than the "sterilized" and "pernicious" International Style architecture promoted by The Museum of Modern Art.[41]

In contrast to the prototypical and demonstrative character of most Midwestern and the few Eastern examples of machine housing of the period, the architects of Southern California found they could actually build for clients houses that partook of the machine. The difference undoubtedly lay with the more liberal, experimental, and (sometimes) hedonistic society that tended to congregate in the Los Angeles area. Certainly the booming economy and the air of fantasy surrounding Hollywood helped to contribute to the situation. Esther McCoy has shown that the clients of Richard Neutra, Rudolph Schindler, and followers were part of an avant-garde in both the arts and private lives.[42] Los Angeles in the 1920s and 1930s appears as the only area in the United States where a true architectural avant-garde existed similar to that of Paris, Utrecht, and Berlin in the 1920s.

6.68 Richard Neutra Von Sternberg House. San Fernando Valley, Calif. 1934–35

Richard Neutra's Lovell House in Los Angeles, while within the International Style idiom, utilized construction technology in a manner far advanced over its European counterparts. Neutra had been attracted to America by the reputation of Frank Lloyd Wright and also by American technological prowess. Shortly after arrival he authored *Wie Baut Amerika?* (1927, *How Builds America?*), which advanced the concept that a new age and a new architecture were being created. Pauline Schindler summed up Neutra's thesis: the new style was "being created not mainly by the professional architect, but by manufacturers of building materials and specialties."[44]

In the mid-1930s Neutra, while retaining certain vestiges of the now-codified International Style idiom, investigated more thoroughly the machine as both image and form-giver for houses. The Beard House, Altadena, California, 1934–35 (figs. 6.66, 6.67), used hollow steel channels for the walls, open-web steel trusses for the roof, and steel web beams as a base for the concrete floor. A plenum thus resulted from the steel shell through which hot or cold air could be circulated. The machine image was further emphasized by painting the exterior a glossy silver-gray and using large areas of clear glazing, some of which could be pulled open to the lush landscape. The interior was carefully detailed, with the main living space containing chromium steel columns, battleship gray linoleum floor covering, brown masonite on the walls, and exposed steel trim. Ironically, a fireplace, not a necessity in Southern California, was included, but Neutra effectively "machined" it with a "radiating aluminum" covering. An early photograph showing Neutra posing in one corner with the magnificent Sierra Madre mountains in the background exhibits his specially designed tubular steel furnishings. Actually, they belonged to Neutra; he moved them from house to house for publicity photographs. His clients, William and Melba Beard, were true machine age modernists. He was the son of the eminent historians and supporters of the machine age, Charles and Mary Beard, and taught engineering at Cal Tech; she was a noted aviator.[45]

The simultaneous "All Steel Residence" built for Joseph von Sternberg, the noted German-American film producer (later lived in by Ayn Rand), in the San Fernando Valley has the same "high tech" look with metal siding and aluminum paint, but is a more dramatic composition (fig. 6.68). Long blank metal walls, one curved in the best streamlined manner, greet the visitor, who pulls up under the raised terrace covering the driveway. A moat surrounds the house

6.69 Rudolph Schindler (1887–1953)
Lovell Beach House near completion.
Newport Beach, Calif. 1925–26

and an "artificial rain device," really a sprinkler, helps to cool the metal patio walls. The long walls—some of them really false fronts—which penetrate the landscape add immeasurably to the apparent size of the house and create a Hollywood stage set illusion.[46]

Rudolph Schindler, also in Los Angeles and a sometimes collaborator with Neutra in the mid-1920s, provided an entirely different image of machine architecture. Schindler had trained directly under Otto Wagner in Vienna and then worked for Frank Lloyd Wright for nearly five years. Schindler lacked Neutra's adroit sense of self-publicity, and he failed to court the Eastern critics and publicists who helped to make reputations. When Schindler heard that The Museum of Modern Art was arranging the *International Style* show he wrote Philip Johnson asking to be included: "I am not a stylist, not a functionalist, nor any other sloganist. Each of my buildings deals with a different *architectural* problem, the existence of which has been forgotten in this period of Rational Mechanization." Johnson replied: "From my knowledge of your work, my real opinion is that your

work would not belong in this exhibition."[47] Schindler's problem—if it was a problem to anyone except a cataloguer of styles—was his romantic, intuitive nature; he sought stimuli, and not formulas like Neutra. He incorporated a great range of influences, from Viennese Secessionist to de Stijl, as well as Wright, European purism of the International Style, and German Expressionism. The result was that he explored a variety of directions and lacked a clear, consistent development as embodied in Neutra's work. Schindler did not see the machine as precise, but rather the means of a crude method of building.

His Doctor Phillip Lovell Beach House, 1925–26 (figs. 6.69, 6.70), investigates the possibility that modern reinforced concrete construction could provide the opportunity for a new spatial enclosure. The concrete frames, "suggested by the pile structures indigenous to all beaches," carried two horizontal decks that opened across the end to the beachfront. Schindler exploited the rough texture of the concrete by using eight-inch-wide Oregon Pine form work, and then used the same wood for the partitions,

floors, trim, and furniture. The building as a form seemed purposely indeterminate, disobeying the usual laws of enclosure with deep voids and extruding projections. He purposely upset the only regularity, the five equally spaced piers, by placing the exterior stairs at markedly different angles. With the Lovell Beach House Schindler explored modern technology in order to create new spatial possibilities.[48]

Deeply disappointed by Johnson's rejection, Schindler made an attempt in the early 1930s to play by the International Style rules; however, by the mid- and late 1930s Schindler was back to his old tricks.

In one of his few writings, "Space Architecture" from 1934, Schindler argued against the idea of a controlling machine age style: "the present machine is a crude collection of working parts, far from being an organism . . . the creaks and jags of our crude machine age must necessarily force us to protect our human qualities in homes contrasting most intensely with the factory." He believed that modern technology freed the architect to create a totally new architecture, "the building as a frame which will help to create the life of the future."[49]

Lacking the well-heeled clients of Neutra, Schindler satisfied himself not with

6.71 Rudolph Schindler
J. Rodriguez House. Glendale, Calif. 1941. Pencil on thin vellum, 17⅛ × 24¼". University Art Museum, Santa Barbara. Architectural Drawings Collection

6.72 Rudolph Schindler
Presentation drawing, William Jacobs House (project). 1936. Pencil and colored pencil on brown paper, 21⅞ × 17½". University Art Museum, Santa Barbara. Architectural Drawings Collection

steel houses (which were abnormally expensive) but with the more mundane products of modern technology: cheap plywood, the two-by-four frame, stucco and lath, and large glass sheets. (Only in the mid-1930s did large plate glass become relatively inexpensive.)[50] Instead of surface play and tarting up the skin with intricate details, Schindler sought overall images which dramatically revealed the changed circumstances of twentieth-century life. He used exploded volumes that emerged as curved roofs, deformed planes, prows, triangles, slanted forms, diagonal frames, and deep voids which seemed unbalanced and even dangerous at times. He attempted to create a totally new spatial experience and image in which no concession was made to tradition and older points of reference. Rafters emerged as architectural elements, glass met fieldstone, and nature in the form of vines dripped from his houses. Certainly the fantasy air of Hollywood must have contributed to Schindler's aesthetic, yet in the end his buildings were more than stage sets, but actually capable of being accomplished.

Gregory Ain, a Los Angeles architect who worked briefly for Schindler and worked for and studied under Neutra for five years, synthesized the social implications of modern architecture. Born into a socialist-oriented family, Ain sought to create inexpensive modern housing utilizing inexpensive modern technology. Schindler's influence was evident in Ain's use of inexpensive materials and the spatial interplay of different volumes; Neutra directed him toward broad plain surfaces enclosing simple forms. Yet, though he recognized Neutra's ambitions and accomplishments, Ain felt Neutra frequently compromised his materials. A private joke between Ain and a fellow Neutra student-employee, Harwell Hamilton Harris, went: "Mr. Neutra, what is the best material to build a steel house out of?"[51]

Ain's Becker House (figs. 6.73, 6.74) in the modern architectural enclave of the Silver Lake area of Los Angeles, 1938, contains right angles and curves in a hillside site. Small and costing about $3,000, the house was constructed out of wood framing and covered with stucco and plywood. The pipe railings and curves gave the house a faintly nautical air. Efficiency of layout was an Ain trademark: the inset for the garage also contains the main entrance. In the interior the volume is emphasized by variations in ceiling height and the continuation of the ceiling plane beyond the window line as a horizontal slab, or prow, that also acted as sunscreen. Space was luminous, open, and easily perceivable. Nothing was intricate in Ain's work; the built-in furniture was of a simple form that added subtle notes of volumetric play.

The Dunsmuir Street Flats, Los Angeles, 1937 (fig. 6.75), are prime examples of Ain's social and humanistic concerns. To fit the long, narrow, trapezoidal site with a gradual grade upslope, Ain created a series of angled cubistic volumes for the individual apartment units. In a sense a horizontal setback, each of the entrances

200

RESIDENCE FOR MR. & MRS. JACOBS. R. M. SCHINDLER - ARCH

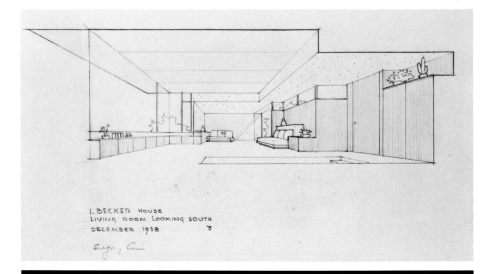

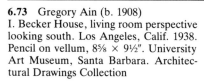

6.73 Gregory Ain (b. 1908)
I. Becker House, living room perspective
looking south. Los Angeles, Calif. 1938.
Pencil on vellum, 8⅝ × 9½". University
Art Museum, Santa Barbara. Architectural Drawings Collection

structurally, the number of building elements was reduced to lower costs. The four-by-four framing studs were carried to the height of the building and along the sides, setting up a rigid frame to be articulated. Based on a four-foot module—the standard lumberyard dimension for materials—all wall openings related to this size, bringing an order and rhythm. Indicating the primacy of the machine, and yet its subservience, the apartment complex appears to rest upon the garages; they greet, but do not intrude.[52]

From buildings and houses conceived of as prefabricated out of steel, glass, and other new materials, to wood-framed dwellings covered in stucco seems a long step backward in the context of a machine architecture. Yet as Ain, Schindler, Wright, and others recognized, mass-production housing was enormously expensive in factory tooling costs, not to speak of transportation costs. To be economically feasible, a tremendous production volume, even by Detroit standards, would be necessary. Finally, much of the expense of housing involved site costs, acquiring the land, placing the foundations, bringing in utilities, and adapting the building to local codes. Some of the concepts of the machine—standardization, regularity, and simplicity—were applicable to the more traditional, carpenter-built structures. While machine processes did make an impact, the overall effect of the machine was more in the rhythm of design and the quest for a new image. The machine liberated architectural imagery in the 1920s and 1930s; however, the real impact of the machine as a process would not be felt until the post-war years, when housing was mass produced by builders at Levitt-style towns across the United States. Machine processes were applicable to any style of house.

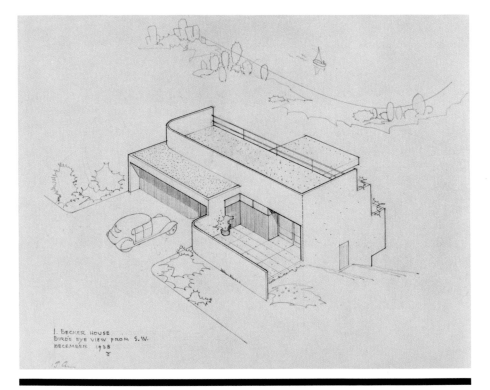

6.74 Presentation sketch for I. Becker House. Pencil on vellum, 8¾ × 10¼". University Art Museum, Santa Barbara. Architectural Drawings Collection

meets exactly the four-foot property setback line on the north side. The major rooms of each unit—including the kitchen—were lighted on three sides. The north side was enclosed with long strip, semi–International Style windows; on the south, large windows and sliding glass doors opened the apartments to individual gardens and porches. Integrated

DUNSMUIR FLATS   STREET SIDE FROM N.E.
1937

6.75 Gregory Ain
Dunsmuir Flats. Los Angeles. 1938. Pen-
cil on vellum, 8¾ × 19″. University Art
Museum, Santa Barbara. Architectural
Drawings Collection

7.1

CHAPTER 7

ENGINEERING A NEW ART

By the twentieth century the machine had radically transformed what Ralph Waldo Emerson once called "the poetry of the landscape."[1] Although visual artists were slow to document changes during the decades after the Civil War, a profound shift of consciousness had occurred by the 1920s. Exposing this new condition through his survey of urban life earlier in the century was the social reformer Lewis Hine. Although hardly a dramatic shot, his 1911 photograph of New York children playing leapfrog over a fire hydrant (fig. 7.2) contrasts visibly with other images from the previous century—Winslow Homer's scenes of boys raiding nests of swallows on the bluffs or lazing in the backyard on a hot afternoon come especially to mind. Even though the harshness of rural life rivaled the blighted cities documented by Hine, Homer's idylls represented modes of play rendered inaccessible to the photographer's street urchins.[2]

With some loose change in their pockets, these same working-class kids could take in a primitive movie at one of the neighborhood storefront theaters proliferating throughout New York. Some twenty years later, a full-grown film in-

dustry had become part of an increasingly complex media network. Consider, for example, Reginald Marsh's mural of *The Press Meeting a Celebrity* (1937), a large fresco for the United States Customs Building in New York (fig. 7.5). A smartly dressed movie star stands casually against the bulwark of a huge ocean liner as she addresses the microphones; meanwhile, a crowd of press photographers lean forward eagerly to film her. Their media ritual occurs on a large floating machine, its billowing stacks rivaling in size the Manhattan skyline in the background. The power of technology is more subtly shown in the manipulation of the celebrity's public image: an aide hidden behind a ventilator releases doves to fly above her head. What new heavenly annunciation is at hand? We can only surmise that this rising star belongs in a Fred Astaire movie with moderne interiors, sophisticated banter, and an elegant dancing partner when the spirit moves her—a product of modern technology at its most glamorous.

While some Americans positively reveled in technology, others were excluded from its promise. The social discrepancy was nowhere more incisively recorded than in Margaret Bourke-White's 1937

7.2 Lewis W. Hine
Leapfrog, New York City. 1911. Gelatin-silver print, 5 × 7″. Collection Walter and Naomi Rosenblum

7.1 Gerald Murphy (1888–1964)
Watch. 1925. Oil on canvas, 78½ × 78⅞″. Dallas Museum of Art. Foundation for the Arts Collection. Gift of the Artist

7.3 Margaret Bourke-White
The Louisville Flood. 1937. Silver print,
9⅞ × 13″. *Life* magazine, Time Inc.

photograph of *The Louisville Flood* (fig. 7.3). Black refugees line up against a billboard advertising "the American Way," symbolized by a white, middle-class family seen through a car windshield. There could be no denying the "World's Highest Standard of Living," symbolized by automobile ownership, were it not for a natural disaster compounding the economic depression of the 1930s.[3]

Technology, then, made its mark upon Americans and no less upon American artists during the 1920s and 1930s. The machine not only broadened subject matter with new images and themes, it also generated new materials and techniques, which suggested formal possibilities previously unavailable. In 1929, for example, some twenty years after an excited public dubbed a small group of artists the "Ashcan School" for their picturesque paintings of urban scenes, Charles Burchfield took the metaphor literally in executing *Still Life—Scrap Iron*, a watercolor of a trash heap and weeds in a culvert (fig. 7.6). Burchfield's predisposition for the junk of a machine civilization strewn over upstate New York evinced a new urban sensibility.

Burchfield's painting demonstrates one way that the machine was expanding traditional categories of art. Artists not only depicted actual ashcans but also picked through them to assemble new objects. Thus Joseph Stella, best known for his paintings of the Brooklyn Bridge, collected scraps of old newspapers and wrappers to make collages with an urban aura. Artists also assembled collages from the perception that human experience might be comprised of interchangeable parts. One of Joseph Cornell's earliest collages shows a man aiming a rifle by resting it on

7.4 Joseph Cornell (1903–1973) *Untitled.* 1930s. Collage, 5⅝ × 3⅝". Estate of Joseph Cornell. Courtesy Castelli Feigen Corcoran

a music stand that serves as a perch for a bird (fig. 7.4). Significantly, the marksman turns out to be Etienne-Jules Marey, the French experimental photographer, shooting his "gun" to capture sequences of motion superimposed on a single frame. Just as Marey revealed fragmented and distorted images hitherto unseen, so Cornell reassembled parts of old engravings and seamlessly pasted them into mysterious incongruities.[4]

7.5 Reginald Marsh (1898–1954)
The Press Meeting a Celebrity. 1937.
Fresco mural. U.S. Customs House, New
York

7.6 Charles Burchfield
Still Life—Scrap Iron. 1929. Watercolor,
21½ × 29⅜″. Collection Charles Rand
Penney

7.7 Marcel Duchamp
The Bride Stripped Bare by Her Bachelors, Even. 1915–23. Oil and lead, wire on glass, 109¼ × 69⅛″. Philadelphia Museum of Art. Bequest of Katherine S. Dreier

In cultivating a new sensibility that required a new way of seeing, the machine called into question traditional cultural values. Thus while American artists responded to a machine world according to their own individual social and economic class, they still kept an eye on Europe. How was the machine to project an American art against the cultural presence of European standards, both academic and avant-garde? While visiting the *Paris Exposition* of 1900, Henry Ad-

ams claimed bafflement and defeat before the mysterious forces of the dynamos on display. Could his American heirs take up his quest for knowledge and negotiate "a new universe which had no common scale of measurement with the old"?[5]

Many Americans were quite willing to transfer their allegiance from nature to technology itself. The switch was not too difficult because American confidence in the powers of technology extended back to the early Republic, when Alexander Hamilton proposed a manufacturing nation in opposition to Jefferson's agrarian ideals. Despite Hamilton's eventual triumph, however, a cultural belief in nature persisted, especially during periods of rapid industrial change, when people held onto familiar conceptions as a precarious stay against the rush of events. As late as 1910, for example, Henri Rousseau could depict an American Indian wrestling an ape in a lush tropical setting. His exotic vision played out an American primitivism of "nature's nation," as American romantics of the early Republic once had it, channeling widespread impressions of a natural paradise into a national identity.[6] Rousseau's contemporaries simply updated this stereotype when they arrived in New York during World War I. America remained a new world, its primitivism located no longer in nature but in a dynamic technology that had taken over the environment. This revised conception persisted into the late 1930s, when Walter Dorwin Teague characterized Americans as "primitives in this new machine age."[7]

Francis Picabia, Marcel Duchamp, and others began straggling into New York in 1915—refugees from the war raging in Europe. Yet New York proved hardly a haven. As Gabrielle Buffet-Picabia later recalled, "Seen from Broadway, the massacres in France seemed like a colossal advertising stunt for the benefit of some giant corporation."[8] Popular entertainment, advertising, corporate interests, and technology formed a complicit web of mass murder on an international scale.

Despite their private reservations, both Picabia and Duchamp publicly praised American technology. The press met them at the dock when they landed, treating them like celebrities due to their participation in the international *Armory Show* in New York two years before. Picabia had actually attended the 1913 exhibition, while Duchamp had scandalized the public with his *Nude Descending a Staircase, No. 2* (fig. 2.8). (The press, having caught the mechanical overtones of the painting, dubbed it *"An Explosion in a Shingle Factory"* and *"The Rude Descending a Staircase, Rush Hour at the Subway."*)[9] In 1915 both artists extolled New York for its skyscrapers, nonexistent in Europe; Duchamp went so far as to dismiss Europe completely. Here was a brave new world that superseded a dying European civilization.

Beneath their optimistic public statements, Picabia and Duchamp were radical iconoclasts who offered American artists an alternative to the shallow enthusiasm of the Italian futurists and the sentimentality of American popular culture.[10] Picabia was thrown into despair and disgust by the war. A pervasive air of nihilism also fed Duchamp's intrinsic skepticism and sense of irony. Neither saw much to celebrate in the carnage, as the futurists apparently did. Picabia's approach to the machine was colored by an acerbic wit and an irony that subverted any possible glorification of technology. Soon after his arrival in New York, he collaborated in the editing of the review *291* (named for Stieglitz's gallery at 291

7.8 Morton Schamberg (1881–1918) *God.* ca. 1918. Miter box and plumbing trap, 10½″ high. Philadelphia Museum of Art. The Louise and Walter Arensberg Collection

7.9 Marcel Duchamp *Fountain.* 1917. Photograph by Alfred Stieglitz in *The Blind Man*, no. 2 (May 1917); original lost. Philadelphia Museum of Art. The Louise and Walter Arensberg Collection Archives

Fifth Avenue). Picabia launched a series of "machine drawings," which were hard-edged and linear, much like advertisements for a Sears, Roebuck catalogue. These machine portraits radically challenged academic standards of subject matter, and in their stark configuration appeared to relinquish any claim to the status of art.

7.10

Duchamp more than matched Picabia in his assault upon the machine with a project he had conceived in Paris. After his arrival in New York he began working on *The Bride Stripped Bare by Her Bachelors, Even* (fig. 7.7), a construction that with its erotic theme and formal implications would have a profound effect on his American associates Charles Demuth and Charles Sheeler. But whereas this large assemblage, informally called *The Large Glass,* was known only to a handful of American artists and writers privy to Duchamp's studio on lower Broadway, the young Frenchman regained notoriety in 1917 with a public gesture.

In order to test the sincerity of his fellow committee members, who had organized a juryless and hence essentially open exhibition, Duchamp submitted a porcelain urinal entitled *Fountain* (fig. 7.9) under the pseudonym of "R. Mutt," supposedly a well-known Manhattan plumber. A shocked committee rejected the urinal, Duchamp resigned, and the public was properly scandalized by the "Richard Mutt Case." *Fountain* was one in a series of what Duchamp called "ready-mades." Such objects required only the artist's signature: Duchamp stressed an artist's *selection* of an artifact for display as the necessary and sufficient condition for its elevation to the status of art. A ready-made required no further manipulation or modification except as an artist might desire.

Duchamp usually chose machine-made objects, often mass-produced and related in kind to machines, which were outside the pale of fine art. Because of its relation to bodily functions, *Fountain* appeared all the more powerful and direct, absolutely primitive in character, and certainly "obscene" to a committee that found itself still bound to notions of Victorian gentil-

ity. Thus the urinal was a radical selection, testing in the extreme both the limits of public taste and the aesthetic principle involved. Duchamp had subverted deeply entrenched cultural norms for art by introducing an artifact from an industrial network into an art network involving studios, galleries, and exhibitions.[11]

Speaking from the intersection of disparate networks at which he stood with his *Fountain,* Duchamp could conclude, "The only works of art America has given are her plumbing and her bridges." Was Duchamp's *Fountain,* then, "a representative piece of American Sculpture," as the poet William Carlos Williams later claimed?[12] Duchamp's irony was elegantly indeterminate. Scorn for academic American art through the elevation of commonplace machine artifacts was undermined by the possibility that they might indeed be taken as objects of aesthetic contemplation both in and out of the art network. During the next two decades American artists would explore Duchamp's ambiguous claim.

It was Dada that broke the silence. Duchamp's gesture shocked the New York art world into taking notice of the presence of the machine in American society. Morton Schamberg, for example, connected a miter box with plumbing parts, and entitled the work *God* (fig. 7.8). His assemblage not only exposed an American obsession with hygiene (later mercilessly exploited by advertising) but also hinted at the way in which the machine

7.10 Man Ray (1890–1976) *Cadeau.* 1921. Mixed media, 5½" × 3½ × 3½". Los Angeles County Museum of Art. The Michael and Dorothy Blankfort Collection

would enter the American home. (Duchamp had been dubbed "Buddha of the bathroom" in the aftermath of the scandal.)[13]

Beyond the immediate thematic possibilities that came to mind, *Fountain* was most important for its material and formal implications. Taking his cue from Duchamp, his close friend, Man Ray selected another domestic artifact—a flatiron—attached to it a vertical row of long tacks, and ironically entitled it *Cadeau* (fig. 7.10). Man Ray also collected ball bearings in an elongated glass jar of the sort for olives. When he arrived in France in 1921, his paintings easily passed customs, whereas *New York 1920,* as he called his bottle of "olives," was not recognized as a work of art. Man Ray told the customs official that it was a "studio decoration," explaining that "sometimes artists didn't have any food, it would give me the illusion that there was something to eat in the house."[14] (Fifteen years later, in *Modern Times,* Charlie Chaplin, strapped into an eating machine to improve the efficiency of factory workers during lunch break, would accidently swallow some nuts and bolts.)

Upon its rejection, *Fountain* was hidden behind a screen at the exhibition site and then taken to "291," where Stieglitz photographed it.[15] Stieglitz had already documented the effect of the machine upon New York City in the 1890s after returning home from a stay in Berlin. Partly because Manhattan was so different from his European idyll, he felt compelled to photograph his new environment. The impulse also came from the camera as a new technology; around the turn of the century Stieglitz energetically expanded the technical boundaries of the camera. No wonder, then, that his involvement with a machine led to images of other machines: trains, airplanes, tugboats, cranes, and New York in the process of constant overhaul were among his favorite subjects until he stopped photographing in the late 1930s.[16]

Animating his project was a longstanding debate over photography: was it possible to create visual works of art with a machine? Stieglitz argued that photography was indeed an art, although the aesthetic implications of his strategy were circuitous. Unlike those photographers who tried to imitate painting in the attempt to establish photography as a visual art, Stieglitz gradually came to advocate "straight" photography: images developed and printed without manipulation of film, paper, and chemicals; images that were direct, uncropped, clear, and sharp rather than soft-focused emulations of the atmospheric neo-Impressionistic paintings then in vogue. This way of seeing was augmented by subject matter that avoided artiness. The raw vitality of Manhattan and its dynamic growth served as a "nonart" subject, one that was uniquely American as well. To qualify photography as art Stieglitz knew that the camera had to eschew painting; but in evading the hegemony of painting, he viewed photography as anti-art. His argument was thus congenial for the proto-Dada gestures of Picabia and Duchamp. *Fountain* and photographer seemed destined to meet.

For Stieglitz and the artists in his group, photography freed painting from the representational image. New York under rapid skyscraper construction continued to be a source of inspiration. When Stieglitz first photographed the Flatiron Building in 1903 he said, "It appeared to be moving toward me like the bow of a monster ocean steamer—a picture of new America still in the making."[17]

The movement in Stieglitz's metaphor, which identified American destiny with technology, was equally evident in John Marin's watercolor *Movement, Fifth Avenue* in 1912 (fig. 7.11), the visual indeterminacy of which extends to all the forms, which explode, disintegrate, and fade. Marin's exuberance in depicting Manhattan continued unabated well into the 1930s. His sense of movement assumed the dimension of a metaphysical imperative that encompassed both the natural and the technological in his art, as he sought "to paint disorder under a big order."

Marin's undivided consciousness was also characteristic of other members of Stieglitz's group. Following his easy movement between cityscape and landscape, Georgia O'Keeffe mounted canvases of New York scenes alongside enlargements of flowers in her exhibitions at Stieglitz's Intimate Gallery in the 1920s. She explained that the juxtaposition was her way of compensating for the displacement of nature by technology: "I will make even busy New Yorkers take time to see what I see of flowers."[18] Such a problem did not exist for O'Keeffe, as evidenced by the overriding organicism of her cityscapes. With *City Night,* painted in 1926, O'Keeffe captured New York in its diurnal rhythms (fig. 7.12). The dark skyscrapers are silhouetted against a deep blue sky, a full moon hovering between the rising buildings. By virtue of her color harmonies, O'Keeffe rendered Manhattan part of Marin's "big order."

With *Silver Tanks and Moon* in 1930 (fig. 7.13), Arthur G. Dove, another artist of the Stieglitz group, projected a sensibility on the order of *City Night.* Although he was more closely associated with nature than the others, partly because he lived on a boat in the Long Island Sound, Dove also painted a remarkable number of canvases involving the machine. Dove's hand, like O'Keeffe's, did not submit to a geometric line, which became instead the trace of a human gesture in the painting. Thus the machine was made organic. Emerson's sanguine view of nature prevailed, as Dove the poet took in everything: gears, ferryboat wrecks, cars in icestorms were measured not to a mechanical precision but to what he called "a flexible form or forma-

7.11 John Marin (1870–1953) *Movement, Fifth Avenue.* 1912. Watercolor, 16⅞ × 13¾". The Art Institute of Chicago. Alfred Stieglitz Collection

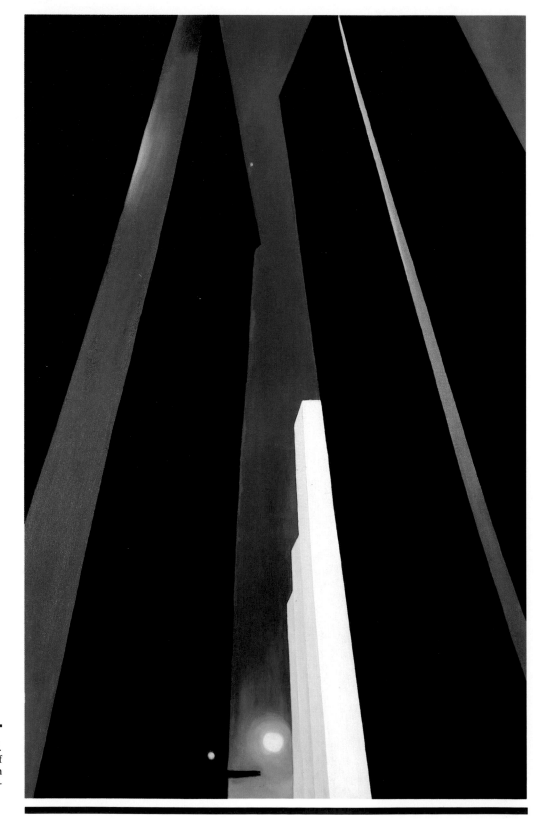

7.12 Georgia O'Keeffe (1887–1986) *City Night*. 1926. Oil on canvas, 48 × 30″. The Minneapolis Institute of Arts. Gift of the Regis Corp., Mr. & Mrs. W. John Driscoll, the Beim Foundation, the Larsen Fund, and by public subscription

7.13 Arthur G. Dove (1880–1946) *Silver Tanks and Moon*. 1930. Oil on canvas, 28⅛ × 18″. Philadelphia Museum of Art. Alfred Stieglitz Collection

7.14 Charles Sheeler
City Interior. 1936. Aqueous adhesive and oil on composition board, 22⅛ × 27". Worcester Art Museum, Worcester, Mass.

tion...governed by some definite rhythmic sense beyond mere geometrical repetition."[19]

In 1922 Stieglitz invited his friends and enemies alike to a symposium on the question "Can a Photograph Have the Significance of Art?" Duchamp, who had abandoned all painting and even work on *The Large Glass* at this time, came to the point: "You know exactly what I think of photography. I would like to see it make people despise painting until something else will make photography unbearable."[20] Implicit in his contempt was the assumption that there were antagonisms between painting and photography.

One artist equally at ease with both painting and photography was Charles Sheeler, who knew Duchamp from the Stieglitz and other avant-garde circles. Sheeler took up photography as a way of supporting himself as a painter. His most important commission came in 1927, when he was asked to photograph Henry Ford's huge River Rouge plant recently completed in Dearborn, Michigan.[21] Not only are those photographs in themselves important documents of American indus-

try, the very act of photography was central to the dynamics of Sheeler's painting. A proponent of straight photography, he printed preternaturally clear images with a sharp focus. (One of his few variations on the straight approach was a triptych entitled *Industry,* involving photomontage of the Rouge plant, which he submitted to a mural exhibition at The Museum of Modern Art in 1932. Fig. 1.2.)

Photography often provided Sheeler with a precise preliminary visual image on which to base his painting, as in the case of *Upper Deck* (fig. 2.6) of 1929. Even though he denied that his paintings had a photographic quality, it is obvious that he strove for a factual exactitude and presence in his work, readily perceived in *City Interior* (fig. 7.14) and *Rolling Power* (fig. 5.24). As one critic noted in 1925, "A picture by Sheeler has the clear, sharp, cold beauty of one of our modern machines, the severe impersonality of a mechanical drawing." The use of machine metaphors in describing Sheeler's painting contributed to the concept of "precisionism," which is not, properly speaking, an avant-garde movement but

7.15 Charles Sheeler
Church Street El. 1920. Oil on canvas,
16⅛ × 19⅛″. Cleveland Museum of Art.
Mr. and Mrs. William H. Marlett Fund

rather a label devised by art historians for a visual style common among some American painters responding to the machine.[22] By its attachment to surfaces the term neglects the depths of ambiguity found in Sheeler's work.

Even though straight photographers claimed to visualize the world without the distortion of art, their prints embodied an aesthetic as much as any pictorial photographer's did. The anti-art of straight photography was congenial to Sheeler's sensibility as a painter. Uneasy under the tutelage of Henry Merritt Chase, who wielded a bravura paintbrush, the young Sheeler had found the *Armory Show* and subsequent viewings of modern art puzzling precisely because of the visual license taken by modern artists.[23] In 1920 Sheeler attempted a simplified, geometric, almost cubist Manhattan in *Church Street El* (fig. 7.15). As the decade went by, however, he increasingly preferred highly representational images of machines and their environment in renunciation of artifice.

A key work in this development was his *Self-Portrait* of 1923, a conté crayon of a telephone set on a table in front of a window with a half-drawn shade (fig. 7.16). The telephone, of course, had been readily accepted as a symbol of modernity. Sheeler's studio-mate, Morton Schamberg, had painted a cubist telephone, its fragmented and shifting elements suggesting the elisions of space achieved by this new means of communication.[24] In contrast, Sheeler's *Self-Portrait* echoes Picabia's witty machine portraits. Bearing only traces of irony, however, Sheeler's image suggests that he tied his identity as a modern artist to the machine. The telephone stands in the foreground; a shadowy figure reflected in the window is discernible. The total image implies that art is a means of communication in which the personality of the artist, if not the artist himself, is concealed or held in abeyance. At most, the artist is but dimly reflected in the work itself.

Sheeler's drawing contrasts significantly with a self-portrait by the Russian avant-gardist El Lissitzky in 1924. His is a photomontage entitled *The Constructor*

7.16 Charles Sheeler
Self-Portrait. 1923. Conte crayon, gouache, and pencil on paper, 19¾ × 25¾". The Museum of Modern Art, New York. Gift of Abby Aldrich Rockefeller

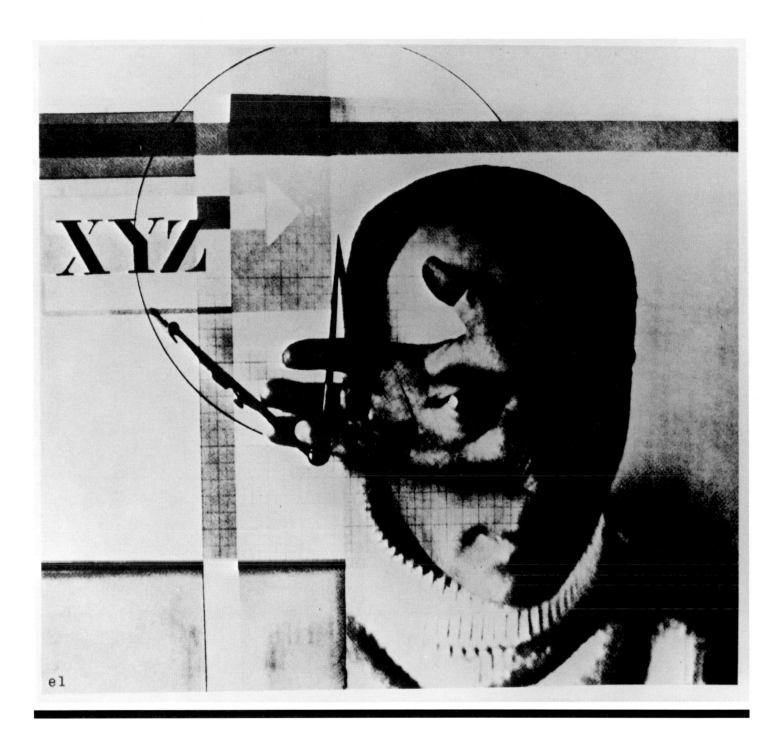

7.17 El Lissitzky [Eliezer Markovitch
Lisitsky] (1890–1941)
The Constructor. 1924. Photomontage

(fig. 7.17), a reference to constructivism, a movement that sought to unite the artist and the engineer. Implicit, too, is a specific conception of art. Superimposed upon the head of El Lissitzky is his hand, which holds a compass. The artist's hand and brain stand at the center of a rational, geometric grid, which suggests the underlying structure of a surrounding world of machines.

Although the world was no less rational for Sheeler, he was self-effacing in the artist's role. No wonder, then, that he admired Duchamp's *Nude Descending a Staircase* specifically for the way its means had been skillfully concealed in making its statement. And statement was everything in Duchamp's *Large Glass,* too, which Sheeler appreciated not for its deceptive veneer of rationality but for its painstaking craftsmanship. The resulting glass assemblage was both literally and metaphorically transparent—a characteristic that also applied to Sheeler's machine paintings. Although Sheeler liked to stress the notion that a painter's will is crucial in building up the successive images of a painting (as opposed to the instantaneous image provided by a camera), he relied heavily upon the geometry of machines to provide internal structure for his images. In addition, he exercised extreme skill in developing an invisible brushstroke to eliminate any vestigial presence of the artist in the painting. His aim was to maintain "precision of statement set down directly with the least possible amount of painting."[25] Sheeler's abnegation of the artist's role combined with his exploration of technology to make him preeminent among American painters of the machine age.

After publishing a single issue of *New York Dada* in 1921, Duchamp and Man Ray embarked for Paris. Dada in New York had been a sporadic affair during the previous six years. In its second, Parisian phase, New York Dada would assume a new, more generalized guise in some quarters as American Dada. Thanks to Duchamp, Man Ray gained entrée among the Parisian Dadaists and introduced them to Matthew Josephson, a young American writer. Josephson soon became aware of their enthusiasm for things American, ranging from skyscrapers and advertising to dime novels, vaudeville, and movies. Unrefined, raucous, and vulgar, these phenomena made little or no claim to art, like Duchamp's sense of American bridges and plumbing. In an advertisement in *Broom,* a little magazine that became his forum for touting an American Dada, Josephson announced "the Age of the Machine": "A new art

7.18

7.19 Stuart Davis
Lucky Strike. 1921. Oil on canvas, 33¼ ×
18″. The Museum of Modern Art, New
York. Gift of The American Tobacco
Company, Inc.

and new literature spring sturdily from the machine civilization."[26] Thus he urged American artists to embrace the machine in the adventurous spirit of Dada and to take the new materials and forms proliferating at an unprecedented rate in America into new realms of creativity.

By 1925 Josephson's American Dada had burned itself out in factional strife, but its importance was far-reaching. During the early 1920s he pulled together a machine age manifesto in the process of development by many artists and writers, either independently or in piecemeal fashion. *Broom,* for example, featured an illustration of Joseph Stella's first painting of the Brooklyn Bridge, dating back to 1918, as well as a photograph of ball bearings by Paul Strand. (In 1921 Strand, who had gotten his start in Stieglitz's magazine *Camera Work* during World War I, began taking pictures of machine parts, emphasizing their power and geometry, as in *Lathe, Akeley Shop, 1923,* fig. 7.18. He later joined forces with Sheeler to film *Manhatta,* a Whitmanesque celebration of New York as the modern city.)

In emphasizing "outdoor billposters" and advertising in magazines and newspapers as well as tabloids, Josephson challenged American artists to be as daring as advertisers (who, as it turned out, would enthusiastically adopt the visual syntax of modern art). Impressed by Dada, Stuart Davis painted in 1921 a series of canvasses with the appearance of enlarged collages: *Lucky Strike* (fig. 7.19), for example, plays with the formal properties of cigarette packs. (Joseph Stella pasted fragments of labels from Luden's coughdrops, Chiclets chewing gum, and Trumpeter cigarettes in his collages.) In 1923 Gerald Murphy, a wealthy American living in France, painted the curtain for *Within the Quota* (fig. 7.20), an American

ballet produced by Les Ballets Suédois, with music by his Yale classmate, Cole Porter. On this large curtain, which resembled a collage, Murphy parodied the front page of American tabloids: "UNKNOWN BANKER BUYS ATLANTIC," "Ex-Wife's Heart-Balm Love-Tangle"—such headlines competed with a "photograph" that set a sleek ocean liner on end against the Woolworth Building (one of John Marin's favorite subjects).[27]

The parodic celebration of the media would eventually yield to satire during the Depression years. The switch was evident in the photographs of Walker Evans. In 1928 Evans's montage of Broadway lights captured the exuberance and glamour of electricity used to serve advertising and entertainment (fig. 7.21). Already adept as an urban photographer (his work in one of his first exhibitions in 1931 was characterized as a mélange "of steel girders, luminous signs and Coney Island bathers"), Evans was also "charged up" by an early Strand photograph of a blind beggar woman on the streets of New York, suggesting a growing interest in the impact of the machine on human beings.[28] Thus his fascination with commercial signs gradually shifted from their formal quality to their human context, as evidenced in *Billboards and Frame Houses, Atlanta, Georgia,* 1936 (fig. 7.22). The erotic promise of Carole Lombard, starring in *Love Before Breakfast,* is undercut by the shabby row houses behind the wall plastered with tattered signs.

Whereas Josephson stressed the new "American flora and fauna" generated by technology, Jean Epstein, another writer for *Broom,* explored some of its more subtle implications. Anticipating Marshall McLuhan by thirty years, he claimed that machines at times become extensions of the self. As a consequence, "spatial

7.20 Gerald Murphy (1888–1964) Scenario, decor, and costumes for *Within the Quota*, produced by Les Ballets Suédois, Paris. 1923. Photograph collection Mr. and Mrs. William M. Donnelly

7.21 Walker Evans
New York City, 1928–1929, "Broadway Composition." 1928–29. Probably 35mm negative

speed, mental speed, multiplication of intellectual images and the deformations of these images" comprised the conditions of modernity.[29] Epstein presupposed a total environment of technology encompassing human action and perception. In 1936 Charles Sheeler would reveal technology as an all-embracing system in *City Interior* (fig. 7.14), its title a metaphor for Henry Ford's River Rouge industrial complex, built to the proportions of a small city and perhaps even more self-contained. Despite the claustrophobic and hermetic connotations of *City Interior,* technology as a system had farflung

7.22 Walker Evans (1903–1975)
Billboards and Frame Houses, Atlanta, Georgia. 1936. Gelatin-silver print, 10 × 8″. Collection Library of Congress

7.23 Berenice Abbott (b. 1898)
Water Front: From Pier 19, East River.
1936. Gelatin-silver print, 10 × 11⅜".
Museum of the City of New York. Federal
Art Project, "Changing New York"

implications, as could be seen in a photograph Berenice Abbott took in the same year: *Water Front: From Pier 19, East River* (fig. 7.23). Her camera swept horizontally from foreground to background, taking in railroad refrigerator cars lined up in front of a docked freighter, all framed by the Brooklyn Bridge. The formal play of interlocking machines in the photograph reinforces the impression of an extensive communications network spanning the globe.

The transportation revolution brought about by the railroad after the Civil War continued into the twentieth century with the development of the automobile and then the airplane. If artists of the nineteenth century harbored ambivalent feelings toward the railroad's encroachment upon the American landscape, those of the twentieth century—painters as disparate as Thomas Hart Benton, Reginald Marsh, and Charles Sheeler—openly celebrated its power. Unlike Sheeler's quietly intense focus on a locomotive's wheels or Marsh's restrained profile of an engine barely in repose (fig. 7.25), Benton's mural *Instruments of Power*, 1930

(fig. 7.24), was flamboyant and even melodramatic in projecting an angulated speeding locomotive from an aggregate of energy-producing machines. An inflated rhetoric is barely constrained by a structure oddly abstract for Benton, self-proclaimed spokesman for the virtues of America's rural heartland as opposed to the "decadence" of modern art. Then again, he had not yet left New York for the Midwest, nor could he shake his urban sensibility.[30]

The automobile was another source of power, although Americans preferred to take its power metaphorically by deriving social status from the kind of car they owned. Picabia and later Man Ray each enjoyed having their pictures taken in sleek, open convertibles. As the automobile became more streamlined in the 1930s, America seemed caught in the wreckage of the depression, recorded by Walker Evans in his odyssey with a camera and compiled in *American Photographs* in 1938. The impact of the automobile on the American landscape was second only to the ravages of poverty. These forces were brought together in

7.24 Thomas Hart Benton (1889–1975) *Instruments of Power*. 1930. Distemper and egg tempera on gessoed linen, 7′8″ x 13′4″. Collection The Equitable Life Assurance Society of the United States, New York

7.25 Reginald Marsh *The Locomotive*. 1934. Fresco, 58 × 43¼″. Hirschl & Adler Galleries, Inc.

Auto Dump Vicinity Easton, Pennsylvania, 1936 (fig. 1.7). Lurching ignominiously, ransacked for usable parts, these abandoned cars huddle rusting in a field behind barbed wire.

More than power, automobiles epitomized speed, as was emphasized by the manifestos of the futurists prior to World War I. By appropriating the fragmentations and elisions of cubism, they painted the blur of speeding cars. Americans had seen their first painting of continuous human motion in the manner of Marey's photographs in Duchamp's *Nude Descending a Staircase, No. 2* at the 1913 *Armory Show*. It was Stuart Davis, however, who captured the subtleties of the automobile's conditioning of human perception, as in his *Windshield Mirror* of 1932 (fig. 7.26). The scene is framed by the windshield, but it is not clear if one is looking through the windshield or back through the rearview mirror. Davis offers shifting views and spatial coordinates through the commonplace experience of driving; similarly, in 1933 the poet Hart Crane would call for a depiction of "the familiar gesture of a motorist in the modest act of shifting gears" rather than "the wonderment experienced in watching nose dives."[31]

Despite public excitement over flight, which became frenzied when Lindbergh successfully landed in France in 1927, artists found it difficult to convey the experience of flying—not just its speed or height, but also its "cosmic rhythm" and "intensity," which would best be served by an "abstract vision," as S. MacDonald-Wright claimed in an essay on the "Influence of Aviation on Art." Paintings most often remained earthbound because artists did not have many opportunities to fly. One exception to this visual inertia was achieved in Arshile Gorky's mural sequence *Aviation: Evolution of Forms Under Aerodynamic Limitations* (1935–36), done under the patronage of the Federal Art Project of the WPA for the Newark Airport in New Jersey. In addition to aerial views, which lent themselves to abstraction, a surviving gouache study (fig. 9.10) indicates that Gorky implied motion through a cubist synthesis of cowl, propeller, landing gear, and struts hovering at an angle on a blue field, conveying, in Gorky's words, "the process of soaring into space, and yet with the immobility of suspension."[32]

As American Dada slowly died in the mid-1920s, another European movement infiltrated the consciousness of American artists. Constructivism, an avant-garde movement born in the Soviet Union in response to the Bolshevik Revolution of 1917, was an attempt to embed avant-garde activity in the development of a new socialist society. To achieve such a heroic goal, Soviet artists called for the creative merger of the artist and the engineer in the service of the revolution.

News of the Soviet avant-garde came sporadically to the United States after the revolution. A central role was played by the Russian-American painter Louis Lozowick, who after visiting Moscow in 1924 wrote several articles on the constructivists and encouraged their exhibition in New York.[33] He claimed that an

7.26 Stuart Davis
Windshield Mirror. 1932. Gouache drawing, 15⅛ × 25″. Philadelphia Museum of Art. Given by Mrs. Edith Halpert

entirely new orientation was in store for the artist, who "should devote his organizing, creative facilities to the productive industrial processes and thus relinquish his parasitic existence." Consistent with this doctrine, Lozowick reported that Alexander Rodchenko "gave up the practice of art" for constructivism.[34]

Rodchenko's gesture had a familiar ring; Duchamp had already abandoned the role of artist and declared himself an engineer in 1921. The two acts, however, were widely dissimilar in intent. Duchamp's gesture was primarily Dada, intended to denigrate art even as he subverted the machine. Although his *Large Glass* held to "a mathematical precision and structural logic" that Lozowick ascribed to the constructivists, Duchamp had an ironic penchant for "slightly distending the laws of physics and chemistry."[35] He also preferred to remain independent of all movements, including Dada, and he was always deeply skeptical of political goals. In contrast, constructivism took its rationalism straight, without irony, in the service of a new social order.

Although the need for artists to take social action on a collective basis was recognized in the 1920s by Jane Heap, co-editor of *The Little Review,* the magazine embraced the anarchism of New York Dada at the outset of the decade. Despite the enlistment of Francis Picabia as a foreign editor for a Picabia number featuring his machine drawings in the spring of 1922, the editors of *The Little Review* were not entirely committed to a Dada view of the machine. One sign of an eventual divergence came in a 1922 issue, which illustrated the sculpture of John Storrs, whose skyscraper iconography implied an American parallel to constructivism.

By the 1920s the skyscraper had become a major symbol of the modern, extending even to the design of furniture. While American painters and photographers had taken the skyscraper to heart, it had not been appropriated by sculptors during the years of World War I. A lone precedent was an assemblage entitled *New York 17* by Man Ray (fig. 7.27). Long metal strips, held together at a streamlined angle by a C-clamp attached to a base, foreshadowed Storrs's metal sculptures of the 1920s, which echo the soaring forms of skyscrapers.

Despite his extensive academic training as a sculptor in Paris, Storrs gradually developed an avant-garde attitude toward his work after the war. In a rare statement published in *The Little Review* in 1922, he railed against the embalming policies of museums and asked for an enlightened patronage that would allow American artists the opportunities already available to scientists and engineers. Storrs called for an integration of artists into the commercial structure of American society. "Let the artists create for your public buildings and homes forms that will express the strength and will to power, that poise and simplicity that one begins to see in some of your factories, rolling-mills, elevators and bridges," he urged.[36]

In the early 1920s Storrs had moved away from traditional stone carving and metal casting by fusing new materials into his sculpture. Illustrated in *The Little Review,* his *Panel with Mirror Insets,* 1921, for example, brings together polychromed stone and mirror glass in elegant patterns crafted on a smooth surface (fig. 7.28). While the zig-zag repetitions and intricate geometry look forward to Art Deco motifs, the title calls attention to the materials synthesized into an abstract relief for an architectural project.

Storrs moved between abstraction and representation in his sculpture. The geometry of the machine gave Storrs a basis for abstraction and simplification. Thus the title of *Composition Around Two Voids,* 1932, stressed the spatial and volumetric form of the work, while its stainless steel composition alluded to a world of machines (fig. 7.30). Similarly, *Study in Pure Form (Forms in Space No. 4)* has a title that emphasizes the work's abstract character even as the elongated assemblage of aluminum, bronze, and copper alludes to a setback skyscraper (fig. 7.29). Storrs's works are all the more remarkable because they cast an illusion of monumentality without challenging the actual size of skyscrapers or industrial machines. Because in the final analysis his sculpture existed outside the socialist context of constructivism, Storrs projected an affluent look for the elite of corporate America—an image that would become increasingly evident in the 1930s in such works as Abel Faidy's assemblage of glossy and elegant machine photographs designed for the reception room of Hedrich-Blessing in Chicago (fig. 9.5).

Abandoning the anarchism that had inspired the eclectic *Little Review,* Jean Heap gradually followed the constructivists in outlining new directions for American artists. Because here they could not expect the government support they received in the Soviet Union, artists needed to start at the grass roots. She geared her argument to the American scene, urging the modern artist to "understand group force: he cannot do without it in a democracy." Mere organization was not enough. Rather, the artist "must affiliate with the creative artist in the other arts and with the constructive men of his epoch: engineers, scientists, etc."[37]

What Heap had in mind culminated in the *Machine-Age Exposition,* which opened in New York on May 16, 1927. She located her show in an unpartitioned office space at Steinway Hall, an ordinary commercial building in midtown Manhattan. One reviewer noted with satisfaction the "significant form" of the space, the "white plaster finish of walls, columns, beams, girders and floor slabs" left unpainted and unadorned, in keeping with

7.28

7.27 Man Ray
New York 17. 1966. Chrome-plated bronze and brass and painted brass vise, 17⅜ × 9¼ × 9¼″. Hirshhorn Museum and Sculpture Garden, Smithsonian Institution, Washington, D.C.

7.28 John Storrs (1885–1956)
Panel with Mirror Insets. 1921. Polychromed stone with mirror glass, 26½ × 14⅛ × 2⅞″. Museum of Art, Carnegie Institute, Pittsburgh. Gift of Dr. and Mrs. Sidney S. Kaufman in memory of Mitchell Kaufman

7.29 John Storrs
Study in Pure Form (Forms in Space No. 4). ca. 1924. Stainless steel, copper, and brass, 14½ × 6½ × 3½″ (with base). Collection Munson-Proctor-Williams Institute, Utica, N.Y.

the machines on display. Heap's project further conformed to the tradition of world's fairs in its optimistic tone, predicated upon a belief in progress. (The next world's fair held in Chicago in 1933–34 would be called *A Century of Progress,* and she intimated prophetic insight by "forecasting the life of tomorrow," just as the main theme of the 1939–40 New York World's Fair would be *Building the World of Tomorrow.*)[38]

At the same time, however, her *Machine-Age Exposition* differed in significant ways from previous world's fairs. As Henry Adams noted in his *Education,* the Paris Fair of 1900 classified artifacts into separate exhibits, so that machines were shown in one hall and art in another. Only the engineer Samuel Langley, head

of the Smithsonian, guided Adams to the Great Hall of Machines for a view of modern power. By 1927, however, Heap and a few artists sensed that engineers and artists had to be brought together. Despite her enthusiasm for engineers, she claimed that they worked in isolation, "practically ignorant of all aesthetic laws"; they needed to learn from artists of the "first rank" who were "organizing and transforming the realities of our age into a dynamic beauty." Thus she decided on an exhibition of "actual machines . . . photographs and drawings of machines, plants, constructions, etc., in juxtaposition with architecture, paintings, drawings, sculpture, constructions, and inventions by the most vital of the modern artists."[39]

7.29

Composition Around Two Voids. 1932.
Stainless steel, 20 × 10 × 6″. Whitney
Museum of American Art, New York.
Gift of Monique Storrs Booz

Fernand Léger designed the cover for
the supplementary issue of *The Little Review* which served as a catalogue for the
show. His design conformed to his dictum
that a "beautiful machine...cannot be
copied." He devised instead an elegant
abstraction whose precise, compass-
drawn circles and interlocking geometric
elements offered, in his words, "the
equivalence" of a mechanical object (fig.
7.31). Consonant with Léger's view that
"the machine belongs to the architectural
order,"[40] photographs of skyscrapers,
factories, and industrial sites dominated
the *Machine-Age* catalogue. There were
plans of Russian industrial architecture,
drawings by Hugh Ferriss, and photographs of a Bauhaus studio, domestic
architecture by Walter Gropius, and Ray-

7.31 Fernand Léger (1881–1955)
Cover design, *The Little Review*, May
1927

7.32 Lewis W. Hine
Sadie at Work, Lancaster Cotton Mill.
1908. Gelatin-silver print, 4¾ × 5″. International Museum of Photography at George Eastman House, Rochester, N.Y.

7.33 Margaret Bourke-White
Amoskeag. 1932. Silver print, 5 × 7″ neg. Collection George Arents Research Library, Syracuse University

mond Hood's American Radiator Building (later painted by Georgia O'Keeffe). While there were only a few photographs of machines in isolation, actual machines on display included a Studebaker crankshaft, an I.B.M. time clock, a Curtiss Aeroplane engine, and a Hyde Windlass propeller.

Although only Naum Gabo and Alexander Archipenko were illustrated in the catalogue, visual artists were featured in the exposition itself. An entry for Storrs

was entitled *Sculpture in Metal Design for Clock Tower,* suggesting his desire to encourage public commissions for the artist engaged in the machine age. Demuth submitted a witty canvas entitled *Business,* while Lozowick included his series of American cities painted when he was abroad during the early 1920s. Even though Duchamp and Sheeler did not enter any work, they served on the artists' organizing committee. The exposition also stressed the decorative arts, which were seen as a way for visual artists to have an impact on everyday life.

While the exposition stimulated curiosity about a new Soviet society, the Soviet trade agency in New York considered the "United States as the embodiment of the highest form of industrial development, the most significant illustration of the Machine Age in actual practice." In such a capitalist environment, then, it was no wonder that the *Machine-Age Exposition* was upstaged by the *Exposition of Art in Trade* sponsored by Macy's department store during the first week in May. The popularity of the Macy exhibition was geared to the promise of consumption, what Lewis Mumford had scornfully dismissed as "bonds, Babbitts, installment buying, speculation in necessities of life, and the bourgeois comforts generally.... " Ironically enough, the exposition was itself finally overshadowed by news of Charles Lindbergh's epochal flight across the Atlantic.[41]

The possibilities of a *Machine-Age Exposition* in the hands of the avant-garde were short-lived. By 1929 Jane Heap and Margaret Anderson decided to terminate *The Little Review.* Their loss of faith in collective avant-garde activity seemed borne out by the fate of constructivism, which did not last much longer in the Soviet Union. Lenin and Trotsky had been either indifferent or ambivalent toward avant-garde art, and with the ascendancy of Stalin the Soviet bureaucracy began to withdraw support from the avant-garde. By 1932 the Soviet state actively suppressed avant-garde movements, including constructivism, in favor of socialist realism, which upheld a positive view of socialism visually depicted in representational terms.

American artists could not ignore the political implications of technology. A machine or a machine-made product might be isolated on a pedestal in an art gallery, but it is the result of technology, which is a human resource, a way of modifying one's environment, and hence inseparable from political, social, and economic issues. These implications had been sensed earlier in the century by Lewis Hine, whose photographs were taken with a reformer's eye, with the intent of changing miserable social conditions through government intervention. Photograph after photograph documented young men, women, and children working in textile mills and factories under deplorable circumstances (see fig. 7.32). When in later years Hine decided to record the epic construction of the Empire State Building, he unabashedly celebrated the workers on the site (see fig. 7.34). *Icarus,* "one of the first men to swing out a quarter of a mile above New York City, helping to build a skyscraper," epitomizes the "daring and imagination" of the workers whom the photographer admired.[42]

Against such scenes of human pathos and courage, Margaret Bourke-White's photograph of a textile mill in Amoskeag, New Hampshire, focuses upon the formal qualities of the looms (fig. 7.33). The photograph implies the productive power of American industry without exposing

7.34 Lewis W. Hine
Icarus—atop Empire State—1931. 1931. Gelatin-silver print, 4 × 5″. International Museum of Photography at George Eastman House, Rochester, N.Y.

7.35 Margaret Bourke-White
Ore-Loading, Great Lakes. 1929. Gelatin-silver print, 19⅛ × 13⅛″. Herbert F. Johnson Museum of Art, Cornell University, Ithaca, N.Y. Gift of Margaret Bourke-White and *Life* magazine

the human sacrifices involved. As a young woman with a strong drive for independence, a photographer imbued with the Protestant ethic, she began her career photographing the industrial landscape of Cleveland, exemplified by *Ore-Loading, Great Lakes,* in 1929 (fig. 7.35). Her photographs celebrate the power and formal beauty of American industry, implicitly sanctioning the status quo. The subse-

7.36 Louis Lozowick
Stage setting for *Gas*. 1926. Pen and ink,
brush and ink, tempera, and pencil on pa-
perboard, 19⁵⁄₁₆ × 12³⁄₈″. National Museum of American Art, Smithsonian Institution, Washington, D.C.

quent appearance of her work in *Fortune* during the 1930s did little to change that impression, even though she allied herself with the radical American Artist's Congress in 1935, protesting social and economic conditions.[43]

Among radicals, Louis Lozowick had been one of the driving forces behind the attempt to bring constructivism to America. His turn to the American scene complied with the initial editorial policy of *The New Masses,* which encouraged an indigenous proletarian culture. His interest in constructivism remained permissible because the Soviet bureaucracy still begrudgingly tolerated avant-garde activity. Influenced by El Lissitzky's geometric abstractions, called "prouns" (an acronym for "Projects for the New Art"), Lozowick devised "machine ornaments," which decorated the catalogue for the *Machine-Age Exposition.* Lozowick's machine ornaments, with their semi-representational allusions to machines, were closer visually to Léger's purist images than to the abstract prouns. *Machine Ornament No. 2* (fig. 1.20), for example, is an elegant geometric configuration, suggesting a heavy machine such as a dynamo. By enlarging these drawings, Lozowick could use them as backdrops for theatrical sets, as in a 1926 production of *Gas* (fig. 7.36), an expressionist drama by Georg Kaiser played in Chicago, or for a fashion show by Lord & Taylor the same year.[44]

An increasing Communist hostility toward the avant-garde was signaled by *The New Masses* as early as 1927. The message must have been clear to Lozowick, who came to see the machine ornaments as problematic on other grounds as well. El Lissitzky's prouns were to be "transfer stations" between abstract images and functional design, which would supposedly lead the Soviet Union to a classless society and a culture imbued with the munificence of technology. In the United States, however, Lozowick's machine ornaments could just as easily lead to advertising logos feeding consumer desires. By 1930 he knew that "the great danger of extreme preoccupation with formalism is that it is likely to degenerate into decoration and ornamentation."[45]

By official Soviet doctrine, form was to be placed in the service of a revolutionary message for the proletariat. From that point of view, Arthur G. Dove's *Hand Sewing Machine* of 1927 (fig. 7.37) would have been deplored because it lacked reference to the machine's role in exploiting immigrant labor. Joseph Cornell's collage (*Untitled,* 1932) would have come under similar attack (fig. 7.38); the ominous psychological implications it attached to the stitched image would not have been considered sufficiently forthright, as opposed to Ida Abelman's loosely structured rendition of her father's memories (*My Father Reminisces,* 1937, fig. 7.39), centrally anchored by a sewing machine and replete with political slogans.

Following party directives more closely from the outset was William Gropper, an artist who had satirized the capitalist order for *The Liberator,* a predecessor of *The New Masses.* Thus he poked fun at an inflationary consumer economy geared to

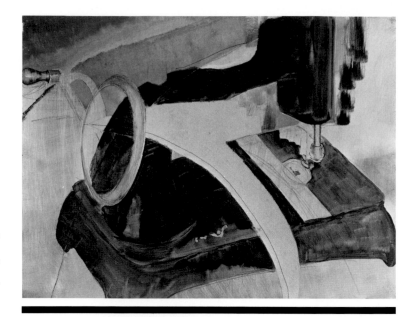

7.37 Arthur G. Dove
Hand Sewing Machine. 1927. Cloth and
paint on metal, 14⅞ × 19¾″. The Metropolitan Museum of Art, New York. Alfred Stieglitz Collection

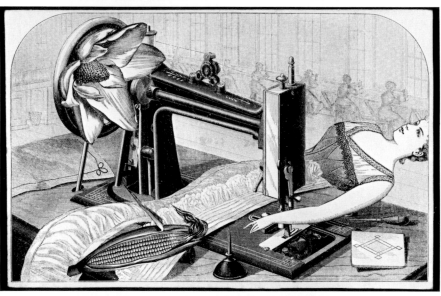

7.38 Joseph Cornell
Untitled. ca 1932. Collage, 5¼ × 8⅛″. Es-
tate of Joseph Cornell. Courtesy Castelli
Feigen Corcoran

7.39 Ida Abelman (b. 1910)
My Father Reminisces. 1937. Lithograph
on paper, 15 × 18¼″. National Museum
of American Art, Smithsonian Institution, Washington, D.C. Transfer from
D.C. Public Library

Work like hell and be happy.

the machine with a cartoon echo of Rube Goldberg. "Work like hell and be happy," runs the caption for an image of a tailor entrapped in a sewing machine and bedeviled by other modern contraptions that efficiently conserve each drop of sweat (fig. 7.40). Here is the efficiency expert Frederick Taylor's "scientific management" with a vengeance.

Goldberg, of course, was famous for his absurd machines. Duchamp had included one of his cartoons in *New York Dada* in 1921 (fig. 7.41). Most likely because of the commercial need to attract a large readership, the cartoonist claimed to be apolitical, though his comic strips often ribbed Americans victimized by their machines.[46] Gropper, however, was capable of probing the dark side of technology with a 1935 cartoon showing an angel of peace hitchhiking alongside a procession of tanks (fig. 7.42).

Facing a crossfire of ideological pressures, Lozowick found himself in an increasingly precarious position because of a need to improvise his radicalism. How could he ignore Soviet antipathy toward an avant-garde emphasis on formal abstraction? "What Should Revolutionary Artists Do Now?" he asked in an article for the December 1930 issue of *The New Masses*. Although a revolution had not yet occurred in the depression-ridden United States, apocalyptic expectations continued to run high. James Rosenberg, for example, envisioned Wall Street on October 29, 1929, the day of the stock-market crash (fig. 7.44): deathlike figures swarm the streets of lower Manhattan, as the skyscrapers threaten to fall, their disintegration a sign of economic entropy rather than a metaphor for energy, as in John Marin's watercolors. As the Depression ground on into 1937, Philip Evergood could paint an *American Tragedy*

7.40 William Gropper (1897–1977) *Work like Hell and Be Happy*. 1922. Cartoon. Reproduced from *The Liberator* (vol. 5, no. 2, 1922, page 8)

7.41 Rube Goldberg (1883–1970) Cartoon from *New York Dada*. 1921. The Alfred Stieglitz Archive in the collection of American Literature, The Beineke Rare Book and Manuscript Library, Yale University, New Haven, Conn.

7.42 William Gropper *Hitchhiker*. 1935. Ink and crayon, 18 × 14″

(fig. 7.43), which dramatized workers and their families in a violent brawl with the police against a backdrop of the closed factory.

Despite catastrophic events, the revolution remained in abeyance. In 1930 Lozowick conceded that radical artists must work within capitalist institutions even while contributing to the revolution-

7.43 Philip Evergood (1901–1973) *American Tragedy*. 1937. Oil on canvas, 29½ × 39½". Private collection

7.44 James Rosenberg (1874–1970) *Dies Irae*. 1929. Lithograph, 13⅞ × 10½". Prints Division, The New York Public Library. Astor, Lenox, and Tilden Foundations

ary movement. Although he granted that caricature was an effective weapon in the class war, he sought "a positive phase" for revolutionary artists. They had to avoid an entrepreneurial individualism catering to the modernistic fashions of capitalism, and offer instead "their services to the working class in its political and economic battles."[47]

In a mural for the Department of the Interior, Gropper again provided an ex-ample by turning from satire to a heroic depiction of American labor at work upon Hoover Dam (fig. 7.46). Here were men dominating their machines on one of the greatest engineering feats of the century. In a similar vein Joe Jones, a young radical painter from Saint Louis, depicted farmers on tractors working their fields (fig. 7.48). Unlike many regionalists—Grant Wood chief among them—who longed for a bucolic past, Jones openly acknowledged the machine in the garden, not as an ominous intruder but as a productive force. (The presence of machine technology in rural areas had been recognized previously by Charles Demuth in *My Egypt* [1927, fig. 2.1], the grain elevators signaling the development of large-scale agribusiness encroaching upon the family farm.)

Lozowick realized that a positive approach did not resolve the question of means. In 1927 he had confidently believed in good constructivist fashion that the delineation of an urban geometry would have universal appeal. By 1931 he pared his universal audience to an urban proletariat. "The American worker inevitably lives and works with cities and machines," he observed.[48] (No wonder,

7.45 Stuart Davis
Swing Landscape. 1938. Oil on canvas,
7'2¾" × 16'5⅛". Indiana University Art
Museum, Bloomington, Ind.

7.46 William Gropper
Construction of the Dam (study for mural, U.S. Department of the Interior). 1937. Oil on canvas, 27⅛ × 87¼″. National Museum of American Art, Smithsonian Institution, Washington, D.C. Transfer from National Park Service

7.47 Ralph Steiner
Portrait of Louis Lozowick. ca. 1930. Gelatin-silver print, 9½ × 7⅝″. The Metropolitan Museum of Art, New York. John B. Turner Fund

then, that Ralph Steiner photographed Lozowick next to giant machinery, with massive gears and screws [fig. 7.47], identifying him, despite suit and tie, as an artist among machines in sympathy with American workers.) Even though abstraction was beyond the pale for the Communist Party, Lozowick was still attracted to formal considerations and saw the need for a balance between avant-garde abstraction and literal transcription.

Tacitly acknowledging the hegemony of American capitalism, Lozowick suggested that the American revolutionary artist should picture the machine environment "more as a prognostication than as a fact," a *projection* of "rationalization and economy which must prove allies of the working class in the building of socialism." In his stress upon the geometry of

the machine—indeed, in his bow toward "the clear cut laconic precision of certain younger artists"—Lozowick approached the anti-art sensibility of Sheeler. Yet he also recommended that revolutionary artists "take liberties with natural appearance whenever their theme requires it" in their quest for "a synthetic style."[49] Thus he underscored the artist's need to build a pictorial reality some years before Sheeler fully grasped such prerogatives.

Lozowick diverged not only from Sheeler, but also from Stuart Davis, who maintained his radical credentials by presiding over the Artists' Union in the 1930s while continuing to develop his own brand of modernism. Davis had intensified his commitment to abstraction in 1927 by nailing an eggbeater to a table as a way of generating pictorial problems for a series of canvases (fig. 2.4). He then turned to the American scene to explore the possibilities of an indigenous American modernism, culminating in a work such as *Swing Landscape,* which he would later call a "colonial cubism" (fig. 7.45).

Lozowick, of course, was engaging in self-description in his *vade mecum* for the revolutionary artist in America. In advocating an urban geometry, he conjured the very forms of his own work. By the 1930s he had moved away from pure abstraction to urbanscapes that included the American worker. In *High Voltage—Cos Cob* (fig 1.9), a canvas of 1930, for example, Lozowick varied the image of an earlier lithograph by adding a worker gazing at the high-voltage electric lines, presumably the product of his labor. Like

7.48 Joe Jones (1909–1963) *Men and Wheat* (mural for U.S. Post Office, Seneca, Kans.). 1940. Oil on canvas, 5 × 12′

Léger before him, Lozowick had switched emphasis from the engineer and the designer to the mechanic working with machines.[50]

Lozowick was not the only American heir of constructivism. During the 1930s, with the rise of a younger generation of American artists, the suppressed Soviet movement left a legacy of abstraction and experimentation with new materials from the industrial order. The political character of constructivism was diluted, however, because Americans had gained a wide range of interrelated European movements from which to choose, from purism and neoplasticism to Bauhaus principles. The situation in America, moreover, was ironic. Abstraction, viewed with deep suspicion by both the Communist Party and a large sector of the American middle class, rather than politics, became the key issue to many young American artists, who lacked exhibition opportunities in an art world still hostile or indifferent to their abstractionism. After some squabbling, they united in an association of American Abstract Artists in 1936 and mounted exhibitions in successive years.[51]

Because these artists had become preoccupied with formal problems, statements in the first *Yearbook* of 1938 took up the aesthetic issues inherent in abstraction, defending its validity, identifying a viable tradition, and explaining its visual presuppositions. *The Yearbook* offered very little in the way of social justification or political vision except in the broadest terms. While constructivist sentiments remained muffled, Rosalind Bengelsdorf acknowledged the "era of science and the machine," claiming that "the machine guided us to a logical combination of simplicity and functionalism. So-called abstract painting is the expression in art of this age."[52] Such passing references were reinforced by the titles of some of the work done by the group. Ilya Bolotowsky, for example, painted a geometric abstraction entitled *Engineer's Dream* (fig. 7.49), while Charles Shaw painted a series of geometric polygonal shapes actually intended to suggest the Manhattan skyline and the setback skyscraper (fig. 7.50). Paul Kelpe was even more explicit in his rendition of *Machine Elements* (fig. 7.51) in 1934.

Among the American Abstract Artists, Ibram Lassaw struggled most persistently with new materials in creating biomorphic forms out of steel and sheet metal (one work involved an electrically lighted shadow box). Exploration of new materials in the constructivist spirit was most extensively undertaken by Charles Biederman, Theodore Roszak, and José de Rivera, three sculptors who were not associated with American Abstract Artists.

7.49 Ilya Bolotowsky
Engineer's Dream. 1930s. Oil on canvas,
38 × 50″. Estate of Ilya Bolotowsky

7.50

7.51 Paul Kelpe (b. 1902) *Machine Elements*. 1934. Oil on canvas, 24 × 24″. The Newark Museum. Charles W. Engelhardt Bequest Fund

Charles Biederman often employed glass and metal within a relief format. In a "New York" series, as in *Work No. 3, New York, 1939* (fig. 7.54), he varied abstract grids within a rectangular frame, echoing Mondrian, whom he had met earlier in Paris.

Roszak constructed objects out of steel, aluminum, and plastic, as well as the more traditional bronze. Working seemingly without effort, he nonetheless left no doubt that these artifacts were *constructed,* with parts carefully machine-tooled and fitted together, as in *Crescent Throat Construction*, 1936, which looks like a drill press (fig. 7.52). Other works, like *Airport Structure*, 1932, resembled futuristic architecture, reflecting his interest in science fiction (fig. 7.53), as did the biomorphic *Chrysalis* (fig. 7.55), which equally resembled a living machine and a Surrealist icon.[53] Just as the sculpture of John Storrs had conformed to the sky-scraper aesthetic of the 1920s, so Roszak shaped his pieces according to the streamlined curves of the 1930s.

Like Roszak, who had owned a tool and die shop in 1932, José de Rivera gained a homegrown knowledge of machines by virtue of an informal apprenticeship as a machinist in Chicago during the late 1920s.[54] *Form Synthesis* of 1930 was his earliest effort in Monel metal, an alloy of nickel, copper, iron, and manganese (fig. 7.56). This highly polished shape has the sleekness of a rocket poised for flight. Despite its monolithic structure, *Form Synthesis* generates a sense of space in its implied motion. In 1938 De Rivera would pursue these possibilities in *Red and Black: Double Element* (fig. 7.57). The curving sheets of polychrome metal resting back to back on a platform are both rectilinear and volumetric, opening and closing, ultimately defining their surrounding space with elegance.

246

7.52 Theodore Roszak (1907–1981)
Crescent Throat Construction. 1936. Sheet
steel, brass, and copper, ht.: 10″. Estate of
Theodore Roszak

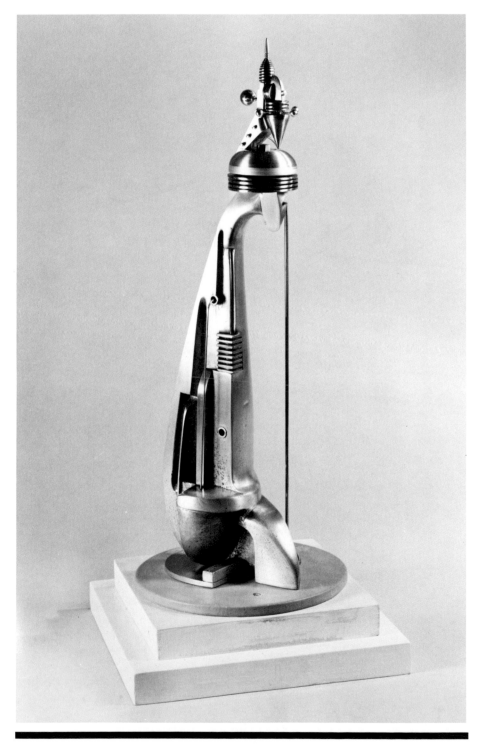

7.53 Theodore Roszak
Airport Structure. 1932. Copper, aluminum, steel, and brass, ht.: 23″. The Newark Museum. Members Fund Purchase

7.54

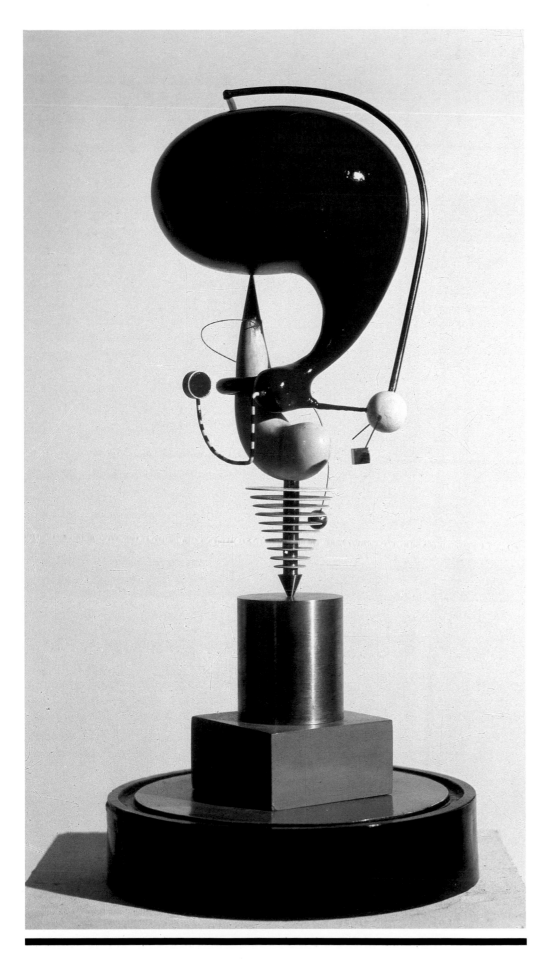

7.54 Charles Biederman (b. 1906)
Work No. 3, New York, 1939. 1939. Painted wood, glass, and metal rods, 32½ × 26¾ × 3¼″. Collection Mr. and Mrs. John P. Anderson

7.55 Theodore Roszak
Chrysalis. 1937. Bronze, steel, and painted wood, ht.: 20″. Collection Sarah J. Roszak

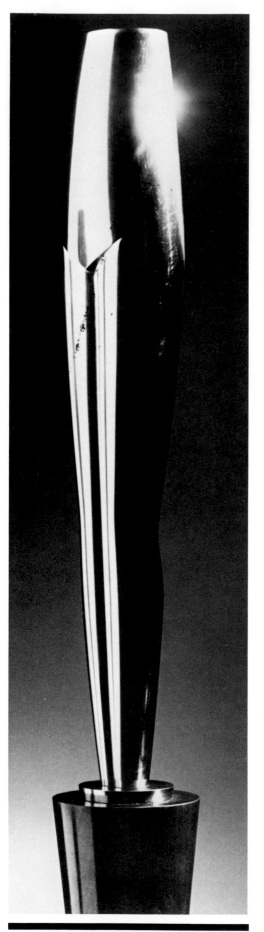

7.56 José de Rivera (1904–1985) *Form Synthesis*. 1930. Monel metal, 18¾″ high. Grace Borgenicht Gallery. Courtesy Mrs. Lita J. de Rivera

Roszak eventually abandoned his constructivist principles on the grounds that productive cooperation between the artist and industry was impossible. He pessimistically concluded that "industry today cannot absorb any genuine esthetic values."[55] While Roszak's disillusionment was precipitated by World War II, the 1939 New York World's Fair (itself a casualty of the war) had earlier indicated the limitations of cooperation in a capitalist society. That the revolutionary possibilities of changing American society would be diluted was disclosed by the role of the industrial designer, who had to find a niche in corporate America in order to work. A large-scale venture like the 1939 New York World's Fair would have been impossible without American business, which provided the material resources for the industrial designer, who in turn conceived the exhibitions and pavilions for the large corporations. It was no accident that the National Cash Register Building, a monumental self-advertisement, rang up daily attendance figures in a prominent display (fig. 7.58). The economic base of the World's Fair was thus a mixed blessing: it generated a blatant commercialism, yet it provided an opportunity for the talents of architects and designers.

The fair also became patron to a broad spectrum of American artists by commissioning work to fit the futuristic theme of the enterprise. Because such commissions were for public display, the mural, which could be integrated with the architecture of the fair, became an appropriate art form. Although murals had often taken political themes during the decade, those chosen for the fair substituted themes of technological progress: hence Ilya Bolotowsky's mural for the Hall of Medical Sciences and Stuart Davis's *History of Communications*. (Only studies of these murals have survived.) The apolitical na-

7.57 José de Rivera
Red and Black: Double Element. 1938.
Painted aluminum, 12 × 18 × 18″. The
Solomon R. Guggenheim Museum, New
York. Gift of Margarete Schultz

7.58 Walter Dorwin Teague
National Cash Register Building. New
York World's Fair. 1939

7.59 Henry Billings (1901–1985) *Ford Mobile Mural* for the New York World's Fair (in process, shown with Billings) 1939. Painted wood and metal, 40 × 70'. The Brooklyn Museum. Gift of Salander O'Reilly Galleries, Inc.

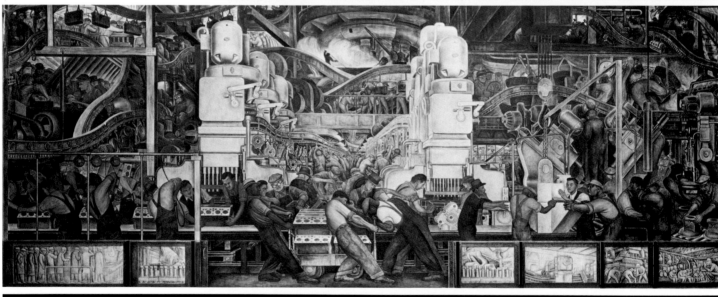

7.60 Diego Rivera (1886–1957) *Detroit Industry, North Wall.* 1933. Fresco, lower panel, 17'8½″ × 45'. The Detroit Institute of Arts. Gift of Edsel B. Ford Fund

ture of the commissioned murals becomes especially evident upon comparing Henry Billings's work for the Ford Building (fig. 7.59) with Diego Rivera's commission for The Detroit Institute of Arts at the start of the decade (fig. 7.60). Despite Billings's credentials as a radical painter, his mural was primarily a complex of abstracted automotive parts, whereas the Mexican muralist's ambitious effort projected a teeming panorama of the River Rouge plant, including laborers, one of whom covertly displays symbols of the Soviet Union.[56]

A positive consequence of the futuristic theme of the New York fair was that avant-garde artists, long ridiculed by the American public, were invited to show their work: Bolotowsky's mural involved biomorphic abstraction while Davis's surface calligraphy created an intricate network of media symbols for the Hall of

7.61 Alexander Calder (1898–1976)
Model for Motorized Outdoor Complex for New York World's Fair. 1938. Painted metal, 14¾ × 19¾ × 9¾". The Pace Gallery

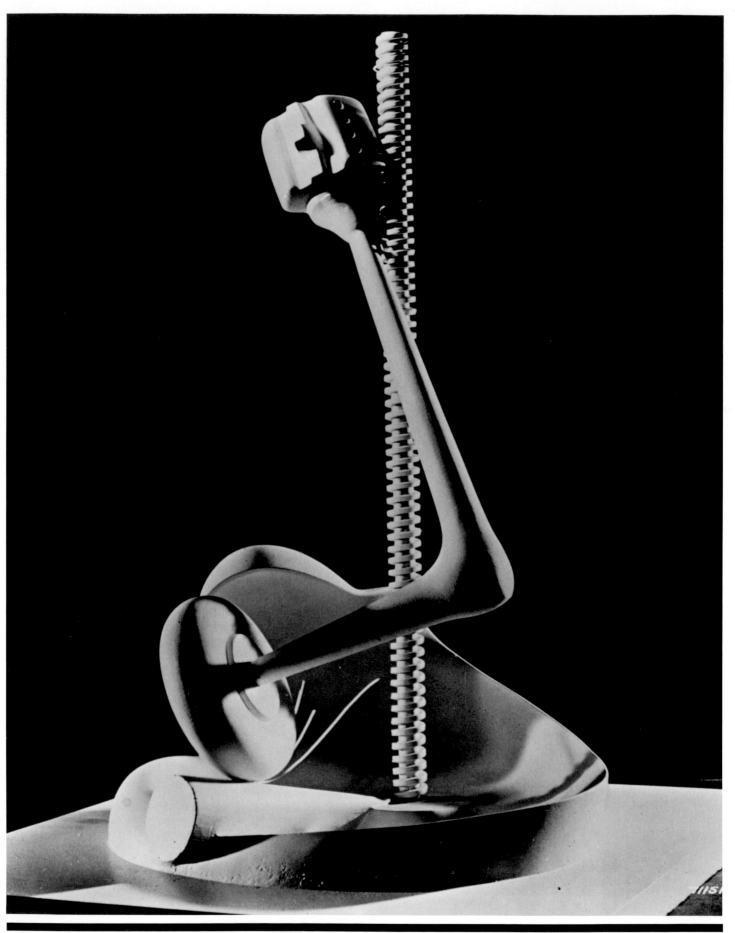

Communications. The fair not only appropriated abstract art but also encouraged artistic innovation with materials. A competition was sponsored by Rohm & Haas, a manufacturer of plexiglass in Philadelphia, and The Museum of Modern Art, the results of which were exhibited in the Hall of Industrial Science, Chemicals, and Plastics.[57]

Critics of the *Machine-Age Exposition* of 1927 had regretted the lack of machines in motion. Genevieve Taggard, for example, suggested that at the very least the show should have included Léger's *Ballet mécanique,* or George Antheil's music played in a darkened room. Another critic went so far as to claim that the visual art looked better on display than did the machines, though he thought they would improve in appearance "on the job," operating in their workplace. He cited Ralph Steiner's photograph of typewriter keys (fig. 2.7) as indicative of how a visual image "can look more dynamic than machinery itself when stationary."[58]

Because of its corporate backing, the 1939 New York World's Fair was able to provide moving exhibits, ranging from machines in operation to entertainment rides. Machine sculpture also gained motion. Henry Billings's mural for the Ford Building was touted by a *Life* feature as "the first three-dimensional mural ever made which actually moves." Of enormous size (forty by seventy feet), the mural was constructed around the image of a Ford V-8 engine, whose operation was seen geared to cosmic forces. (Bearing similar universal implications was Alexander Calder's *Model for Motorized Outdoor Complex for New York World's Fair,* fig. 7.61.) In front of the Ford Building was Isamu Noguchi's magnesite eighteen-foot-tall *Chassis Fountain,* an assemblage of enlarged automobile parts (fig. 7.62). Water cascading down a vertical screw lent the illusion of motion. During World War I the art dealer Robert Coady had referred to machines as "moving sculpture."[59] In less than a quarter-century, American sculpture had caught up with machines.

One of the most popular amusement rides at the 1939 World's Fair was the parachute jump. Yearning for flight, people enjoyed the ascent and fall. With World War II in full swing, the military commandeered the ride to train paratroopers. Hart Crane had caught the risky promise of flight in the opening passage of his magnificent "Proem: To Brooklyn Bridge": "How many dawns," the narrator asks, "chill from his rippling rest / The seagull's wings shall dip and pivot him . . . Then, with inviolate curve, forsake our eyes / As apparitional as sails that cross / Some page of figures to be filed away; / —Till elevators drop us from our day. . . ."[60] The freedom of the bird, soaring through a compressed time, and the cinematic shift from expansive sky and ocean to cramped office space suggest an imagination seeking to mythologize this new machine world.

In 1939 Ralston Crawford optimistically suggested Walt Whitman's open road in *Overseas Highway* (fig. 9.1). In 1940 Clarence Carter depicted a young woman kneeling before the "altar" of a giant steel press in *War Bride,* initially called

7.62 Isamu Noguchi (b. 1904) *Chassis Fountain* (Fountain for Ford Exposition Building, New York World's Fair). 1939. Magnesite, ht.: 18′, dia.: 12′. Original lost

255

7.63 Clarence Carter (b. 1904)
War Bride. 1940. Oil on canvas, 36 × 54″.
Museum of Art, Carnegie Institute, Pittsburgh. Richard M. Scaife American
Painting Fund and Paintings Acquisitions
Fund

"Bride in a Mechanized World" (fig. 7.63). The ominous juxtaposition of a white-gowned bride and the darkly gleaming press looming above her has the surreal quality of a dream, as it indeed was. While teaching painting at the Carnegie Institute of Technology, Carter was invited on a tour of the steel mills: "That night," he recounted, "I dreamed I painted a picture that was very vivid in my mind.... Some of the girls in my Senior painting classes were getting married before the boys would be leaving to go into the coming war. This got mixed into my dream of painting of the steel mill which became the sanctuary."[61] What a strange sanctuary! In one year's time, the infinite stretch of Crawford's open road had reached this dead end. Was technology a force for human growth or destruction?

If the machine were an entirely rational product, such a question might summon a rational, logical answer. Yet Carter, like Crawford, was engaged in myth. Dreams do not require logic, and one need not sleep in order to dream. The machine, then, elicited responses drawn from dreams. Sometimes this occurred openly, as in Joseph Cornell's collage, which echoes a surrealist fondness for "a chance encounter, on a dissecting table, of a sewing machine and an umbrella."[62] This dreamlike quality was no less true of paintings with a severe appearance of rationality—Carter's neat rows of stamped steel sheets or Crawford's precise lines leading to the horizon. The rhetoric of composition and color obscures the need to question where Crawford's highway will lead: the open road is one embodiment of the American Dream. Carter's metallic "sanctuary" barely conceals two flanking gargoyle-like forms, much as the huge central dynamo in Fritz Lang's film classic *Metropolis* changes into a devouring beast in the frenzied imagination of the boss's son.

Even more than Lang's melodramatic vision, the subtle encroachment of machines in everyday life threatened ties with the past by challenging traditional values. American artists approached this problem in a number of ways. There was, first of all, an opportunity to record the mythic imagination as it absorbed the machine. Thus, for example, Edward Hopper included the advertising logo of the now-familiar Mobil flying red horse in his depiction of a lonely roadside gas station (fig. 7.66).[63] The use of Pegasus by a modern corporation suggests one of the ways the impact of radical change was softened by traditional terms.

Another approach was to monumentalize the machine. Gerald Murphy, for example, enlarged and exposed the innards of a pocket watch (fig. 7.1). Its labyrinthian impact is stunning, as we see the mechanism that incessantly regulates our lives in an industrial society—itself become an intricate system. Berenice Abbott also engaged in monumentalization

7.64 Berenice Abbott
Brooklyn Bridge, Water and Dock Streets, Brooklyn. 1936. Gelatin-silver print, 11⅜ × 10″. Museum of the City of New York. Federal Art Project, "Changing New York"

7.65 Berenice Abbott
Manhattan Bridge: Looking Up. 1936. Gelatin-silver print, 19¼ × 15¼″. The Art Institute of Chicago. WPA Art Program

by her angle of vision in photographing the *Manhattan Bridge: Looking Up* (fig. 7.65). Yet she must have realized that having accentuated the aesthetic dimension of the bridge she also isolated it from any past that it might have had. Abbott's project of photographing *Changing New York*, as she entitled her book of photographs, exposed the history of this most modern of cities, whose technology seemed to continually obliterate the past.[64] Thus in another photograph (fig. 7.64), she situated the Brooklyn Bridge between an old warehouse in the foreground and the New York skyline in the back, thereby visualizing the history of technology as it took place in New York.

The Brooklyn Bridge was not the most modern of bridges. Yet it served as a locus of mythmaking for many artists because its heroic history extended back to the nineteenth century. (Hart Crane thought that it could metaphorically bridge past and present.) John Marin was the first to paint it, prior to World War I. With World War II impending, Louis Guglielmi detonated the Brooklyn Bridge in a nightmare image of death and destruction (fig. 7.67). It was Joseph Stella, however, who engaged in the most extensive mythic re-creation of the Brooklyn Bridge, overflowing from successive paintings to prose, often poetic statements accompanying his vision of technology. Stella's project matched that of Crane, who spent his life as a poet attempting to transform the Brooklyn Bridge into a symbol that might bear the deepest cultural aspirations and values of Americans. (After failing to obtain illustrations from Stella, Crane used the photographs of Walker Evans for his first edition of *The Bridge*.)[65]

258

7.66 Edward Hopper (1882–1967)
Gas. 1940. Oil on canvas, 26¼ × 40¼″.
The Museum of Modern Art, New York.
Mrs. Simon Guggenheim Fund

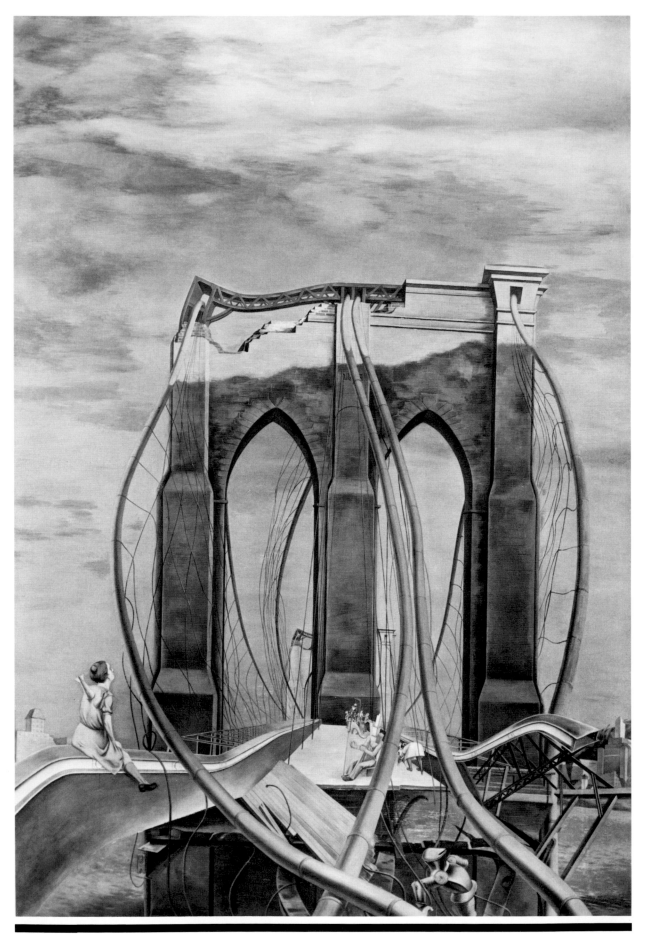

7.67

Stella painted different versions of the Brooklyn Bridge between the two world wars. His first painting captured the shimmering surfaces of the bridge, lifting the viewer into its heights and down into the depths of its brilliant center cast as a diamond. Subsequent versions were less cubistic and more linear if not schematic in appearance. His most ambitious project involved five panels entitled *The Voice of the City of New York Interpreted* (fig. 7.68), begun in 1920 and finished in 1922. Stella deployed an urban iconography, ranging from the outer panels of the Port of New York and the Brooklyn Bridge to the "Great White Way" of Broadway flanking a central panel of skyscrapers. Comprising Stella's *summa,* the hieratic composition of this polyptych took on the coloration of stained-glass windows in an attempt to translate secular achievement into religious terms.

Stella expressed his mythic quest with an extravagance of sexual and religious metaphors, which he intensely experienced as a mode of knowledge.[66] In a similar fashion, Carter's dream mixed his female art students with machines, and machines with the act of painting, itself a way of creating meaning. The cognitive powers of art had been acknowledged earlier in the century by Henry Adams after his profoundly disturbing experiences at Paris in 1900. Overwhelmed by the huge dynamos on view in the Hall of Machines, Adams wrote, "the pen becomes a sort of blind-man's dog, to keep him from falling into the gutters." Yet he understood that the force of the dynamos was a transmogrification of the spiritual force of the Roman Catholic Virgin, herself a purified symbol of pagan sexual powers. Calling Diana of the Ephesians an "animated dynamo," Adams saw the dynamo itself as "an occult mechanism," with its own sexual energy.[67]

Although Adams claimed that "all the steam in the world could not, like the Virgin, build Chartres," he knew nonetheless that American artists would remain hopelessly outdated unless they came to terms with the machine. In 1911 Duchamp also sensed obsolescence at the annual Parisian *Salon d'Aviation.* Increasingly agitated by the motors and propellers on display, he turned to Brancusi and declared: "Painting is finished. Who can do anything better than this propeller? Can you?" First responding with his ready-mades, Duchamp then turned to the construction of his *Large Glass,* which bound up sexual and religious motifs no less ambiguously than had Adams in his chapter on the dynamo and the Virgin in the *Education.*[68]

The insights of Duchamp and Adams rallied many American artists during the 1920s and 1930s around the prime cultural images of the dynamo and the Virgin in their perceptions of the sexual and religious implications of the machine. An early precedent was set by Francis Pica-

7.67 O. Louis Guglielmi (1906–1956) *Mental Geography.* 1938. Oil on panel, 35¾ × 24″. Collection Mr. and Mrs. Barney A. Ebsworth

7.68 Joseph Stella
The Voice of the City of New York Interpreted. 1920–22. Oil and tempera on canvas, five panels; side panels each 88½ × 54″; center panel 99¾ × 54″. The Newark Museum. Felix Fuld Bequest Fund Purchase, 1937

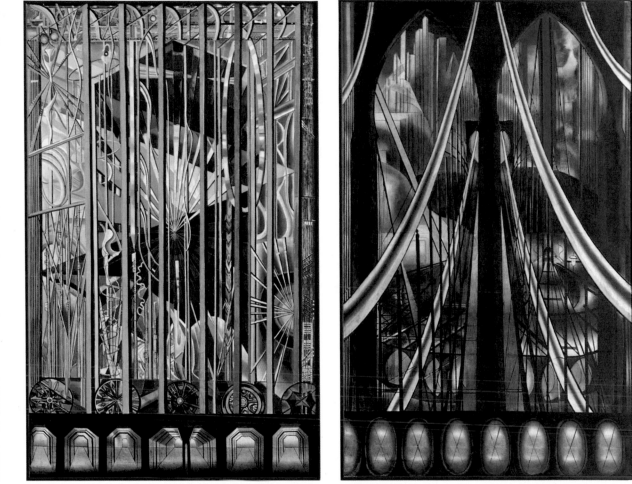

7.69 Isamu Noguchi
One Thousand Horsepower Heart. ca.
1938. Painted plaster. Original lost

7.70 Alfred Stieglitz
Georgia O'Keeffe. 1933. Palladium print,
9½ × 7¾". The Metropolitan Museum of
Art, New York. On loan from the Collection of Georgia O'Keeffe

bia's machine portrait of *A Young American Girl in a State of Nudity,* a precise linear drawing of a spark plug bearing the trademark "Forever." With its echo of Duchamp's attribution of a "desire-magneto" to the Bride, this conflation of electric and sexual energy subverted Adams's prediction that "an American Venus would never dare exist."[69]

During the 1920s sexual images proliferated in great variety. By exaggerating his larger-than-life female figures, Gaston Lachaise cast a *Dynamo Mother* in the image of Adams's "animated dynamo," exceeding the sole requirement that she be "fecund."[70] Such blatant sexuality was muted by the witty eroticism of Demuth's work or the elegant display of Georgia O'Keeffe's arm photographed against the polished hubcap of her 1932 Ford V-8 (fig. 7.70). The permutations of sexuality and technology were but a metonym for anthropomorphic machines. If Hine could lend his photograph of a worker inside a turbine the title *Heart of the Turbine* (fig. 7.72), Noguchi imagined a *One Thousand Horsepower Heart* (fig. 7.69), the human organ itself mechanized. The resonance of the machine metaphor was such that vehicle and tenor were interchangeable: machines could assume human identity just as human beings could be mechanized.

In 1922 Paul Strand's acknowledgment of the machine as the "new God" simply ratified the religious implications of previous work like Schamberg's witty assemblage of plumbing parts and looked forward to Joseph Stella's icons, among others. Noguchi offered a modern version of Haniwa pre-Buddhist figures he had been drawn to in Japan with an aluminum *Miss Expanding Universe* (fig. 7.71) (named by his close friend Buckminster Fuller), soaring with expansive benedic-

7.71 Isamu Noguchi
Miss Expanding Universe. 1931. Aluminum, 40⅞ × 34⅞″. The Toledo Museum of Art, Toledo, Ohio. Museum Purchase Fund

tion.[71] For good measure Hine subtitled his *Heart of the Turbine* "Worker at His Shrine." The photographer's religious metaphor went beyond Adams's ambiguities to an affirmation of American labor and the machine. The positive implications of such mythologizing were most clearly identified with Sheeler's work. Sheeler himself photographed not only the Ford plant at the Rouge but also the Cathedral at Chartres during the 1920s. His Ford photographs appeared in the magazine *transition* under the caption of the "industrial mythos." In 1932 Sheeler was described as the "Fra Angelico among contemporary painters" in renouncing "the symbolism of the Virgin for that of the dynamo": "His work has the same ascetic, faithful approach to the forms and masses of industrialism as had the Florentine monk toward the religious imagery of his day."[72]

The mythmaking inherent in the dynamo and the Virgin, the desire to sustain vestiges of traditional meaning in the face

7.72 Lewis W. Hine
Heart of the Turbine. 1930. Gelatin-silver print, 4¾ × 6⅞″. International Museum of Photography at George Eastman House, Rochester, N.Y.

of discontinuity, has persisted through Clarence Carter's *War Bride* to the present. But even at the height of such mythologizing, there were undercurrents of skepticism. In reviewing MacKnight Black's *Machinery*, Edward Dahlberg sardonically asked, "Are Dynamos Bosoms?" Such machine metaphors, he thought, belonged on the "literary junk yard."[73]

Dahlberg's rejection, though harsh, was based on the same presupposition underlying a "postscript" to a series of arti-

7.73

7.74 A. Stirling Calder (1870–1945) *Fountain of Energy, Equestrian Group.* 1915. Artificial travertine. For *Panama-Pacific International Exhibition,* San Francisco. Destroyed

cles on Henry Adams written by the young poet Louis Zukofsky for *Hound and Horn* in 1930. In his postscript "Beginning Again with William Carlos Williams," Zukofsky implicitly called for an artist who could live with ease in a world of machines and accept their reality without the need to mythologize. Within Adams's terms, the artist must accept the multiplicity of the dynamo in place of the unity of the Virgin. Zukofsky had Williams in mind. The older poet and doctor moved readily among the industrial wastes of New Jersey, treating his poor patients in Paterson and then making quick trips into Manhattan to catch the most recent avant-garde event. During World War I, on his way to visit Marsden Hartley at his studio, he heard sirens and quickly jotted down "The Great Figure," on "a red / firetruck / moving / tense . . . through the dark city." A decade later, Charles Demuth turned the poem into a "poster portrait" of his friend. *I Saw The Figure Five in Gold* (fig. 7.73) magnificently locates the poet in the urban landscape, a labyrinthian welter of skyscrapers and flashing signs, the most prominent being the "figure five" of the fire engine moving through the streets.[74]

Against Demuth's vibrant portrait of the poet at one with the machine, Williams later wrote a "Sketch for a Portrait of Henry Ford," depicting him as "a tin bucket" full of "heavy sludge" and "steel grit." The dented bucket swung round at increasing speed, its handle suddenly "gives / way and the bucket / is propelled through / space. . . ."[75] The precise use of language image recalls Picabia's machine portraits in rejecting overt allegory so that the image resides complete in itself. The laconic statement of an impending disaster suggests Williams's capacity to live with the chaos of multiplicity.

The promise of technology was fulfilled, however, by another artist living comfortably among machines in a world beyond Adams. It was Alexander Calder, born into a family of sculptors, who decisively parted from the outmoded attitudes of a previous generation, represented by his father's contorted allegorical figures so prominent at the 1915 *Panama-Pacific International Exposition* in San Francisco. The elder Calder's

7.73 Charles Demuth *I Saw the Figure Five in Gold.* 1928. Oil on composition board, 36 × 29¾". The Metropolitan Museum of Art, New York. The Alfred Stieglitz Collection

7.75 Alexander Calder
A Universe. 1934. Motor-driven mobile: painted iron pipe, wire, and wood with string, ht.: 40½″. The Museum of Modern Art, New York. Gift of Abby Aldrich Rockefeller

7.76 Alexander Calder
Praying Mantis. 1936. Painted wood, rod, and wire, ht.: 78″. Wadsworth Atheneum, Hartford, Conn. The Henry and Walter Keney Fund

statuary symbolizing electricity and other scientific discoveries inadequately conveyed the new world at hand (see fig. 7.74). Standing in a long American tradition of tinkerers, his son was able to conceive of sculpture that actually moved, creating a complex motorized *Universe* (fig. 7.75) in 1934 or a *Praying Mantis* (fig. 7.76) swaying in metal and wire in 1936.

Certainly Calder's debts to surrealism and constructivism, not to mention Mondrian and Duchamp, should not be denied. Biomorphic shapes, constructed forms, the concept of kinetic art—such cross-fertilization with the European avant-garde occurred during Calder's stay

in Paris during the late 1920s. Such a beginning in Europe was ambiguous, as it would be for any American, because Europe was the origin necessarily acknowledged for the promise of a new American culture. Beginnings and endings thus came full circle in Calder, who astonished the Parisians with his marvelous wire figures and the play of his circus, having grown up from his childhood tinkering with wire shapes and making toys for his family and friends.[76] Culminating in the mobile, these forms are such that they no longer signal their machine origins. In returning to nature, technology became the natural once again in Calder's work.

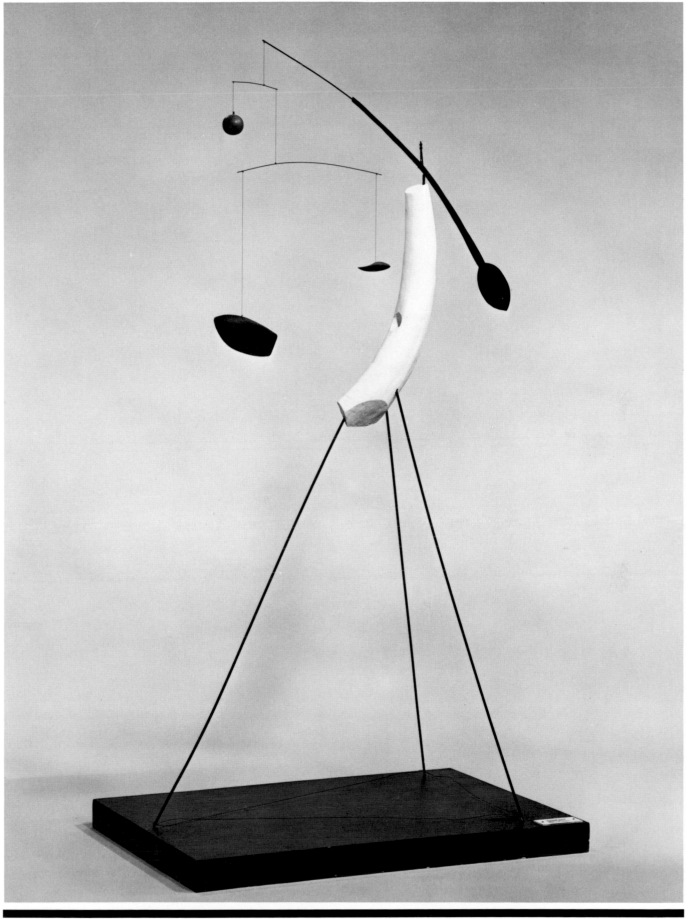

7.76

8.1

CHAPTER 8

DESIGN FOR
THE MACHINE

The 1920s and 1930s are usually seen as a unit—the years between the two great wars—even though there were obvious differences. Although the machine was the major motivating force throughout the period, the approaches and reactions to it changed from decade to decade, and so too did the art evolve. The 1920s was a decade of transition, dislocation, hope, and fear. There was an uneasiness in the air, a restlessness, but also an exuberance, expressed in the art of the period with its zig-zags, lightning bolts, cubist and geometric designs, verticality, and stepped contours. The gates from the executive office of the Chanin Building reflect, perhaps as well as any object, the agitation, energy, sense of motion and speed, and the power of the machine—albeit the whole resting somewhat precariously on narrow stacks of coins (fig. 8.1). In retrospect, they can be seen as a prophetic statement of things to come.

But the bubble, a popular decorative motif of the 1920s, was about to burst. With the devastating effects of the Depression, existing insecurities dissolved into a general disillusionment. Yet at the same time this crisis created a national unity of purpose, a need to find a way to assuage the ensuing panic. A feeling emerged that if everyone pulled together, with the help of the machine behind them, a better tomorrow could be achieved. From this unity of response developed values, beliefs, and symbols that became identified as uniquely American. Streamlining, with its sense of speed, became the symbol of the decade (see fig. 8.2). Emphasis shifted from the vertical to the horizontal, accentuated by parallel lines. Cubist, jagged-stepped outlines were replaced by smooth and rounded corners more conducive to the conservative and consolidating mood of the 1930s.[1]

The machine age in America was ultimately the product of business and the middle class. Americans clung tenaciously to their potpourri of historical styles—and, in fact, still do. After World War I, however, new motivating forces were at work. The old traditions continued, but like it or not the world was changing. The areas most resistant to change were the home and its appurtenances. As is usual, progressive experimentation was initiated by painters and sculptors. Architects followed closely behind, with the skyscraper and factory finally achieving their full-blown twentieth-century form. It should

8.1 Rene Chambellan (1893–1955), designer, with Chanin Co. Architectural Department
Entrance gates to the Executive Suite, 52nd floor, Chanin Building. New York. 1928. Wrought iron and bronze

8.2 Henry Dreyfuss (1904–1972) Thermos Pitcher and Tray. 1935. Manufactured by American Thermos Bottle Co., Norwich, Conn. Aluminum, steel, glass, and rubber, ht. of thermos: 7¼"; base dia.: 5¼". The Brooklyn Museum. Gift of Paul F. Walter

8.3 Vase. ca. 1930. Designer and manufacturer unknown. Mold-blown glass, 11¾ × 6 × 4". Collection Eric Brill

not be a surprise that the last holdout was the domestic structure. In a rapidly changing world the home was the last bastion of stability and continued traditions. Still, Americans could not resist improvements made in the design and function of new appliances. Modern design sneaked into the home by way of the back door, through the garage, the kitchen, and the bathroom, without much notice or resistance (see fig. 8.4).

The term decorative arts has never been totally satisfactory, although no one has come up with a better name for the applied arts—furniture, silver, ceramics, glass, metalwares, costumes, textiles, and jewelry. The meaning in the twentieth century has expanded to include many different kinds of objects. With the advent of electricity and other technological developments, a whole host of new machines and forms evolved. Furthermore, they were often made out of materials that had never before been considered in artistic terms. A perfect example is the radio. In the 1920s it was housed in wood, period-reproduction cabinets; there was uncertainty as to whether this new communication wonder should be disguised as a piece of traditional furniture or exposed as a new modern machine with a grace and beauty of its own. Gradually, as technology evolved in the 1930s and the size of the chassis became smaller, manufacturers found the courage, due to financial pressures, to design cases that more closely conformed to the radio's function and were cheaper to produce.[2] Plastic became a popular medium for the cases.

To get around the problem of what should be considered a decorative art in the twentieth century, many historians and curators lump everything under the rubric "design." The point is that any use-

8.4 Kraetsch and Kraetsch Kitchen, Butler House. Des Moines, Iowa. 1936

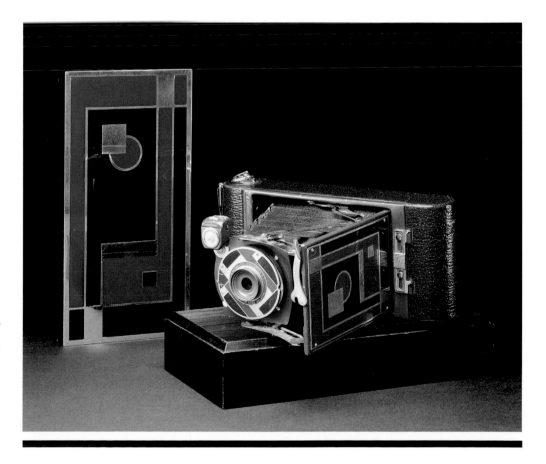

8.5 Walter Dorwin Teague Camera and Box (model no. 1A Gift Camera). 1930. Manufactured by Eastman Kodak Co., Rochester, N.Y. Camera: Chrome-plated and enameled metal, leather, and paper, 3½ × 8 × 6½″. Box: Wood, enameled and inlaid with metal, 2⅜ × 8⅞ × 4⅜″. The Brooklyn Museum. H. Randolph Lever Fund

8.6 Walter Dorwin Teague Vase. ca. 1930. Manufactured by Corning Glass Works, Steuben Division, Corning, N.Y. Blown glass, acid etched and engraved, ht.: 6½″; dia.: 7½″. Collection Inglett-Watson & Ken Forster

ful object that displays a beauty of line and form can fall under the definition of decorative arts. A study of the decorative arts of the period reinforces the argument that there was a motivating force that had a major impact on all aspects of our culture. One cannot look at the Sears radio (fig. 8.7) and the Electrolux vacuum cleaner (fig. 8.8) without realizing that they were made at the same time, and that there was a strong family resemblance among all the progressive arts of the 1920s and 1930s.

The impact of the machine, of course, is not exclusive to the twentieth century, nor to America for that matter. Throughout the nineteenth century, Americans loved to simplify and standardize machines. There was even an appreciation of the machine's physical beauty. Europeans had always admired American efficiency and resourcefulness. It was noted that where "Americans consciously sought to produce beauty . . . they had signally failed. Where they had succeeded—unconsciously—was in the field of applied science." Oscar Wilde, after a visit to America in 1883, commented that:

> There is no country in the world . . . where machinery is so lovely as in America. I have always wished to believe that the line of strength and the line of beauty are one. That wish was realized when I contemplated American machinery. It was not until I had seen the waterworks at Chicago that I realized the wonders of machinery; the rise and fall of the steel rods, the symmetrical motion of great wheels is the most beautifully rhythmic thing I have ever seen.[3]

There are two major differences between the American Industrial Revolution in the nineteenth century and the twentieth-century machine age: the rapidity and magnitude of the changes wrought by the machine in the 1920s and 1930s; and the use of the machine to produce objects that did not imitate designs of the past. The machine was criticized through most of the nineteenth century

8.7 Clarence Karstadt "Silvertone" Radio (model 6110). 1938. Manufactured by Sears, Roebuck and Co., Chicago. Plastic housing, 6½ × 11¾ × 6½". Collection Eric Brill

for producing inferior imitations of hand-made objects. It often seemed impossible that a standard of aesthetics could ever be applied to anything made by the machine. This was essentially true as long as we relied on historical styles for our inspiration and believed that "beauty could be revived only by reviving the handicraft tradition."[4] Charles R. Richards, the director of the American Association of Museums in 1924, perfectly summed up the state of the decorative arts in the early 1920s:

> As a nation we are artistically immature. We have always been dependent for our artistic culture on the older art of Europe.... We are not yet ready for any considerable excursion into the untried. This, however, will not always be so. As a country we grow rapidly. Some day we shall come of age artistically and then we can expect expression in the field of industrial art comparable to what we already have achieved in architecture and the scenic art of the stage.

Richards went on to bemoan the fact "that we are so inclined to look on the field of applied art as a branch of human activity in which creative achievement is finished and to decry the possibility of any

new avenues of expression. We hold no similar attitude toward painting or sculpture, nor toward poetry or music. Why is it that in this particular field only the old is sacrosanct?"[5]

Americans isolated themselves from the various progressive design movements that had been developing in Europe since around 1900. Lack of cultural confidence prevented them from responding to avant-garde art. Not convinced they had a culture, Americans looked to the past, whether it was their own or European. The American Arts and Crafts movement is often credited with being our first attempt at modernism. It is true that the furniture of Gustav Stickley and others like him introduced the idea of simple, unadorned design;

8.8 Lurelle Guild (b. 1898) Vacuum Cleaner (model 30). 1937. Manufactured by Electrolux Corp., Dover, Del. Chrome-plated, polished, and enameled steel, cast aluminum, vinyl, and rubber, 8½ × 23 × 7¾". The Brooklyn Museum. Gift of Fifty-50

8.10

Unfortunately, the American Designers' Gallery, like so many other arts organizations, could not survive the crushing blow of the Depression.

Throughout these early experimental years there was confusion, enthusiasm, and abhorrence for the many guises of modern art. In 1928 an editorial writer in *The New Republic* noted:

There are signs, here and there, of a panicky attempt to be modern; and the result is what might be expected. Instead of arriving experimentally at modern designs, by a steady adaptation of traditional forms to new taste and needs, as the European craftsmen have done, the American manufacturer, having lost the power of fresh design by his years of silly imitation, exercises neither restraint nor imagination in honestly facing his new problems.... It makes people of taste think that all modern design is a bad joke; and, when it becomes a laughing-stock, it makes other manufacturers confirmed in their utter dependence upon copycatting the designs of the past. But our manufacturers apparently know no middle term between monastic sterility and an imperial orgy; and the fact is, one alternative is just as ridiculous as the other.[24]

It is not surprising that in the late 1920s and the 1930s American experiments with modern design appear in a confusing array of different styles. Even though there had been important developments and exhibitions in America of European avant-garde painting and sculpture (such as the *Armory Show* of 1913), Americans, for the most part, had no previous experience with the various European avant-garde movements. Furthermore, a schism in this country had developed between the fine and decorative arts during the first two decades of this century. During the last quarter of the nineteenth century, there had been a conscious collaboration between architect, painter, sculptor, and artisan in America and Europe; in this atmosphere the division between major and "minor" arts became less distinct. This interrelationship of the arts was continued and strengthened in Europe through various modern movements such as the Wiener Werkstätte, the German Werkbund and Bauhaus, Dutch de Stijl, French purism, and Russian constructivism. In America, however, collaboration of the arts was essentially sustained by artists making expensive, one-of-a-kind, handmade objects. After World War I, only a few could afford these luxuries. The decorative arts fell into a deep sleep of ignorance where machine-made copies of previous styles and periods reigned supreme.

It took a period of time to sort through, digest, and integrate the new progressive expressions, and ultimately to develop an expression that suited American taste and life-styles. Some contemporary commentators were aware of both the difficulties and the excitement of living through an age of transition:

Much silly work has been produced and there has been much aesthetic "wastage," though it may be pointed out that this experimental period exactly corresponds to the present experimental state of science, of politics, and indeed, of social existence. And yet it is a marvelous period in which to live. There is a certain amount of disorder which is inseparable from the creation of new things: but there is a romance in the present day, both in its life and art for which there is hardly any parallel in the past.[25]

8.10 Ilonka Karasz (1896–1981) Rug. ca. 1928. Cotton warp, wool weft, 107 × 109½". The Metropolitan Museum of Art, New York. Gift of Theodore R. Gamble, Jr., in honor of his mother, Mrs. Theodore Robert Gamble

PAUL T. FRANKL   **NEW YORK CITY**

8.17 Paul T. Frankl
Page from *Form and Re-Form* (New York: Harper and Brothers, 1930)

genta, or a vivid purple become merely rich and striking when toned down with surroundings of dull silver."[37] Metallic lusters became an important decorative device; the illusion of space was created by using mirrors. The skyscraper became such an important symbol of America's originality and prowess that the form appeared in almost every medium from a lowly scale (fig. 8.20) to a sophisticated silver tea service (fig. 8.18). The setback also became a popular decorative device, as seen in a silver-plated mirror and brush set from 1928 (fig. 8.19).

The frenzied energy and vivaciousness of New York was also expressed in many different ways and in many different me-

diums. Ruth Reeves, one of the leading modern textile artists of the period, designed the pattern "Manhattan" (fig. 8.24), one of twenty-nine textile designs commissioned by W. & J. Sloane in 1930. "Manhattan" captured the hustle and bustle of the city, incorporating what were becoming recognized as American symbols—skyscrapers, factories, airplanes, boats, trains, automobiles, and bridges. This fairly literal representation, block-printed on cotton, was to be used for curtains or wallcoverings. In contrast, the pattern of an elegant silk and mink evening wrap abstracted both the setback skyscraper and the sense of motion (fig. 8.23). Viktor Schreckengost captured the excitement of New Year's Eve in New York in a glazed porcelain punch bowl depicting skyscrapers, boats, and cocktail glasses (fig. 8.25).

A painting entitled *Rhapsody in Blue* equates the frenzy of life in New York with the syncopated rhythms of jazz— both are seen as symbols of a new American age. This painting was used as an ad for Steinway pianos (fig. 8.26); an accompanying blurb stated that "In any discussion of the future of American music, George Gershwin's 'Rhapsody in Blue' sooner or later becomes the center of controversy. Many believe it to be the first significant departure in the establishment of a native school of composition. Certainly, it is among the most ambitious and successful of all experiments in the American idiom."[38]

As early as 1925 an article in *The Decorative Furnisher* made the connection between jazz music, jazz pictures, jazz clothes, and jazz decorations. "Jazz is, as to music, 'a medley of sounds,' and, as to costume and decoration, 'a medley of color and of design.' A few scattered notes would make the definition a 'riot' of

8.18 Louis W. Rice
"Skyscraper" Tea Service. 1928. Manufactured by Bernard Rice's Sons, Inc., New York, as part of their "Apollo Studio" line. Silver-plated metal, teapot ht.: 6½"; sugar ht.: 4½"; creamer ht.: 4⅞". Collection John P. Axelrod

8.19 Louis W. Rice
Brush and Mirror. 1928. Manufactured by Bernard Rice's Sons, Inc., New York, as part of their "Apollo Studio" line. Silver-plated metal, brush length: 10¼"; mirror length: 15". Historical Design Collection, Inc.

8.20 Joseph Sinel (1889–1975)
Scale. 1929. Manufactured by International Ticket Scale Corp., New York. Chrome-plated and painted metal and glass, 77 × 15 × 25". Wolfson Collection

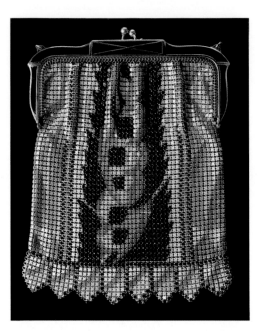

8.21 Handbag. ca. 1925. Manufactured by Whiting and Davis, Co., Inc., Plainville, Mass. Metal mesh, 7 × 5⅛ × ¼″. The Brooklyn Museum. Gift of Dr. Annella Brown

8.22 Evening Slippers. ca. 1925. Manufactured by Bob, Inc. Leather with stones. The Metropolitan Museum of Art, New York. Gift of Mrs. R. C. Jacobsen

8.23 Evening Wrap. ca. 1928. Designer and manufacturer unknown. Silk and mink. The Metropolitan Museum of Art, New York. Gift of the Fashion Group, Inc.

8.23

8.24 Ruth Reeves (1892–1966) Textile, "Manhattan" Pattern. 1930. Manufactured by W. and J. Sloane, New York. Block-printed cotton, 80¼ × 35⅛". Collection John P. Axelrod

8.25 Viktor Schreckengost (b. 1906) Punch Bowl. 1931. Manufactured by Cowan Pottery, Rocky River, Ohio. Porcelain, ht.: 11¾″; rim dia.: 16⅝″. Cooper-Hewitt Museum, the Smithsonian Institution's Museum of Design, New York. Gift of Mrs. Homer D. Kripke

8.26 Earl Horter (1885–1940) Illustration for Steinway Piano Advertisement. 1928. From *House & Garden* (March 1928)

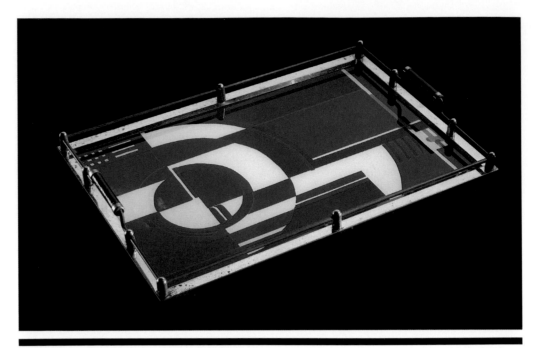

8.27 Tray. ca. 1935. Designer and manufacturer unknown. Chrome-plated metal, reverse-painted glass, and painted wood, 1½ × 12 × 18″. Collection Charles Senseman

8.28 Beach Umbrellas from Troy Sunshade Products catalogue. 1929. Troy Historical Society and Troy Miami County Public Library, Troy, Ohio

8.29 Illustrations of Fabric Samples from Troy Sunshade Products catalogue. 1929. Troy Historical Society and Troy Miami County Public Library, Troy, Ohio

TROYSCO FABRICS
HAND APPLIED DESIGNS ON RADIANT CLOTH
Width 27 in. Per Yard $1.50

No. 7302 BLACK (Throw*) No. 7304 Black (Teary*) No. 7306 BLACK (Teens*) No. 7500 TROPICAL ORANGE (Truth*) No. 7505 TROPICAL ORANGE (Tenet*)

No. 7604 BLUE (Towed*) No. 7609 BLUE (Tuque*) No. 7705 GREY (Tense*) No. 7709 GREY (Tench*)

sounds or a 'riot' of color."[39] These abstracted expressions of excitement, exploration, and nervousness found their way into all aspects of life, from a painting to a pair of shoes (fig. 8.22) and a metal mesh evening purse (fig. 8.21). The new trend of strong colors, "weird designs and brevity of materials" in women's fashion was related to so-called jazz decoration, which Hollywood had been promoting in the movies.[40]

A mistaken impression is that the palette of this period was essentially red, white, black, and silver. They were popular colors, but as can be seen from the 1929 Troy Sunshade Products catalogue, there was a dizzying array of color and pattern choices; even the lowly beach umbrella was decked out in the latest Parisian fashion (see figs. 8.28, 8.29). In *Fortune* magazine's first issue in February 1930, a long article on "Color in Industry" indicated that since 1925 there had been a big change in the use of color, particularly for objects that never had color before—cars, beds, bathroom fixtures, toilet paper, appliances. Paint manufacturers such as E. I. duPont de Nemours developed quick-drying lacquers, which were increasingly used to decorate furniture.[41] The same article claimed: "Nearly everyone likes bright colors. And, in this post-war period of broken precedents, of weakened traditions, it is not surprising that old chromatic inhibitions should be shaken off, and that the American people should gratify its instinct for color by bathing itself in a torrent of brilliant hues."[42]

This effervescent, jazz-age spirit was expressed in many different ways. Cubism, a style borrowed from contemporary French painting and sculpture, perfectly expressed this mood of restlessness and exploration. As usual, Americans were not interested in the style's intellectual theories, but in its decorative shapes. Erik Magnussen, a Danish silversmith who worked for the Gorham Manufacturing Company from 1925 until 1929, designed a remarkable three-piece silver cubist-inspired coffee set in 1927 (fig. 8.31). Its planes are broken up into irregularly shaped triangles, whose shapes are further contrasted by the use of gilt and oxidized brown. This unconventional design was exhibited several times, and was pictured in *The New York Times*, where it was entitled "The Lights and Shadows of Manhattan."[43] Emotions ran to extremes on a design like Magnussen's. Some thought its cubist-inspired form inventive and modern, while others found it bizarre, eccentric, and ridiculous. Americans rejected a good deal of early modernism because it was not functional, straightforward, or simple—characteristics that had appealed to Americans since the seventeenth century.

The editorial writer in the January 4, 1928, issue of *The New Republic* must surely have been describing the Magnussen silver service and a matching serving spoon and fork:

I came upon a display of Modern American silverware on Fifth Avenue the other day which was both painful and funny. It was funny because the

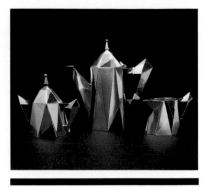

8.31 Erik Magnussen (1864–1961) "Cubic" Coffee Set. 1927. Manufactured by Gorham Co., Providence, R.I. Silver with gilt and oxidized panels, coffee pot ht.: 9½". Private collection

8.30 Donald Deskey Table Lamp. ca. 1927–29. Manufactured by Deskey-Vollmer, New York. Chrome-plated steel and frosted glass, 12¼ × 4¼ × 5⅛". Collection John C. Waddell

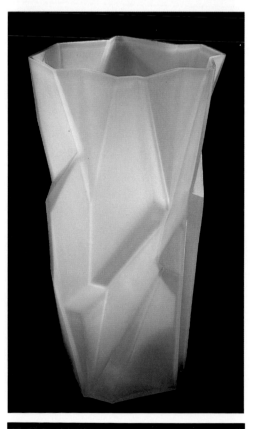

8.32 Vase. ca. 1928. Possibly manufactured as part of "Ruba Rombic" line by Consolidated Lamp and Glass Company, Coraopolis, Pa. Mold-blown glass, ht.: 15½". Collection Charles Senseman

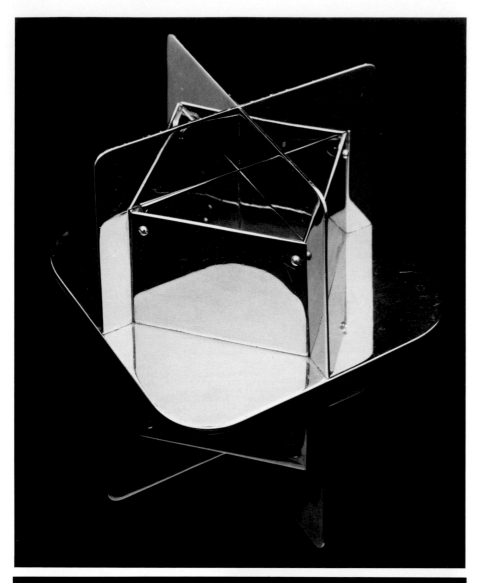

8.33 William Lescaze
Pencil Holder. 1932. Designed for the PSFS Building, Philadelphia. Manufacturer unknown. Chrome-plated metal, 3½ × 5½ × 5½". The Brooklyn Museum. Promised Gift of Nelson Blitz, Jr.

8.34 Egmont Arens (b. 1887)
Table Lamp. 1928. Prototype made by the designer. Chrome-plated metal, ht.: 10"; base dia.: 7". The Brooklyn Museum. Promised Gift of Nelson Blitz, Jr.

manufacturer had obviously gritted his teeth and said to the designer: "Go as far as you like!" It was painful because the designer had applied a cubistic technique to surfaces that, in the sheer nature of things, cannot be treated cubistically; and because, instead of deriving his design from the actual function of a tea set and a salad set, he had sought to derive it, the advertisement placard said, from the skyscrapers of New York! Our skyscraper worship has produced some pretty sad results; but I think this cubistic claptrap in silver is about the worst I have seen.[44]

Although the writer's viewpoint was not universal, it would become so by the mid-1930s. In any case, whether because of this attitude or the coffee set's expense, this seems to be the only one made.

Magnussen was not alone in his cubist approach. The Consolidated Lamp and Glass Company designed around 1928 a line of glassware they called "Ruba Rombic" (fig. 8.32). As an advertisement stated, Rubaiy means epic or poem, and Rombic means irregular in shape.[45] In the July 1928 issue of *Garden and Home Builder*, Ruba Rombic is described as "Something entirely new in modern table glass...so ultra-smart that it is as new as to-morrow's newspaper."[46] Even Howe and Lescaze, one of the first architectural firms to espouse the functional International Style, designed a cubist-influenced, desk-top pencil holder (fig. 8.33). Egmont Arens, an industrial designer known for his lighting fixtures, created a playful lamp integrating cubist planes with metallic geometry (fig. 8.34). Howe and Lescaze and Arens used cubism as a point of departure to design useful objects in the form of abstract sculpture.

8.35 Gear Table for lobby of A. O. Smith Research and Engineering Building. 1929–31. Aluminum, steel, and glass, 25 × 36"

8.36 Carpet. ca. 1930. Designer and manufacturer unknown. Wool, 27¾ × 48¼". Collection Peter and Judy White

The lobby of the A. O. Smith Research and Engineering Building (fig. 3.9) in Milwaukee, designed by Holabird and Root, graphically illustrates the diversity of stylistic forces. These range from the liberal approach to the machine, as seen in the glass and metal table (fig. 8.35), to the cubist pattern of the floor, to the almost classical, straightforward seating furniture and walls. Artists and designers were bombarded from all directions, not only in terms of the various imported European avant-garde styles, but in terms of the radical transformations in their own lives caused by the machine. The result was a period of exploration, imitation, inventiveness, playfulness, and gradual American synthesis of many different styles.

Department stores across the nation continued to play an important role in disseminating the new styles to a wider audience in the late 1920s and 1930s. The American Federation of Arts organized traveling exhibitions of modern decorative arts. The Metropolitan Museum of Art mounted an extremely popular show in 1929 entitled *The Architect and the Industrial Arts*. This museum exhibition was unique in that eight prominent architects—Armistead Fitzhugh (landscape architect), Raymond M. Hood, Ely Jacques Kahn, Eugene Schoen, Joseph Urban, Ralph T. Walker, John W. Root, Eliel Saarinen—plus Leon V. Solon, a ceramic designer, organized and planned almost every detail of the presentation. There were thirteen room arrangements that addressed some of the practical problems of contemporary living, although in one critic's opinion they were mainly for the more affluent.[47] In retrospect, the room settings seem to be the epitome of what would later be regarded as modernistic, a debased form of modernism. As a group these interiors were remarkably cohesive. Their emphasis on verticality, angularity, zig-zags, rhythmic patterns, and the use of both luxury and new materials perfectly summed up the mood of the 1920s.

The next industrial art exhibition organized by the Metropolitan Museum was in 1931. This time, instead of custom-made objects, everything in the show was either mass-produced or at least available in some quantity on the open market. (This must have been the Metropolitan's nod to the Depression, because by 1934 the museum had reverted back to inviting specific designers to create settings and objects specially for that exhibition.)

The big event of 1931, though, was not at the Metropolitan, but at The Brooklyn Museum, where an exhibition by the members of the American Union of Decorative Artists and Craftsmen, better known as AUDAC, was held. AUDAC, formed in 1928, was the most ambitious professional group of the period, "an organization of designers, architects, artists, engaged in designing for individual needs, commercial organizations, industrial firms, heads of stores, and manufacturing establishments and all other persons interested in the industrial, decorative and applied arts."[48] Its membership by 1931 included more than a hundred well-known artists/designers, plus a host of industrial designers, many of whom are unfortunately little remembered today. Through publi-

cation of *The Annual of American Design 1931*, with essays by a diverse group of authors representing various points of view, AUDAC presented: "a very significant sociologic truth—that the machine need not enslave man; that its standardization need not lead to rigid repetition, and that its mass producing need not exclude esthetic considerations."[49]

AUDAC organized two shows of its members' work. The first was held in 1930 at the Grand Central Palace in Manhattan, the second and more important one the following year at The Brooklyn Museum. The range of material shown was greater than in any previous industrial design exhibition—furniture, radio cabinets, fabrics, photographs, typography, decorative paintings and graphic arts, architectural models and designs, and a Monel metal sink by Gustav Jensen. One particularly perceptive critic, Blanche Naylor, felt that "this exhibition indicates that today's designers are developing an original school of American design which is worthy to stand beside the best efforts of other lands."[50] Only two years after the Metropolitan Museum's *Architect and the Industrial Arts* exhibition, there was a marked progression toward a more machine-style aesthetic. Russel Wright showed a cocktail shaker that had been reduced to basic geometric forms (fig. 8.37). Its beauty lay in the simplicity of these forms, their relationship to one another, and the seductive and reflective quality of the chrome surface.

8.37 Russel Wright
Cocktail Shaker. ca. 1930. Manufactured by Russel Wright, Inc., New York. Chrome-plated pewter, ht.: 9″; width: 4⅞″; base dia.: 2¾″. Collection George H. Waterman III

8.38 Walter Dorwin Teague
Shop Front from *Design for the Machine*,
Philadelphia Museum of Art. 1932. Executed by Friedland-Newman, Inc. Courtesy Philadelphia Museum of Art

The AUDAC exhibition received a tremendous amount of press coverage from New York to Omaha.[51] The show was extended an extra three months because of its popularity. Unfortunately, this was AUDAC's last hurrah. Art organizations like AUDAC (or the even shorter-lived Contempora, Inc.—one New York exhibition in 1929) made important contributions to the public awareness of modern design. But they all fell victim to the harsh economic realities of the 1930s. The vanguard modern artists/designers had had a real sense of mission and freedom of expression during the 1920s, but the Depression dashed this sense of adventure.

In 1932 the Pennsylvania Museum (now the Philadelphia Museum of Art) held an exhibition boldly entitled *Design for the Machine*. Walter Dorwin Teague designed a shop front heralding features that would come to typify much of the 1930s design—horizontal lines, rounded corners, and bold typography (fig. 8.38). Before a design formula crystalized there were times, particularly in the early 1930s, when art and the machine became seemingly interchangeable. Leading in this area were a number of progressive manufacturers. The Tesla Coil, a high-frequency discharge demonstrator made by the Welch Scientific Company (fig. 8.40), was a functional machine; however, it looks not unlike a piece of abstract sculpture. The complexity of such machines fascinated designers, as evidenced by the imaginative Pattyn Products Company's machine age lamp (fig. 8.41). Figure 8.43 could at first glance be part of a system of gears, but is actually an inventive brass and copper bracelet. The Stehli Silk Corporation in 1925 gave artists free reign to tell "the story that contemporary American art should be telling to the

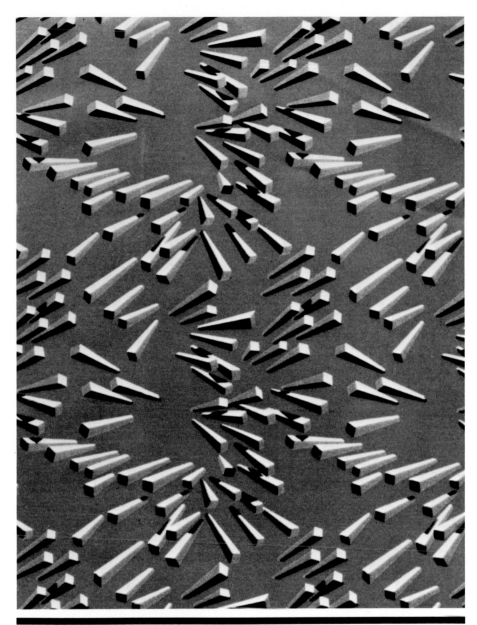

American people."[52] Charles B. Falls, using a lowly peg as his design motif, created a dynamic and vibrant pattern in silk (fig. 8.39). Americans also responded to the simple geometric forms of machine parts and their materials by creating beautiful abstract sculpture, such as the table lamp by an unknown artist (fig. 8.44).

As the Depression set in, traditional patronage of the arts shifted from the church and the rich private collector to business. The Chicago *Century of Progress Exposition* of 1933–34 marked the symbolic end of this first phase of modernism. Despite the fact that the buildings had futuristic titles such as "The House of Tomorrow," the fair represented a hun-

8.39 Charles Buckles Falls (1874–1960) "Pegs." 1927. Manufactured by Stehli Silk Corp., New York. Printed silk crepe-de-chine, 40 × 70″. The Newark Museum

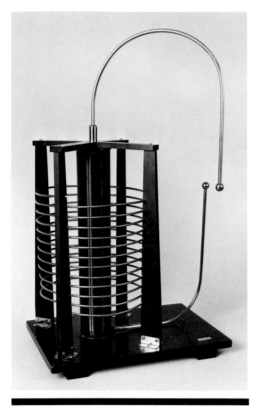

8.40 Nikola Tesla (1856–1943) Tesla Coil (High-Frequency Discharge Demonstrator). 1931. Welch Scientific Co., Chicago. Copper and wood, 29 × 18½ × 12½″. Collection Jim Greer and Dyan Economakos

8.41 Table Lamp. ca. 1935. Probably manufactured by Pattyn Products Co., Detroit. Chrome-plated and enameled steel and brass, glass, ht.: 20″; dia. of shade: 8″. The Brooklyn Museum. H. Randolph Lever Fund

8.42 John Vassos, designer and illustrator, Ruth Vassos (1895–1970), author *Ultimo* (New York: E.P. Dutton & Co.). 1930. 10⅜ × 7¾ × ½″. The Brooklyn Museum. H. Randolph Lever Fund

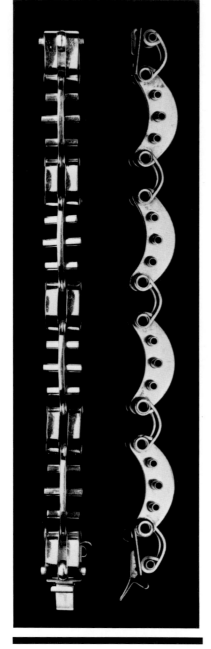

8.43 Bracelet (top and side views). Mid-1930s. Designer and manufacturer unknown. Brass and copper-plated metal, 7¼ × ½ × ½″. Historical Design Collection, Inc.

8.44 Table Lamp. ca. 1930. Designer and manufacturer unknown. Aluminum, ht.: 18¼″; shade dia.: 13¾″. Collection Inglett-Watson & Ken Forster

dred years of American technological progress: it was in effect a report on our progress to that moment. The brightly colored cubist buildings reflected the spirit of the late 1920s, while the sponsorship of the pavilions by large corporations indicated the patronage change. The emphasis was on consumerism and labor-saving machines. In effect, the debate over modernism—its existence, its appropriateness for America, and the merits of its aesthetic qualities—became secondary to the need for economic recovery. The means to economic recovery was the machine in its many manifestations. This meant that America had accepted, if begrudgingly, modernism.

AMERICANIZATION: 1934–41

The impact of the Depression only served to magnify the radical transformations and feelings of dislocation during the 1920s. The spirit of adventure, invention, and experimentation during the initial phase of the machine age led to fragmentation and different points of view, which in turn led to a need for a single definable American culture. "The search for culture was the search for meaningful forms, for patterns of living. That search began in the 1920s and culminated in the 1930s.... By 1927 the words 'modern' and 'streamlined' were being used not only in reference to design of particular objects, but also to a quality of living, a life-style. They are the words of the new machine order looking for a culture."[53] The desire was for an ideal style that would represent America and at the same time bring order to the seeming chaos of the moment. By the 1930s it seemed that the machine represented the only means

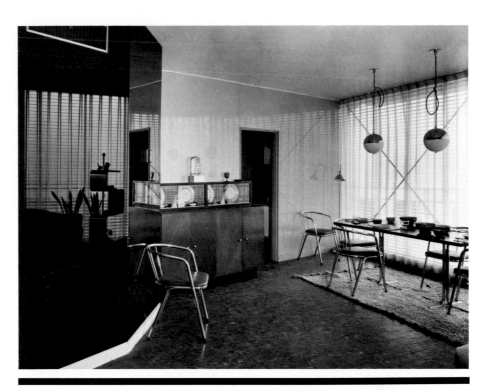

to a better future. Paradoxically the machine's rise to prominence was accompanied by a growing conservatism, a fear of the loss of individualism. John and Ruth Vassos, in their 1930 book *Ultimo* (fig. 8.42), depict in their gray-and-white illustrations and accompanying text a mechanized world in which man has lost his uniqueness. This book, and others that they published, expressed the fear that instead of man controlling the machine, the machine would control man.

Deceptions were needed to allay fears. Just as the beautiful and colorful cover of *Ultimo* gives no hint of the stark, cold, and forbidding landscapes that lurk inside, so too did the general public disguise the machine. Colonial Revival styles, popular since the 1880s, became even more so. Modern man felt nostalgia for a past age when life appeared simpler and it seemed possible to control one's own destiny. This explains, in part, the reluctance to modernize the home except for functional areas like kitchens and bathrooms: a man's "castle" was not a "machine for living," but a retreat from the realities and confusion of modern life. Of course there were also aesthetic reasons for the resurgence of the style's popularity; its forms were simple, functional, and classical, traits characteristic of 1930s design.

8.45 George Fred Keck
Interior, House of Tomorrow. *Century of Progress Exposition.* Chicago. 1933

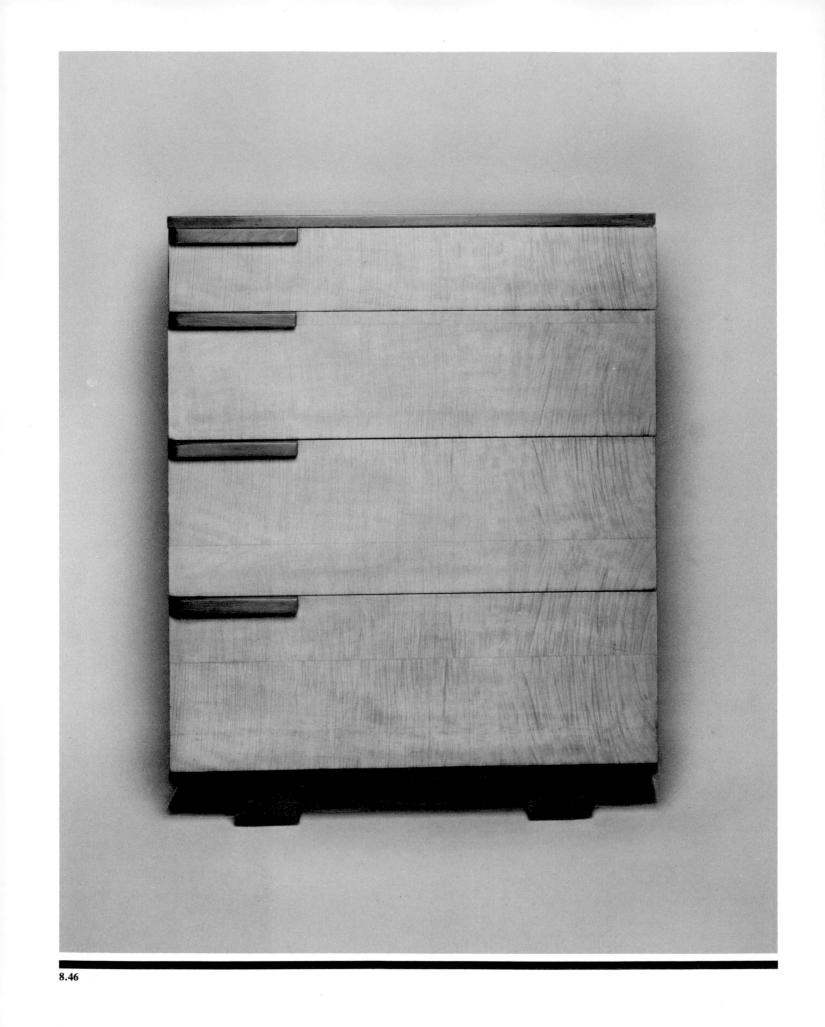

By 1936 the modern style was described as simple, honest, functional, practical, comfortable, convenient, sanitary, and durable—characteristics seen in everything from furniture to stoves. Functionalism, the idea that the form and appearance of an object derive entirely from its purpose and use, was implicit in all descriptions of modern design in the 1930s. But there were divergent opinions as to how this idea should be expressed. The Museum of Modern Art's *Machine Art* exhibition of 1934, unlike the 1927 *Machine-Age Exposition*, received enormous publicity. There were over four hundred objects listed under the categories of: "Industrial Units," "Household and Office Equipment," "Kitchenware," "House Furnishings and Accessories," "Scientific Instruments," and "Laboratory Glass and Porcelain." Actual machine parts were displayed on pedestals along with appliances and other objects that had never before been given such enthusiastic endorsement as art by a museum. The exhibition, viewed by its young curator, Philip Johnson, and the museum's director, Alfred H. Barr, Jr., as the true expression of modern as opposed to the French-inspired modernistic, reflected the Modern's long-standing bias toward Bauhaus-oriented functionalism, or the International Style.[54] It was the parts or inner workings of a machine that served as the inspiration and symbol for this new modern age.

Many of the objects shown in the exhibition are still as "modern" and "functional" as they were in 1934. Cocktail glasses designed by Walter Dorwin Teague are classics (fig. 8.51). Boiling flasks used by scientists are still made in the same efficient form and produced from the same durable material, Pyrex glass, an important twentieth-century innovation for

kitchenware (fig. 8.50). Even George Sakier's lavatory panel had a straightforward, geometric simplicity that seems timeless (fig. 8.48). The Museum of Modern Art became a staunch exponent of the "form follows function," "less is more" aspect of modernism that until the 1970s was generally regarded as the only true form of modernism. Ironically, the exhibition that really established this identity for the museum, *Machine Art*, was made up almost entirely of American objects, yet the museum, in its exhibitions and collecting policy, has promoted European expressions of functional modernism as the only true form of this style.

Americans in the 1930s were looking for a uniquely American expression or symbol of the machine age. It was left to a new type of designer, an American invention, the industrial designer, to create a suitable modern image.[55] This "new breed of folk heroes" recognized the form

8.47 Walter Dorwin Teague Gas Range. 1934. Manufactured by Floyd-Wells Co., Royersford, Pa.

8.46 Gilbert Rohde (1894–1944) Chest of Drawers. 1933–34. Manufactured by Herman Miller, Zeeland, Mich. English sycamore and sucupiro, 41½ × 34 × 19″. The Brooklyn Museum

8.48 George Sakier (b. 1930) Lavatory Panel from Arco Panel Unit System. 1933. Designed for the Accessories Company, Inc., New York, division of American Radiator Company

8.49 Clifford Brooks Stevens (b. 1911) and Edward P. Schreyer "Petipoint" Iron. 1941. Manufactured by Waverly Tool Company, Sandusky, Ohio. Metal and plastic, 4⅞ × 5 × 10″. The Brooklyn Museum. Gift of Larry Whitely

8.50 Boiling Flasks. Before 1934. Manufactured by Corning Glass Works, Corning, N.Y. Glass, tallest ht.: 15″; shortest ht.: 5¾″. The Museum of Modern Art, New York. Gift of the manufacturer

8.51 Walter Dorwin Teague Cocktail Glasses. Before 1934. Manufactured by Corning Glass Works, Steuben Division, Corning, N.Y. Glass, left: 3⅜ × 3″; right: 3 × 2¼″. The Museum of Modern Art, New York. Gift of Corning Glass Works

of the transportation machine—automobiles, trains, airplanes—as the perfect American metaphor for this new age. If one word other than machine could describe this period, both literally and figuratively, it would be "speed." For the 1920s speed represented the frantic tempo of a world in transition. This caused both angst and excitement. For the 1930s speed or streamlining became a symbolic means to achieve a society of order and "confidence in the face of complexity."[56] What started out as a means to an end—economic recovery—became a reassuring sign of a progressive society in control of its destiny. Horizontal lines, curved corners, smooth surfaces, and frictionless parts all contributed to a feeling of confidence, efficiency, and reliability that soothed people's trayed and jagged nerves. Beyond the economic considerations there was also a genuine concern for improved design in all aspects of daily life, from the most expensive custom-made luxury item to the most ordinary mass-produced object. To the general public of the 1930s streamlining was the ultimate statement of modern design. It got to the point where it did not matter whether streamlining had a practical application or not. It became one of the symbols of the new era, and a particularly American symbol. The style ranged from the ridiculous to the sublime. Today an aerodynamically designed pencil sharpener or iron may seem absurd, serving no particular function (see figs. 1.4, 8.49). On the other hand, Peter Müller-Munk's chrome pitcher (fig. 8.52), with its perfect pouring spout, is streamlining at its most elegant and practical, a perfect harmony of efficiency, material, and the machine process. At the time, all types of streamlining were seen as serving an important function. As Lewis Mumford said in 1934,

8.52 Peter Müller-Munk (1904–1967) "Normandie" Pitcher. 1935. Manufactured by Revere Copper and Brass Co., Rome, N.Y. Chrome-plated brass, 12 × 3 × 9½". The Brooklyn Museum. H. Randolph Lever Fund

"simplification of the externals of the mechanical world is almost a prerequisite for dealing with its internal complications."[57] Simplification equaled control.

A number of important industrial designers established independent offices in the later 1920s. These jacks-of-all-trades became the link between the engineer and the businessman. Their importance grew with the recognition that appearance was a factor in sales. This point was dramatically demonstrated when, in 1927, Henry Ford agreed to style and color change in his previously unalterable

8.53 W. Archibald Welden (1900–1970)
Saucepan. 1939. Manufactured by Revere
Copper and Brass Co., Rome, N.Y. Cop-
per-clad stainless steel

automobiles. The need to stimulate the
economy further promoted the idea of
yearly style changes, thereby placing the
industrial designer in a position of tremendous influence. The ramifications of
their ideas, whether in fact they only created the surface design of an object or actually made practical improvements in its
function, affected almost all aspects of
daily living. Their legacy lives on in the
important role industrial designers continue to play in our society, as well as in
objects they designed that are still in use
today, such as the Waring blender, designed by Peter Müller-Munk, and Revere pots and pans, designed by W.
Archibald Welden (fig. 8.53). Today
most Americans are familiar with the
names of Deskey, Loewy, Teague, Bel
Geddes, and Dreyfuss, mainly because
these industrial designers were almost as
good at self-salesmanship as at design.
Their fame has tended to obscure the
many other talented designers, such as
Nathan George Horwitt, Gilbert Rohde,
Wolfgang and Pola Hoffmann, Peter
Müller-Munk, Walter von Nessen, Egmont Arens, Kem Weber, Robert Heller,
Paul Lobel, Lee Simonson, Kurt Versen,
Warren McArthur, Alexander Kachin-
sky, Winold Reiss, Ilonka Karasz, Ruth
Reeves, Walter Kantack, Henriette Reiss,

Joseph Aronson, and Frederick Kiesler—
a list by no means complete.

Streamlining, as both style and symbol,
suited the austere tenor of the times. Expensive materials were replaced by
cheaper and newer ones that could be
easily molded for mass production. There
was an elimination of ornamentation, a
paring down of forms. As early as 1930
Nathan George Horwitt designed the
"Beta" chair with flowing, curved, re-
peating lines that gracefully and inven-
tively approached the problem of the
cantilevered form (fig. 8.54). Only two
prototypes were made, one of which was
shown in the Modern's *Machine Art* exhibition. While Americans were celebrating
their "modernistic" progress at the Chicago World's Fair in 1934, they were introduced to two streamlined trains, the
Union Pacific's *M10,000* and the Burlington *Zephyr* (see figs. 5.13, 5.11). That
same year Chrysler introduced their
streamlined car, the *Airflow*, which did
not become a commercial success, but
contributed to the growing awareness of
this new style. Gradually allusions to and
visual manifestations of speed appeared
in all the arts. Even *Vogue* magazine dictated that to be fashionable a woman's
"profile will have the windswept fleet
lines of a speedboat or aeroplane."[58] The
constant refinement to find the ideal form
of least resistance against air and water
ultimately led to the teardrop shape, the
source of inspiration for Kem Weber's
1934 armchair (fig. 8.55). With its grand
sweeping arms, Weber's chair has a force-
ful sculpted form. This particular aerody-

8.54 Nathan George Horwitt (b. 1898) "Beta" Chair. 1930. Prototype designed for The Howell Company, Geneva, Ill. Chrome-plated tubular steel, upholstered, 26 × 22⅞ × 27½". The Brooklyn Museum. Gift of the designer

8.55 Kem Weber
Armchair. 1934. Manufactured by Lloyd Manufacturing Co., Menominee, Mich. Chrome-plated steel, wood, and leather, 29 × 28½ × 39". Collection Charles Senseman

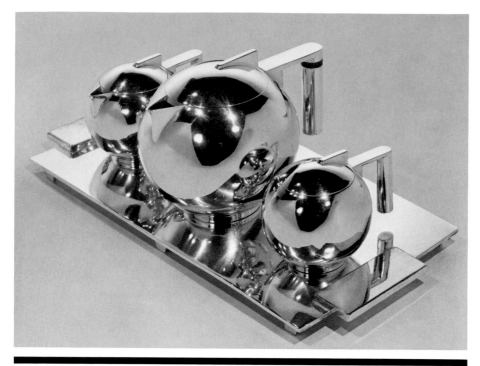

8.56 Paul Lobel (1899–1983)
Tea Service. c. 1930. Silver plate, wood inset, teapot: 6 × 6 × 8¼"; tray, 18 × 8⅛ × 1". Manufactured by Wilcox Silver Plate Co., International Silver Co., Meriden, Conn. The Metropolitan Museum of Art, New York. Gift of M. H. Lobel and C. H. Lobel, 1983

8.57 Paul Schreckengost (1908–1983)
Pitcher. ca. 1938. Manufactured by Gem Clay Forming Co., Sebring, Ohio. Glazed earthenware, 7½ × 11½ × 4". Collection Jim Greer and Dyan Economakos

namic shape appeared in every material from silver to ceramics. Streamlining ranged from extremes of phallic and teardrop forms to gently rounded corners as seen in Gilbert Rohde's table lamp (fig. 8.59). Even Frank Lloyd Wright, in the architecture and furnishings of the Johnson Wax Building, was seduced by the allure of this pervasive style (see fig. 8.58).

Streamlining summed up the contradictions of the 1930s. There was an almost naive faith in the power of the machine to make America a unique and better place. At the same time, there was also a growing conservatism. As Jeffrey Meikle states:

> the streamlined style expressed not only a phallic technological thrust into a limitless future. Its dominant image, the rounded, womblike teardrop egg, expressed also a desire for a passive, static society, in which social and economic frictions engendered by technological acceleration would be eliminated. Streamlining was paradoxically a style of retreat and consolidation as well as one of penetration and forward progress.[59]

The closer Americans came to realizing that we actually had a culture, the more determined we were to hang on to it. There sprung up a sense of commitment and of community. "It was during this period that we find, for the first time, frequent references to an 'American Way of Life.' The phrase 'The American Dream' came into common use."[60] Perhaps for the first time there was a feeling that we were developing a true American culture, which would come to fruition only after World War II, when we came into our own politically, economically, and culturally.

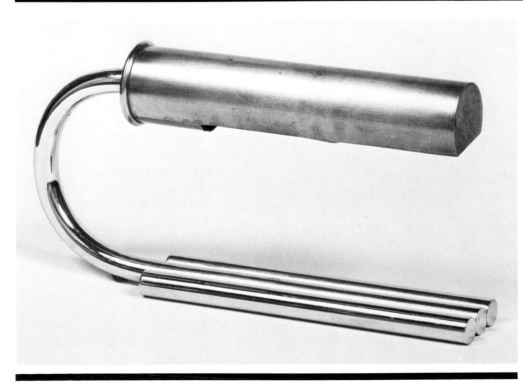

8.58 Frank Lloyd Wright
Desk and Chair. ca. 1936–39. Manufactured by Steelcase, Grand Rapids, Mich. Enameled and brass-plated steel and walnut, desk: 33½ × 35 × 84″; chair: 34½ × 23½ × 19½″. The High Museum of Art, Atlanta

8.59 Gilbert Rohde
Table Lamp. ca. 1933. Manufactured by Mutual-Sunset Lamp Manufacturing Co., Inc., Brooklyn. Chrome-plated steel and brass, 7 × 14 × 2¼″. Collection Inglett-Watson & Ken Forster

A NEW ERA

In the brief span of some two decades decorative arts changed more radically than in any other previous period. Technology not only affected traditional forms, but also created the need for totally new ones. New economic realities and technological advancements such as the greater availability of electricity brought dramatic changes and endless challenges to designers and industry. The ease of transportation and the relocation of a large percentage of the population to cities had a major impact on how people lived. Even by 1922 a writer commented how the "high rents and increased cost of living necessitate constant moving and make it increasingly difficult to establish permanent homes. The young people seem to pitch their tents like the Nomads."[61] Living spaces became smaller as more and more Americans began to live in apartments or small suburban developments. Servants were a thing of the past except for the very rich. Versatility of space and furniture became necessities, cost and durability became issues. No matter how tenaciously Americans hung on to their period reproductions, there was no way to escape the effects of the modern movement. Gradually there was a rebellion

against stuffy, dark interiors, over-draped windows, dust-collecting curlecues, and styles of decoration that are foreign in mood and manner to the spirit of present day living. It [modern design] aims at decorative simplification that creates a natural background for the personality of those living with it. It fits in with the reality of apartment house dwelling and its space limitations. It has been furthered by science, which has developed revolutionary new methods of production, and has utilized expressive new materials such as chromium, aluminum, bakelite, monel metal, new lacquers, cellophane, cork, etc.[62]

In the quest for comfort and affordable furnishings, experiments were made with mass-production techniques utilizing both old and new materials. Many of these so-called "new" materials had either been invented or discovered by the nineteenth century, but neither the technology nor the need for their domestic use had existed until the 1920s. Metal, in one form or another, has played an important role in the history of decorative arts since ancient times. During the nineteenth century cast iron was popular for outdoor and some indoor furniture. Bronze, brass, silver, pewter, and tin were used for accessories from decorative sculpture to tablewares. Gold, the most highly prized of all metals, was used occasionally by the rich, primarily for ceremonial or presentation pieces. During the twentieth century there was a radical change in the types of metals employed and the way in which they were used. For instance, Norman Bel Geddes "was proud of his designs for Simmons because they did not perpetuate the use of metal as an ersatz substitute for wood. In 1929 he declared, 'In creating these Simmons designs [see fig. 8.60] I have always kept in mind the medium in which I was working and believe that the furniture immediately reveals itself as metal.' "[63] This idea of "truth to materials"

8.60 Norman Bel Geddes Vanity and Mirror (in "Exposition Yellow"). ca. 1929–32. Manufactured by The Simmons Co., Chicago. Enameled steel, chrome-plated metal, brass, and wood, overall 57 × 44 × 19″. Collection Jim Greer and Dyan Economakos

8.61 Gilbert Rohde
Desk. ca. 1934. Manufactured by Troy
Sunshade Co., Troy, Ohio. Chrome-plated steel, painted wood, and plastic, 29 ×
42 × 22″. The Brooklyn Museum

represented a major shift in thinking and approach to design from the previous century. It was now permissible to allow any material, no matter how vulgar or cheap it had seemed in the past, to be itself.

The history of metals, their technological development, and varied uses in relation to decorative arts has yet to be written. In America by the late 1920s, custom-made examples of chromed or nickel-plated tubular steel furniture and lighting devices appeared in exhibitions and were made for private commissions. But the first designers and manufacturers to mass produce these objects are still unknown.

Chromium was discovered by a French chemist, Vauquelin, in 1798. He is given credit for its name, which derives from Latin, "chroma," meaning color or brilliance. Chromium is not found in a free state but must be extracted, a process which at first was difficult and expensive. It was valued commercially for its hardness, capacity to form alloys, appealing color and brilliance, and resistance to corrosion and heat. Its usefulness for projectile coverings and armor-plate was proven

during World War I, when domestic production increased by almost eighty-fold. After the war new markets were sought for the metal.[64]

With the introduction of chrome-plating for commercial use in 1925, the metal developed a slow but steady popularity. Nickel was also used for plating, but it was not as hard as chrome and required frequent polishing. Consequently, it was used more often as an underplating for chrome. Chromium perfectly suited the desire for durable, functional, and simple furnishings. It was also a perfect medium in an age when light became such an important decorative device. A contemporary critic proclaimed: "This era of light in environment is synonymous with the present-day enlightment of civilization, and can promise to be no less enduring. Nor can it have a better emblem of endurance than Chromium."[65] Chrome began to appear in objects as disparate as desks, clocks, and armchairs.

A number of companies started producing chromed tubular steel furniture in the late 1920s, but there was great resistance to its domestic use. It was consid-

314

8.62 John Vassos
"RCA Victor Special" Portable Phonograph. Mid-1930s. Manufactured by RCA, New York. Aluminum and various metals, Closed, 8 × 15½ × 17¼". Collection Dr. William S. Greenspon

8.63 Kem Weber
Table Clock. 1934. Manufactured by Lawson Time, Inc., Pasadena, Calif. Chrome-plated metal and plastic, 4½ × 8¾ × 3½". Collection John P. Axelrod

8.64 Lurelle Guild
Compote. 1934. Manufactured by Kensington, Inc., New Kensington, Pa. Aluminum and plastic, ht.: 6″; dia.: 13½″. Alan Moss Ltd.

8.65 Warren McArthur (1885–1961)
Armchair. ca. 1935. Manufactured by Warren McArthur Corp., New York. Aluminum, rubber, and upholstery, 31 × 22¼ × 22″. Private collection. Courtesy Catherine Kurland

8.66 Gilbert Rohde
"Semi-Arm" Chair. ca. 1934. Manufactured by Troy Sunshade Co., Troy, Ohio. Chrome-plated steel and leatherette, 30 × 21 × 21¼″. Washburn Gallery

ered perfectly suitable for offices and hospitals, but too sterile and impersonal for the home. The 1933 Chicago World's Fair, with its extensive showing of tubular steel furniture, contributed to a gradual acceptance of metal furniture for any interior.[66] Steel was seen as a symbol for modern life. According to the literature of one manufacturer, it was "natural therefore that the modern spirit should express itself in striking, radically different kinds of furniture—and that the furniture should be of steel, for this is the age of steel, and steel sounds the keynote of practicability, energy and strength which dominates our modern life."[67]

Aluminum was also employed exten-

sively during this period. Like chromium, aluminum was difficult and expensive to extract. In fact, until an American, Charles Martin Hall, discovered in 1886 an electrolytic process making commercial production possible, aluminum was too costly. In forty years aluminum evolved from a laboratory curiosity to an industrial staple.[68] The impetus for its development came from both its uses in transportation and World War I. Although aluminum is a relatively soft metal, it was combined with various alloys to increase its industrial and commercial value. Eventually aluminum was used for everything from furniture, lighting fixtures, interior architectural decoration, to appliances and accessories such as buttons, picture frames, candlesticks, tableware, and kitchen utensils.

Stainless steel, which contains 18 percent chromium and 6 percent nickel, was also popular, particularly for cooking utensils, cutlery, and flatware. Monel, an alloy of nickel and copper, was first developed in 1905. Stronger than pure nickel, it was used primarily for industrial purposes, but gradually worked its way into the home through the kitchen in the form of sinks, appliances, furniture, cabinet door-pulls, and trim.

The popular metals of the period all had common characteristics: their history was relatively recent, and their "white" color, reflective qualities, and ability to be reduced to simple forms expressed the era's identification with speed and efficiency.

316

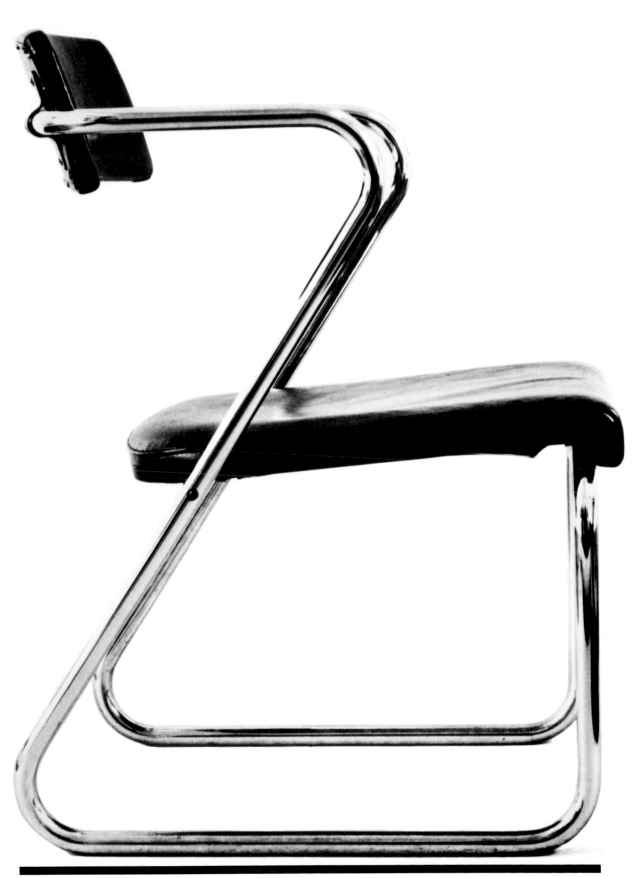

8.66

8.67 Peter Pfisterer (b. 1907)
Table Lamp. ca. 1935–40. Chrome-plated
and enameled metal, wood, 6¾ × 13½ ×
3½″. Historical Design Collection, Inc.

8.68 Donald Deskey
Table Lamp. ca. 1927–29. Manufactured
by Deskey-Vollmer, New York. Brass,
7½ × 9 × 5″. Collection Diane Wolf

Electricity had a profound effect on almost every aspect of human existence. It represented the epitome of modernism, from the prosaic electric ice crushers to the power and potential ramifications of the TVA. On the most personal level the development of artificial, electric lighting had the greatest effect on people's day-to-day lives. As lightbulbs became less cumbersome, the designer could become more imaginative in both the types of fixtures and the use and purpose of the light. At first it was difficult for the designer to break away from the traditional forms used to house candles and gas. It took a while to realize that totally new forms were needed, and that light itself could be used as a decorative device. Beginning in the late 1920s, lighting fixtures ceased to resemble anything from the past. Some of the new materials, such as chromium and aluminum, became staples of the lighting industry because of their reflective qualities. The bulb itself could become part of the design. It was now possible to duplicate natural light, create light of any color, focus light of any intensity on a particular spot, or use it indirectly. This versatility encouraged architects and designers to use light as an interior and exterior decorative device, to create a mood ranging from subtle to dramatic. Department stores were quick to see its advantages as an effective selling device. The planners of the Chicago World's Fair proclaimed the progress of the twentieth century in a flood of colored lights that dramatically illuminated the buildings of the exposition. By the 1930s lighting had come of age. Its flexibility, cleanliness, and inexpensive effectiveness made it a perfect medium for the machine age.

Electricity revolutionized life in the factory, office, and home. The housewife

8.69 Kurt Versen (b. 1901) Adjustable Floor Lamp. ca. 1930. Manufactured by Lightolier. Copper-plated metal, ht.: 60⅛"; shade dia.: 14". The Brooklyn Museum. H. Randolph Lever Fund

8.70 Gilbert Rohde
Clocks. 1932–33 (center foreground, ca. 1935). Manufactured by Herman Miller Clock Company, Zeeland, Mich. Left to right: Collection Charles Senseman; Collection Ilon Specht Case; (center and center foreground) Collection John P. Axelrod; (right, rear) Collection Paul F. Walter; (right foreground) The Brooklyn Museum. H. Randolph Lever Fund; Collection Charles Senseman

was inundated with a wide variety of labor-saving devices and gadgets—clothes- and dishwashing machines, electric refrigerators, stoves, vacuum cleaners, irons, toasters. At first these new electrical wonders were housed in the antiquated forms of their ancestors. Each technological advance required not only an engineer or scientist, but an artist to give it an appropriate modern housing. The industrial designer styled the outer shape to suit the modern interior mechanism, often improving the efficiency as well as the design. With a series of clocks designed for Herman Miller around 1932–33, Gilbert Rohde transformed an ancient device, one that had been revered throughout history, into a modern idiom (fig. 8.70). In using both old and new materials he reduced the elements necessary for telling time to a minimum, with circles and squares often replacing numerals.

Plastic, a material synonymous with the machine age, came into its own during the 1930s. Synthetic plastics were invented in the nineteenth century. The first to become a commercial success was celluloid,

invented by an American, John Wesley Hyatt, in 1868. Its most popular nineteenth-century use was for toiletry articles made to look like ivory, and it became an important ingredient in the manufacture of camera film. The plastic that was to initiate the modern use of this synthetic material was Bakelite. Invented by Leo H. Baekeland in 1907, it was primarily used as an electrical insulator, remaining hidden through most of the 1920s in radios, airplanes, automobiles, telephones, and electric power lines. The expiration of Baekeland's patent in 1927 encouraged development of cheaper, more colorful, and more versatile plastics.

Although plastic began to come out of hiding in the late 1920s, in the form of tabletops and decorative objects, it was not until the Depression and the increasing role of the industrial designer that its full potential was explored. The growth of plastics coincided with the development of objects which had no historical precedent, such as radios. Radio companies turned to plastic not for the beauty of the material, particularly, but "to reduce pro-

8.71 Harold L. Van Doren (1895–1957) and J. G. Rideout (d. 1951)
Radio. 1930–33. Manufactured by Air-King Products Co., Brooklyn. Plastic, metal, and glass, 11¾ × 8⅞ × 7½". The Brooklyn Museum. Purchased with funds donated by The Walter Foundation

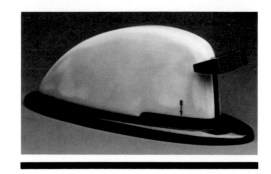

8.72 Lester L. Wheeler and William H. Gref, with Orlo Heller of Bortic Studios, New York.
"Aristocrat" Stapling Machine. 1937. Manufactured by E. H. Hotchkiss Co., Norwalk, Conn. Cast phenolic resin case manufactured by Catalin Corp., New York. 2⅝ × 7½ × 2¼". Collection Ilon Specht Case

8.73 Armchair. 1939. Manufactured by Pittsburgh Plate Glass Co., Ford City, Pa., possibly designed by Louis Dierra of PPG. Glass and upholstery with metal fittings, 29 × 22⅜ × 22½". The Brooklyn Museum. H. Randolph Lever Fund

8.74 Gilbert Rohde (attributed to) Lounge Chair. ca. 1934. Manufacturer unknown. Chrome-plated steel and leather, 32½ × 26½ × 34". Collection Alan Moss Ltd.

duction costs, and to eliminate finishing and assembly operations."[69] Harold Van Doren and John Gordon Rideout designed one of the first plastic radio cabinets for the Air-King Products Company in 1933 (fig. 8.71). The plastics industry also benefited from streamlining. Easy to mold, the material became synonymous with this American style.

The overwhelming transformation of almost every aspect of our society had, like it or not, an impact on the way we lived and the etiquette we observed. According to Paul Frankl, "Like the whole structure of our society, our manners have changed radically. Restraint and formality have been superseded by a greater ease in speech, in gesture, in more natural positions of repose. As Aldous Huxley has pointed out in one of his delightful essays, we have learned the art of 'lolling.' There is an honesty, a frankness, a directness in our social relations that can only be described as 'modern.' "[70] This relaxation was another direct consequence of the Depression, a great equalizer. Exotic woods, elaborately carved; silver; porcelain; expensive fabrics; and precious stones for jewelry were simply unaffordable for most. Economics pushed traditional luxury objects out of reach and furthered acceptance of the new materials and technology.

Furniture, whether made from traditional materials such as wood or new materials like chrome, glass, plastic, or cork, reflected this functional approach in its honesty of construction and materials, elimination of fussy details (whether decorative motifs or fancy upholstery techniques), practicality, flexibility, and comfort. "In 1928, with the invention of latex foam, a complete revolution in upholstery techniques was set in motion,

8.75 Walter Dorwin Teague Interior, Ford Building. New York World's Fair. 1939

opening up new design possibilities in regard to chair shape, construction and comfort."[71] The proportions and use of furniture changed in order to accommodate smaller living spaces with lower ceilings, but also to suggest informality, intimacy, and relaxation.

Neoclassicism was a strong force in design, as was repeatedly noted by contemporary writers. The paring down of forms often resulted in a strong classical feeling in objects and interiors. This interest in classicism is not surprising, for, as already noted, the classical reference made it eas-

ier to assimilate the staggering changes Americans confronted every day.

In this more informal atmosphere new materials covered our walls, furniture, and floors. Along with plastics, many synthetic fibers were developed, the most important of which was rayon. Since the nineteenth century inventors had tried to develop an "artificial silk." When in the 1920s it was realized that rayon had a potential far greater than simply as an imitation of silk, the industry flourished. Rayon could act like almost any natural fiber and be woven to imitate almost any

type of textile from gossamer-thin glass curtains to brocades and velvets. Its impact was felt by both the fashion world and interior decoration. Throughout the late 1920s into the 1930s, there was growing interest in textured and woven fabrics, as texture became as important as pattern in upholstery and window fabrics. Rayon and other synthetic yarns were also used in conjunction with natural fibers. Textured plaids became very popular. Coated materials, such as duPont's Fabrikoid, were also extensively used as a substitute for leather. Coated, washable wallpapers, linoleum for floors, a new, so-called seamlock technique for greater ease of manufacturing carpets, and Formica for counter and tabletops all indicated the desire for convenience, ease of upkeep, and less expensive ways to decorate.

This new informality extended to the ways people entertained, with ramifications in a number of industries. Silver, which for hundreds of years had been considered the appropriate material for flatware and hollow ware, was usurped by a number of new cheaper metals. This is not to say silver totally disappeared—grandmother's silver pattern and tea service were obviously not discarded—but the purchasing of new silver was severely curtailed. The silver industry attempted to make their styles more contemporary, but newer, less expensive metals began to take silver's place on the dining room table. Even Emily Post, the guardian of proper etiquette, told her readers "No metal, it seems to me, is quite so complete an answer to the housewife's prayer as chromium—appealing not only to the eye, but to practical requirements, because... it stays brilliantly polished to the end of time. Another beauty of chromium to most of us is that really lovely things can be had at a comparatively small expense."[72]

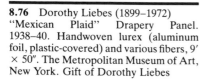

8.76 Dorothy Liebes (1899–1972) "Mexican Plaid" Drapery Panel. 1938–40. Handwoven lurex (aluminum foil, plastic-covered) and various fibers, 9′ × 50″. The Metropolitan Museum of Art, New York. Gift of Dorothy Liebes

A number of different companies began to mass-produce chrome, copper, aluminum, and nickel-plated accessories. As these new materials became popular for everyday use, manufacturers sought new markets. The Chase Brass & Copper Company, producer of industrial parts, started a "Specialty Line" in 1930 (fig. 8.79). The line flourished until World War II, when all Chase's energies were diverted to war production; it was never revived. In a short span, however, Chase produced a wide variety of objects, including lamps, tableware, smoking accessories, bookends, and watering cans. Chase used some in-house designers, but also commissioned designs from artists such as Russel Wright and Walter von Nessen. This was a formula followed by other manufacturers. One of the interesting aspects of the work done at Chase was the adaptation of existing industrial parts to the design of the new specialty items. Von Nessen took brass plumbing elbow joints and created amusing animal bookends, and the classical fluting design in many of his tea services and other tableware was inspired by extruded industrial piping.[73] Nothing was sacred.

Traditional porcelain dinner services were replaced by earthenware. Russel Wright's "American Modern" pattern (see fig. 2.27) was *the* present to give a young bride in the late thirties. Glass place settings were extremely sophisticated and worked well with the reflective qualities of chrome. Flowers were just as beautiful in glass or metal vases as in porcelain. Plastic dishes and flatware presented a colorful display, and were wonderfully practical for family use. The hostess could even self-confidently greet her guests in plastic jewelry (fig. 8.82).

Changing etiquette and social habits created the need for new forms. Prohibition (which extended from 1920 to 1933),

8.77 Russel Wright
Flatware. 1933. Manufactured by Russel Wright, Inc., New York. Sterling silver

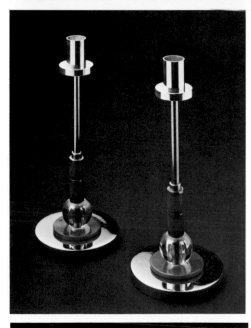

8.78 Candlesticks. ca. 1935. Manufactured by M. Goldsmith Co., Brooklyn. Plastic, chrome-plated iron, and steel, ht.: 10″; base dia.: 4¼″. The Brooklyn Museum. H. Randolph Lever Fund

8.79 "Specialty" Line Items. ca. 1930–36. Manufactured by Chase Brass & Copper Co., Waterbury, Conn. All objects company design unless otherwise noted. Left to right: candle holder; Walter von Nessen, bookend; Gerth and Gerth, candle holder; watering can; tea service; bookend; coffee urn; Russel Wright, pancake and corn set. Chrome, copper-plated, or lacquered brass, copper, steel, or aluminum with plastic fittings. Top left, Historical Design Collection, Inc.; lower right, The Brooklyn Museum. Gift of Paul F. Walter; all others Collection Ilon Specht Case

8.80 George Sakier
Vases. ca. 1929. Manufactured by Fostoria Glass Co., Moundsville, W.Va. Molded glass, tallest, ht.: 9⅜″; dia.: 3½″; shortest, ht.: 4⅜″; dia.: 6¾″. Collections John C. Waddell (center pair) and Alan Moss Ltd. (both ends)

8.81 Walter Dorwin Teague
Tableware. ca. 1934. Manufactured by Corning Glass Works, Steuben Division, Corning, N.Y. Glass

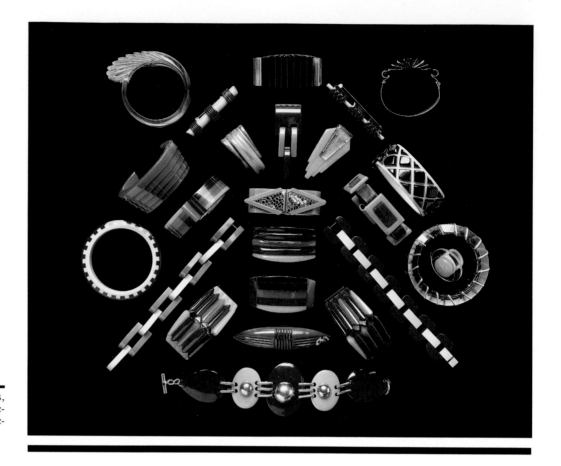

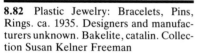

8.82 Plastic Jewelry: Bracelets, Pins, Rings. ca. 1935. Designers and manufacturers unknown. Bakelite, catalin. Collection Susan Kelner Freeman

8.83 Wolfgang Hoffmann (1900–1969) Table. 1935. Manufactured by The Howell Company, St. Charles, Ill. Chrome-plated steel and glass, 16⅞ × 25⅝". Collection Inglett-Watson & Ken Forster

the government's vain attempt to prohibit the manufacture, transportation, and sale of alcoholic beverages, forced people to drink at home, thus helping to create a new social event—the cocktail party—which in turn necessitated new types of furniture and accessories. The cocktail table was one such new form (fig. 8.83). It was low, so that the host could serve while seated comfortably, and easily cleaned, so that the guests could put their glasses down without fear of stains. Of course, the craze for mixed drinks created the need for cocktail shakers and matching glasses, produced in glass and various forms of metal (see fig. 8.84). Even soda water received a new machine age form to accompany the sophisticated world of the cocktail (fig. 8.85). And for the convenience of moving liquor bottles, shakers, glasses, and all the other paraphernalia necessary for mixed drinks, there were cocktail or beverage carts (fig. 8.87).

Smoking also became a symbol of the new social code. Men no longer retired to the library for their cigars, pipes, and cigarettes after dinner, as women finally began to smoke openly. Advertisements and movies reinforced the glamorous aspects of this insidious habit. A whole array of smoking accessories developed—ashtrays of all sizes and shapes, cigarette holders, and lighters (see fig. 8.86).

Responses to the change in the social status of women, and the breaking away from the protective code of the Victorian era, were expressed in many different ways. The body was no longer confined in corsets or padded with bustles. Dresses in the 1920s rejected fitted form altogether and were shortened to expose the legs. Form would return in the 1930s, not to restrict, but to emphasize the natural curves of the body. Hair was shortened for ease

8.84 Norman Bel Geddes Cocktail Shaker, Glasses, and Tray. 1937. Manufactured by Revere Brass and Copper Co., Rome, N.Y. Chrome-plated metal, shaker ht.: 12¾". The Brooklyn Museum. Gift of Paul F. Walter

8.85 Norman Bel Geddes "Soda King" Syphon Bottle. ca. 1935. Manufactured by Walter Kidde Sales Co., Bloomfield, N.J. Chrome-plated and enameled metal with rubber fittings, ht.: 10"; dia.: 4¼". The Brooklyn Museum. H. Randolph Lever Fund

8.86 W. J. Campbell
Climax Cocktail Smoker. 1934. Manufactured by Climax Machinery Co., Indianapolis. Steel and aluminum, ht.: 26½″; dia. 16½″. Collection John P. Axelrod

8.87 Gilbert Rohde
Beverage Cart. ca. 1934. Manufactured by Troy Sunshade Co., Troy, Ohio. Chrome-plated steel, painted wood, and cork, 33 × 33¾ × 18¾″. The Brooklyn Museum. H. Randolph Lever Fund

of care and more importantly as a symbolic statement of women's growing independence. Sexuality also came out of hiding. Aspects of a woman's personal life, which in the nineteenth century had remained secret, perhaps even to her husband, were now out in the open. Ironically, the more freedom women achieved, the more emphasis was placed on their feminine sexuality (maybe for fear from both women and men that women would lose it). Advertising promoted beauty aids, and cosmetics became an important business. A need arose for a table at which to store and apply these beauty aids. A woman's vanity, a furniture form which was not new but had almost disappeared during the nineteenth century, was resurrected (fig. 8.88). This form in the past had been called a dressing table; its renaming in the twentieth century was more appropriate to its new use.

The machine age in America represented for both men and women a rite of passage through a technological maze to a cultural coming-of-age. The use of the machine in all of its many manifestations could not help but be acknowledged. The machine was new. It was unfamiliar. Its capabilities and potential were unknown. It was exciting and threatening; it was overwhelming, all-consuming, and inescapable. It was discovered, explored, exploited, glorified, and at times vilified. America's obsession with the machine lessened by the end of the 1930s as we became more comfortable with it. This did not mean we had conquered it or were even aware of the extent of its future potential, both positive and negative. With familiarity, though, there was a release from a material focus on the machine itself. Designers began to realize that just because machine technology was used to make a chair, for example, the chair need

not resemble a machine. As Lewis Mumford so perceptively stated in 1934, "the passage of the machine into art was in itself a signal of release, a sign that the hard necessity of practice, the preoccupation with the immediate battle was over—a sign that the mind was free once more to see, to contemplate, and so to enlarge and deepen all the practical benefits of the machine."[74] And so indeed did artists and designers begin to free themselves from the physical shackles of the machine image.

8.89 Ilya Bolotowsky
Untitled (study for a mural). ca. 1939. Oil on canvas, 29⅝ × 47½″. The Newark Museum. John J. O'Neill Bequest Fund

8.90 Installation view of furniture by Charles Eames and Eero Saarinen, *Organic Design in Home Furnishings* exhibition, The Museum of Modern Art, New York. 1941. Courtesy The Museum of Modern Art, New York

By 1937 the economy had improved. No longer were designers forced to produce designs in the proven-marketable machine image. In addition there was a growing new aesthetic spirit, as seen in the surrealistic work of Jean Arp and Joan Miró in Europe, and in the biomorphic art of Isamu Noguchi, Alexander Calder, Stuart Davis, and Ilya Bolotowsky in America. The same technology that made it possible to mold forms into streamlined shapes could be adapted to produce biomorphic ones. Geometric regularity, whether straight-lined or curved, was gradually being replaced by irregular fluid outlines. Materials such as wood, which, because of its strong traditional associations, had been largely ignored by avant-garde designers, were looked at again with new eyes. Alvar Aalto, the Finnish architect and furniture designer, had been working with molded plywood throughout the 1930s. His one-man show at The Museum of Modern Art in 1938 had a major impact on American designers. Eero Saarinen and Charles Eames won first prize in The Museum of Modern Art's competition, *Organic Design in Home Furnishings*, held in 1940–41 for both "organic" and "aggregate"

8.91 Isamu Noguchi
"Radio Nurse" (short-wave radio transmitter for home or hospital use). 1938. Manufactured by Zenith Radio Corp., Chicago. Housing molded by Kurz-Kasch, Inc. Bakelite plastic housing, 8 × 6½ × 6½″. Collection Fifty-50

solutions to furniture forms (see fig. 8.90). The importance of the side- and armchairs is that they looked nothing like machines, and yet they were totally dependent on machine technology. Though not strictly the first plywood chairs to be molded in two directions, they were the first such chairs to be widely known for this new technique.[75] New technology made it possible to create compound curves resulting in a sculptural form that was both strong and light. Springs were replaced by a foam rubber pad for com-

8.92 Walter Dorwin Teague
Desk Lamp. ca. 1939. Manufactured by
Polaroid, Cambridge, Mass. Aluminum,
metal, and plastic, 12¾ × 11½ × 10¼″.
The Brooklyn Museum. H. Randolph
Lever Fund

8.93 Gilbert Rohde
Living Room, *Contemporary American
Industrial Design* exhibition, The Metro-
politan Museum of Art, New York. 1940.
From *Magazine of Art* (June 1940)

fort. These chairs (despite the unresolved
problems of how to attach the legs) were
harbingers of the new direction furniture
design would take after the disruption of
the war. The goals of strength, comfort,
and lightness were becoming a reality.[76]

The Metropolitan Museum's *Contemporary American Industrial Art* exhibition
in 1940 illustrated the profound change
that was occurring in this country during
the late 1930s. If one did not know the
date of Gilbert Rohde's living room for
this show (fig. 8.93), one would assume
that it had been designed in the 1950s. Already in place are the gooseneck lamp
with an amoeba-shaped shade, a freely
flowing curved fireplace wall, biomorphic
rug, shaggy upholstery, and the ubiquitous tapered wire legs of the chair and
table.

334

8.94 Karl Ratliff
"Twin-O-Matic" Waffle Iron. 1937 (Exhibited at New York World's Fair, 1939). Manufactured by Manning-Bowman & Co., Meriden, Conn. Various metals and plastic, 7 × 12 × 11¼". Alan Moss Ltd.

Belief in the limitless future potential of the machine had both its positive and negative aspects. During the 1930s this almost blind faith in the power of the machine to make the world a better place helped hold a badly shattered nation together. People were easily lulled into a false sense of security by the utopian visions of the future which bombarded them from every direction. Many objects took on futuristic forms as if they were going to be propelled into outer space. These science-fiction fantasies contributed to an almost naive approach to serious problems and a denial of the problems that could already be foreseen.

As Americans innocently gaped at the wonders of the *World of Tomorrow* at the New York World's Fair, Europe was plunged into an horrendous war. Insulated by our geographic distance and naiveté, Americans had no comprehension that in two years our world would be turned upside down by this conflagration. Grover A. Whalen, president of the fair, could in all sincerity write that this exposition shows "the immediate necessity of enlightened and harmonious cooperation to preserve and save the best of our modern civilization. We seek to achieve or-

8.95 Russel Wright
Coffee Urn. ca. 1935. Custom-made by Russel Wright, Inc. (later Russel Wright Accessories), New York. Spun aluminum and walnut, 16 × 15 × 12". Collection Paul F. Walter

derly progress in a world of peace; and toward this end many competent critics have already noted marked progress."[77] This astounding innocence is all the more remarkable when one remembers that we were already in the process of creating the ultimate machine that could destroy the world—the nuclear bomb.

We were eager for the future. Despite the doomsayers most people felt that the machine could not help but make the world a better place. Most fascinating is the fact that the actual future was developing where anyone could see it, but,

8.96 Gilbert Rohde
Fashion of the Future ("Man of the next century will revolt against shaving and wear a beautiful beard...His hat will be an antenna...His socks—disposable. His suit minus tie, collar, buttons"). Vest is Rohm-Haas plexiglass. Anton Bruehl photograph for *Vogue* (February 1939)

8.97 John Vassos
Television Console, Model TRK-12. 1939. Manufactured by RCA, New York. Wood, glass, and metal parts, 39 × 34½ × 20″. Collection Arnold Chase

ironically, very few recognized it. Gilbert Rohde predicted that the man of the twenty-first century would throw off his drab and confining suit and tie and express himself in a practical, colorful jumpsuit (fig. 8.96). This garment would have both a heating and air-conditioning system and be able to send and receive radio transmissions. To the public of 1939 this was a fantastic, but possible vision of the future. Today, it is an image rich in associations with the 1930s' almost quaint view of the world to come. Buck Rogers and his exploits in space come quickly to mind. Meanwhile, Americans were officially introduced, in 1939, to a new electronic medium, television. It was difficult

to recognize at the time, however, that this novelty, housed in its ungainly and conventional-looking case, would ultimately transform society.

The machine age was a time of contradictions and ironies, of hopes and fears. It was also a period of growth and maturity. The unifying and defining factor was the machine. The decorative arts developed from handmade machine-looking objects to biomorphic forms that were totally dependent on machine technology. Throughout this difficult journey Americans demonstrated their creativity and ingenuity.

Recognition of America's contribution to design during the 1920s and 1930s has been slow in coming. Russel Wright in 1938 issued a challenge that is only recently being met:

Why can't someone, A Museum of Modern Art or a New York World's Fair, put on an exhibit in which they would dramatize all design that is American? First, let them parade those unconscious developments, free from any aesthetic inferiority complexes. Our bridges. Our roads. Our factory machinery. Our skyscrapers. Let them throw a spotlight on our shining bathrooms and our efficient kitchens. Roll out our trick cocktail gadgets—our streamlined iceboxes—our streamlined pencil sharpeners....Let them put a magnifying glass (if they feel they need it) over these things to find the American character....Let them do this without recourse to European standards in their selection. It has never been done. But I know that they will find that there is a distinct American character of design in all that is American and that our home furnishings tie in to this character. Not until then, will we know of what elements this American character consists.[78]

9.1

CHAPTER 9

THE MACHINE AGE AND BEYOND

The machine age in America, the years prior to 1941, occurred when the public, led by artists, designers, and industrialists, believed that the machine could make a beneficent impact upon art and life. A utopian faith in technology reinforced a long-standing American ideal of creating a new world, even during the Depression. With America's entry into the raging world war and the horrific resolution at Hiroshima and Nagasaki, it became all too evident that the optimistic future of the machine age needed to be rethought. An American fascination with the machine and technology continued after 1945, but with a new sense of urgency: the machine now threatened to run out of control.

The machine age was central to the development of modernism in the twentieth century. The word "modern," instead of being synonymous with "contemporary" or "up-to-date"—its nineteenth-century definition—came to mean in the 1920s and 1930s an identifiable and special sensibility that called for a complete break with the past. The features of the machine, its ahistorical, nontraditional, impersonal, and abstract character, seemed to mandate an art and culture with similar outlines.

The results of this machine age modernism could be seen in the radical transformations that took place in America between the wars. Vast industrial complexes, high-voltage power lines, new parkways, superhighways, and bridges came to dominate the landscape. To the painter Ralston Crawford, the industrialization of the natural landscape was symbolic of "the emancipation of the times," promising the elimination of poverty from the world. Crawford's *Overseas Highway* of 1939 (fig. 9.1) captures the excitement of a totally new environment stretching across the Florida Keys in the late 1930s. As Crawford explained, "I felt that I was quite literally going to sea in my car."[1]

By the 1930s American transportation changed its look. Automobiles became rolling sculpture with their new, integrated bodies. Streamlining overtook trains, boats, buses, trucks, and planes, making them speedier, more comfortable, and more accessible. Americans could tow monocoque aluminum-riveted trailers, metaphorically linked with flight by the *Airstream* manufacturer. At the 1939 New York World's Fair, Brooks Stevens introduced the future with a motorized home on wheels (fig. 9.2). Lining the new

9.1 Ralston Crawford (1906–1978) *Overseas Highway.* 1939. Oil on canvas, 28 × 45″. The Regis Collection

9.2 Clifford Brooks Stevens (b. 1911)
Research Car, New York World's Fair.
1939

9.3 Douglas D. Ellington and R. J.
Wadsworth, chief architects, Hale Walker, town planner
Business Center, Movie Theater, and
Housing, Greenbelt, Md. 1935–41. Collection Library of Congress. Farm Securities Administration, Office of War
Information

roads were sleek and efficient machine-produced service stations and diners.

Although the various proponents of streamlining, the International Style, and stripped classicism competed for architectural dominance, their idioms held in common an essential abstraction and simplification derived from the machine. While the ideal of a completely machine-made or mass-produced architecture remained largely elusive, all the architectural idioms sought to embody the machine and its processes in their image. Instead of visually complex exteriors—the hallmark of Victorian and other traditional architecture—the new buildings appeared simpler on the outside and yet enjoyed mechanically more complex interiors, with labor-saving and comfort-enhancing machinery. Through air conditioning, ventilation, and new materials, the building could protect the inhabitants from the extremes and at the same time be open to nature.

The quest for a totally new and socially responsive environment led to a number of experiments. In the 1930s architectural reform found implementation in several of Roosevelt's New Deal programs, notably the Resettlement Administration and the Housing Division of the PWA. For the first time in American history, the federal government took responsibility for providing adequate housing for the population. The results varied, from large, socially repressive housing blocks in the Williamsburg section of Brooklyn to revolutionary new towns near Cincinnati, Los Angeles, Milwaukee, and Trenton.

Greenbelt, Maryland, about thirteen miles from Washington, D.C., was perhaps the best-known and most successful among planned towns (fig. 9.3). Designed and constructed between 1935 and 1941, Greenbelt offered a harmonious environment comprised of open space, recreational areas, a civic and business center, and domestic housing for 3,500, which quickly grew to over 7,000 inhabitants. The town was situated in a large arc surrounding an open field at one end of a lake; motor and pedestrian traffic were rigorously separated. Modern in style, most buildings of Greenbelt were constructed out of concrete block, painted white and trimmed with raised brick for abstract ornamental detail. The community succeeded: a cooperative store was established, and residential groups successfully oversaw the future direction of the town.[2]

The ideal of the planned town lay dormant in the years immediately following World War II, not to rise again until the 1960s. The suburb, so lovingly portrayed in the movie *The City*, became the goal of many Americans. Similarly, the old industrial city with its rotting slums became the scene of urban renewal after the war.[3]

Whereas public and commercial buildings were readily given over to machine age abstraction, after World War II most American single-family housing remained stylistically tied to traditional exteriors. With the new power sources, especially hydroelectricity, however, the machine entered the American household, bringing new comforts, new ways of living, and new entertainment (fig. 9.4). Certainly not every American could afford or even admired the shapes and forms of the new furnishings—the chromium tubular tables, the speedboat-shaped chairs, the abstractly patterned glassware. In some of its manifestations the new design was aimed at an elite taste fostered by designers and curators like Frankl and Barr for the purpose of revolutionizing the interior decor of an entire house. Committed modernists sought a unity for their interiors: a Theodore Roszak sculpture and a Donald Deskey torchère lamp not only existed harmoniously but were difficult to

tell apart. Most Americans of all classes, however, remained safely ensconced in their overstuffed chairs and ate at their Grand Rapids reproduction dining-room suite. Into this traditional (though mass-produced) interior, technology brought entertainment. Now the family could gather at the radio—and eventually the television—every evening.

A more extensive revolution occurred in the American bathroom and kitchen. The bathroom evolved from a subject never mentioned in polite company to a fantasy of white enamel, porcelain, and chrome fixtures. The machine truly dominated the kitchen, for there one could sit

9.4 Lester T. Beall (1903–1969) *Light* poster for Rural Electrification Administration. 1937. Silkscreen, 40 × 30″. The Museum of Modern Art, New York. Gift of the designer

9.5 Abel Faidy
Reception Room for Hedrich-Blessing.
Chicago. 1935–36

in a chromium tubular chair without self-consciousness and be surrounded by a refrigerator, stove, toaster, blender, dishwasher, washing machine, and clothes dryer, all products of industrial design promoted by corporations intent upon developing a new market.[4]

Americans thus came to inhabit new spaces conceived in novel ways not only at home but also in the workplace, especially in the corporate offices in large cities. Abel Faidy's design for the Hedrich-Blessing Studio emphasized the machine-like camera and the merchandising value of product display (fig. 9.5). Located in a windowless interior space of a large Chicago office building, the design created an expansive feeling by using black and chrome furniture, walls of mirror glass and glass block, and a photographic mural. The narrow space seemed infinite. An assemblage of photographs appropriately tilted in a cubist manner, the mural illustrated buildings of Walter Dorwin Teague and Holabird and Root, the Burlington *Zephyr*, a Gilbert Rohde clock, and a scientist at his microscope. Despite lending an illusion of infinite office space, the mirrors also reflected a controlled image of a smooth and efficient, clean and bright machine to which the human being had to conform.[5]

In addition to manufacturing sleek corporate images, the machine age provided a world of illusion and fantasy through mass-produced entertainment for the radio and film. The hopes and dreams of millions fastened onto film personalities who became idols of the silver screen in movie palaces throughout the country (fig. 9.7). Cedric Gibbons, a committed modernist architect and movie set designer, fittingly conceived the Oscar as a statue with the sleek metallic form of a Brancusi, yet the icon was a quintessentially American machine age figure, mass-produced and featureless, a robot rising out of a film reel can (fig. 9.6).

American artists celebrated this new world created by machines in their paintings, sculpture, and photographs. Led by Alfred Stieglitz, photographers documented the presence of skyscrapers, bridges, dynamos, and other now-familiar icons of the machine age. Painters and sculptors soon followed this initial exploration with images that revealed the speed, power, and geometric forms of machines. By the 1930s artists were aware of two developments: the spread of the machine throughout the United States beyond urban areas, and the interconnectedness of technology. Walker Evans, Stuart Davis, and Charles Demuth were only a few of the artists who explored the impact of the machine in rural America. Charles Sheeler best visualized the machine as a total system in his photographs and paintings of Henry Ford's River Rouge plant.

9.6 Cedric Gibbons (1893–1960)
Oscar. ca. 1928. Britannia alloy, gold plated, ht.: 13″ (including base)

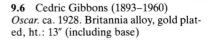

9.7 Frederick Kiesler
Interior, Film Guild Cinema. New York. 1928

9.8 Robert Lepper (b. 1906) Mural for Mining Industries Building, West Virginia University, Morgantown, W.Va. 1940–42. Egg emulsion on canvas, 12 × 48′

These two trends in technology were dramatically brought together in Robert Lepper's large mural for West Virginia University (fig. 9.8). His original intention—to paint a regional mural in the vein of the American Scene movement—dissolved as he began to grasp the national economic importance of the West Virginia mineral industry. Composed of individual studies of specific machines drawn from actual duPont and Union Carbide plants in Charleston (fig. 9.9), the mural took as its theme the extraction of coal and gas, their transformation into energy, and their ultimate distribution to industry and home. This interweaving of the mechanical and the living, the organic and the inorganic, created a panorama of the machine age in one specific locality yet tied it to a larger national scene. Its only rival was Diego Rivera's Ford murals in Detroit a decade earlier.[6]

Because American artists, unlike industrial designers, usually were not patronized by large corporations, they felt fewer constraints about taking a critical stance toward the machine. Then, too, they had first become aware of the machine and its aesthetic possibilities through Marcel Duchamp and Francis Picabia in New York during World War I. As a consequence, American artists regarded the machine not only as an elegant, geometric form with utopian possibilities, but also as a destructive and irrational entity. Most crucially, however, the very flexibility of their expressive forms allowed artists to make complex statements about technology, to discern its subtle changes upon human sensibility, and to explore its mythic possibilities.

Thus Arshile Gorky's mural project for Newark Airport became a meditation on the "plastic symbols of aviation" and the origin of all mechanics (fig. 9.10). Although there were correspondences between Gorky's paintings and actual airplanes, his complex of ten panels went beyond naturalistic rendition. Working from photographs, Gorky took the mechanical parts of airplanes and in some panels transformed them into biomorphic elements; as he imagined it, "the engine becomes in one plane like the wings of a dragon." In two panels devoted to "Activities on the Field," he abstracted airplane parts for their symbolic value, then distorted and reintegrated them into a unified surface structure he hoped would convey a "miraculous new vision of our time."[7]

The virtual destruction of Gorky's high achievement at Newark is emblematic of the mixed legacy left by American artists of the machine age. Dada, of course, was short-lived, though Duchamp in his silent and subversive existence was picked up again by Pop artists during the 1960s. Constructivism never really gained a footing in America, despite the efforts of Jane Heap and Louis Lozowick. Geometrical abstraction in painting remained a small movement throughout the 1930s, eventually overshadowed by abstract expressionism after 1945; its heritage only began to be appreciated in the 1960s with the emergence of Minimal Art. The substantial achievement of the Department of the Treasury's Art Section and the WPA mural program in placing mural paintings and sculpture in public buildings across the United States was pluralistic in style; most tended toward American Scene narrative, with machines taking equal billing with cows and farmers. This mural movement came to an end with World War II. A generation later a new mural movement took up ethnic politics rather than technological themes.

Stieglitz's group dispersed by the 1940s, largely because it had been comprised of an older generation of modernists. Charles Demuth died of diabetes at the height of his powers; Georgia O'Keeffe's departure to the Southwest moved her away from urban themes; and Stieglitz's retirement as a photographer crippled the cohesive force of the group. The development of individual artists was equally mixed. Some, like Theodore Roszak, became disillusioned with the prospect of creating art out of technology, while others, like Alexander Calder, continued to explore possibilities initiated in the 1930s to such an extent that we no longer think of their work as technological but "natural." Sheeler continued to paint after the war but with a greater license and poetic turn, as though the task of looking steadily and clearly at machines had belonged to an earlier, specific moment in time. What has become known in retrospect as a "precisionist" style was carried on by Ralston Crawford, who was just starting out in the late 1930s.

An enduring legacy of the machine age in the arts occurred in the institutional realm of art education, which underwent a revolution. Although the best-known changes involved the immigration of leading European designers, the way had been well prepared with extensive curricular revisions and the establishment of several new schools in New York, Los Angeles, Dayton, Pittsburgh, and elsewhere during the 1930s. In 1935 at the Carnegie Institute of Technology, the first program in industrial design began under the leadership of Wilfred Readio. Robert Lepper, the most theoretical instructor on the faculty, initiated a basic course of visual analysis. Taking field trips to large factories in Pittsburgh, students tried to determine basic machine processes and then align them with Lep-

9.9 Robert Lepper
Bottling Machine (study from mural at West Virginia Univerity). 1941. Oil on masonite, 42 × 35″. Private collection

per's "elements of visual perception"—"line, area, volume, space, value, and texture." The abstract quality Lepper sought in design was not unlike Johannes Itten's and Moholy-Nagy's Bauhaus courses, although the American's ideas came independently. In seeking to go beyond the mere manufacture of style, Lepper was, ironically enough, criticized by some industrial designers for not turning out stylists. His theorizing has become commonplace in American art and design schools since World War II.[8]

Both industrial design and advertising art were fundamental to the new age of mass consumption and mass information. As foreseen by Matthew Josephson and his Dada friends in the early 1920s, American taste was in the process of becoming mass-produced and homog-

enized, shaped by professionals whose roles were virtually unknown prior to World War I. Through advertising artists, avant-garde concepts of art and design were spread on the pages of magazines and billboards across the country. The industrial designer, a product of the 1920s and 1930s, consciously determined to reshape consumer products. Aware that traditional distinctions between "fine" art and commerce had become blurred, Josephson urged artists' participation in the burgeoning mass media.[9]

His call was heeded by only a few painters, Stuart Davis and Gerald Murphy among them, who played with the visual possibilities of advertising. During the Depression photographers were more willing to view critically the inherent contradictions of advertising art. This period of conscious exploration and experimentation gradually brought about the Americanization of our culture, setting the stage for the 1940s and 1950s, when America assumed world leadership, not only culturally, but politically and economically. By the time of our entry into World War II, the climate in which Europe looked to us for design inspiration was already in place. American designers came to age just at the time the European community was thrown into chaos. Already in the mid-1930s European artists, designers, and architects were pouring into the United States to escape political tyranny at home.

Waiting to greet them was a new breed of critic and museum curator—exemplified by Lewis Mumford and Alfred H. Barr, Jr. Instead of being standard-bearers for old world art and culture, these new pacesetters rejected the past and set out to convert American taste to their own view of modernism, defined by the machine. A wide range of avant-garde

9.10 Arshile Gorky (1904–1948)
Study for a mural for Administration
Building, Newark Airport. Newark, N.J.
1935–1936. Gouache on paper, 13⅝ ×
29⅞″. The Museum of Modern Art, New
York. Extended loan from the United
States WPA Art Program

ideas and experiments gradually became institutionalized, not only by The Museum of Modern Art, but by other museums, art schools, and commercial corporations. Thus the abstraction of organic forms, long associated with Surrealism and known as biomorphism, came to dominate the advanced design of machine-made domestic products. Frederick Kiesler speculated on anthropomorphism, which he called "correalism and biotechnique," and was the first designer of the machine age to attempt to systematize human form and its measurements into a guide for furniture production. In his "kinetic" installation for Peggy Guggenheim's Art of This Century Gallery in 1942 (fig. 9.11), the furniture took on an organic, kidney-shaped form which could be adopted for chairs, display stands, cocktail tables, and beds. The kidney-shaped swimming pool would become ubiquitous in backyards across the United States in the 1940s and 1950s.[10]

The machine age in America was politically complex and ultimately contradictory. Only a few American avant-garde artists committed to machine age abstraction adopted a left-wing political posture. Most Americans interested in abstraction were attracted to the formal achievements of the Russian constructivists as distinct from their political ideology. Unfortunately, the ascendancy of Stalin and socialist realism by the early 1930s terminated political hopes for the proponents of abstraction in the Soviet Union and led to the promotion of social realism by the Communist Party in the United States. Thus the dominant wing of the American left came to affirm the machine in representational terms.

Ironically, then, abstraction was appropriated as the language of big business and the corporate elite. That The Museum of Modern Art, controlled by and representing some of the largest American fortunes, could actively propagandize the International Style, or the Bauhaus, indicated a new ideological context for European machine age art. American corporations adopted the streamlined look while also transforming avant-garde experimentation into formulas for buildings, products, and advertising in support of capitalist enterprise. As a fundamental resource of society, the machine was intrinsically political. A machine rationality could be emphasized by Marxist and capitalist alike for the enhancement of an ordered society just as the force of the machine could be symbolically exploited for its emotive power in advertising. Carried to an extreme, the force of the machine could be identified with a totalitarian state on the right *or* the left.

Given the unprecedented impact of machine technology upon American society during the 1920s and 1930s, political approaches barely resolved the problems that arose. Ultimately, the machine in America helped to generate a new consumerism with increased government regulation, establishing a hybrid of capitalism and socialism committed to mass production and mass consumption. George Santayana's claim that Americans were idealists working on matter was at no time more evident than during the machine age of the 1920s and 1930s. The idealism, the optimism, and, some might say, the naiveté of Americans would be severely tested in the creation of a machine world. The concern Paul Strand had noted in 1922 still remained: "the machine must be humanized unless it in turn dehumanize us." On that imperative the machine age in America would move.[11]

9.11 Frederick Kiesler
Art of This Century Gallery. New York.
1942. Surrealist Gallery with Frederick
Kiesler seated in foreground. Berenice
Abbott photograph

CHAPTER 1

America and the Machine Age

1. Paul Strand, "Photography and the New God," *Broom* (November 3, 1922), pp. 252, 257.
2. Stuart Chase, *Men and Machines* (New York: Macmillan, 1929), p. 1; Sheldon Cheney and Martha Cheney, *Art and the Machine* (New York: Whittlesey House–McGraw-Hill, 1936), pp. 8, 26.
3. Constance Rourke, *Charles Sheeler, Artist in the American Tradition* (New York: Harcourt, Brace, 1939), p. 137.
4. André Siegfried, *America Comes of Age* (New York: Harcourt, Brace, 1927), p. 347.
5. The term "machine age" was widely used at the time. Warren Susman, "Introduction," in *Culture and Commitment, 1929–1945*, Warren Susman, ed. (New York: Braziller, 1973), pp. 1–24, uses the term. Reyner Banham, *Theory and Design in the First Machine Age*, 2nd ed. (New York: Praeger, 1967), deals exclusively with European architecture and identifies the period as approximately 1909–29. Gilman M. Ostrander, *American Civilization in the First Machine Age: 1890–1940* (New York: Harper & Row, 1970), stretches the term, but he does not deal to any degree with machines or the visual arts. In 1927 *The New York Times Index* began using "Machine Age" as an entry. "Machine Age" also appeared in *The Reader's Guide to Periodical Literature*, starting in 1929. Charles A. Beard, "Introduction," in *Whither Mankind*, Charles A. Beard, ed. (New York: Longmans, Green, 1928), p. 14; John C. Burnham, "Watson, John Broadus," in *The Dictionary of American Biography*, Supplement 6 (New York: Scribner, 1980), p. 672; Stephen Fox, *The Mirror Makers: A History of American Advertising and Its Creators* (New York: Morrow, 1984), p. 86.
6. United States Bureau of Census, *Historical Statistics of the United States*, vol. 2 (Washington, D.C.: Government Printing Office, 1975), pp. 796, 827; Alan Balfour, *Rockefeller Center, Architecture as Theatre* (New York: McGraw-Hill, 1978), pp. 19–21.
7. Paul Goodman and Frank Otto Gatell, *America in the Twenties* (New York: Holt, 1972), p. 75.
8. James J. Flink, *The Car Culture* (Cambridge: M.I.T. Press, 1975), pp. 18, 140; Bureau of Census, *Historical Statistics*, vol. 2, pp. 716, 718, 710; Robert S. and Helen M. Lynd, *Middletown in Transition: A Study in Cultural Conflicts* (New York: Harcourt, Brace & World, 1937), pp. 265–67; Wilbur J. Cash, *The Mind of the South* (New York: Vintage Books–Random House, 1941), p. 260.
9. Paul Fussell, *The Great War and Modern Memory* (New York: Oxford Univ. Press, 1975).
10. David A. Hounshell, *From the American System to Mass Production, 1800–1932* (Baltimore: Johns Hopkins Press, 1984); John F. Kasson, *Civilizing the Machine: Technology and Republican Values in America, 1776–1900* (New York: Penguin, 1977), pp. 155–58; John Kouwenhoven, *The Arts in Modern American Civilization* (New York: Norton, 1967 [1948]), pp. 15–53; Herwin Schaefer, *Nineteenth Century Modern, The Functional Tradition in Victorian Design* (New York: Praeger, 1970); Leo Marx,

The Machine in the Garden (New York: Oxford Univ. Press, 1964).
11. Walt Whitman, "Song of the Exposition" [1876], in *Leaves of Grass and Selected Prose* (New York: Holt, 1949), p. 167; Horatio Greenough, *Form and Function: Remarks on Art, Design, and Architecture*, Harold A. Small, ed. (Berkeley: Univ. of Calif. Press, 1947); Henry Adams, *The Education of Henry Adams* [1918], (New York: Modern Library, 1931), p. 308.
12. Alan Trachtenberg, *Brooklyn Bridge, Fact and Symbol* (New York: Oxford Univ. Press, 1965); Robert Coady, "American Art," *The Soil* (December 1916), p. 1.
13. Walter Pach, "Art," in *Civilization in the United States*, Harold E. Stearns, ed. (New York: Harcourt, Brace, 1922), p. 241.
14. Lewis Mumford, "Machinery and the Modern Style," *The New Republic*, 27 (August 3, 1921), p. 265; Mumford, "The City," in *Civilization in the United States*, Stearns, ed., p. 12.
15. James Parton Haney, "Our Needs and Opportunities in the Industrial Arts," *The American Magazine of Art*, XI (December 1919), pp. 59–60.
16. Margaret Bourke-White, *Portrait of Myself* (New York: Simon & Schuster, 1963), p. 40, and quoted in "Men and Machines Exhibition Challenges Art," *The New York Times* (October 26, 1930), VIII:15.
17. Louis Lozowick, "The Americanization of Art," in *Machine-Age Exposition Catalogue*, printed in *The Little Review*, XI (1927), pp. 18–19; reprinted in Janet Flint, *The Prints of Louis Lozowick, a Catalogue Raisonné* (New York: Hudson Hills, 1982), pp. 18–19.
18. Thomas Tallmadge, *The Story of Architecture in America* (New York: Norton, 1927), p. 296; George Santayana, "The Genteel Tradition in American Philosophy [1911], *Winds of Doctrine* (London: Dent, 1913), p. 188; quoted in Carl Zigrosser, *The Complete Etchings of John Marin* (Philadelphia: Philadelphia Museum of Art, 1969), pp. 16–17; Hugh Ferriss, *The Metropolis of Tomorrow* (New York: Ives Washburn, 1929), p. 16; and quoted in Dorothy Norman, *Alfred Stieglitz: An American Seer* (New York: Random House, 1973), p. 80.
19. Fred Austin, "Skyscrapers—America Produces Its First Jazz Ballet," *The Dance Magazine* (April 1926), p. 24; *The New York Times* (August 7, 1928), 25:2; Richard Striner, "Machine, Dance: An Intellectual Sidelight to Busby Berkeley's Career," *Journal of American Culture*, 7 (1984), pp. 60–68.
20. Sinclair Lewis, *Babbitt* (New York: Grosset & Dunlap, 1922), pp. 68, 69; Macknight Black, *Machinery* (New York: Horace Liveright, 1929), pp. 8, 15.
21. J. H. [Jane Heap], "Machine-Age Exposition," *The Little Review*, XI (Spring 1925), p. 22; Harry Crosby, *Shadows of the Sun: The Diaries of Harry Crosby*, Edward German, ed. (Santa Barbara: Black Sparrow, 1977), p. 146.
22. Wanda M. Corn, *Grant Wood, The Regionalist Vision* (New Haven: Yale Univ. Press–Minneapolis Institute of Arts, 1983), p. 82; Marlene Park and Gerald E. Markowitz, *Democratic Vistas, Post Offices and Public Art in the New Deal* (Philadelphia: Temple Univ. Press, 1984).
23. Philip Lippincott Goodwin, *Rooftrees, or

the Architectural History of an American Family* (Philadelphia: Lippincott, 1933), p. 61.
24. Norman Bel Geddes, *Horizons* (Boston: Little, Brown, 1932), p. 3; Walter Dorwin Teague, "Why Disguise Your Product?" *Electrical Manufacturing*, 22 (October 1938), p. 47.
25. Henry Ford, "Machinery, The New Messiah," *The Forum*, 79 (March 1928), p. 363.
26. Alfred H. Barr, Jr., "Foreword," in *Machine Art* (New York: Museum of Modern Art, 1934), n.p., and Chase, *Men and Machines*, p. 328.

CHAPTER 2

Machine Aesthetics and Styles

1. Loewy's charts appeared in Cheney and Cheney, *Art and the Machine*, pp. 25, 99, 126, 137, 237. Some of them were altered in the intervening years; see Raymond Loewy, *Industrial Design* (Woodstock, N.Y., Overlook Press, 1979), pp. 74–76.
2. Teague, "Why Disguise Your Product?" p. 110; some examples out of many are "Editorial— Appearance Counts," *Product Engineering*, 1 (June 1930), p. 284, and R. E. Hellmund, "An Engineer's Approach," *Electrical Manufacturing*, 22 (October 1938), p. 50.
3. I have been stimulated and influenced in this approach by George Kubler, *The Shape of Time: Remarks on the History of Things* (New Haven: Yale Univ. Press, 1962), and Reyner Banham, "Machine Aesthetic," *The Architectural Review*, 117 (April 1955), pp. 225–28.
4. Paul T. Frankl, *Form and Re Form* (New York: Harper & Bros., 1930), p. 51; Frankl, "Furniture for the House of Tomorrow," *Architecture*, LXIX (April 1934), p. 192.
5. Rudolph Rosenthal and Helena L. Ratzka, *The Story of Modern Applied Art* (New York: Harper Bros., 1948), pp. 167–74; Walter Littlefield Creese, "American Architecture from 1918 to 1933 with Special Emphasis on European Influence" (Ph.D. Dissertation, Harvard Univ., 1949), pt. II, pp. 1–7; Karen Davies, *At Home in Manhattan: Modern Decorative Arts, 1925 to the Depression* (New Haven: Yale Univ. Art Gallery, 1983), p. 10.
6. Quoted in Museum of Modern Art and Philadelphia Museum of Art, *Marcel Duchamp*, Anne D'Harnoncourt and Kynaston McShine, eds. (New York: Museum of Modern Art, 1973), p. 256. See also, Milton J. Brown, *American Painting from the Armory Show to the Depression* (Princeton: Princeton Univ. Press, 1955); on geometrical simplification, see Reyner Banham, *Theory and Design in the First Machine Age*, and Kurt Roland, *A History of the Modern Movement* (New York: Van Nostrand Reinhold, 1973).
7. "Modernism in Industrial Art," *The American Magazine of Art*, XV (October 1924), p. 540. Arthur Pulos, *American Design Ethic* (Cambridge: M.I.T. Press, 1983), p. 304; United States Commission on International Exposition of Modern Decorative and Industrial Art, Paris, 1925, *Report of the Commission Appointed by the Secretary of Commerce to visit and report upon the International Exposition of Modern Decorative and Industrial Art in Paris, 1925* (Washington, D.C.: Department of Commerce, 1926), pp.

48, 78, 79; Helen Appleton Read, "The Exposition in Paris," *International Studio*, 82 (November 1925), p. 96.

The terms "Art Moderne, "modernistic," and "modernist" were in fairly wide usage until the 1960s, though frequently used with disparagement, as explained below. The term "Art Deco" with direct reference to the 1925 Paris exhibition was first used in 1966 during a Paris exhibition devoted to the subject, as one of the subtitles to the catalogue: Musée des Arts Décoratifs, *Les Années '25': Art Deco/Bauhaus/Stijl/Esprit Nouveau*. (Paris: Musée des Arts Décoratifs, 1966). Bevis Hillier, *Art Deco of the 20s and 30s* (London and New York: Studio Vista and Dutton, 1968), helped to popularize the term; see pp. 11–12 for 1920s objects with an appearance similar to, or deriving from, those in the 1925 exhibition. Subsequently, Martin Battersby, *The Decorative Twenties* (London and New York: Studio Vista and Walker, 1969), used "Art Deco" for design up to the 1925 exhibition, and "new modernism" for work after. In the United States, Elayne H. Varian, *Art Deco* (New York and Bloomfield Hills: Finch College Museum of Art and Cranbrook Academy of Art, 1970), helped to expand the term to the 1930s. The Finch-Cranbrook show was enlarged for The Minneapolis Institute of Arts, text by Bevis Hillier, *The World of Art Deco* (New York: Dutton, 1971). On page 23, Hillier gives an account of the term. The term "Art Deco" which originally applied to only work derived from the 1925 Paris exhibition had become greatly enlarged and now in some usage includes practically anything designed between 1918 and 1941. See Richard Guy Wilson, "Defining Art Deco," *Art Deco Society of New York News*, 3 (Fall 1983), p. 2.

8.   The exhibition is well covered in contemporary photographs; for the best collection see *Exposition Internationale des Arts Décoratifs et Industriels Modernes* (Paris: Larousse, 1929), 13 vols.

9.   Read, "The Exposition," p. 93; and Helen Appleton Read, "Creative Design in Our Industrial Art," *International Studio*, 83 (March 1926), p. 56.

10.   P. M., "Paul Poiret's Famous Criticism," *Arts and Decoration*, 18 (November 1922), pp. 60, 64.

11.   "We tend to go into raptures over certain primitive forms.... The fact that some native form may be a religious symbol means nothing." Ely Jacques Kahn, *Design in Art and Industry* (New York: Scribner, 1935) p. 35. See also "The American Indian's Contribution to Design," *House Beautiful*, 67 (April 1930), pp. 437, 480–82; M. D. C. Crawford, "Primitive Art and Modern Design," *Creative Art*, 3 (December 1928), p. xli; and Allen True, "Color Decoration at the Boulder Dam Power Plant," *The Reclamation Era*, 26 (January 1936), p. 13.

12.   Fernand Léger, "The Esthetics of the Machine," *The Little Review*, IX (Autumn–Winter, 1923–24), pp. 55, 57. Elizabeth Turner, "American Artists in Paris, 1920–1929" (Ph.D. Dissertation, Univ. of Virginia, 1985), p. 85; Louis Lozowick, "Fernand Léger," *The Nation*, 121 (December 16, 1925), p. 712. See also, Bernadette Constensou, ed., *Léger et l'Esprit Moderne* (Paris: Musée d'Art Moderne de la Ville de Paris, 1982).

13.   Le Corbusier, *Towards a New Architecture* (New York: Praeger, 1960 [1927]), p. 121.

14.   Ibid., p. 89; "On Our Library Table," *The Architect*, 9 (December 1927), p. 287; Ralph Walker, "A New Architecture," *Architectural Forum*, 48 (January 1928), pp. 4, 1.

15.   Frankl, *Form and Re-Form*, pp. 31, 33; Walter Dorwin Teague, "Designing for Machines," *Advertising Arts* (April 2, 1930), p. 50; Walter Dorwin Teague, *Design This Day; The Technique of Order in the Machine Age* (New York: Harcourt, Brace, 1940), figs. 69, 70, p. 161 (see also pp. 141–60 and 263–73).

16.   Letter, Wilmar Soss of Dunhill to Philip Johnson, Jan. 29, 1934; letter Philip Johnson to Nelson Rockefeller, Jan. 31, 1934, in Museum of Modern Art, Archives.

17.   Philip Johnson, "History of Machine Art," *Machine Art*, n.p. For a later attack, see John McAndrew, " 'Modernistic' and 'Streamlined,' " *Museum of Modern Art Bulletin* (December 1938), pp. 2–3.

18.   Paul T. Frankl, *New Dimensions* (New York: Payson & Clarke, 1928), pp. 16–17; Frankl, *Form and Re-Form*, pp. 41–49.

19.   Le Corbusier, *Towards a New Architecture*, pp. 99–119; C. G. Holme, "The Influence of the Air," *Creative Art*, 5 (October 1929), pp. 725–28; Joseph J. Corn, *The Winged Gospel, America's Romance with Aviation, 1900–1950* (New York: Oxford Univ. Press, 1983); Cheney and Cheney, *Art and the Machine*, p. iv; see also, Teague, *Design This Day*, fig. 78, p. 165.

20.   Interview with Albert Dean, Budd Company, May 31, 1984. See also, Stan Grayson, "The All-Steel World of Edward Budd," *Automobile Quarterly*, 16 (Fourth Quarter 1978), p. 362; Hounshell, *From the American System*, p. 294; Charles C. Carr, *ALCOA, An American Enterprise* (New York: Rinehart, 1952), pp. 166–69, 179–80; and Jeffrey L. Meikle, *Twentieth Century Limited, Industrial Design in America, 1925–1939* (Philadelphia: Temple Univ. Press, 1979), pp. 80–81.

21.   "Frank Lloyd Wright and Hugh Ferriss Discuss This Modern Architecture," *Architectural Forum*, 53 (November 1930), p. 536. See also *Contempora Exposition of Art and Industry* (New York: Art Center, 1929), n.p.; and Paul Lester Wiener, "Creative Architecture of Erich Mendelsohn," *Architectural Forum*, 53 (November 1930), pp. 611–12. Wiener was the founder and director of Contempora, an international organization comprised of Germans (Bruno Paul), Frenchmen (Paul Poiret), and Americans (Wright, Mumford, Ferriss, and others). See also Rosenthal and Ratzka, *The Story of Modern Applied Art*, pp. 186–87; Cheney, *The New World Architecture*, pp. 97, 107; Clarence P. Hornung, "Architecture as a Source in Modern Design," *Advertising Arts*, 15 (July 9, 1930), pp. 41–45; and Bel Geddes, *Horizons*, p. 24.

22.   "Design Decade," *Architectural Forum*, 73 (October 1940), p. 221.

23.   "Streamlining Glorified," "Same Girl—Five Ways," and "Streamline the Silhouette," in *Sunday News* (September 8, 1935); and "Streamlining the Stars," *Screenland* (January 1935); all in Arens Collection, Arents Research Library, Syracuse University; Lewis Mumford, *Technics and Civilization* (New York: Harcourt, Brace, 1934), p. 253.

24.   Teague, *Design This Day*, figs. 24, 21.

25.   Eliot Noyes, *Organic Design* (New York: Museum of Modern Art, 1941), inside front cover and passim. For definition of organic see Bel Geddes, *Horizons*, p. 18, Le Corbusier, *Towards a New Architecture*, p. 268, and Cheney, *New World Architecture*, pp. 34, 379; "An Entirely New Type of Chair is Presented in Exhibition of Organic Design Opening at _____," Museum of Modern Art, publicity release, Contemporary Modern Art Society of Cincinnati, Univ. of Cincinnati Archives, Organic Design file.

26.   Frederick Lewis Allen, *Since Yesterday* (New York: Bantam, 1961 [1939]), pp. 111–12; see also, "Sex: The Case Against Mae West," in *Culture and Commitment, 1929–1945*, Susman, ed., pp. 107–14; Teague, *Design This Day*, figs. 18, 19, 17, p. 53.

27.   I do not mean to imply that sexual imagery first appears in car advertising in 1938. Clearly it occurred in the late 1920s, as in the "Body by Fisher" advertisements in which stylish young women frequently appear; but the car as a sex symbol used overtly in advertisements appears to be a 1930s innovation.

28.   Alfred H. Barr, Jr., ed., *Fantastic Art, Dada, Surrealism* (New York: Museum of Modern Art, 1936); and Russell Lynes, *Good Old Modern* (New York: Atheneum, 1973), pp. 143, 144.

29.   Roy Sheldon and Egmont Arens, *Consumer Engineering* (New York: Harper & Bros. 1932), p. 102; Russel Wright, quoted in Pulos, *American Design Ethic*, p. 292, and William J. Hennessey, *Russel Wright, American Designer* (Cambridge: M.I.T. Press, 1983), pp. 37–38.

30.   Frank Lloyd Wright, "The Logic of Contemporary Architecture as the Expression of This Age," *Architectural Forum* (May 1930), quoted in Frederick Gutheim, ed., *Frank Lloyd Wright on Architecture* (New York: Grosset & Dunlap, 1941), p. 141; Frank Lloyd Wright, *An Organic Architecture, The Architecture of Democracy, the Sir George Watson Lectures of the Sulgrave Manor Board for 1939* (Cambridge: M.I.T. Press, 1970), p. 39.

31.   Review of *Technics and Civilization*, *Time* (May 7, 1934), p. 77; and Mumford, *Technics and Civilization*, pp. 353, 370–71.

32.   Lewis Mumford, *The Culture of Cities* (New York: Harcourt, Brace, 1938), p. 453; see also, pp. 282, 356–57, 372–73, and figs. 25–28, 32.

CHAPTER 3

Selling the Machine Age

1.   *The New York Times* (May 1, 1927), I:11. See also, R. H. Macy and Co., *The Catalogue of the Exposition of Art in Trade at Macy's* (New York: R. H. Macy Co., 1927), which says on the cover, "The Exposition Follows the Plan of the Exhibitions Held by the Metropolitan Museum of Art"; and William H. Baldwin, "Modern Art and the Machine Age," *The Independent*, 119 (July 9, 1927), p. 35, figs. 35–38. "A Reaction in Our Art," *The New York Times* (May 3, 1927), p. 24. Elizabeth L. Cary, "Art in Trade," *The New York Times* (May 8, 1927), p. 25.

2.   Yossef Gaer, "Louis Lozowick," *B'Nai Brith*, 41 (June 1927), pp. 378–79; Barbara Beth Zabel, "Louis Lozowick and Technological Optimism of the 1920s" (Ph.D. Dissertation, Univ. of Virginia, 1978), p. 165. And "Little Review Papers," box 6, file 17, Univ. of Wisconsin–Milwaukee, Univ. Archives. "Bel Geddes," *Fortune*, 2 (July 1939), p. 51; Davies, *At Home in Manhattan*, p. 86, conveniently summarizes the exhibits. John Cotton Dana, "The Cash Value of Art in Industry," *Forbes* (August 1, 1928), pp. 16, 18, 32.

3.   Paul T. Frankl, "Merchandising the Modern Idea in Decoration," *Advertising & Selling* (December 26, 1928), p. 36.

4.   Robert Paul Thomas, "Style Change and the Automobile Industry During the Roaring Twen-

ties," in *Business Enterprise and Economic Change*, Louis P. Cain and Paul J. Uselding, eds. (Kent, Ohio: Kent State Univ. Press, 1973), pp. 118–38; Daniel J. Boorstin, *The Americans, The Democratic Experience* (New York: Vintage, 1974), pp. 89–164.

5. These changes are well covered in Meikle, *Twentieth Century*, pp. 104–7.

6. Thorstein Veblen, *The Theory of Business Enterprise* (New York: Scribner, 1904); Malcolm Cowley, *Exile's Return* (New York: Viking, 1951), p. 61; Alfred P. Sloan, Jr., *My Years with General Motors* (New York: MacFadden, 1965), pp. 150–52; Allan Nevins and Frank Ernest Hill, *Ford, Expansion and Challenge: 1915–1933* (New York: Scribner, 1957), p. 465.

7. Lewis, *Babbitt*, pp. 74–75, 95.

8. Frederick Lewis Allen, *Only Yesterday* (New York: Bantam, 1959 [1931]), p. 125; Henry Ford and Samuel Crother, *My Life and Work* (New York: Doubleday, 1923), p. 146; Henry Ford, "Machinery—The New Messiah," *The Forum*, 79 (March 1928), p. 362.

9. H. L. Mencken, *A Carnival of Buncombe*, Malcolm Moos, ed. (New York: Vintage, 1960); Lewis Mumford, *Sticks & Stones* (New York: Boni Liveright, 1924), ch. 8; and Chase, *Men and Machines*.

10. Richard H. Pells, *Radical Visions and American Dreams: Culture and Social Thought in the Depression Years* (New York: Harper, 1973); "Purpose," *Fortune*, 1 (February 1930), p. 38.

11. David F. Noble, *American by Design: Science, Technology and the Rise of Corporate Capitalism* (New York: Oxford Univ. Press, 1977), p. 111; see entire ch. 7; M. Luckiesh, "Simulating Sunlight; A New Era of Artificial Lighting," *Transactions of the American Institute of Electric Engineers*, 49 (April 1930), pp. 511–18; Mary Jacobs, "How Shall We Live in the Future?" *Scientific American*, 146 (February 1932), pp. 71–74; "The Philosophy of Customer Research," *Product Engineering*, 8 (May 1937), pp. 162–65; Boorstin, *The Americans*, pp. 148–49.

12. "Research and Engineering Building of the A. O. Smith Corporation, Milwaukee, Wis.," *Architectural Forum*, LV (November 1931), pp. 527, 526; E. W. Burgess, *The Smith Research and Engineering Building, Bulletin No. 215* (Milwaukee: A. O. Smith Corp., 1930), p. 8.

13. Robert W. Rydell, "The Fan Dance of Science: The Prescriptive Function of Science at the 1933–34 and the 1939–40 World's Fairs," *ISIS* (1985). I am indebted to Professor Rydell for much of the material in the following paragraphs. On the NRC see also, Noble, *American by Design*, pp. 152–56; Allen D. Albert, "The Architecture of the Chicago World's Fair of 1933," *The American Architect*, 135 (April 5, 1929), pp. 421–30; "Preliminary Studies for the Chicago World's Fair," *Pencil Points*, 10 (April 1929), pp. 217–28; *Official Guide* (Chicago: A Century of Progress, 1933), p. 11; and *Official View Book, A Century of Progress Exposition* (Chicago: Reuben H. Donnelley Corp., 1933), n.p.

14. Quoted in Rydell, "The Fan Dance" pp. 7, 23. The quotation is taken from my transcription of *The City*. I have been unable to discover a surviving text.

15. Quoted in Meikle, *Twentieth Century*, p. 208.

16. Quoted in Frank S. Presbrey, *The History and Development of Advertising* (Garden City: Doubleday, Doran & Co., 1929), pp. 619–25; Susman, *Culture and Commitment*, pp. 142–43; Stephan Fox, *The Mirror Makers: A History of American Advertising and Its Creators* (New York: Morrow, 1984), pp. 120–26. Fox's book is the best history of American advertising.

17. "Commercialism in Art," *The American Magazine of Art*, 15 (February 1924), p. 92; Carl Sandburg, *Steichen the Photographer* (New York: Harcourt, Brace, 1929), p. 51; Paul Rosenfield, "Carl Sandburg and Photography," *The New Republic*, 62 (January 22, 1930), pp. 251–52.

18. Paul Strand, "Steichen and Commercial Art," *The New Republic*, 62 (February 19, 1930), p. 21.

19. Earnest Elmo Calkins, *Business the Civilizer* (Boston: Atlantic Monthly–Little, Brown, 1928), p. 136. This book is a collection of many of Calkins's articles and speeches. Calkins, *"and hearing not—,"* *Annals of an Adman* (New York: Scribner, 1946), p. 201. See also, Calkins, "Beauty the New Business Tool," *The Atlantic Monthly*, 140 (August 1927), p. 146; Calkins, "Art as a Means to an End," *Advertising Arts* (January 8, 1930), pp. 17–23. Leon Clark, "René Clarke," *Advertising Arts* (July 15, 1930), pp. 57–62; James D. Herbert, "Come into the Kitchen," *Advertising Arts* (April 2, 1930), pp. 30–31.

20. Ralph M. Hower, *The History of an Advertising Agency* (Cambridge: Harvard Univ. Press, 1949). Susan Fillin Yeh, "Charles Sheeler and the Machine Age" (Ph.D. Dissertation, City Univ. of New York, 1981), pp. 137–38; *The Rouge; The Image of Industry in the Art of Charles Sheeler and Diego Rivera* (Detroit: Detroit Institute of Arts, 1978), p. 11; Charles W. Millard III, "Charles Sheeler, American Photographer," *Creative Photography*, VI, no. 1 (c. 1968), n.p.; Samuel M. Kootz, "Ford Plant Photos of Charles Sheeler," *Creative Art*, 8 (April 1931), pp. 264–76. Photographs by Sheeler used as advertisements for the Ayer Agency appear in Art Director's Club, *Seventh Annual of Advertising Art* (New York: Book Service Co., 1928), pp. 18, 132. Charles T. Coiner, "How Steinway Uses Modern Art," *Advertising Arts* (April 2, 1930), pp. 1–8; *A. M. Cassandre Posters* (St. Gall, Switzerland: Zollikofer and Co., 1948), n.p.

21. *Edward Steichen* (Millerton, N.Y.: Aperture, 1978), p. 8; Fox, *The Mirror Makers*, pp. 90–94; Jennifer Davis Roberts, *Norman Bel Geddes; An Exhibition of Theatrical and Industrial Designs* (Austin, Texas: Univ. of Texas at Austin, 1979), p. 27; Meikle, *Twentieth Century*, pp. 51–52; Norman Bel Geddes, "Designing the Office of Today," *Advertising Arts* (January 8, 1930), p. 48; Walter Rendell Story, "The Decorator as a Minister of Trade," *The New York Times Magazine* (June 23, 1929), p. 19. See also, "A Modern Room for a Modern Purpose," *The American Architect*, 136 (July 20, 1929), pp. 96–102; "A Dramatic Background for Modern Business," *Theatre Arts Monthly*, 13 (September 1929), p. 712.

22. Nathaniel Pousette-Dart, "The Evolution of American Advertising Art," *Art Director's Club: Twentieth Annual of Advertising Age* (New York: Watson-Guptill, 1941), pp. 9–15; M. F. Agha, "Graphic Arts in Advertising," *Modern American Design*, R. L. Leonard and C. A. Glassgold, eds. (New York: Ives Washburn, 1930), pp. 139–40; Ray Sullivan, "Modern Layout in Advertising," *Western Advertising*, 18 (February 5, 1931), pp. 16–17; Charles Everett Johnson, *The Six Essentials of Advertising Art* (Palms, Calif.: Walter T. Foster, 1931); Interview, author with H. E. B. Anderson, Austin Company (April 23, 1984); and Martin Greif, *The New Industrial Landscape: The Story of the Austin Company* (Clinton, N.J.: Main Street

Press, 1978), pp. 103–5.

23. L. Sandusky, "The Bauhaus Tradition and the New Typography," *PM*, IV (July 1938), pp. 1–35; M. F. Agha, "Sans-serif," *Advertising Arts* (June 1931), pp. 41–47; Leonard and Glassgold, eds., *Modern American Design*, pp. 152–53; "Lucian Bernhard," *PM*, III (April 1937), pp. 33–38.

24. Michael Schudson, *Advertising: The Uneasy Persuasion* (New York: Basic Books, 1984).

25. "Both Fish and Fowl," *Fortune*, 9 (February 1934), p. 90.

26. Pulos, *American Design Ethic*, pp. 260–66; Rosenthal and Ratzka, *The Story of Modern Applied Art*, p. 163; Charles R. Richards, *Art in Industry* (New York: Macmillan, 1929), p. 10; Lucian Bernhard, "Putting Beauty into Industry," *Advertising Arts* (January 8, 1930), pp. 33–40; Kenneth H. Condit, "Appearance Counts," *Product Engineering*, 2 (September 1931), p. 418.

27. "Both Fish and Fowl," p. 98.

28. "Color in Industry," *Fortune*, I (February 1930), p. 85; Sheldon and Arens, *Consumer Engineering*, pp. 102–3; Donald Dohner, "Color for Attention," in "What You Can Do With Color," *Product Engineering*, 3 (January 1932), pp. 17–18; Howard Ketcham, "Product Appeal Through Correct Color," *Product Engineering*, 6 (July 1935), p. 258; see also, "The Science of Colors," p. 256.

29. Letters, Robert Lepper to author, January 20, 1984, and February 3, 1984; "Designing Things Better," *Business Week* (November 7, 1936), p. 41; Letter, Lenore Swoiskin, archivist, Sears, Roebuck, to author, December 14, 1983; "Department Announces 50 Birthday Presents," *Sears News-Graphic* (February 8, 1936); Cheney and Cheney, *Art and the Machine*, pp. 251–70.

30. Raymond Loewy, "Modern Metals in Modernising," *The Iron Age*, 138 (June 13, 1935), p. 29; see the photo of Lurelle Guild's studio in "Both Fish and Fowl," p. 91.

31. T. J. Maloney, "Case Histories in Product Design-X," *Product Engineering*, 5 (June 1934), p. 219; "Best-Dressed Products Sell Best," *Forbes* (April 1, 1934), pp. 13–19; "Profiles, Artist in a Factory," *The New Yorker* (August 28, 1931), p. 22; *Advertising Arts* (July 9, 1930), pp. 12–13.

32. The careers of most of these designers are treated in Pulos, *American Design Ethic*; Meikle, *Twentieth Century*; and "Fish and Fowl." See also, Raymond Loewy, *Never Leave Well Enough Alone* (New York: Simon & Schuster, 1951), pp. 50–51, 64; David Gebhart and Harriet von Brenton, *Kem Weber* (Santa Barbara: The Art Galleries, Univ. of Calif., Santa Barbara, 1969); "Ten Men in Your Life," *House and Garden* (September 1947), p. 122; and Harold Van Doren, *Industrial Design*, (New York: McGraw-Hill, 1940).

33. Charles R. Richards, *Industrial Art and the Museum* (New York: Macmillan, 1927), pp. v, 55, 69; Richard F. Bach, "American Industrial Art at the Metropolitan Museum," *Architectural Record*, 55 (March 1924), p. 690.

34. "Beauty and the Machine," *The Survey* (March 15, 1924), pp. 304–5.

35. Royal Cortissoz, "A Contemporary Movement in American Design," *Scribner's Monthly* (May 1929), p. 588; "1931 Industrial Art Show," *Business Week* (October 29, 1931), p. 28; "A Parade of Contemporary Achievements at the Metropolitan Museum," *Arts and Decoration*, 43 (December 1934), pp. 13–25; Metropolitan Museum, *Contemporary American Industrial Art:*

1934 (New York: Metropolitan Museum, 1934).
36. Leonard and Glassgold, eds., *Modern American Design*, was published for the American Union of Decorative Artists and Craftsmen; see pp. 132–33 for the 1930 exhibit. On the Brooklyn exhibit see American Union of Decorative Artists and Craftsmen, *AUDAC Exhibition, May–June 1931* (Brooklyn: The Brooklyn Museum, 1931); "The AUDAC Exhibition," *The Brooklyn Museum Quarterly*, 18 (July 1931), pp. 93–97; and Blanche Naylor, "American Design Progress," *Design* (September 1931), pp. 82–89.

CHAPTER 4

The Machine in the Landscape

1. "Remaking the World," *Collier's*, 95 (March 16, 1935), p. 60.
2. Duncan Aikman, "New Pioneers in the Old West's Deserts," *The New York Times Magazine* (October 26, 1930), p. 7.
3. P.H. Elwood, Jr., "State Parks and Highways," *Landscape Architecture*, 22 (October 1931), p. 25.
4. "Design Decade," *Architectural Forum*, 73 (October 1940), p. 318; See also, "Streamlined Mountain Thoroughfare," *Better Roads*, 10 (July 1940), pp. 13–14, 31–32.
5. Sigfried Giedion, *Space, Time and Architecture* (Cambridge: Harvard Univ. Press, 1941), pp. 550, 553–54.
6. "Unfit for Modern Motor Traffic," *Fortune*, 14 (August 1936), pp. 85, 89.
7. *Ibid.*, pp. 85–92, 94, 96, 99; See also, Jean Labutut and Wheaton A. Lane, eds., *Highways in our National Life* (Princeton: Princeton Univ. Press, 1950); Mark S. Foster, *From Streetcar to Superhighway: American City Planners and Urban Transportation* (Philadelphia: Temple Univ. Press, 1981); and Thomas H. MacDonald, "Highways and Railroads," *Scientific American*, 146 (April 1932), pp. 222–25.
8. "Unfit for Modern Motor Traffic," pp. 91–92.
9. Benton MacKay and Lewis Mumford, "Townless Highways for the Motorist: Proposal for the Automobile Age," *Harper's*, 163 (August 1931) p. 355.
10. *Ibid.*, p. 347.
11. H.V. Hubbard, *Parkways and Land Values*, vol. XI of *Harvard City Planning Studies* (Cambridge: Harvard Univ. Press, 1937), p. xii.
12. Gilmore D. Clarke, "Modern Motor Ways," *Architectural Record*, 74 (December 1933), p. 431. Clarke notes he is quoting Edward M. Bassett.
13. *Ibid.*, p. 431, again quoting Bassett.
14. For the history of parkways see: Clay McShane, "De la rue à l'autoroute, 1900–1940," *Les Annales de la recherche urbaine*, nos. 23–24 (July–December, 1984), pp. 17–29 [Professor McShane kindly gave me a longer version of his paper]; Isabele Gournay, "Influence américaine sur l'environment routier français," *Monuments historiques*, no. 134 (September 1984), pp. 61–66; Norman T. Newton, *Design on the Land* (Cambridge, Belknap Press–Harvard Univ. Press, 1971), ch. 39. See also, the citation in note 9 above.
15. Jay Doner, "Principles of Westchester's Parkway System," *Civil Engineering*, IV (February 1934), pp. 85–87; Stanley W. Abbot, "Ten Years of the Westchester County Park System," *Parks and Recreation*, XVI (March 1933), pp. 307–10; Clarke, "Modern Motor Ways," pp.

430–37.
16. Gilmore D. Clarke, "Our Highway Problem," *American Magazine of Art*, 25 (November 1932) pp. 286–90.
17. Gilmore D. Clarke, "New Bridges Mean Opportunity for Architects," *American Architect*, 143 (September 1933), pp. 56–61; Clarke, "The Mount Vernon Memorial Highway," *Landscape Architecture*, 22 (April 1932), pp. 179–80; and Clarke, "The Parkway Idea," *The Highway and the Landscape*, W. B. Snow, ed. (New Brunswick, N.J.: Rutgers Univ. Press, 1959), pp. 35–55.
18. "Parks and Highways of Long Island," *Architectural Record*, 74 (December 1933), pp. 426–29, 438. See also, Robert A. Caro, *The Power Broker: Robert Moses and the Fall of New York* (New York: Knopf, 1974), pp. 169 *et seq.*
19. Carl W. Condit, *American Building Art: The Twentieth Century* (New York: Oxford Univ. Press, 1961), pp. 282–83.
20. David Brodsly, *L.A. Freeway: An Appreciative Essay* (Berkeley: Univ. of Calif. Press, 1981).
21. Charles Downing Lay, "New Towns for High-Speed Roads," *Architectural Record*, 78 (November 1935), pp. 352–54.
22. Frank Lloyd Wright, *The Disappearing City* (New York: William Farquar Payton, 1932); republished in an expanded version as *When Democracy Builds* (Chicago: Univ. of Chicago Press, 1945); again republished even more expanded as *The Living City* (New York: Horizon Press, 1958).
23. Peter M. Wolf, *Eugène Hénard and the Beginning of Urbanism in Paris, 1900–1914* (The Hague: International Federation for Housing and Planning, and Paris: Centre de Recherche d'Urbanisme, 1968).
24. Luciano Caramel and Alberto Longatti, *Antonio Sant'Elia* (Como: Villa Communale Dell'Olo, 1962).
25. Le Corbusier, *Urbanisme* (Paris: G. Cres, 1925); translated into English by Frederick Etchells as *The City of Tomorrow and Its Planning* (New York: Payson & Clark, 1929). His *Vers une Architecture* (Paris: G. Cres, 1923), translated into English by Frederick Etchells as *Towards A New Architecture* (New York: Warren and Putnam, 1927), pp. 55 *et seq.*, shows some of his ideas. For discussion of Le Corbusier's ideas on the city and highways, see also Frank Pick, "The Way of To-Morrow and the Traffic Problem," *Creative Art*, 5 (September 1929), pp. 624–28.
26. In particular there was the famous Moses King, *King's Views of New York* (Brooklyn: Moses King, Inc., 1911), front cover, republished in many places such as *King's Views of New York 1896–1915, & Brooklyn 1905* (New York: Arno Press, 1977), p. 1.
27. Hugh Ferriss, "Civic Architecture of the Immediate Future," *Arts & Decoration*, 18 (November 1922), pp. 12–13.
28. Ferriss, *The Metropolis of Tomorrow*, pp. 118, 130, 143.
29. *The Architectural Record*, 73 (January 1933), p. 15.
30. Egmont Arens, "The Roadway Housing Plan," draft of talk with illustrations; and "What is the Matter with Our Automobile Highway System?" draft of a talk, both c. 1934. Arens Collection, George Arents Research Library, Syracuse University, Syracuse, N.Y.
31. "Unfit for Modern Motor Traffic," p. 99.
32. Miller McClintock, "Of Things to Come," in *New Horizons in Planning, Proceedings of the National Planning Conference, Detroit, Michi-

gan, June 1–3, 1937* (Chicago: American Society of Planning Officials, 1937), pp. 34–38; and "At the Wheel," *The New York Times* (June 6, 1937), p. 12.
33. Norman Bel Geddes, *Magic Motorways* (New York: Random House, 1940); Meikle, *Twentieth Century*, p. 208.
34. Lincoln Kirstein, *Murals by American Painters and Photographers* (New York: Museum of Modern Art, 1932); Dorothy Crafly, "Murals at the Museum of Modern Art," *The American Magazine of Art*, 25 (August 1932), pp. 93–102.
35. David B. Steinman and Sara Ruth Watson, *Bridges and Their Builders* (New York: Putnam, 1941), pp. v, 374, 375. See also, Paul Zucker, *American Bridges and Dams* (New York: Greystone Press, 1941).
36. Wilbur J. Watson, *A Decade of Bridges, 1926–1936* (Cleveland: J.J. Jansen, 1937); *Bridge Designing, Selection of Designs from the 1929–1930 Student Competition* (New York: American Institute of Steel Construction, 1930); "Prize Winning Bridges," *Architectural Record*, 72 (July 1932), p. 16; Alan Trachtenberg, *Brooklyn Bridge, Fact and Symbol* (New York: Oxford Univ. Press, 1965).
37. Condit, *American Building*, pp. 121–25; Watson, *A Decade of Bridges*, pp. 1–3; "Bayonne Bridge..." *Architectural Record*, 72 (December 1932), pp. 346, 361–65.
38. Watson, *A Decade of Bridges*, p. 80.
39. Elizabeth B. Mock, *The Architecture of Bridges* (New York: Museum of Modern Art, 1949), p. 87.
40. Aymar Embury II, "The Aesthetics of Bridge Design," *Pencil Points*, 19 (February 1938), pp. 116–17. See also, Condit, *American Building*, pp. 135–38; and Watson, *A Decade of Bridges*, pp. 44–52.
41. Condit, *American Building*, pp. 140–41; Robert Moses, *Bronx-Whitestone Bridge* (New York: Triborough Bridge Authority, 1939).
42. Quoted in Michael J. Crosby, "The Background of the Bridges," *Architecture*, 74 (March 1985), p. 152. See also, Richard Dillon, *High Steel: Building the Bridges Across the San Francisco Bay* (Millbrae, Can: Celestial Arts, 1979).
43. Irving F. Morrow, "Beauty Marks Golden Gate Bridge Design," *Architect & Engineer*, 128 (March 1937), pp. 21–24; Crosby, "The Background of the Bridges"; Condit, *American Building*, pp. 143–46. See also, Irving F. Morrow, "Why Modern Architecture," *Architect & Engineer*, 146 (September 1941), pp. 31–36, 41.
44. J.B. Priestley, "Arizona Desert," *Harper's Monthly Magazine*, 174 (March 1937), p. 365.
45. For the general history of dams see: Norman Smith, *A History of Dams* (London: P. Davies, 1971); Allen H. Cullen, *Rivers in Harness: The Story of Dams* (Philadelphia: Chilton Books, 1962); Julian Hinds, "Continuous Development of Dams Since 1950," Paper N. 2605; and K.B. Keener, "Dams Then and Now," Paper No. 2606, *Transactions, American Society of Civil Engineers*, CL (1953), pp. 489–535. See also, T.W. Mermel, *Register of Dams in the United States* (New York: U.S. Committee on Large Dams, 1963), and Condit, *American Buildings*, ch. 8.
46. "Boulder Dam: Engineering Triumph," *The Literary Digest*, 122 (October 17, 1935), pp. 19–20.
47. Condit, *American Building*, p. 247.
48. On the history of Hoover Dam, see: U.S. Department of the Interior, Bureau of Reclamation, *Boulder Canyon Project, Final Reports* (Boulder City, Nevada; Washington, D.C.; and

Denver: Bureau of Reclamation, 1938–50), 7 parts and 23 bulletins. There is extensive literature on Hoover Dam's political and economic context and also some interpretations, all of which is summarized in Richard Guy Wilson, "Machine-Age Iconography in the American West: The Design of Hoover Dam," *Pacific Historical Review*, 54 (November 1985), pp. 463–93.

49. "The Dam," *Fortune*, 8 (September 1933), p. 78. There were numerous photographers associated with the project, but Ben Glaha stands out. See Ben Glaha, "Boulder Dam, The Photographs of Engineering Works," *U.S. Camera*, I (January–March 1939), pp. 18–23, 78–79; "Glaha Complimented," *The Reclamation Era*, 25 (July 1935), p. 152; "Photographs Exhibited," *The Reclamation Era*, 25 (August 1935), p. 168; "Photographs Exhibited," *The Reclamation Era*, 25 (September 1934), p. 185; and Willard Van Dyke, "The Work of Ben Glaha," *Camera Craft* (April 1935), pp. 166–72. Glaha's work was exhibited nationwide in 1935. In 1938 Cliff Segerblom became the official bureau photographer for the dam and is responsible for the excellent photographs of the test dam, of the spillways, and valve outlet houses; author interview with Cliff Segerblom, May 15, 1984.

50. Alson Clark, "The 'Californian' Architecture of Gordon B. Kaufmann," *Society of Architectural Historians Southern California Chapter Review*, 1 (Summer 1982), pp. 1–8; "Gordon B. Kaufmann Obituary," *Southwest Builder and Contractor* (March 4, 1949), p. 7; Harris C. Allen, "It Can Happen Here: A Classical Scholar Learns a Modern Language," *Architect and Engineer*, 129 (May 1937), pp. 13–34; Gordon B. Kaufmann, "The Architecture of Boulder Dam," *Architectural Concrete* 2, no. 3 (1936), pp. 3–4. See also, Wesley R. Nelson, "Ornamental Features of Boulder Dam," *Compressed Air Magazine* 43 (June 1938), pp. 5615–20.

51. Oskar Hansen, "The Sculptures at Boulder Dam—Part II: Split Second Petrified on the Face of the Universal Clock," *The Reclamation Era*, 32 (March 1942).

52. The literature on the TVA is enormous. For my study I have relied on: Tennessee Valley Authority, *Annual Reports* (1934–42); R. L. Duffus and Charles Krutch, *The Valley and Its People* (New York: Knopf, 1946); Arthur E. Morgan, *The Making of the TVA* (Buffalo: Prometheus, 1974); Daniel E. Lillienthal, *TVA Democracy on the March* (New York: Harper, 1953).

53. Professor William Jordy has in preparation a study of TVA's planning and the town of Norris; he has shared some of this information with me. Marian Moffett and Lawrence Wodehouse, *Built for the People of the United States; Fifty Years of TVA Architecture* (Knoxville: Univ. of Tenn., 1983), which contains essays by Jordy and Professor Creese (who also has a study of TVA in progress), conveniently summarizes material. TVA architecture was extensively published in the 1930s. See also, Marian Moffett and Lawrence Wodehouse, "Noble Structures Set in Handsome Parks: Public Architecture of the TVA," *Modulus*, 17 (1984), p. 75–83; Harry B. Tour, "TVA—Ten Years of Concrete," *Architectural Concrete*, 9 (July 1943), p. 22–29; F. A. Gutheim, "Tennessee Valley Authority, A New Phase in Architecture," *Magazine of Art*, 33 (September 1940), pp. 516–31; and Talbot F. Hamlin, "Architecture of the TVA," *Pencil Points*, 20 (November 1939), pp. 720–44.

54. For information on Wank see Frederick Gutheim, "Roland Wank, 1898–1970," *Architectural Forum*, 133 (September 1970), pp. 58–

59; Walter L. Creese, "The TVA as an Allegory," in Moffett and Wodehouse, *Built for the People*, pp. 59–63.

55. See Alfred Fellheimer, "Contemporary Design in Architecture," *Pencil Points*, 13 (June 1932), pp. 383–89. Denny Carter, "Paul Philippe Cret and the Union Terminal," in *Art Deco and the Cincinnati Union Terminal* (Cincinnati: Art History Department, Univ. of Cincinnati, 1971), pp. 10–15, attempts to claim Cret as the main designer. Evidence does not support this assertion.

56. Creese, "The TVA as an Allegory," p. 60; see also, "TVA Postscripts," *Magazine of Art*, 34 (May 1941), pp. 260–63.

57. Quoted in Moffett and Wodehouse, "Noble Structures," p. 77.

58. Roland A. Wank, "Integrated Design is a Joint Responsibility," *Pencil Points*, 25 (October 1944), pp. 48–53; Wank, "Nowhere to Go but Forward," *Magazine of Art*, 34 (January 1941), pp. 6–12; Wank, "Architecture in Rural Areas," *Pencil Points*, 23 (December 1942), pp. 47–53; Wank, "Some Recent Work of the Tennessee Valley Authority," *Pencil Points*, 22 (July 1941), pp. 475–82.

59. "The Norris Dam," *Magazine of Art*, 31 (March 1935), pp. 158–61. The 1920s engineers design is shown in Moffett and Wodehouse, *Built for the People*, p. 8; see also, "Tennessee Valley Authority," *Architectural Forum*, 71 (August 1939), pp. 73–114, especially p. 83.

60. Kenneth Reid, "Design in TVA Structures," *Pencil Points*, 20 (November 1939), p. 764; see the entire article, pp. 690–719.

61. "Tennessee Valley Authority," *Architectural Forum*, p. 76.

62. Adams, *The Education of Henry Adams*, p. 380.

CHAPTER 5

Transportation Machine Design

1. Bel Geddes, *Horizons*, p. 24. See also, Carlton Atherton, "Speed Determines New Forms," *Design*, 35 (April 1934), pp. 4–7; Buford Pickens, "Speed," in *Development of Contemporary Civilization*, William J. Bossenbrook, ed. (New York: D. C. Heath, 1940), pp. 372–73; "The Automobile of Our Age," *Design*, 37 (December 1935), p. 35; and Gordon M. Buehrig and Jackson Williams, *Rolling Sculpture* (Newfoundland, N.J.: Haessner, 1975), p. 84. For general background see Robert C. Reed, *The Streamline Era* (San Marino, Calif.: Golden West Books, 1975).

2. Paul A. Hanle, *Bringing Aerodynamics to America* (Cambridge: M.I.T. Press, 1982). For background see Roger E. Bilstein, *Flight in America, 1900–1983* (Baltimore: Johns Hopkins Univ. Press, 1984).

3. Rene Francillon, *Lockheed Aircraft Since 1913* (New York: Putnam, 1970).

4. Richard F. Smith, "The Intercontinental Airliner and the Essence of Airplane Performance," *Technology & Culture*, 24 (July 1983), pp. 248–49; Bush, *The Streamlined Decade*, pp. 3–36.

5. Bel Geddes, *Horizons*, pp. 110–21.

6. Linda Wellesley, "Flying De Luxe," *Airwoman*, 12 (February 1935), p. 7; "Decoration by Ounces and Inches," *Arts and Decoration*, 42 (April 1934), pp. 30–31; "Atlantic Clipper has Modern Interiors," *Life* (August 23, 1937), p. 39; Roberts, *Bel Geddes*, pp. 34–36.

7. Douglas Robinson, *Giants in the Sky: A History of the Rigid Airship* (Seattle: Univ. of Washington Press, 1973).

8. Boeing, "Model Specification and History," courtesy of Boeing Aircraft Company.

9. Bilstein, *Flight in America*, pp. 89–92; *Airplanes Must Fly. The Story of the Development of the Douglas Transports* (Santa Monica: Douglas Aircraft [c. 1937]).

10. *Douglas Transport DC-2* (Santa Monica: Douglas Aircraft [c. 1935]), pp. 3, 13.

11. Quoted in Paul Wilson, *Chrome Dreams: Automobile Styling Since 1893* (Radnor, Pa: Chilton, 1976), pp. 68–69, 142.

12. Stephan Bayley, *Harley Earl and the Dream Machine* (New York: Knopf, 1983); Thomas L. Hibbard, "Early Days at GM Art & Colour," *Special-Interest Autos*, 23 (July–August 1974), pp. 41–43, 54; "Aerodynamics and Streamlining," Preliminary Proof from the 1935 *Automobile Buyer's Guide*, Customer Research Staff, General Motors, Detroit, in Arens Collection, Arents Research Library, Syracuse Univ.

13. Bel Geddes, *Horizons*, pp. 52–63.

14. Ralf J. F. Kieselbach, *Streamline Cars in Europe/USA: Aerodynamics in the Construction of Passenger Vehicles 1900–1945* (Frankfort, Germany: Kohlhammer, 1982), vol. II, pp. 154–57. This book gives a complete treatment of American streamlined cars. See also, Mike Lamm, "Dymaxion," *Car Life* (May 1968), pp. 29, 50–53; and Strother MacMinn, "American Automobile Design," in Gerald Silk, *Automobile and Culture* (New York: Abrams, 1984), pp. 209–51.

15. Alexander Klemin, "How Research Makes Possible the Modern Motor Car," *Scientific American*, 151 (August 1934), p. 108.

16. "There Are No Automobiles," *Fortune*, 2 (October 1930), pp. 73–77; *Story of the Airflow Cars* (Detroit: Chrysler Corporation Engineering Office, 1963); George L. McCain, "Dynamics of the Modern Automobile," *S.A.E. Journal* (Transactions), 35 (July 1934), pp. 248–56; Howard S. Irwin, "The History of the AIRFLOW Car," *Scientific American*, 210 (August 1977), pp. 98–104.

17. Wilson, *Chrome Dreams*, p. 158; Meikle, *Twentieth Century*, pp. 148–51; Norman Bel Geddes, Minutes of Meeting: 'Q' Account, September 18, October 19, 24, 25, 1933, Bel Geddes Collection.

18. Ernest Kanzler, "The Gentle Gentleman of the Industry, Edsel Ford," *Ward's Quarterly*, 1 (Summer 1965), pp. 68–70, 127; Holden Koto, "Living with Style," 32 (May–June 1975), pp. 40–45; and Lorin E. Sorensen, "The Fishleigh Fords," *Special-Interest Autos*, 39 (March–April 1977), p. 56; "Lincoln Zephyr" *Ford News*, 15 (November 1936), pp. 730–36; File, "Auto—Ford—Experimental—1930–39," Edison Institute, Ford Archives.

19. File, "Auto—Lincoln—1938—Cont. Prototypes," and "1939 Photo File, Cont.," Ford Archives.

20. Barrett Andrews and Edward Longstreth, "The Motor's Changing Silhouette," *Arts and Decoration*, 44 (May 1936), pp. 36, 56.

21. F. Hol Wagner, Jr., "Shovelnoses," *Burlington Bulletin*, no. 13 (Fourth Quarter 1984), pp. 1–48; Ralph Budd, "Railroading Moves Ahead," *Atlantic*, 155 (May 1935), pp. 534–44; Richard Overton, *Burlington Route, History of the Burlington Lines* (New York: Knopf, 1965), pp. 396–97; Zenon Hansen, "Zephyr 9900," *The Railroad Capital* (April 1984), pp. 1–11. I am especially indebted to Mr. Hansen for research assistance in this section.

22. "Five and a Half Years of the Streamliners," *Railway Age*, 107 (October 14, 1939), pp.

551–94; "The Streamliners—After Six Years," *Business Week* (February 10, 1940), pp. 47–54; "March of the Streamliners," *Railway Age*, 111 (November 22, 1941), pp. 829–48.

23. For background see Bush, *The Streamlined Decade*, ch. 5; Bel Geddes, *Horizons*, p. 70.

24. O.G. Tietjens and K.C. Ripley, "Air Resistance of High Speed Trains," *Railway Mechanical Engineer* (February 1932), pp. 61–63; "Design and Application Trends in Railroad Motor Trains," *S.A.E. Journal* (Transactions), 35 (November 1934), pp. 408–14; William D. Middleton, "The Brill Bullet," *Trains Magazine* (July 1966), pp. 26–29; Otto Kuhler, *My Iron Journey: An Autobiography of a Life with Steam and Steel* (Denver: Intermountain Chapter, National Railway Historical Society, 1978), p. 217.

25. Harold E. Ranks and William W. Kratville, *The Union Pacific Streamliners* (Omaha: Kratville Pub., 1974), pp. 11–15; E. E. Adams, "Union Pacific Light-Weight High-Speed Train," *Railway Mechanical Engineer* (December 1933), pp. 419–24; "Union Pacific Installs Light-Weight High Speed Train," *Railway Age*, 96 (February 3, 1934), pp. 184–96. On May 9, 1935, Adams, Stout, and two other Pullman engineers filed a patent, serial number 56,754, for the *M10,000*, which was granted on June 16, 1936. Information courtesy of Zenon Hansen. See also, "Round and Light," *Fortune*, 8 (August 1933), pp. 64–66.

26. "All Records Shattered!" *Aluminum News-Letter* (November 1934), p. 8.

27. "Pioneer Without Profit," *Fortune*, 15 (March 1937), pp. 82–87, 128, 130, 132, 134.

28. Interview, May 31 and August 28, 1984, with Albert Dean; Interview, August 28, 1984, with Walter Dean; I am also indebted to John Derrah of the Budd Company and Richard Jansen, University of Vermont. See also, "Light-Weight Design with Shot-Welded Stainless Steel," *Product Engineering*, 5 (July 1934 and August 1934), pp. 242–45, 293–95; "Burlington 'Zephyr' Completed at Budd Plant," *Railway Age*, 96 (April 14, 1934), pp. 533–44; E. C. Anderson, "The Burlington Zephyr," and R. Eksergian, "The Design of Light-Weight Trains," *Transactions of the American Society of Mechanical Engineers*, 56 (September 1934), pp. 659–701.

29. Interview with Albert and Walter Dean, August 28, 1984.

30. Karl R. Zimmermann, *The Remarkable GG1* (New York: Quadrant Press, 1977), pp. 15–17.

31. Lucius Beebe, *Highiron* (New York: Appleton-Century, 1938), p. 9.

32. Bush, *The Streamlined Decade*, pp. 69–72; Jim Scribbins, *The Hiawatha Story* (Milwaukee: Kalmbach Pub., 1970); Kuhler, *My Iron Journey*, pp. 225–26.

33. Raymond Loewy, *The Locomotive: Its Esthetics* (London: Studio, 1937), figs. 62–63, 66–83; Otto Kuhler, "Applied Design in Railroad Equipment," *Railway Age*, 99 (November 30, 1935), p. 713; Bush, *The Streamlined Decade*, pp. 74–75, 88–90.

34. "The Mercury, Henry Dreyfuss, Designer," *Architectural Forum*, 65 (August 1936), pp. 119–24; Lucius Beebe, *20th Century Limited* (Berkeley: Howell-North Books, 1962); "Power. A Portfolio by Charles Sheeler," *Fortune*, 22 (December 1940), pp. 73–83; "New Trains," *Architectural Forum*, 69 (September 1938), pp. 175–82.

35. Franklin M. Reck, *On Time: The History of Electro-Motive Division of General Motors Cor-*poration (La Grange, Ill.: Electro-Motive, 1948), pp. 87–159; Jim Boyd, "The Men Who Styled the Streamliners," *Railfan & Railroad*, 5 (November 1984), pp. 32–43; Stanley Repp, *Super Chief... Train of the Stars* (San Marino: Golden West, 1980); Paul Cret, "Streamlined Trains," *Magazine of Art*, 30 (January 1937), pp. 17–20; John F. Kirkland, *Dawn of the Diesel Locomotive in America* (Chicago: Interurban, 1983).

36. David P. Morgan, "The Diesel That Did It," *Trains* (February 1960), pp. 23–35; Daniel J. Mulhearn and John R. Taibi, *General Motors F-Units* (New York: Quadrant Press, 1982).

37. For illustrations and background information see: William H. Miller, Jr., *The Great Luxury Liners, 1927–1954* (New York: Dover, 1981); and John Malcome Brinnin, *The Sway of the Grand Saloon* (New York: Delacorte, 1971).

38. Bel Geddes, *Horizons*, pp. 35, 38; Bel Geddes, "Streamlining," p. 562.

39. Miller, *The Great Luxury Liners*, p. 35; and *Matson Log*, February 1980, p. 154.

40. Bush, *The Streamlined Decade*, pp. 48–52.

41. Robert Speltz, *The Real Runabouts* (Lake Mills, Iowa: Graphic Publishing, 1977), pp. 6–12.

CHAPTER 6

Architecture in the Machine Age

1. "Contemporary Architecture: A Symposium," *Journal of Proceedings of the 63rd Annual Convention of the AIA, May 21–23, 1930*, pp. 23–55. Excerpts were printed in *Architectural Forum*, 53 (July 1930), pp. 49–50; and Howe's talk in *T-Square Club Journal*, 1 (March 1931).

2. Richard Oliver, *Bertram Grosvenor Goodhue* (Cambridge: M.I.T. Press, 1983).

3. Harvey Wiley Corbett, "Zoning and the Envelope of the Building," *Pencil Points*, 4 (April 1923), pp. 15–18.

4. Ralph T. Walker, "A New Architecture," *Architectural Forum*, 48 (January 1928), pp. 1–4; "Architecture of To-day: An American Architect's View," *Creative Art*, 5 (July 1929), pp. 460–65. See also, Ralph Walker, *Ralph Walker, Architect* (New York: Henahan House, 1957). Lewis Mumford, "American Architecture Today," *Architecture*, 57 (April 1928), p. 185.

5. Walter H. Kilham, Jr., *Raymond Hood* (New York: Architectural Book Pub., 1973); and Robert A. M. Stern with Thomas P. Catalano, *Raymond Hood* (New York: Institute for Architecture and Urban Studies and Rizzoli, 1982).

6. Raymond Hood, "What is the Price of Beauty," *Liberty Magazine* (December 7, 1929), pp. 65–66; and "The Spirit of Modern Art," *Architectural Forum*, 51 (November 1929), pp. 445–48.

7. Personal communication, Wallace K. Harrison to author, March 16, 1981.

8. Alan Balfour, *Rockefeller Center, Architecture as Theater* (New York: McGraw-Hill, 1978), pp. 137–52. See also, Carol Herselle Krinsky, *Rockefeller Center* (New York: Oxford Univ. Press, 1978).

9. Siegfried Giedion, *Space, Time and Architecture* (Cambridge: Harvard Univ. Press, 1941), pp. 845–53.

10. Theodore James, Jr., *The Empire State Building* (New York: Harper, 1975). See also, "Skyscrapers: The Paper Spires," *Fortune*, 2 (September 1930), pp. 54–55, 58, 119–21.

11. The draftsman was J. Beckening Vinckers, whose work is shown in Leon V. Solon, "Modernism in Architecture," *The Architectural Record*, 60 (September 1926), pp. 193–201. See also,

"Francis S. Swales, Draftsmanship and Architecture, as Exemplified by the Work of William Van Alen," *Pencil Points*, 10 (August 1929), p. 526.

12. Kenneth Murchison, "The Chrysler Building as I See It," *American Architect*, 138 (September 1930), p. 24. See also, Cervin Robinson and Rosemarie Haag Bletter, *Skyscraper Style* (New York: Oxford Univ. Press, 1975), pp. 21–22.

13. Personal communication, Wallace K. Harrison to author, May 5, 1981.

14. William Chaitkin, "The Stainless-Steel Illuminated Indian," in *Essays Presented to D. Kenneth Sargent* (Syracuse: School of Arch., Syracuse Univ., 1971), pp. 11–28.

15. For background and a complete picture of the exhibit see, Richard Guy Wilson, "International Style: the MoMA Exhibition," *Progressive Architecture*, 63 (February 1981), pp. 92–105.

16. Henry-Russell Hitchcock and Philip Johnson, *The International Style* (New York: Norton, 1932), pp. 158, 74–75.

17. Esther McCoy, *Vienna to Los Angeles: Two Journeys* (Santa Monica: Arts & Architecture Press, 1979), p. 8.

18. Hitchcock and Johnson, *International Style*, p. 20.

19. Kenneth K. Stowell, *Architectural Forum*, 56 (March 1932), p. 253.

20. "A Shop-Fabricated Residence," *Architectural Forum*, 55 (August 1931), pp. 220, 238; "Aluminaire: A House for Contemporary Life," *Shelter*, 2 (May 1932), pp. 54–56; Personal communication with Albert Frey, May 17, 1984.

21. Christian Hubert and Lindsay Stamm Shapiro, *William Lescaze* (New York: Institute for Architecture and Urban Studies and Rizzoli, 1982), p. 30.

22. Norman Bel Geddes, "The House of Tomorrow," *Ladies Home Journal*, 48 (April 1931), pp. 12–13, 162; Bel Geddes, *Horizons*, pp. 128–29.

23. "House of Richard H. Mandel," *Architectural Forum*, 63 (August 1935), p. 67. See also, "Off the Record," *Fortune*, 12 (October 1935), pp. 28, 34.

24. "Butler Residence," *Architectural Forum*, 67 (September 1937), pp. 180–86.

25. Michael F. Zimny, "Robert Vincent Derrah and the Nautical Moderne" (M.A. Thesis, Univ. of Virginia, 1982).

26. "Super Terminal," *Bus Transportation* (April 1940), pp. 166–68; Hans Wirz and Richard Striner, *Washington Deco* (Washington, D.C.: Smithsonian Institution Press, 1984), pp. 179–80.

27. Ivan Rodriguez and Margot Ammidown, *From Wilderness to Metropolis: The History and Architecture of Dade County (1825–1940)* (Miami: Metropolitan Dade County, 1982), pp. 135–43; Laura Cerwinske, *Tropical Deco* (New York: Rizzoli, 1981).

28. Talbot Hamlin, "A Contemporary American Style," *Pencil Points*, 19 (February 1938), pp. 99–106.

29. Theo B. White, *Paul Philippe Cret: Architect and Teacher* (Philadelphia: Art Alliance, 1973); and Travis C. McDonald, "Modernized Classicism: The Architecture of Paul Philippe Cret in Washington, D.C." (M.A. Thesis, Univ. of Virginia, 1980).

30. Martin Greif, *The New Industrial Landscape*, p. 103.

31. Quoted in W. Hawkins Ferry, *The Legacy of Albert Kahn* (Detroit: Detroit Institute of Arts, 1970), p. 23. See also, Grant Hilderbrand, *Designing for Industry: The Architecture of Albert Kahn* (Cambridge: M.I.T. Press, 1974).

32. Daniel I. Vieyra, *Fill'er Up* (New York: Collier, 1979).

33. "A Standardized Filling Station Unit," *Architectural Record*, 70 (December 1931), p. 458; "Service Stations," *Architectural Forum*, 65 (October 1936), p. 315.

34. Marquis James, *The Texaco Story* (Texas Company, 1953), p. 66; "Standardized Service Stations Designed by Walter Dorwin Teague," *Architectural Record*, 82 (September 1937), pp. 69–72; Meikle, *Twentieth Century*, pp. 125, 128.

35. Buckminster Fuller, *4-D Time Lock* (1929; reprint edition, Albuquerque: Biotechnic Press, 1979); R. Buckminster Fuller and Robert Marks, *The Dymaxion World of Buckminster Fuller* (Garden City: Doubleday, 1973), pp. 15–21; Theodore Morrison, "The House of the Future," *House Beautiful*, 66 (September 1929), pp. 292–93, 324, 326, 328, 330.

36. Henry Dubin, "Construction of the Battle-deck House," *Architectural Forum*, 55 (August 1931), pp. 227–31; Letter Le Corbusier to M. Stein, July 11, 1928, copy in possession of Arthur Dubin, Chicago.

37. [George Fred Keck], *House of Tomorrow* (Chicago: Neo-Gravure Co. [1933]), exhibition pamphlet. See also, Narciso G. Menocal, *Keck & Keck, Architects* (Madison, Wis.: Elvehjem Museum of Art, Univ. of Wisconsin, 1980).

38. Quoted in Thomas M. Slade, " 'The Crystal House' of 1934," *Journal of the Society of Architectural Historians*, 29 (December 1970), p. 351.

39. "Mass-Produced Houses in Review," *Fortune*, 7 (April 1933), p. 80.

40. *Tomorrow's Homes for the Many* (New York: Revere Copper and Brass, n.d.), pamphlet; Meikle, *Twentieth Century*, pp. 132–33.

41. Frank Lloyd Wright, "Foreword Concluded," *Architectural Forum*, 68 (January 1938), p. 100; see also, pp. 79–83.

42. McCoy, *Vienna to Los Angeles*.

43. Quoted in Thomas Hines, *Richard Neutra and the Search for Modern Architecture* (New York: Oxford Univ. Press, 1982), p. 65.

44. *Ibid.*, pp. 119–20; Arthur Drexler and Thomas S. Hines, *The Architecture of Richard Neutra* (New York: Museum of Modern Art, 1982), pp. 62–65; W. Boesinger, ed., *Richard Neutra, 1923–1950* (New York: Praeger, 1966), pp. 30–33.

45. Hines, *Richard Neutra*, pp. 132–38.

46. Quoted in David Gebhard, *Schindler* (New York: Viking, 1971), p. 116.

47. R. M. Schindler, "A Beach House of Dr. P. Lovell at Newport Beach, California," *Architectural Record*, 66 (September 1929), pp. 257–61.

48. Schindler, "Space Architecture," in *Dune Forum*, quoted in Gebhard, *Schindler*, pp. 194–95.

49. Albert A. Hopkins, "Glass and the Machine Age," *The Glass Industry*, 13 (September 1932), pp. 145–47.

50. Esther McCoy, *The Second Generation*, (Salt Lake City: Gibbs M. Smith, 1984), p. 82. See also, David Gebhard, Harriet Von Breton, and L. Weiss, *Architecture of Gregory Ain* (Santa Barbara: Univ. of California, 1980).

51. McCoy, *Second Generation*, pp. 96–98.

CHAPTER 7

Engineering a New Art

1. "The Poet," *Selections from Ralph Waldo Emerson*, Stephen E. Whicher, ed. (Boston: Houghton Mifflin, 1957), p. 229.

2. For a grim view of life in rural Wisconsin around the turn of the century, see Michael Lesy, *Wisconsin Death Trip* (New York: Random House, 1973). Hine is socially and culturally situated in Alan Trachtenberg, "Ever—the Human Document," in *America & Lewis Hine: Photographs, 1904–1940* (Millerton, N.Y.: Aperture, 1977); see also, Judith Mara Gutman, *Lewis W. Hine and the American Social Conscience* (New York: Walker, 1967).

3. Ironic juxtaposition kept cropping up in photographs taken during the depression because the social disparities were difficult to ignore. See, for example, Dorothea Lange's photograph of a couple carrying their belongings down a desolate highway past a billboard advising "Next time try the train" to Los Angeles, the city of one's dreams. For an account of documentary activity among artists during the depression, see William Stott, *Documentary Expression and Thirties America* (London: Oxford Univ. Press, 1973).

4. The relation of photography to collage is addressed by Susan Sontag, *On Photography* (New York: Farrar, Straus, 1977). See also, William C. Seitz, *The Art of Assemblage* (New York: Museum of Modern Art, 1961).

5. Adams, *The Education of Henry Adams*, p. 381.

6. Perry Miller, *Nature's Nation* (Cambridge: Harvard Univ. Press, 1967), pp. 197–207. For a discussion of the cultural implications of the debate between Hamilton and Jefferson, see Marx, *The Machine in the Garden*. Among Rousseau's jungle paintings, *Tropical Landscape: An American Indian Struggling with an Ape* (1910) is unique in its explicit rendition of a "noble savage," which had a long European tradition kept alive by literary and visual reports of North American Indians.

7. Walter Dorwin Teague, quoted in Meikle, *Twentieth Century*, p. 183. For an overview of Dada and primitivism in America, see Dickran Tashjian, *Skyscraper Primitives* (Middletown: Wesleyan Univ. Press, 1975).

8. Gabriel Buffet-Picabia, "Some Memories of Pre-Dada: Picabia and Duchamp," in Robert Motherwell, ed., *The Dada Painters and Poets* (New York: Wittenborn, 1967), p. 259. For Picabia in America, see William A. Camfield, *Francis Picabia: His Life and Times* (Princeton: Princeton Univ. Press, 1979).

9. Milton Brown, *The Story of the 1913 Armory Show* (Greenwich, Ct.: New York Graphic Society, 1963), p. 110.

10. For the standard account of futurism, see Joshua Taylor, *Futurism* (New York: Museum of Modern Art, 1961). Popular views of technology in the nineteenth century are touched upon in John F. Kasson, *Civilizing the Machine* (New York: Grossman, 1976).

11. For a useful theoretical account of the social networks of art, see Jacques Maquet, *Introduction to Aesthetic Anthropology* (Reading, Ma.: Addison-Wesley, 1971).

12. Marcel Duchamp, "The Richard Mutt Case," *The Blind Man*, No. 2 (May 1917), p. 5; Williams, *Kora in Hell* (Boston: Four Seasons Company, 1920), p. 10. For Williams and Duchamp, see Tashjian, "Seeing Through Williams: The Opacity of Duchamp's Readymades," *The Library Chronicle*, Series 29 (1984), pp. 35–48.

13. Louise Norton, "Buddha of the Bathroom," *The Blind Man*, p. 6.

14. *Self-Portrait* (Boston: Atlantic–Little, Brown, 1963), p. 110.

15. The urinal can be traced to Stieglitz's "291" Gallery after it was removed from the Independents Exhibition. In a note to Henry McBride, the art critic, Stieglitz wrote: "I wonder whether you could manage to drop in at 291 Friday some time. I have, at the request of [Henri] Roche, [John] Covert, Miss [Beatrice] Wood, Duchamp and Co., photographed the rejected 'Fountain.' You may find the photograph of some use.—It will amuse you to see it.—The 'Fountain' is there too.—" (ALS, 19 April 1917, Henry McBride Papers, Archives of American Art, Microfilm, Frame 445).

16. For Stieglitz as a leader of an emerging American avant-garde during World War I, see William I. Homer, *Alfred Stieglitz and the American Avant-Garde* (Boston: New York Graphic Society, 1979); for an account that quotes him extensively, see Dorothy Norman, *Alfred Stieglitz, An American Seer* (New York: Random House, 1973); for a family biography, see Sue Davidson Lowe, *Stieglitz: A Memoir/Biography* (New York: Farrar Straus, 1983).

17. Stieglitz quoted in Norman, *Alfred Stieglitz*, p. 45.

18. Dorothy Norman, ed., *The Selected Writings of John Marin* (New York: Pellegrini & Cudahy, 1949), p. 46; Georgia O'Keeffe, "About Myself," in *Georgia O'Keeffe: Exhibition of Oils and Pastels, An American Place*, (January 22–March 17, 1939).

19. Dove's statement, made on the occasion of an exhibition of his paintings in 1933, is quoted in Frederick S. Wight, *Arthur G. Dove* (Berkeley: Univ. of Calif. Press, 1956), p. 64.

20. "Can a Photograph Have the Significance of Art?" *Manuscripts*, 4 (December 1922), p. 2.

21. Sheeler's project at the Ford plant has been studied in detail by Mary Jane Jacob and Linda Downs, *The Rouge: The Image of Industry in the Art of Charles Sheeler and Diego Rivera* (Detroit: Detroit Institute of Arts, 1978).

22. Sheeler, *Autobiography*, in Charles Sheeler Papers, Archives of American Art, Microfilm, Frame 66; Dudley Poore, "Current Exhibitions," *The Arts*, VII, no. 2 (February 1925): p. 115; for a study of Sheeler's photography, see Charles W. Millard III, *Charles Sheeler: American Photographer*, a special issue of *Contemporary Photographer*, VI, no. 1 (1967). See also, Martin Friedman, *The Precisionist View in American Art* (Minneapolis: Walker Art Center, 1960); and Karen Tsujimoto, *Images of America: Precisionist Painting and Modern Photography* (Seattle: Univ. of Washington Press, 1982).

23. In his *Autobiography* Sheeler disapproved that "in all of our schooling at the Academy the direction was that of acquiring the greatest possible dexterity regardless of content" (Frame 55). Of the work of Picasso and the cubists, Sheeler claimed, "They were very strange pictures which no amount of description, of which I had considerable in advance, could prepare me for the shock of coming upon them for the first time" (Frames 62–63).

24. For a close contextual study of Sheeler's *Self-Portrait*, see Susan Fillin Yeh, "Charles Sheeler's 1923 'Self-Portrait,' " *Arts*, 52, no. 5 (January 1978), pp. 106–9; Morton Schamberg, who died in the influenza epidemic of 1918, has been studied most recently by William Agee, *Morton Livingston Schamberg* (New York: Salander-O'Reilly Galleries, 1982).

25. Sheeler, *Autobiography*, Frames 94–95, 107. Sheeler claimed with approval that "Marcel Duchamp's Nude Descending a Staircase was the most controversial picture in the [1913 Armory] show. It represented the very antithesis of what we had been taught. For in it the statement was

all important and the means by which it was presented skilfully concealed" (Frame 72). Sheeler admired Duchamp's "remarkable ability of the hand to carry out the orders of the eye" in executing the *Large Glass* (Frames 78–79).

26. The advertisement appeared on the back inside cover of *Broom*, 5, no. 1 (August 1923).

27. For a detailed account of Murphy's theater projects as well as his paintings, see William Rubin, *The Paintings of Gerald Murphy* (New York: Museum of Modern Art, 1974). Stella's collages are discussed in Irma B. Jaffe, *Joseph Stella* (Cambridge: Harvard Univ. Press, 1970), pp. 88–92.

28. Letter to Hanns Skolle, June 28, 1929, quoted in *Walker Evans at Work*, with an essay by Jerry L. Thompson (New York: Harper & Row, 1982), p. 25.

29. "The New Conditions of Literary Phenomena," *Broom*, II, no. 1 (April 1922), pp. 3–10.

30. Benton's *Instruments of Power* was one of the ten murals he was asked to paint in a commission entitled *America Today* for the New School for Social Research in New York in 1929. Benton's return to Missouri, the state of his birth, in 1935, was a symbolic affirmation of his Midwestern, hence for him his "true" American identity. For a general survey of American Scene painting, see Matthew Baigell, *The American Scene* (New York: Praeger, 1974).

31. So as to grasp the full impact of technology, Crane urged artists to go beyond "the power and beauty of machinery" to a level of expression derived from "the unconscious nervous responses of our bodies" ("Modern Poetry," in Waldo Frank, ed., *The Collected Poems of Hart Crane* [New York: Liveright, 1933], pp. 175–79).

32. S. MacDonald-Wright, "Influence of Aviation on Art: The Accentuation of Individuality," *Ace: The Aviation Magazine of the West*, 1, no. 2 (September 1919), pp. 11–12; Gorky, "My Murals for the Newark Airport: An Interpretation," in Ruth Bowman, *Murals without Walls: Arshile Gorky's Aviation Murals Rediscovered* (Newark, N.J.: The Newark Museum, 1978), p. 15.

33. Lozowick's first essay on the Soviet avant-garde was "The Russian Dadaists," *The Little Review*, VII, no. 3 (September–December 1920), pp. 72–73; for a detailed account of the Société Anonyme, Inc., which was the first organization to exhibit the Soviet avant-garde in the United States, see Robert L. Herbert, Eleanor S. Apter, and Elise K. Kenney, eds. *The Société Anonyme and the Dreier Bequest at Yale University* (New Haven: Yale Univ. Press, 1984); see also, Susan Noyes Platt, *Modernism in the 1920s: Interpretations of Modern Art in New York from Expressionism to Constructivism* (Ann Arbor: UMI Research Press, 1985).

34. "A Note on Modern Russian Art," *Broom*, IV, no. 3 (February 1923), p. 202; for an overall view of the Russian avant-garde during and after the 1917 Revolution, see John E. Bowlt, "The Failed Utopia: Russian Art 1917–32," *Art in America*, 59 (July–August 1971), pp. 40–51; for constructivism, see Willy Rotzler, *Constructive Concepts: A History of Constructive Art from Cubism to the Present* (New York: Rizzoli, 1977); for Lozowick and the constructivists, see Barbara Zabel, "The Precisionist-Constructivist Nexus: Louis Lozowick in Berlin," *Arts*, 56, no. 2 (October 1981), pp. 121–27; Joan Marter, "Constructivism in America: The 1930s," *Arts*, 56, no. 10 (June 1982), pp. 72–80.

35. *The Bride Stripped Bare by Her Bachelors, Even*, a typographic version by Richard Hamilton of Marcel Duchamp's *Green Box*, translated by George Heard Hamilton (New York: Wittenborn, 1960), n.p.

36. "Museums or Artists," *The Little Review*, IX, no. 2 (Winter 1922), p. 63.

37. "Comments," *The Little Review*, IX, no. 2 (Winter 1922), p. 22.

38. Herbert Lippmann, "The Machine-Age Exposition," *The Arts* XI, no. 6 (June 1927), p. 325; Heap, "Machine-Age Exposition," p. 24; for a history of the 1939 New York World's Fair, see Helen A. Harrison, *Dawn of a New Day* (New York: New York Univ. Press, 1980).

39. "Machine-Age Exposition," *The Little Review*, XII, no. 1, Supplement (May 1927), p. 36. This is a somewhat abridged version of her essay that appeared in the Spring 1925 issue.

40. Léger, "The Esthetics of the Machine, Part II," *The Little Review*, IX, no. 4 (Autumn-Winter 1923–1924): 55; "The Esthetics of the Machine, Part I," *The Little Review*, IX, no. 3 (Spring 1923), 46.

41. "New Architecture Develops in Russia," *The New York Times* (May 29, 1927) II:1; Lewis Mumford, "The Bourgeois Girls Like Their Ham Sliced Thin," *New Masses*, 3, no. 5 (September 1927), p. 23.

42. *Men at Work: Photographic Studies of Modern Men and Machines* (New York: Macmillan, 1932), n.p.

43. See "American Artists' Congress," *New Masses* (October 1, 1935), p. 33, for its call against "the destructive forces of war and fascism." When Margaret Bourke-White was later called up by HUAC in the 1950s, she protested a political innocence during the 1930s. See Robert E. Snyder, "Margaret Bourke-White and the Communist Witch Hunt," *Journal of American Studies*, 19, no. 1 (April 1985), pp. 5–25. The entire fiasco was ironic in light of her mainstream American values, as evidenced in her memoir, *Portrait of Myself* (New York: Simon & Schuster, 1963).

44. Lozowick's debt to Léger is emphasized by Flint, *The Prints of Louis Lozowick: A Catalogue Raisonné*, p. 16. Lozowick described his stage design for *Gas* in "'Gas' A Theatrical Experiment," *The Little Review*, XI, no. 2 (Winter 1926), pp. 58–60. He found the subject of *Gas* amenable because he could adapt it to the American scene, though he was apparently unenthusiastic about German expressionist drama (Flint, *The Prints of Louis Lozowick*, pp. 17–19).

45. Lozowick, "Lithography: Abstraction and Realism," *Space*, 1 (March 1930), p. 32. In 1929 Lozowick wrote an essay tracing the artistic and social development of El Lissitzky from a proponent of a national art before the 1917 Revolution to the advocate of an international constructivism after 1917. Lozowick noted the speed with which constructivist principles were absorbed by bourgeois culture: "When the interior decorators of Europe and America utilized the experiments with materials for purposes of ostentatious display, that is, for purposes directly contrary to the constructivists' original idea, the school was facing a crisis." Lozowick approved of El Lissitzky's decision, like Rodchenko's before him, to abandon art for the manufacture of posters ("El Lissitsky," *transition*, no. 18 [November 1929], pp. 285–86). See Alan C. Birnholz, "El Lissitzky, the Avant-Garde, and the Russian Revolution," *Artforum*, XI, no. 1 (1972), pp. 70–76.

46. The standard biography is Peter C. Farzio, *Rube Goldberg: His Life and Work* (New York: Harper & Row, 1973).

47. "What Should Revolutionary Artists Do Now?" *New Masses*, 6, no. 7 (December 1930), p. 21; "Art in the Service of the Proletariat," *Literature of the World Revolution*, no. 4 (1931), p. 126.

48. *Ibid*. In 1927 Lozowick had claimed that "the whole of mankind is vitally affected by industrial development" so that the artist's "potential audience will be practically universal" ("The Americanization of Art," p. 19).

49. "Art in the Service of the Proletariat," p. 127. Lozowick would write a favorable review of Sheeler ("American Artist," *New Masses*, XXIX, no. 3 [October 11, 1938], pp. 25–26).

50. For a discussion of Léger's emphasis upon the mechanic/worker, see Christopher Green, *Léger and the Avant-Garde* (New Haven: Yale Univ. Press, 1976), pp. 192–211.

51. Work on those involved with the American Abstract Artists group has been published piecemeal. An encapsulated history can be found in Susan C. Larsen, "The American Abstract Artists: A Documentary History, 1936–1941," *Archives of American Art Journal*, 14, no. 1 (1974), pp. 2–7; see also, John R. Lane and Susan C. Larsen, eds., *Abstract Painting and Sculpture in America, 1927–1944* (New York: Abrams, 1983).

52. "The New Realism," *American Abstract Artists Yearbook, 1938*, in *American Abstract Artists: Three Yearbooks (1938, 1939, 1946)* (New York: Arno Press, 1969), p. 22.

53. Joan Marter, "Theodore Roszak," in Lane and Larsen, eds., *Abstract Painting and Sculpture*, p. 213. See also, Joan M. Marter, "Theodore Roszak's Early Constructions: The Machine As Creator of Fantastic and Ideal Forms," *Arts*, 54 (November 1979), pp. 110–13; Gregory Gilbert, "Theodore Roszak," in Jennifer Toher, ed., *Beyond the Plane: American Constructions, 1930–1965* (Trenton: New Jersey State Museum, 1983), pp. 89–92.

54. The standard study of José De Rivera is Joan M. Marter, *José De Rivera*, intro. by Dore Ashton (Madrid: Taller Ediciones, 1980).

55. "Some Problems of Modern Sculpture," *Magazine of Art*, 42 (February 1949), p. 56; Roszak also discussed his sense of the weaknesses of constructivism in "In Pursuit of an Image," *Quadrum*, 2 (November 1956), pp. 49–60.

56. For an analysis of Rivera's Detroit murals, see Jacob and Downs, *The Rouge*; also, Max Kozloff, "The Rivera Frescoes of Modern Industry at the Detroit Institute of Art: Proletarian Art Under Capitalist Patronage," *Artforum*, 12, no. 13 (November 1973), pp. 58–64; for a general study of public commissions of avant-garde art, with some references to the 1939 New York World's Fair, see Greta Berman, "Abstractions for Public Spaces, 1935–1943," *Arts*, 56, no. 10 (June 1982), pp. 81–86; Joan M. Marter, "Modern American Sculpture at the New York World's Fair, 1939," in Joan M. Marter, Roberta K. Tarbell, and Jeffrey Wechsler, *Vanguard American Sculpture, 1913–1939* (New Brunswick, N.J.: Rutgers Univ. Art Gallery, 1979), pp. 141–49.

57. Alexander Calder took first prize with a polychromed forerunner of his stabiles. See "Plexiglass Sculpture Prizes Are Awarded," *Pencil Points*, 20, no. 6 (June 1939), pp. 56–57.

58. Taggard, "The Ruskinian Boys See Red," *New Masses*, 3, no. 3 (July 1927), p. 18; Herbert Lippmann, "The Machine-Age Exposition," p. 325.

59. "Mobile Mural," *Life*, 6, no. 11 (March 13, 1939), p. 42; Coady, *The Soil*, 1 (January 1917), p. 55.

60. "Proem: To Brooklyn Bridge," *The Collected Poems*, pp. 3–4.
61. "War Bride," *Dreamworks*, 4, no. 2 (1984–85), p. 107.
62. The surrealists took the image from Isidore Ducasse, a young French poet who as the "Comte de Lautreamont" had written *Les Chants de Maldoror* just before he died in 1870 (Marcel Jean, ed., *The Autobiography of Surrealism* [New York: Viking, 1980], pp. 43–52).
63. Mobil launched its promotion of the logo in 1934 by updating an image from Greek mythology: "Pegasus Flies Again!" ran the *Fortune* ad, explaining "How the Winged Horse of Ancient Greece became the Symbol of a Modern American Institution" (*Fortune*, IX, no. 4 [April 1934], p. 143).
64. See Berenice Abbott, *New York in the Thirties*, with text by Elizabeth McCausland (New York: Dover, 1973), originally published as *Changing New York* (New York: Dutton, 1939). Having rescued Eugene Atget's photographs of Paris (recounted in Julien Levy, *Memoir of an Art Gallery* [New York: Putnam, 1977], pp. 90–95), Abbott must have recognized the need for a similar documentation of New York City.
65. For the Crane/Evans connection, see Gordon K. Grisby, "The Photographs in the First Edition of *The Bridge*," *Texas Studies in Literature and Language*, 4 (Spring 1962), pp. 5–11; Trachtenberg, *Brooklyn Bridge: Fact and Symbol*, pp. 185–93; for Crane and Stella, see Irma B. Jaffe, "Joseph Stella and Hart Crane: The Brooklyn Bridge," *The American Art Journal*, 1 (Fall 1969), pp. 98–107; George Knox, "Crane and Stella: Conjunction of Painterly and Poetic Worlds," *Texas Studies in Literature and Language*, 12, pp. 689–707.
66. Stella's sexual attitudes have been discussed by Jaffe, *Joseph Stella*, pp. 78–79.
67. *The Education of Henry Adams*, p. 381.
68. Duchamp's assertion was quoted in K. G. Pontus Hulten, *The Machine As Seen at the End of the Mechanical Age* (New York: Museum of Modern Art, 1968), p. 140. The original source is "La Vie dans l'oeuvre de Fernand Léger," an interview with Dora Vallier, *Cahiers d'Art* (Paris), 29, no. 2 (1954), pp. 133–77. For a comparison of Adams and Duchamp, see Dickran Tashjian, "Henry Adams and Marcel Duchamp: Liminal Views of the Dynamo and the Virgin," *Arts*, 51, no. 9 (May 1977), pp. 102–7.
69. *The Education of Henry Adams*, p. 385.
70. *Ibid.*, p. 384.
71. Joan M. Marter, "Interaction of American Sculptors with European Modernists: Alexander Calder and Isamu Noguchi," in *Vanguard American Sculpture, 1913–1939*, p. 115; see also, Isamu Noguchi, *A Sculptor's World*, foreword by R. Buckminster Fuller (New York: Harper & Row, 1968), pp. 19–21.
72. Ernest Brace, "Charles Sheeler," *Creative Art*, XI, no. 2 (October 1932), p. 97. The laconic quality of Sheeler's paintings and photographs made them vulnerable to disparate interpretation, depending upon their context. On the cover of *Ford News* in 1929, for example, a Sheeler photograph appeared to glorify the industrial order. On the other hand, Henry McBride later thought that Sheeler's work expressed an alienation caused by technology. (See discussion in *Skyscraper Primitives*, p. 223.) Six of Sheeler's Ford photographs also appeared in an unlikely source like *transition*, no. 18 (November 1929), p. 123, with the caption, "Charles Sheeler: The Industrial Mythos." Eugene Jolas, editor of *transition*, had become interested in the American

machine age through a Jungian lens.
73. "Are Dynamos Bosoms?" *The New Republic*, 59, no. 761 (July 3, 1929), pp. 187–88; Zukofsky, "Henry Adams: A Criticism in Autobiography," *Hound and Horn*, III, no. 3 (April–June 1930), pp. 333–57; III, no. 4 (July–September 1930), pp. 518–30; IV, no. 1 (October–December 1930), pp. 46–72; "Beginning Again with William Carlos Williams," *Hound and Horn*, IV, no. 2 (January–March 1931), pp. 261–64. For a brief allusion to Zukofsky and a discussion of Williams in the Adams context, see William Wasserstrom, *The Ironies of Progress: Henry Adams and the American Dream* (Carbondale: Southern Illinois Univ. Press, 1984), pp. 184–213.
74. "The Great Figure," *The Collected Earlier Poems*, p. 230. For an account of the friendship between Williams and Demuth, see Dickran Tashjian, *William Carlos Williams and the American Scene* (Berkeley: Univ. of Calif. Press, 1978), pp. 66–72.
75. Williams's poem, which remains uncollected, appeared in *Matrix*, II, no. 6 (November–December 1940), p. 20.
76. Siegfried Giedion perhaps sums up Calder best: "None other in contemporary art was born into this American experience, which lies, as we often stress here, in a particular relation, a gearing of the American man with the machine, with mechanism, with the mobile. No other people is in such close touch with these abstract structures. Calder absorbed the modern means of expression, slowly amalgamating them with his own background until, by 1931, he had attained the sensitivity to states of equilibrium that he stressed in his 'mobiles' " (*Mechanization Takes Command*, p. 477).

CHAPTER 8
Design for the Machine

1. I. Warren Susman, *Culture as History: The Transformation of American Society in the Twentieth Century* (New York: Pantheon, 1984), p. 160. I thank Warren Susman for his insightful discussion on the differences between the character of the 1920s and 1930s.
2. Lockwood Barr, "Radio: Furniture or Specialty?" *Good Furniture and Decoration*, 36, no. 2 (February 1931), pp. 87–91.
3. Kouwenhoven, *The Arts in Modern American Civilization*, p. 173; as quoted in Kouwenhoven, *The Arts in Modern American Civilization*.
4. Philip Johnson, "Decorative Art a Generation Ago," *Creative Art*, 12, no. 4 (April 1933), p. 297.
5. Charles R. Richards, "In Defense of the Modern Movement in European Industrial Art," *American Magazine of Art*, 15, no. 12 (December 1924), p. 633.
6. Johnson, "Decorative Art," p. 297.
7. Frank Lloyd Wright was the one figure to participate in the Arts and Crafts movement and also be an early proponent of the machine. However, his influence was felt more strongly in Europe than at home.
8. Interview, Christopher Wilk with author, November 1985.
9. Dianne Hauserman, "John Cotton Dana: The Militant Minority of One" (M.A. Thesis, New York Univ., 1965), pp. 100–102.
10. *Ibid.*, pp. 58–65; "Contemporary Art in Current Exhibitions," *Good Furniture*, 32, no. 5 (May 1929), p. 241.
11. Davies, *At Home in Manhattan*, p. 88. An

excellent book on American decorative arts from 1925 to 1932.
12. C. Adolph Glassgold, "The Modern Note in Decorative Arts," *The Arts*, 13, no. 4 (April 1928), p. 225; Davies, *At Home in Manhattan*, pp. 10, 84–91.
13. Glassgold, "The Modern Note," p. 225.
14. Mrs. Ripley Hitchcock, "Industrial Art as a Personal Responsibility," *American Magazine of Art*, 13, no. 10 (October 1922), pp. 327–29; "Art and Industry—an Industrial Arts Survey," *American Magazine of Art*, 14, no. 2 (February 1923), p. 81.
15. Lord & Taylor, *An Exposition of Modern French Decorative Art* (New York: Lord & Taylor, February 1928), n.p.
16. Glassgold, "The Modern Note," p. 225.
17. Davies, *At Home in Manhattan*, p. 86; Glassgold, "The Modern Note," p. 227.
18. Lord & Taylor, *An Exposition*.
19. *Ibid.*
20. R. H. Macy & Co., *An International Exposition of Art in Industry* (New York: R. H. Macy & Co., 1929), n.p.
21. *The Machine-Age Exposition Catalogue*, *The Little Review*, XI (1927), p. 36.
22. *American Designers' Gallery, Inc.* (New York: American Designers' Gallery, 1929), n.p.; "Exhibit of American Designers' Gallery: An Ambitious Program in Art Moderne," *Good Furniture*, 32, no. 1 (January 1929), p. 45.
23. Shepard Vogelsgang, "Contemporary Interior Design Advances," *Good Furniture*, 32, no. 5 (May 1929), p. 229.
24. Glassgold, "The Modern Note," p. 229.
25. "Art in the Machine Age—II," *Creative Art*, 3, no. 2 (August 1928), p. 79.
26. Donald Deskey, conversation with author, May 1983.
27. Interview, Jennifer Toher, David A. Hanks and Associates, New York, with author, September 1985.
28. Athena Robbins, "Furniture Goes to Market," *Good Furniture and Decoration*, 36, no. 2 (February 1931), p. 97.
29. Advertisement for Ypsilanti Fleckron chromium plated steel furniture, *Furniture Record*, 60, no. 5 (May 1930), p. 33.
30. Davies, *At Home in Manhattan*, p. 46.
31. Michael Komanecky and Virginia Fabbri Butera, *The Folding Image* (New Haven: Yale Univ. Art Gallery, 1984), p. 246, n. 7.
32. *Ibid.*, pp. 243–44.
33. R. W. Sexton, *The Logic of Modern Architecture* (New York: Architectural Book Pub., 1929), p. 92. As quoted in Davies, *At Home in Manhattan*, p. 65.
34. "American Modernist Furniture Inspired by Sky-scraper Architecture," *Good Furniture*, 29, no. 3 (September 1927), p. 119.
35. *Ibid.*
36. "American Modern Art, Its History and Characteristic," *Good Furniture*, 27, no. 4 (October 1926), p. 173.
37. *Ibid*, pp. 173–74.
38. Steinway and Sons, New York, advertisement, *House and Garden*, 50, no. 3 (March 1928), back cover.
39. Robert N. Hunter, "The New Note in Decoration," *The Decorative Furnisher*, 68, no. 6 (September 1925), p. 79.
40. *Ibid.*, p. 110a.
41. "Color in Industry," *Fortune*, 1, no. 1 (February 1930), pp. 85–94.
42. *Ibid.*, pp. 88–90.
43. Charles Carpenter, Jr., *Gorham Silver 1831–1981* (New York: Dodd, Mead, 1982), p. 259.

44. As quoted in Glassgold, "The Modern Note," p. 229.

45. Hazel M. Weatherman, *Colored Glassware of the Depression Era 2* (Ozark, Mo.: Weatherman Glass Books, 1974), p. 48. A label on a perfume bottle, c. 1928, in the collection of The Chrysler Museum, Norfolk, Va. (63.114.1), "Consolidated Lamp & Glass Co., Coraopolis, Pa.," declares "Ruba Rombic—an epic in Modern Art."

46. Shirley Paine, "Shop Windows of Mayfair," *Garden and Home Builder*, 47 (July 1928), p. 510. Referred to in Davies, *At Home in Manhattan*, p. 58.

47. Shepard Vogelsgang, "Toward a Contemporary Art," *Good Furniture*, 32, no. 3 (March 1929), pp. 117–28.

48. American Union of Decorative Artists and Craftsmen, *AUDAC Exhibition*.

49. C. Adolph Glassgold, "Modern American Industrial Design," *Arts and Decoration*, 35, no. 3 (July 1931), p. 31.

50. Blanche Naylor, "American Design Progress," *Design*, 33, no. 4 (September 1931), p. 89.

51. Clipping file, The Brooklyn Museum.

52. Kneeland L. Green, "Modern Life of Ordinary Things Designs: Americana Fabrics," *Creative Art*, 4, no. 2 (February 1929), p. 104.

53. Susman, *Culture as History*, pp. 188–89.

54. Lawrence Sidney, "Clean Machines at the Modern," *Art in America*, 72, no. 2 (February 1984), p. 135.

55. Cheney and Cheney, *Art and the Machine*, pp. 58–59, offers an excellent contemporary definition of an industrial designer.

56. Sidney, "Clean Machines at The Modern," pp. 134–35; Meikle, *Twentieth Century*, p. 186.

57. Mumford, *Technics and Civilization*, p. 357.

58. "Vogue Forecasts a Wind-Swept Spring,"

Vogue (January 15, 1934), p. 19. Source courtesy of Kevin L. Stayton.

59. Meikle, *Twentieth Century*, p. 185.

60. Susman, *Culture as History*, p. 154.

61. Hitchcock, "Industrial Art as a Personal Responsibility," p. 328.

62. *ABC of Modern Age Furniture* (New York: Modernage Furniture Co., 1933), p. 3.

63. Davies, *At Home in Manhattan*, p. 113.

64. Carleton Ryder, "The Light and Color of Chromium," *Good Furniture and Decoration*, 36, no. 5 (May 1931), p. 269; "Chromium," *The Encyclopaedia Britannica*, vol. 5 (London: The Encyclopaedia Brittannica Co.).

65. *Ibid.*, p. 275.

66. Sharon Darling, *Chicago Furniture: Art, Craft and Industry 1833–1983* (New York: Norton, 1984), p. 314.

67. The Howell Company, Geneva, Ill., *Modern Chromsteel Furniture*, catalogue, 1933, n.p.

68. "Aluminum," *Fortune*, 1, no. 2 (March 1930), pp. 68–71, 134, 136–37.

69. Meikle, *Twentieth Century*, p. 98.

70. Paul T. Frankl, "Why We Accept Modernistic Furniture," *Arts and Decoration*, 39, no. 2 (June 1928), p. 58.

71. *Modern Chairs 1918–1970* (Boston: Boston Book and Art Publisher, 1971), p. 15.

72. Kimberly Sichel, "Walter Von Nessen, Early Post Modernist," *Industrial Design*, 31 (May/June 1984), p. 41.

73. R. S. McFadden, "Designers' Ability Salvages Waste," *Design*, 35, no. 3 (September 1933), p. 22; Sichel, "Walter Von Nessen," p. 41.

74. Mumford, *Technics and Civilization*, p. 326.

75. Christopher Wilk, "Furnishing the Future. 1925–1946," in Derek Ostergard, ed., *Bent Wood and Metal Furniture 1850–1946* (New York: American Federation of Arts, 1986), n.p., discusses a little-known armchair design by Alvar Aalto around 1931–32 that is bent in two directions and which predates the Eames and Saarinen furniture.

76. Arthur Drexler, *Charles Eames Furniture from the Design Collection* (New York: Museum of Modern Art, 1973), p. 12.

77. *Official Guide Book of the New York World's Fair* (New York: Exposition Pub., 1939), p. 5.

78. Martin Greif, *Depression Modern: The Thirties Style in America* (New York: Universe Books, 1975), p. 43, as quoted (and condensed) in Davies, *At Home in Manhattan*.

CHAPTER 9
The Machine Age and Beyond

1. Quoted in Barbara Haskell, *Ralston Crawford* (New York: Whitney Museum of American Art, 1985), p. 51; Jack Cowart, "Recent Acquisition: *Coal Elevators* by Ralston Crawford," *The St. Louis Art Museum Bulletin*, 14 (January–March 1978), p. 11.

2. Clarence Stein, *Towards New Towns for America* (Cambridge: M.I.T. Press, 1957), pp. 119–87. See also, Clarence Arthur Perry, *Housing for the Machine Age* (New York: Russell Sage Foundation, 1939); and Catherine Bauer, *Modern Housing* (Boston: Houghton Mifflin, 1934).

3. A critical view of this development is: Jane Jacobs, *The Death and Life of Great American Cities* (New York: Vintage, 1961).

4. A critical view of this development is: Dolores Hayden, *The Grand Domestic Revolution* (Cambridge: M.I.T. Press, 1981).

5. "Hedrich-Blessing Studio, Chicago, Illinois, Abel Faidy, Architectural Designer," *Architectural Forum*, 65 (July 1936), p. 22.

6. Interview, Robert Lepper with Wilson, January 9, 1985; Correspondence, Lepper to Wilson, March 15, 1984; and Lepper, "Description of the Theme for the Mural in the Auditorium of the Mineral Industries Building—West Virginia University," October 1941, typescript. See also, William T. Schoyer, "Robert Lepper's Industrial Realism," *Carnegie Alumnus* (October 1941), pp. 4–5; Edward Alden Jewell, "In the Realm of Art, Pittsburgh Opens Its Big Annual," *The New York Times* (October 26, 1941), X:9; and Penelope Redd, "Carnegie Institute's Exhibit," *Pittsburgh Sun Telegraph* (October 19, 1941), clipping.

7. Frederick J. Kiesler, "Murals without Walls: Relating to Gorky's Newark Project," *Art Front*, 2 (December 1936), pp. 10–11; Gorky, "My Murals for the Newark Project: An Interpretation," in *Murals Without Walls*, pp. 13–14; see also, Ethel K. Schwabacher, *Arshile Gorky* (New York: Macmillan-Whitney Museum of American Art, 1957), pp. 70–78.

8. Gilbert Rodhe, "The Design Laboratory," *American Magazine of Art*, 35 (October 1936), pp. 638–43, 686; E. M. Benson; "Wanted: An American Bauhaus," *American Magazine of Art*, 37 (June 1934), pp. 307–11; Pulos, *American Design Ethic*, p. 400. Interview, Lepper with Wilson, January 9, 1985; Correspondence, Lepper to Wilson, January 20, 28, 1984; Lepper, "Apprenticeship for Industrial Design," *Art Instruction*, 2 (September 1938), pp. 9–12.

9. Matthew Josephson, *Portrait of the Artist As American* (New York: Octagon Books, 1964), reprint of 1930 edition), pp. 307–8.

10. Kiesler, "On Correalism and Biotechnique," *Architectural Record*, 86 (September 1939), pp. 60–75; "New Display Techniques for Art of This Century," *Architectural Forum*, 78 (February 1943), pp. 49–53; Peggy Guggenheim, *Art of This Century* (New York: Universe Books, 1979), pp. 271–72, 274–75. See also, "Kiesler's Pursuit of an Idea," *Progressive Architecture*, 42 (July 1961), pp. 104–23.

11. Strand, "Photography and the New God," p. 257.

This is only a selection from the wealth of published material devoted to the machine age.
Further references are contained in the notes that accompany each chapter.

Banham, Reyner. *Theory and Design in the First Machine Age.* New York: Praeger, 1967.

Bel Geddes, Norman. *Horizons.* Boston: Little, Brown & Co., 1932.

Brodsly, David. *L.A. Freeway: An Appreciative Essay.* Berkeley: University of California Press, 1981.

Brown, Milton W. *American Painting from the Armory Show to the Depression.* Princeton: Princeton University Press, 1955.

Bush, Donald J. *The Streamlined Decade.* New York: George Braziller, 1975.

Cheney, Sheldon. *The New World Architecture.* New York: Tudor Publications Co., 1930.

Cheney, Sheldon, and Cheney, Martha Chandler. *Art and the Machine: An Account of Industrial Design in 20th Century America.* New York: McGraw-Hill, 1936.

Clark, Robert Judson, et al. *Design in America, The Cranbrook Vision 1925–1950.* New York: Harry N. Abrams, Inc., 1984.

Condit, Carl. *American Building Art: The Twentieth Century.* New York: Oxford University Press, 1961.

Davidson, Abraham A. *Early American Modernist Painting 1910–1935.* New York: Harper & Row, 1981.

Davies, Karen. *At Home in Manhattan: Modern Decorative Arts, 1925 to the Depression.* New Haven, Conn.: Yale University Art Gallery, 1983.

Detroit Institute of Arts. *Detroit Style: Automotive Form 1925–1950.* Detroit: Detroit Institute of Arts, 1985.

Ferriss, Hugh. *The Metropolis of Tomorrow.* New York: Ives Washburn, 1929.

Flink, James J. *The Car Culture.* Cambridge, Mass.: M.I.T. Press, 1975.

Frankl, Paul T. *Form and Re-Form.* New York: Harper & Bros., 1930.

———. *New Dimensions.* New York: Payson & Clarke, 1928.

Giedion, Siegfried. *Mechanization Takes Command.* New York: W. W. Norton, 1969.

Greif, Martin. *Depression Modern: The Thirties Style in America.* New York: Universe Books, 1975.

Harrison, Helen A., ed. *Dawn of a New Day. The New York World's Fair, 1939/40.* New York: New York University Press, 1980.

Hitchcock, Henry-Russell. *Modern Architecture: Romanticism and Reintegration.* London: Payson & Clarke, 1929.

Hitchcock, Henry-Russell and Johnson, Philip. *The International Style: Architecture Since 1922.* New York: W. W. Norton Co., 1932.

Homer, William I. *Alfred Stieglitz and the American Avant-Garde.* Boston: New York Graphic Society, 1979.

Hulten, K. G. Pontus. *The Machine as Seen at the End of the Machine Age.* New York: Museum of Modern Art, 1968.

Hurley, B. F. Jack, ed. *Industry and the Photographic Image.* New York: Dover, 1980.

Lane, John R., and Larson, Susan C., eds. *Abstract Painting and Sculpture in America, 1927–1944.* Pittsburgh and New York: Museum of Art, Carnegie Institute, and Harry N. Abrams, Inc., 1983.

Leonard, R. L., and Glassgold, C. A., eds. *Annual of American Design.* New York: Ives Washburn, 1930.

Marter, Joan M.; Tarbell, Roberta K.; and Wechsler, Jeffrey. *Vanguard American Sculpture, 1913–1939.* New Brunswick, N.J.: Rutgers University Art Gallery, 1979.

Marx, Leo. *The Machine Age in the Garden: Technology and the Pastoral Ideal in America.* New York: Oxford University Press, 1968.

Meikle, Jeffrey L. *Twentieth Century Limited: Industrial Design in America, 1925–1939.* Philadelphia: Temple University Press, 1979.

Mumford, Lewis. *Technics and Civilization.* New York: Harcourt, Brace & Co., 1934.

Museum of Modern Art. *Machine Art.* New York: Museum of Modern Art, 1934.

Park, Edwin Avery. *New Backgrounds for a New Age.* New York: Harcourt, Brace & Co., 1927.

Park, Marlene, and Markowitz, Gerald E. *Democratic Vistas: Post Offices and Public Art in the New Deal.* Philadelphia: Temple University Press, 1984.

Pulos, Arthur J. *American Design Ethic: A History of Industrial Design to 1940.* Cambridge, Mass.: M.I.T. Press, 1983.

Pultz, John, and Scalista, Catheline B. *Cubism and American Photography.* Williamstown, Mass.: Sterling & Francine Clark Art Institute, 1981.

Reed, Robert C. *The Streamline Era.* San Marino, Calif.: Golden West Books, 1975.

Robinson, Cervin, and Bletter, Rosemarie Haag. *Skyscraper Style: Art Deco New York.* New York: Oxford, 1975.

Sidney, Lawrence. "Clean Machines at The Modern." *Art in America* 72, no. 2 (February 1984).

Silk, Gerald, et al. *Automobile and Culture.* New York: Harry N. Abrams, Inc., 1984.

Sironen, Marta K. *A History of American Furniture.* East Stroudsburg, Pa.: Towse Publishing Co., 1936.

Steinman, David B., and Watson, Sara Ruth. *Bridges and Their Builders.* New York: G. P. Putnam's Sons, 1941.

Stott, William. *Documentary Expression and Thirties America.* New York: Oxford University Press, 1973.

Susman, Warren I. *Culture as History: The Transformation of American Society in the Twentieth Century.* New York: Pantheon Books, 1984.

Tashjian, Dickran. *Skyscraper Primitives.* Middletown, Conn.: Wesleyan University Press, 1976.

Teague, Walter Dorwin. *Design This Day: The Technique of Order in the Machine Age.* New York: Harcourt, Brace & Co., 1940.

Tsujimoto, Karen. *Images of America: Precisionist Painting and Modern Photography.* Seattle, Wash.: University of Washington Press, 1982.

Weber, Eva. *Art Deco in America.* New York: Exeter, 1985.

Wilson, Paul. *Chrome Dreams: Automobile Styling Since 1893.* Radnor, Pa.: Chilton Book Co., 1976.

INDEX

PHOTOGRAPH
CREDITS

The authors and publishers wish to thank the following photographers, institutions, collectors, and all others who have graciously consented to the reproduction of their photographs (references are to figure numbers).

Abramson-Culbert Studio, 2.3; Albert Kahn Associates, Inc., 1.8, 3.11, 6.51, 6.52; J. Alexander, Commission of Fine Arts, 4.10; Altoona Area Public Library, 5.19; American Airlines, 5.6; *The American Architect,* vol. 128, 2.11; A. O. Smith Corporation, Milwaukee, 8.35; Armen, 3.1, 8.39; Arrasmith, Judd, Rapp & Associates, 6.41; The Austin Company, 3.21, 6.48, 6.49, Dirk Bakker, Detroit Institute of Arts, 1.3; Noel Barnhurst, 8.97; Beckett Associates, 6.39; E. Benn Ltd. (from Mendelsohn, *Structures and Sketches,* 1924), 2.19; Ruth Bernhard, courtesy Mrs. Frederick Kiesler, 9.7; Michael Bleichfeld, 1.6; Breger & Associates, 8.6, 8.44, 8.59, 8.83; Irving Browning, 6.22; Buckminster Fuller Institute, 5.9, 6.58; Burlington Northern, 5.15; Caltrans, 4.6, 4.11; Thomas B. Catalano, courtesy

Whitney Museum of American Art, 6.12; Chevron Corporation, 6.55; courtesy Chicago Historical Society 6.20; Chrysler Historical Collection, 5.10, 5.11; City of New York, Parks and Recreation, 4.5; Geoffrey Clements, 7.42, 7.50; Coca-Cola Bottling Plant of Los Angeles, 6.40; Condé Nast Publications, 3.25; © 1939 (renewed 1967) Condé Nast Publications, Inc., 8.96; Cranbrook Archives, 6.2; Culver Pictures, 1.22; Dennis Anderson Photography, 8.67; Discovery Hall Archival Collections, South Bend, Ind., 2.26; Doubleday & Co. (from Frankl, *Space for Living,* 1938), 2.23; from *Walker Evans: At Work* (used by permission), 7.21; Federal Works Agency, Section of Fine Arts, 7.48; Sigurd Fisher, courtesy Haines Lundberg Waehler, successor firm, 6.5, 6.6; from *Fortune* (October 1935), 6.36; The Frank Lloyd Wright Memorial Foundation, 2.28; General Motors Design, 2.24, 5.7; George Arents Research Library, Syracuse University, 8.77; Richard Goodbody, courtesy Catherine Kurland, 8.61; Goodyear Tire & Rubber Company, 2.16; Pedro E. Guerrero, 6.65; John Gutmann, 1.17; Hedrich-Blessing, 6.37, 6.60, 6.61, 6.63, 8.4, 8.44, 9.5; Henry Ford Museum and Greenfield Village, 5.13, 5.14; Holabird and Root, 3.8, 3.9, 5.18, 6.20; William N. Hopkins, Hopkins Associates, 8.27, 8.32, 8.55; © Wolfgang Hoyt/Esto, 7.5; Scott Hyde, 8.25; Fons Iannelli, courtesy Kelmscott Gallery, 1.5; Isabey, 7.21; Ives'Washburn (from Bernard and Glassgold, *American Modern Design,* 1931), 3.22; Kalmbach Publishing Co., Milwaukee, 5.20; Mrs. Frederick Kiesler, 9.11; Knoedler Gallery, 7.61; Jerry Kobylecky, 8.40, 8.57, 8.60, 8.88; Sandra Kocher, 6.34; © Lawrence S. Williams, Inc., 6.1; William Lebovitch, 6.46; Schecter Lee, 1.4, 2.27, 5.28, 8.2, 8.3, 8.5, 8.7, 8.8, 8.13, 8.16, 8.18, 8.19, 8.21, 8.25, 8.30, 8.31, 8.34, 8.36, 8.37, 8.41, 8.42, 8.43, 8.49, 8.52, 8.54, 8.62, 8.63, 8.64, 8.68–74,

8.78, 8.79, 8.80, 8.82, 8.84, 8.85, 8.87, 8.91, 8.92, 8.94, 8.95; Robert Lepper, 9.8; Life Picture Service, 7.35; F. A. Lincoln, courtesy The Isamu Noguchi Garden Museum, 7.69; Lockheed Corporation, 5.2; ® George Long, A.M.-P.A.S., 9.6; Luckhaus Studios, courtesy Dione Neutra, 6.66, 6.67, 6.68; Richard Margolis, 7.6; Matson Navigation Company, 5.26; Jeffrey Meikle, 2.25, 3.4, 3.5, 3.24, 5.29; Milwaukee Road Collection, Milwaukee Public Library, 2.18, 5.21; Moulin Studios, San Francisco, 4.15, 4.16, 4.17, 4.18; Chuck Murphy, 8.46; Museum of the City of New York, 6.9, 6.11, 6.18; Museum of the City of New York, Gottscho-Schleisner Archive, 4.13, 6.16, 6.17; Museum of the City of New York, Print Archives, 7.62; Museum of Modern Art (from *Machine Art,* 1934), 8.48; National Fine Arts Commission, 6.44; Nebraska Governor's Office, 6.3; Dione Neutra, 6.32; New York City Parks Dept., 4.5; N.Y.O.P. R.H. P.—Taconic Region, 4.4; *New York Post,* 1.28, 7.58; New York Public Library, 3.17; Niagara Mohawk Power Company, 6.23, 6.24, 6.27; Ken Novack, 8.86; Pan American World Airways, 5.3; Philadelphia Savings Fund Society, 6.31; Phototeque, 1.21; Port Authority of New York and New Jersey, 4.9, 4.12; Raymond Loewy International, 2.2; Redyref-Pressed and Welded, Inc., New York, 1.11; Revere Copper and Brass, Inc., Clinton, Ill., 8.53; © Cervin Robinson, 6.8, 6.10, 6.19; Rockefeller Center, 6.13; Santa Fe Southern Pacific Corp., Chicago, 5.25; Roberto Schezen, 8.1; Schreiner, courtesy Texaco, 6.56; Cecil B. Scott, 4.25; SITES, Joe A. Goulait, 3.15; Smithsonian Institution, 4.14; W. J. Stettler, 7.60; Brooks Stevens, 9.2; Herbert Striner, 6.26; Studio Nine, Inc., 8.65; Tennessee Valley Authority, 4.24, 4.26, 4.27, 4.30, 4.31; Tennessee Valley Authority, Charles Krutch, photographer, 4.28; U.S. Dept. of the Interior, Bureau of Reclamation, 2.12, 4.19, 4.22, 4.23, 4.29; University of California, Berkeley, Architectural Slide Library, 7.74; University of California, Los Angeles, 6.33; University of California, Santa Barbara, 6.69, 6.70; University of Virginia Library, 7.31; University of Wisconsin, 8.9; Gretchen Van Tassel, 9.3; VEB Verlag der Künst, Dresden, 7.17; Walter Dorwin Teague Associates, 8.47, 8.75, 8.81; Katherine Wetzel, 8.14; Richard Guy Wilson, 6.31, 6.50; Worsinger Photographs, 3.2; Wurts Brothers Photography, courtesy Richard Wurts, 1.29; Zabriskie Gallery, 7.52

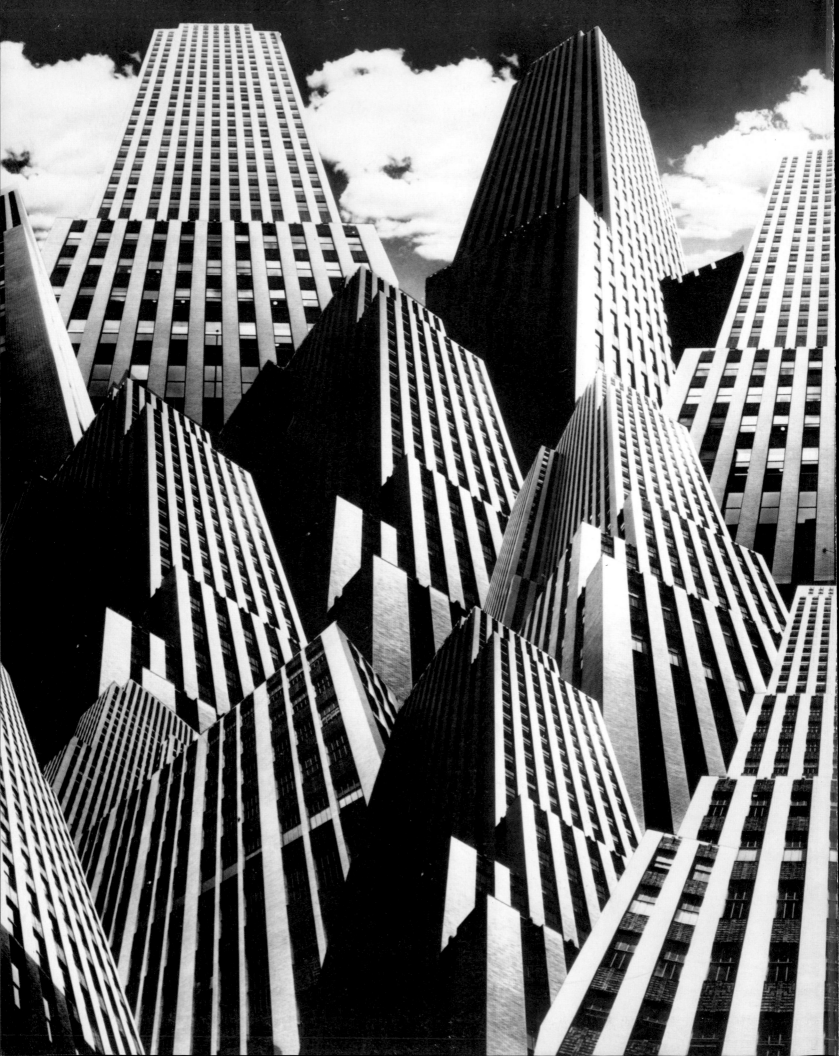